Mike Donlin

Mike Donlin

A Rough and Rowdy Life
from New York Baseball Idol
to Stage and Screen

Steve Steinberg and Lyle Spatz

University of Nebraska Press : Lincoln

The University of Nebraska Press is part of a land-grant institution with campuses and programs on the past, present, and future homelands of the Pawnee, Ponca, Otoe-Missouria, Omaha, Dakota, Lakota, Kaw, Cheyenne, and Arapaho Peoples, as well as those of the relocated Ho-Chunk, Sac and Fox, and Iowa Peoples.

Library of Congress Cataloging-in-Publication Data
Names: Steinberg, Steve, author. | Spatz, Lyle, 1937– author.
Title: Mike Donlin: a rough and rowdy life from New York baseball idol to stage and screen / Steve Steinberg and Lyle Spatz.
Description: Lincoln: University of Nebraska Press, [2024] | Includes bibliographical references and index.
Identifiers: LCCN 2023039388
ISBN 9781496238962 (hardback)
ISBN 9781496240224 (epub)
ISBN 9781496240231 (pdf)
Subjects: LCSH: Donlin, Mike. | Baseball players—New York (State)—New York—Biography. | New York Giants (Baseball team)—History. | Baseball—New York (State)—New York—History—19th century. | Baseball—New York (State)—New York—History—20th century. | Actors—United States—Biography. | BISAC: SPORTS & RECREATION / Baseball / History | BIOGRAPHY & AUTOBIOGRAPHY / Entertainment & Performing Arts
Classification: LCC GV865.D585 S74 2024 | DDC 796.357092 [B]—dc23/eng/20230831
LC record available at https://lccn.loc.gov/2023039388

Set in Miller by A. Shahan.

To Colleen, who has always given
me the space to travel to the early
twentieth century, whether in a
Seattle coffee shop, on a Greek island,
or another corner of the world.

     —ss

To Rona, who found me at my
lowest point and brought love, joy,
and laughter back into my life.

     —LS

You learn eventually that, while there are no villains, there are no heroes either. And until you make the final discovery that there are only human beings, who are therefore all the more fascinating, you are liable to miss something.

—PAUL GALLICO, sportswriter and novelist (1897–1976)

CONTENTS

ILLUSTRATIONS

ACKNOWLEDGMENTS

We thank Rob Taylor, our editor at the University of Nebraska Press, for his faith in our research and writing, and his assistant, Courtney Ochsner, for her support with the myriad of details that brought this book to fruition. We thank our readers for their input: Maury Bouchard, Judy Cash, Bill Lamb, and Gabriel Schechter. Gabriel did two separate reviews of the manuscript and provided many pages of suggestions and corrections.

We thank Judy Cash, for her tireless efforts in discovering and verifying incidents in Mike Donlin's life, and Jennifer McCord, for her advice and guidance in helping us shape our story and navigate the changing world of publishing.

Dr. Stephen Boren helped us in understanding the medical problems of both Mike Donlin and Mabel Hite, and the state of medical knowledge at the time. Oscar Andy Hammerstein supplied us with information on his family's vaudeville theater and the world of vaudeville as it existed in the early twentieth century. Daniel Winkler provided insight into both Christian Science and the rise of motion pictures. Professor Richard Crepeau gave perspective on the nature of heroes and how they are viewed.

The members of the Society for American Baseball Research (SABR) continued to be an invaluable resource for expertise on baseball history. The Billy Rose Theatre Division of the Performing Arts branch of the New York Public Library was a wonderful source of photos and material on the show business careers of Mike and Mabel. Especially valuable were the library's Robinson Locke scrapbooks. The *Retrosheet* website allowed us to examine countless box scores and some play-by-plays of games from more than a century ago. We used *Baseball-Reference* as our source for Major and Minor League statistics.

We have assembled unique photographs, drawing on the personal collections of Andrew Aronstein, Jim Chapman, David Eskenazi, Dennis

Goldstein, Tom Hufford, Michael Mumby, and Steve Steinberg. We have also drawn on the *Boston Herald-Traveler* Photo Morgue of the Boston Public Library, the George Grantham Bain Collection at the Library of Congress, the Chicago Daily News Collection of the Chicago History Museum, and the National Baseball Hall of Fame Library of Cooperstown, New York. We also have photos from the Margaret Herrick Library of the Academy of Motion Pictures Arts and Sciences, the Lazarnick Collection of the Detroit Public Library, the Trefts Collection of the Missouri History Society, and Transcendental Graphics/The Rucker Archive.

HISTORICAL NOTES

The authors spell "Pittsburgh" and the names of that city's newspapers with the "h" at the end of the word. In the early twentieth century the spelling appeared both ways and changed during our story.

The word "theater" and the names of theaters were often spelled "theatre."

The authors italicize stage productions and movie names per the *Chicago Manual of Style*. In newspapers of the era they were often in quotation marks.

"Base ball" was often spelled as two words during this era. While the authors write it as one, we have left the two-word spelling when it appears in quotes.

Player ejections by umpires are an ongoing work-in-progress by *Retrosheet*. The early twentieth-century data are incomplete, and ejections are likely understated.

Mike Donlin appeared in many movies uncredited. Some are listed in databases; others (brief appearances) are not. While the Internet Movie Database (IMDB.com) lists him in more than seventy films, the number likely is closer to one hundred.

Mike Donlin

PART 1

Mike before Mabel

1

....

Growing Up with Tragedy

Some people seem to glide effortlessly through life, from one success to another. Others seem doomed to heartbreak, with adversity and even tragedy shadowing them. Mike Donlin was one of these "others," and his struggles with misfortune may have driven his inner strife. Yet he never conceded defeat in life and succeeded in sport, entertainment, and love. Legendary sportswriter Damon Runyon noted, "He never asked the world for anything but an even break in his life."[1]

Humorist and actor Will Rogers said of Donlin, "Bad health, bad luck, but always that something that made him the real fighter."[2] Rogers was putting a positive spin on the words "real fighter" for his old friend. Donlin, particularly before he married, was a hot-headed brawler who drank too much, traits that got him into trouble with authority.

"One of the greatest baseball players that ever wore a cleated shoe," Runyon wrote of Donlin, "and one of the most picturesque characters ever produced by the old game."[3] In every season that he played regularly Donlin was a dominant offensive player, one of the best in the National League.[4] Yet he left it at the height of his fame for the woman he loved. He went on to a career on the stage and then in motion pictures, where he became a beloved friend of many in Hollywood.

Michael Joseph Donlin was born on May 30, 1878, in Peoria, Illinois, and grew up in Erie, Pennsylvania.[5] His older siblings were born in Erie, and the family returned there after his birth. Their father's job likely prompted the family's brief move to Peoria. Michael's father, John (Jack), was born in Ireland in the early 1840s and worked as a railroad brakeman before becoming a railway conductor. Michael's paternal grandfather, who brought his family from Ennis, County Clare, Ireland, also worked for the railroads. Michael's mother, Margaret (Maggie) Cayton Donlin, was born and raised in Erie, around 1849.

The railroads were a place of opportunity for newly arrived Irish Catholics; British laws and an agrarian economy had kept them mired in poverty.[6] The website of the Irish Railroad Workers Museum states, "A free, young America spoke to these men. . . . Railroads were an industry that welcomed them to take on work, however modest, and rise to wherever their strong backs and wits could take them."[7]

Though they barely survived in their native country, Ireland's Catholics loved their lands and rarely abandoned them—until the Great Famine of 1845–49. Their primary crop and source of sustenance and livelihood, the potato, was susceptible to a fungus known as potato blight. Because so much of the population depended on that one highly nutritious crop, "the stage was set for a demographic catastrophe should nature intervene," wrote Irish historian Kevin Kenny.[8] In 1846 virtually the entire crop was destroyed. To add to the tragedy, landlords were evicting families that could no longer pay their rent. The British government provided vastly inadequate relief, a source of bitterness that remains to this day.[9] More than one million Irish, most of them Catholics, died from starvation and famine-related illnesses.

In the 1840s almost half of America's immigrants—more than one million people—came from Ireland.[10] Their poverty made it impossible for them to become independent farmers. And many no longer wanted a rural existence: land had been "the symbol of oppression and insecurity, of unbroken want and misery."[11] So they gravitated to towns, where they helped and were helped by the rise of big-city political machines.

But the Irish brought with them a predilection that nineteenth-century writer and politician John Francis Maguire foresaw in 1868: "Drink. This fatal tendency to excessive indulgence [was] the main cause of all the evils and miseries and disappointment that have strewn the great cities of America with those wrecks of Irish honor, Irish virtue, and Irish promise."[12] Kenny explained this fondness for alcohol: the more one drank—in public—the more Irish and the more of a man he became.[13]

Jay P. Dolan elaborated on this connection. Intemperance flowed from the "stem family tradition" among the Irish. The oldest son received the family inheritance, and it led younger sons to spend their spare time drinking with their friends. "They carried this tradition to the United States, where the ubiquitous saloon became a drinking club for young men," Dolan wrote.[14] But while these are explanations for why the Irish drank so heavily, what remains unanswered, wrote Kenny, is why the same intake of alcohol generated higher rates of alcoholism among the Irish than other ethnic groups.[15]

In the 1850s a nativist political group called the Know-Nothing Party arose to fight immigration and the rising influence of Catholics. In the 1880s and 1890s, as immigration surged from Eastern and Southern Europe, "being from the British Isles, the Irish were now considered acceptable and assimilable to the American way of life."

Michael's grandfather was killed in a railroad accident in 1875.[16] His mother, Margaret, died in a horrific train accident on a trestle bridge near Erie on June 29, 1885. This occurred just two weeks after Michael's aunt Jennie died of pneumonia at age thirty-four.[17]

Margaret Donlin was traveling in the caboose with her young children, son Joseph and daughter Nellie. The train was stopped as the engine had pulled past the bridge and was switching railcars, with the caboose and flatcar in the back, sitting over the trestle. "Run for your lives! There's a train close upon us," the brakeman yelled, as he realized a freight train was bearing down on the caboose.

The brakeman helped them to a flatcar in front of the caboose. But instead of the caboose being crushed, "it was driven against the flat car with such force as to double it like an oxbow, breaking the couplings at one end and throwing the car over the edge of the bridge, where it hung by one end."[18] The impact hurled Margaret toward the creek eighty feet below. She fell forty feet with her baby in her arms, and she landed on telegraph wires that cut into her flesh and stripped it from her ribs. After an hour the wires gave way, and Margaret fell into the ravine. She died the next day, but her daughter Nellie was saved when her dress was caught by a tree branch. Son Joseph escaped with minor injuries by running into a railcar.[19]

Michael's father, whose work required him to travel for extended periods, put the two surviving children, along with three of their siblings, into an Erie orphanage. Seven-year-old Michael went to live with another Erie Irish family, the Murphys.

In the next five years, before Michael turned thirteen, he lost his three remaining grandparents. All had been born in Ireland. In 1890 Michael's uncle James, a freight train conductor, was killed when he was struck by a train. (One account reported that it was the same engine that had killed Michael's grandfather in 1875.)[20] Two years later another of his father's brothers, a railroad telegrapher and the first Donlin born in the United States, died of tuberculosis at age thirty-six.[21] That same year, 1892, Michael's cousin James, who was three years younger than Michael, also passed away.

Early in 1894 fifteen-year-old Michael became an orphan when John Donlin died suddenly, a week after a minor operation. He had survived a railroad accident fifteen years earlier, when he fell on the tracks and eighteen rail cars passed over him.[22] Just two years after John's death, Michael's aunt Alice died, and two years after that, in 1898, Michael's little sister Nellie, who had survived the train accident that killed her mother, died at age fifteen.[23] All these Donlins are buried in Erie's Trinity Cemetery in the Donlin and Cayton family plots.[24]

These were the losses Michael Donlin suffered before his twenty-first birthday. The instability and insecurity they contributed to his personality can only be surmised. There would be many more family deaths in his next twenty-one years.

Michael was living with his maternal uncle, William Cayton, when his father died.[25] It is not clear when he moved from the Murphy to the Cayton household. Eddie Murphy was about Michael's age and later played for the St. Louis Cardinals from 1901 to 1903. In 1908 he told an Akron reporter, "Donlin is a fine fellow. We were raised together, Mike being brought up in my home."[26]

Throughout Donlin's life there would often be competing forces driving his conduct. Instances of antisocial behavior—aggressiveness, braggadocio, excessive drinking, shortness of temper, and even outbursts of violence—were juxtaposed with how those close to him thought of him, that he was indeed a "fine fellow." St. Louis sports editor Sid Keener, who knew Donlin from the day he began his Major League career until the day he died, wrote, "He was in numerous brawls—on the ballfield, around corners, or in saloons. And yet, despite his desire to go out and look for trouble, everyone who knew Mike Donlin admired him."[27] He was a fascinating and complicated man.

2

....

"I'm Going to Be a Sensation in Baseball"

Mike Donlin was not a well child.[1] In 1908 he spoke of his weak constitution as a youth. While the account was laced with a morbid sense of humor, it likely was based on fact. "Up to the time I was fifteen or sixteen, all the leading undertakers of the village took more than a passing interest in me. . . . I was the puniest kid in town, and my relatives always kept their mourning rags within reach." He went on to explain that by playing baseball, "[I] gradually got away from the graveyard and built myself up."[2]

Donlin was a machinist by trade and worked at the Erie City Iron Works but was not happy with a job that forced him to spend so much time indoors.[3] He also traveled on the railroads, where he earned money by selling "everything from Parisian novels to tragic train cigars."[4] His friend Eddie Murphy recalled, "We struck out and drifted south, but soon after going to New Mexico, I decided to return home. Mike kept going."[5]

Donlin, now known as Mikey or Mike, took jobs at hotels and stores in smalls town and competed in footraces on the side. He developed a following by winning many contests and earned money from tips by those who had wagered on him.[6] But he had a serious accident in one race when the organizers used a heavy fishing line for the finish tape. As he hit it, Donlin turned to look back at his opponents. The line was high and taut and cut into his neck.[7] It was time for him to turn his sights to another athletic endeavor.

At some point in the mid-1890s Mike's friends told him to "turn his attention towards baseball."[8] Tom Kelly, the University of Oregon baseball coach from 1909 to 1911, recalled pitching for Santa Clara College against Donlin.[9] Kelly remembered Donlin as "an ideal young ball player, fast on his feet, and [he] hit like a catapult. He was the typical wild Irish kid, imbued with that natural baseball sense and confidence that spell success." The youngster already had a flair for showmanship: his bat was painted red, white, and blue, and Donlin called it his "Dewey."[10] This was shortly after Admiral George Dewey's 1898 victory at Manila Bay in the Spanish-American War.

Accounts of Donlin's baseball beginnings are sketchy. He was playing semipro ball in Nevada and New Mexico in 1896 and 1897. In 1913 he told a reporter that his first game had been in Las Vegas; this may have been as early as 1896.[11] Donlin explained his start in baseball to another reporter in 1920. There was a city league of four clubs in Los Angeles in 1897, with doubleheaders each Sunday. "An opportunity to play a game every Sunday for a cut of the gate looked good to me," he said.[12]

When Donlin sat down with screenwriter Jean Plannette in 1930 and looked back on his life, he elaborated on his Los Angeles start. He was heading to the gold fields of Alaska in 1897 when he saw a poster advertising a doubleheader at Fiesta Park. He found the manager of one of the teams, said he was a pitcher, and was paid $9 to play in the twin bill against a Black team. "Mike still refuses to say just how many hits the negroes were able to score against the new-born twirler. His hitting caused a sensation," wrote Plannette.[13] The Trilbys, known as the "Colored Terrors," played against white teams in Los Angeles. When his club was in San Diego a few weeks later, Donlin agreed to join that city's team for $60 a month.[14]

In 1898 Donlin played his first professional game, in the resurrected California League.[15] Attendance was hampered that summer by attention focused on the Spanish-American War.[16] Donlin started the season with San Jose and was primarily a pitcher, one who threw and batted left-handed. He was a dangerous hitter who also played some outfield. One California paper called him the "Eastern wonder" and "the phenomenal left-arm winger of Southern California."[17] He joined the Watsonville team in midseason. "Little is known regarding the club's ability. Outside of Donlin, it is impossible to figure on the team at present."[18]

In July Mike surfaced as a star performer. Early in the month he struck out sixteen San Francisco batters.[19] At the end of the month he beat the league-leading Sacramento Gilt Edges, named after the city's lager beer, with a two-hitter. Some years later Jim Byrnes, who appeared in ten Major League games, recalled facing Donlin in California: "What Donlin did to us was cruel. He had that old roundhouse curve of his working like a charm, and he struck out nineteen of our men. But that was not all. He went at bat four times and drove the leather over the right-field fence for three home runs."[20]

The sportswriter for the *San Francisco Call* was Joe Corbett, brother of the former heavyweight boxing champion Gentleman Jim Corbett. "The gentleman [Donlin] is not new to the fans, having demonstrated his abilities on a former occasion when acting in the same capacity for the 'Florists' of San Jose. He was very good on that occasion, but yesterday he was simply great."[21]

Reporters noted that Donlin's "swagger" and "braggadocio," as well as his wildness on the mound, were holding him back.[22] A San Francisco sportswriter used sarcasm to make his point: "Donlin, with a judicious application of cold compresses to his head to reduce the enlargement, and more experience in the box, will become a good pitcher."[23]

Donlin was issuing a lot of walks, but he had control issues with more than his pitching. Newspapers usually did not disclose "misbehavior" by ballplayers, but before one late summer game Donlin's behavior could not be covered up. In front of a big crowd on August 21 he "bore signs of having lately had a tussle with John Barleycorn" and insisted his manager pay him the money he was due.[24] When Donlin was informed that his pay was current, he "abused [manager H. D.] Baxter in a vile manner and refused to play ball." Baxter suspended him for thirty days without pay. "He has been royally treated—in fact far better than he deserves," the article continued. "His conduct is all against him. He has been no sooner out of one local scrape than he has got himself into another."[25] But the star was reinstated a few days later after he apologized.[26]

In early October Mike struck out fifteen Beachcombers in beating Santa Cruz. "Donlin was simply invincible. . . . It must be admitted that Donlin pitched National League ball against which even the Baltimores would have vainly endeavored to struggle for supremacy."[27] A week later he one-hit San Jose, 6–1.

A late October game between Watsonville and Santa Cruz at the latter's Dolphin Park on the beach generated much local excitement, and the crowd included four hundred fans from Watsonville. Donlin's ineffectiveness made it no contest, as the Beachcombers won easily, 9–3. "He was as wild as a March hare, and . . . free passes were numerous. . . . When Donlin left, he was badly rattled."[28]

A week later Donlin was a member of the Beachcombers. In those early days of the league players moved from team to team with dizzying frequency. In his first start for Santa Cruz he struck out thirteen men in a 1–0 loss to league-leading Sacramento. "This was an example of what Donlin may accomplish when retaining his mental equilibrium and attending strictly to business. There is a great future ahead for this little giant."[29]

Many Santa Cruzians looked forward to having Donlin back in 1899. But Joe Corbett explained that Mike had left Watsonville because he became "intoxicated" with his success. He was unable to "live through the adulation of his admirers . . . [and] became inflated with the idea that he could run the town of Watsonville. . . . In the town at night, when everyone was sleeping, Donlin would cut loose, and who would dare reprimand him?"[30] Finally the club decided to release him.

A few years later veteran Santa Cruz baseball observer Bill Hathaway spelled out "intoxication" in a more critical vein. "Mike made good, but he was a hail-fellow, well-met, and after every winning game, he drank too deeply from the cup and was unfit for action the following day." Santa Cruz signed him, but "once again he slipped," said Hathaway. "He was arrested for drinking too heavily, hauled into court and sentenced to six months in the County jail." Donlin promised to remain sober, got a suspended sentence, and returned to the club.[31]

In 1899 the league slimmed down from eight to six teams. After Donlin beat Oakland on April 22, a San Francisco sportswriter suggested he was a genuine Major League prospect. "There is no company in the National League that is too fast for him. He draws the cork with his left hand, has amazing curves, great speed, and absolute control of the ball. . . . Yesterday Donlin made the Oakland wing shots look like bogus beer checks."[32]

Just over a month later Donlin got headlines from another San Francisco paper after he beat the city's Athletics. "Donlin showed during the game that he is very likely the best all-round player in the league. He is certainly the best pitcher, as good as the best batter. . . . He has splendid control, particularly of straight balls, a wide inshoot."[33] A local Santa Cruz paper called Donlin the "[Willie] Keeler of the league."[34]

There were some bumps along the way. In mid-June Donlin blew an 8–0 lead against the Sacramento Gilt Edges. He "lost his nerve when the Sacramento crowd jeered him. He grew warm, angry, livid, and then went into the air. It was awful, and the crowd howled and howled."[35]

Donlin was dominating the league and helping Santa Cruz maintain first place to such an extent that stories began to appear that other California League clubs were "scheming" to get rid of him by having a big-league club acquire him. On June 24 his photo appeared on the front page of the *Sporting News*, along with word that he had accepted an offer from manager Patsy Tebeau of the St. Louis Perfectos (renamed the Cardinals in 1900). "The great southpaw" lost only one game that season and was also the California League's best "batsman," with a .421 batting average, said the caption.[36]

Donlin had a local booster who helped pave the way for his promotion to the National League. "No man ever burglarized his way into the league with a smaller kit and in such a strange way as Mike Donlin," wrote John Sheridan in the *St. Louis Republic* in early 1900.[37] "The St. Louis Club was in a bad way all season. It needed pitchers and outfielders," wrote A. H. Noyes, a California *Sporting News* reporter and friend of Donlin. "Here was a man who was both, and a grand batsman as well."[38]

Tebeau directed inquiries about Donlin to Noyes, but communications were awkward and disjointed because Noyes was in jail at the time for an alcohol-related offense.[39] Whenever a wire was sent west, Donlin had to make the trip to the jail to consult with Noyes. Perhaps Tebeau thought Donlin was the one in jail; desperate for the promising player, he wired back, "Send Anyhow."[40] This confusing story morphed over the years into one in which Donlin was in jail at the time, and this was not the case according to Sheridan's contemporary account.[41]

Donlin demanded a big salary from the Perfectos. He eventually signed for an annual salary of $2,100, and the owners of the Beachcombers got $500.[42] Perhaps thinking too much about his promotion and not enough about the game at hand, Donlin was hit hard in his final start for Santa Cruz. He staggered to a 10–6 win after surrendering a 5–0 lead. "They Make Tebeau's $500 Donlin Look Like Thirty Cents," shouted a headline in a San Francisco paper.[43]

Santa Cruz fans did not want to see Donlin go. "They will probably never forgive the management there for selling Donlin. He was recognized as the mainstay of the team and was almost worshipped by the baseball public," wrote a St. Louis reporter.[44] But Beachcombers co-owner and manager Oscar Tuttle admitted at the end of the season that he had no choice. "I had to release Donlin because I needed the money."[45]

When Donlin left the Beachcombers, they were in first place with an 18-10 record; they would finish the season at 35-49. While statistics are somewhat sketchy, Donlin was reported to have hit .402 and posted a 10-4 record with Santa Cruz.[46]

Donlin's flair for self-promotion began early in his career. In a 1945 article boxing writer and sports cartoonist Hype Igoe recalled meeting the young Donlin. The Santa Cruz club, also known as the Sand Crabs, was playing at San Francisco's Recreation Park. "There was a 17-year-old [sic] center fielder on the team. How he could belt the quince!" said Igoe.[47] After hitting a home run and two triples, the young ball player approached Igoe.

Mister, I was wondering if you'd put a picture of me in the paper. They tell me that you are an [San Francisco] Examiner sports artist. That's a big paper. It counts. Now, if you can print a picture of me in the Examiner, I know those big baseball owners back East, in New York, say, will see it and send for me. I'm going to be a sensation in baseball. I KNOW I am. I'm a great player NOW. . . . Now, here's one of my pictures, pal. You can print this but be sure to get my name under it. That's important, too![48]

Igoe's editor did not run the photo, but Igoe recalled being impressed. "He was so earnest, so sure of his future." It was only about ten years later, when Igoe attended a ball game at the Polo Grounds, that he realized the publicity-seeking youngster was Mike Donlin.[49]

3

....

The Making of Mike Donlin

Mike Donlin arrived in St. Louis with the conceit and audacity of a player who believed he was destined for stardom. Sid Keener was a youngster on the welcoming committee that greeted him. In 1933 he recalled that "slim, trim athletic figure, possessing an inimitable swagger to his walk" getting off a streetcar and announcing, "I'm Mickey Donlin, the best ball player that ever came out of California, and I've got instructions to call on a fellow named Tebeau."[1]

When Donlin entered the clubhouse, manager Patsy Tebeau was with future Hall of Famers Cy Young, Bobby Wallace, and Jesse Burkett. He addressed Tebeau: "'Listen, manager. We gotta understand each other right from the jump. I ain't 'Mike.' My name's 'Mickey,' and I want it to be 'Mickey' from you and all the other fellows on this ball club.'[2] Tebeau was startled by the aggressive entrance of the player he had never seen before," Keener continued. "He told Burkett, 'Jesse, I think it will be up to you to tone down this busher.' Jesse delighted in putting a rookie over the hurdles."

Donlin then picked up a bat and knocked a couple of Cy Young's pitches into the bleachers. "I doubt if more than ten drives were hit that far in the entire history of the Cardinals' old ball park," marveled Keener.[3]

Donlin was pleased that Tebeau would be his first Major League manager. As a youngster, he had been a fan of the National League's Cleveland Spiders. "I was brought up in Erie, Pennsylvania, and the old Cleveland team was my pet one. I never saw the old Spiders in action, but I thought of them by day and dreamed of them by night."[4] Tebeau was one of the stars of that Cleveland team and their player-manager from 1891 to 1898.

Looking back, in 1911, at that first meeting in 1899, Donlin admitted he was a little frightened of Tebeau, known as "the leading scrapper of them all." But "It was going to be up to me to prove that I was of good Irish stock," said Donlin. "I quickly figured it out that I would have to fight myself into popular favor. . . . I guess Pat Tebeau . . . admired my nerve."[5] Donlin soon made his way to the offices of the *Sporting News*, which had a wall adorned with the photos of baseball's stars. J. G. Taylor Spink, whose family owned the weekly and was its publisher from 1914 to 1962, recalled that Donlin "flew into a terrible rage. 'Where the hell is my picture?' he shouted."[6]

A *St. Louis Post-Dispatch* columnist wrote in 1899, "Donlin looks like an athlete. He is squarely built, and his flesh is firm and solid. He is muscled like an ox and is quick and graceful in his movements. He is 5 feet 11 inches in height and weighs 175 pounds . . . and nothing gives him greater pleasure than a good round of applause from the grandstand."[7] Another St. Louis writer gave a far more revealing description, unusual writing for a baseball reporter in 1901: "He had a tongue for the wine when it was red, the whiskey when it was yellow, and the beer when it was amber; likewise a shrewd eye for the talking soubrette. Sober, a genial Irishman; loaded, a fighting Mick; he was not a really bad or unlikable fellow. He always did wrong while always meaning right. He could commit more sins against more commandments of God and man than anyone alive. . . . Mike loved the passing scrap and never ducked the street brawl when he could stop it with his face."[8]

Frank and Stanley Robison, already owners of the National League's Cleveland Spiders, bought the St. Louis Perfectos before the 1899 season. This was the era of "syndicate ball," when an owner could control more than one team. The purchase brought sighs of relief from the league's management and other owners because it rid the organization of saloon proprietor Chris Von der Ahe, who had owned the St. Louis club since 1892. Known as the Browns, his teams were terrible; from 1895 to 1898 they posted a combined record of 145-398.

With creditors and lawsuits closing in on Von der Ahe, he declared bankruptcy, and his club was sold by court order. The Robisons created a clean break from the previous owner with new uniforms and a new team name, the Perfectos. They were disappointed with the support Cleveland fans had been giving the Spiders and decided to focus their efforts on their newly acquired team in the larger city.[9] They moved virtually the entire talent of the Spiders' club, including Young, Burkett, and Wallace, to St. Louis. With almost no good players remaining, the 1899 Spiders had a 20-134 record and earned the moniker of Major League Baseball's worst team ever.[10]

St. Louis fans welcomed the new roster with an Opening Day crowd of fifteen thousand. The Perfectos led the league for the first month of the season but soon faded and fell from first to sixth place within a month. A *Sporting News* editorial dealt with the taunts the team was getting from hometown fans and the improper responses of the players to such criticism.[11] In mid-June Tebeau went so far as to issue an apology to the fans for the club's play.[12] This was the background to the young California phenom's being brought to Tebeau's attention.

Mike Donlin's Major League debut came on July 19, 1899, in relief, with three innings of shutout ball in a loss to the defending champion Boston Beaneaters. He then played a solid game in the field at shortstop and at bat with a triple in a win over Brooklyn. The *St. Louis Post-Dispatch* featured a likeness of Donlin (before photographs were common in newspapers), "who has made such a hit with the St. Louis club."[13] That same day the reporter for the city's morning paper, the *Globe-Democrat*, gushed, "Donlin's work at short field yesterday was surprisingly good. . . . [He] is particularly fast on his feet, and he gets down to first as fast as Burkett or Keeler. . . . Donlin is a natural player and gives every indication of being a star."[14]

In two more appearances as a pitcher that season, Donlin was wild (giving up thirteen walks) and was hit hard, and his pitching career virtually came to an end.[15] On August 29 he made his only start. He walked nine men as the Washington Nationals cruised to a 13–7 win. "Walk followed walk, and to vary the monotony, Donlin would occasionally hit a batter, make a wild pitch, or a balk."[16] What made the game more notable was that he led off and hit a home run, his third in the past four games. Four days later he hit another home run, as well as a single and double.

When Tebeau moved Donlin to shortstop, he sparkled in his first game, handling six chances cleanly. But he made six errors in his next two games at that position. On Sunday, July 30, with Cy Young pitching in front of an overflow home crowd of eighteen thousand, Donlin made three miscues at shortstop and one at first base. "Donlin, at short, made several inexcusable errors, but when considering that the youngster is not an infielder, they could readily be excused."[17]

At first base, a less demanding position for a fielder and one more suited to a left-handed thrower, Donlin was not much better, with nine errors in thirteen games. On August 7 Tebeau moved him to center field.

He settled there, where he appeared in fifty-one of his sixty-six games. His fielding was still weak.[18]

Donlin knew he would be tested by Burkett, who was famous for his ornery disposition and foul language. "The Crab" had been "the meanest player on the infamously rowdy Cleveland Spiders." He used so many expletives that newspapers could not print most of his outbursts. A typical censored one was the following: "Why you blank, blankety-blank, do you know what I think of you? I think you are the blankest blank-blank that ever came out of the blank-blankest town in the blank-blank land."[19]

Even the cocky Donlin admitted he came close to quitting when he was the focus of Burkett's razzing. "Jesse Burkett sized me up as a fresh Bush Leaguer and made life miserable for me. I determined to jump the club that night and go back to California." But Wallace, the Perfectos' mild-mannered shortstop, steadied Donlin. "Don't let Burkett bluff you any longer," Wallace told him. "You may have to fight. Burkett will battle, but you look husky enough to take care of yourself."[20]

The following week, in Pittsburgh, Donlin caught a fly ball Burkett thought was his. "He roared like a bull and threatened to knock my block off," recalled Donlin. On the carriage ride back to the hotel Donlin shoved Burkett, who said, "What's the matter, kid, you ain't exactly looking for trouble with me?" Donlin replied, "That's exactly what I'm after, you big sour stiff."[21] F. C. Lane, the longtime editor of *Baseball Magazine*, told this story in his 1925 book, *Batting*, as an example of how courage plays a role in a ballplayer's progress. "That affair was the making of Mike Donlin."[22]

Donlin and Burkett still had some bumps in their relationship, but Donlin held firm. In early August he lashed out: "You have gone the limit with me, Burkett. . . . I ain't hunting trouble, but you and I will mix the next time you call me, and I'll back myself to lick you." Tebeau was impressed. "He is plucky to the core."[23]

Once Donlin passed that test, Burkett became a sort of a mentor to him. After he had a bad day at shortstop, with the fans booing him, Donlin recalled, "Jesse Burkett may be a 'crab,' but he was the first man to brace me up when the roasts were coming good and plenty from the stands."[24]

Donlin overcame his jitters—or hid them well. The July 29 issue of *Sporting News* stated, "That young Californian, Donlin, is made of the right stuff. He has made his way in life since early boyhood. He has the confidence born of success in every line he has undertaken."[25]

In early August Donlin got into a fight with catcher Ossee Schrecongost at the St. Louis train station as the team was leaving for Pittsburgh. "Schreck" was upset that a couple of Donlin's low throws had hit him in the shins. He triggered the brawl with a comment about "fresh kids with $10,000 arms and two-cent heads who broke into the league before they knew the first rudiments of the game." Donlin knocked him down twice and was winning the fight when Schreck picked up an iron railroad coupling pin. The brawl was broken up before he could use it.[26]

A *Sporting News* reporter commented on the practice of veterans making life hard on rookies and said that such a practice was "responsible for the failure of many promising players. Very few of them have the pluck of Donlin, and they become broken in spirit by the nagging tactics of the big bullies."[27] Donlin told Jean Plannette that his only real friends on the team were pitchers George Cuppy and Cowboy Jones. "The rest of the boys spent their time thinking of new ways of ribbing me."[28] Even Burkett did not relent. "I've got my eye on you," he told Donlin, "and if you show a streak of yellow, I'll help that gang of knockers chase you back to the coast."[29]

Patsy Tebeau had a reputation for rowdiness that rivaled that of Baltimore's John McGraw. When the Orioles came to St. Louis in early September, Tebeau reinforced that reputation. The *Baltimore Sun* reported that Tebeau's "pent-up malice" toward the Orioles went to "disgraceful lengths" in the September 1 game, when he openly stated to the Orioles players, "We are after you and are going to spike you if we can." St. Louis players repeatedly jump-slid into first base during the game, leading with raised spikes. When a fight broke out in the ninth inning between Orioles base runner Aleck Smith and Perfectos second baseman Cupid Childs, "Donlin, the fresh youngster who is said to pride himself on his pugilistic abilities," rushed in from center field and tried to hit Smith. The crowd poured onto the field as Tebeau was shouting at Childs and Donlin, "Hit, him, hit him."[30]

Frank Patterson of the *Sporting News* reported that Tebeau and Burkett also encouraged fans to throw eggs and stones at the Orioles that day. The conduct was "the most dastardly, mean, cowardly, and contemptible that it has ever been my misfortune to see in any ball player on the diamond."[31] How McGraw would have reacted can only be imagined, but he was at home in Baltimore, tending to his critically ill wife.[32]

A few days later, on September 7, Tebeau attacked umpire Arlie Latham over a disputed call in the field. Donlin, who already had been ejected for arguing balls and strikes, rushed Latham and would have attacked him too had Bobby Wallace not stopped him.[33] Donlin did not stop there. The *Sporting News* reporter cryptically wrote of "vile pantomimic actions by which he expressed his opinion of Latham. It was the most outrageous exhibition of vulgarity ever seen on a ball field."[34]

While the *Sporting News* reporter acknowledged Donlin's potential, he leveled harsh criticism at the rookie. "A certain amount of reserve is expected from a minor league graduate during his first season in the fastest company, and Donlin, instead of respecting the time-honored rule, never loses a chance to make himself offensively prominent in every way. He has frequently shown his contempt for the old heads, and the day of reckoning will come." The reporter suggested that Donlin would be taught a lesson when his club headed east, and it would not be a surprise if he ended up in a hospital while on the road trip.[35]

The Perfectos finished the 1899 season in fifth place, where they had been when Donlin arrived. Meanwhile, he became part of the best outfield in baseball. He batted .323 (playing center field and leading off almost exclusively); Emmet Heidrick hit .328, and Burkett hit .396. Cy Young led the pitching staff with a 26-16 record; Donlin finished at 0-1.

In his book on the Irish in American sports, Patrick Redmond wrote, "The lack of opportunities for advancement for the Irish meant professional sports offered an escape, real or metaphoric, for every poor urban immigrant of Irish descent. . . . [Sports offered] wealth and heroic status."[36] Donlin planned to follow a long line of Irish baseball stars, led by the colorful Mike "King" Kelly, who had excelled in the late nineteenth century. But there was an obstacle in his path: Donlin himself. As a *Sporting News* reporter noted at the end of the season, in the veiled language that was common at the time, if Donlin "did not take care of himself" and if "he keeps up the convivial pace," he would drop out of the league in another season.[37]

4

....

"Provided He Takes Care of Himself"

In late 1899 the National League downsized from twelve to eight clubs. But the league's problems went beyond an excessive number of teams as scandals, mismanagement, and infighting among owners were rampant. The *Sporting News* became increasingly critical of the way the league was conducting its business. An editorial just before the start of the 1899 season declared, "What's the matter with these National League magnates? What a shame it is that the greatest of sports . . . should be in the hands of such a mal-odorous gang as these magnates have proven themselves to be. . . . [League meetings were characterized by] mudslinging, brawling, corruption, breaches of confidence, dishonorable conspiracies, [and] threats of personal violence."[1]

As Harold Seymour wrote in his history of the game in the nineteenth century, the league was a "monopolistic maze with an interlocking ownership which made competition among them a farce."[2] The Baltimore Orioles had been the powerhouse team of the 1890s until most of the club's talent was transferred to Brooklyn before the 1899 season by the common ownership group of the two clubs. The Orioles' star third baseman, John McGraw, along with catcher Wilbert Robinson, refused to leave Baltimore, primarily because they lived there and owned a successful café in town. McGraw, only twenty-five years old, took over as manager of the depleted team and led it to a surprising 86-62 record.

"The surprising success of the Baltimore Club has made its manager, John J. McGraw, the most prominent figure in baseball," wrote the *Sporting News*. "So capable a critic as [Brooklyn] Manager Hanlon has often declared that this big, little man has never had within his recollection an equal as an inside player and as a run-getter."[3] Another writer of the baseball weekly described McGraw's personality as "one of the hustling, never-say-die players who carries the crowds with him, and while possibly is excessively aggressive on some occasions."[4]

But after his Baltimore club was eliminated in the league's contraction, McGraw had no choice but to relocate for the 1900 season. Frank Robison wanted him to join his St. Louis club, now known as the Cardinals. McGraw finally agreed (as did Robinson), but only after Robison agreed to delete from the contract the reserve clause, which bound a player to his club from year to year. McGraw told Robison, "I'll give you the best I have while I am here. . . . I am sorry, Frank, but I can play with you for only one season."[5] McGraw told sportswriter Bozeman Bulger, "I saw many opportunities for myself and wanted to be in position to seize the one that I liked best."[6] He also garnered the largest salary ever paid to a ball player, $10,000.[7]

But Robison had created an awkward situation. McGraw was joining the club as captain and field leader, while Patsy Tebeau remained as manager. "What a pity," wrote Frank Patterson in the *Sporting News* later that year, "that Mr. Robison's friendship for Tebeau should have robbed the liberal fans of St. Louis of the great baseball that team, with McGraw leading, could have given them this summer."[8] Patterson called McGraw "the most valuable manager the game has ever known."[9]

Most observers considered the strengthened St. Louis club a pennant contender.[10] Veteran Patsy Donovan, a sensational fielder and base runner, as well as a consistent .300 hitter, was acquired from Pittsburgh and joined Emmet Heidrick and Jesse Burkett in the outfield. They were solid hitters; all would hit above .300 in 1900, led by Burkett's .363. All were good fielders, not known as a strength of Donlin's, who started the season on the bench. Third baseman Bobby Wallace moved to shortstop to allow McGraw to assume his regular position. Wallace would spend most of the rest of his Hall of Fame career at short.

Donlin moved into the starting lineup in early May, when Heidrick hurt his leg. Donlin's defensive shortcomings surfaced early. On May 8 he "longingly rubbered" a fly ball, an error that opened the door for four Cincinnati runs.[11] But he also scored two runs, one on his first home run of the season, and St. Louis won. A week later he misjudged a fly ball, which led to an inside-the-park home run and a Cardinals' loss.[12]

Later in May Donlin excelled in a series at the Polo Grounds.[13] On May 20 he helped Cy Young beat the Giants with two long throws, one to home plate and the other to McGraw at third, to eliminate runners. One St. Louis reporter predicted Donlin would become the league's best outfielder, "provided he takes care of himself and fails to complacently regard the wine when it is red and the beer when it is amber."[14] Another St. Louis correspondent, likely John Sheridan, was more forthcoming:

> Donlin is a gay gallant not at all averse to a finish bout with World's Champion James J. Bacchus, the man whom they have all tackled and never yet got a decision over, given a black eye, or handed a knock-down. Also, that he is a devout worshiper, a constant genuflector upon the time-worn steps of Venus' altar. Well, I must admit I like a kid who loves the ladies, God bless 'em all. But I never could see what a fellow could gain, especially an athlete, in these catch-as-you-can, no-hold-barred bouts with Hall Adali Bacchus. . . . Let Donlin eschew fun and stick to business, and they will all have to tip their chapeaus to him.[15]

Yet, as a *Sporting News* writer pointed out, such shortcoming did not impinge on Donlin's rising popularity: "The fans idolize the dashing, fleet-footed Donlin."[16]

As the season moved into June, Donlin continued to gather accolades for his play. "'Mickey' Donlin, the Erie–Santa Cruz phenom, is setting the entire East on fire by his swift playing," wrote a reporter for the *St. Louis Globe-Democrat*. "On all sides he is being described as 'the grandest young player in the league,' 'the king of all youngsters,' etc. . . . His fielding, which had a decidedly saffron tinge to it in '99, is now really first class, and he is showing a 'whip' of the Heidrick, Wagner type. And as for hits, he is getting them in bunches every day."[17] Donlin had just stroked five hits in a game in Boston when he was only a double away from the cycle.

As the midpoint of the season approached, the Cardinals experienced more injuries and more losing. Rowdyism continued to be prevalent throughout the league, but in St. Louis John McGraw was not berating umpires with his usual passion. As "ringleader" of the rowdy Baltimore Orioles of the 1890s, McGraw was known as a "rough, unruly man who is constantly playing dirty ball. He has the vilest tongue of any ball player."[18] Yet he had been uncharacteristically subdued all this season. To his credit McGraw did not want or try to undermine Tebeau. As the Cardinals slid

MIKE DONLIN, Outfielder,
ST. LOUIS. 1900.

1. Mike Donlin began his Major League career in St. Louis as a pitcher in 1899. He soon found a home in the outfield, where he was one of four Cardinals who batted above .300 in 1900, led by the .363 of Jesse Burkett, a career .338 hitter, just above Donlin's .333. At that time this was still the primary way images were presented in publications. National Baseball Hall of Fame Library, Cooperstown, New York.

down in the standings, there were calls for Tebeau to be fired, but the loyal Robison resisted.

On June 17 the Cardinals were trounced by the Reds, 14–2, and it was Donlin who led the battle with an umpire. He hurled epithets at Adonis Terry; even a St. Louis paper was critical: "Profanity should not be permitted. It hurts the game and is an insult to the ladies, and there were many of them in the stands Sunday."[19] Two days later another loss to Cincinnati pushed St. Louis into last place. This time Terry tossed Donlin, and it was a shove of the umpire—not just words—that earned his ejection. An editorial in the *Sporting News* said that Tebeau countenanced the "outrageous conduct," and it asked, "Will President Robison give rowdyism his sanction by permitting his players to bulldoze and threaten umpires?"[20]

Until 1898 only one umpire officiated a game. While a second was added that season, owners complained of the cost and went back to just one arbiter for the 1900 season.[21] But just three games into the season, a *Sporting Life* reporter wrote, "It is apparent that the magnates have made a fatal mistake in abolishing the double umpire system. . . . The plays are made so fast that it is almost impossible for one man to judge balls and strikes and to take care of base decisions at the same time."[22] The following season the league would return to the two-umpire system.

At around 3 a.m. on Sunday morning, June 24, Donlin's lack of restraint imperiled not only his career but also came close to costing him his life. He entered a St. Louis saloon with pitcher Gus Weyhing; it was likely not their first visit to a bar that night. An older man with a long, red beard was drinking with a young friend, and Donlin began to tease him with "uncalled-for boisterousness on his art of 'joshing' the elderly gentleman." Along with his comments about the old man's "chin lilies," Donlin ran his fingers through them.[23]

The two men left the bar, but Donlin and Weyhing followed them. Donlin continued with his taunts. The young friend suddenly pulled out a knife, came up from behind, and slashed Donlin across his face. A *Sporting Life* writer described the wounds in detail: "Two bad cuts across the throat, one along the right side of his face, running vertically down his cheek close to the ear, one across his check under the eye, a slight gash across the nose, and the fingers of both hands are seriously slashed and cut."[24] He got these last cuts wrestling the knife away from his assailant. Fortunately the gashes were not deep (though scars would remain for his lifetime), but the hand wounds were expected to keep Donlin out of action for three or four weeks.

Donlin returned just a week later, but on July 4 he badly sprained his knee, an injury that put him on crutches for two weeks. To compound the Cardinals' woes, McGraw broke his finger sliding home in the same game. The team continued to sputter. Rather than appear on the coaching line, McGraw spent a lot of time at the thoroughbred racetrack across the street. Criticism of his doing so appeared in the *Sporting News*.[25]

In early August *Sporting Life* wrote, "Individually the St. Louis team is the greatest in the world today. Collectively, it is the worst."[26] Shortly after McGraw joined the club, he said, "I have been going very slowly in suggesting changes and advocating team work because Tebeau is manager, and I do not want to nor will I make myself offensive to him."[27] More recently McGraw told a friend, "To play winning ball would require very radical changes in the team's style of play, and these changes I have no authority and power to make."[28]

On August 19, when his club's record stood at 42-50, Patsy Tebeau resigned. "I could not make the team play the ball it seemed capable of playing. I tried every trick I knew and found myself unable to get proper results."[29] While Tebeau played an aggressive type of game, he did not enforce discipline. "The crop of four o'clocks [players who stayed out late carousing] increased this year until the Donlin carving incident of the man with the auburn whiskers opened the eyes of the St. Louisans to the fact that the flower of the Cardinals were [*sic*] a lot of night-blooming cereuses."[30] An unnamed St. Louis player said, "There is no use to try to duck it. Booze is the cause of our being where we are. . . . I am surprised that some of the newspaper boys suppress stories about us."[31]

Despite Robison's urging, McGraw declined to take over as manager. "I am sorry, Frank, but I can't take it," he said.[32] He was smart enough not to take over a demoralized team near the end of the season—especially when he knew he would be leaving in 1901. A *Sporting News* editorial reminded readers, "He was an artist, a leader, a general of the game in Baltimore; he has been and is a 'hired hand' in St. Louis."[33] He batted .344 for the Cardinals and led the league with an on-base percentage of .505. "He played good ball, and let it go at that."[34]

Who ran the club for the final few weeks of the season? McGraw and Patsy Donovan made the lineups and selected the pitchers.[35] Frank Robison appointed his concessions manager, Louis Heilbronner, as the de jure manager. But as Fred Lieb pointed out in his history of the Cardinals, Heilbronner "could no more command the respect of those ex-Spiders than a fly could win the affection of a real spider."[36] Big pitcher Jack Powell threatened to lock the tiny and rotund manager in the team safe, but prankster Mike Donlin went further.

McGraw told Heilbronner that the club would win more games if Donlin did not fight with umpires and get tossed so often. The five-foot-tall manager decided to fine Donlin the next time he was ejected. When umpire Hank O'Day tossed the outfielder, Heilbronner told him, "You're fined $100 for getting put out of the game." Donlin was furious. "I am, am I? You little shrimp. I'll show you." Donlin grabbed him and carried him to the water barrel. "Take the cover off the water bucket, Mac," he said to McGraw. "I am going to drown this insect of a manager."[37] Heilbronner later said: "And I think he would have done it except for two things. McGraw didn't lift the lid off the water barrel, and I cancelled the fine in mid-air."[38]

The Cardinals ended the season tied for fifth place with the Chicago Cubs, with a 65-75 record. Donlin hit .326 with ten home runs in only seventy-eight games; his .507 slugging average was the team's best. The *Sporting News* reported that only four Cardinals (McGraw, Robinson, Young, and Donovan) received their final paychecks of the season. The others had theirs withheld because "[keeping] late hours, dissipation, and gambling" resulted in the poor play.[39] Frank Robison also mentioned just four players who had behaved properly, but Burkett and not Young was in his account. "I am totally disgusted with the way the players acted during the season just closed," he said.[40]

Donlin headed to California for the offseason. He captained and played for a San Diego team that won the championship of the Southern California Winter League.[41] But in late January 1901 Donlin was replaced as captain because of his outbursts against umpires.[42] A report from Santa Cruz noted that "Micky Donlin's style of registering a kick was distasteful to the effete Southerners, and to soothe their sensitive feelings, threw up the sponge."[43]

Donlin's popularity and talent still led to efforts among California fans to raise money to keep him in the state year round.[44] There were reports that Donlin had signed with a Los Angeles team.[45] He did not mind such publicity. While he likely intended to play in the Major Leagues in 1901, he declared that he would play in the California League if the St. Louis club did not give him a big raise over the $300 a month he was paid in 1900.[46]

Even when Donlin was in San Diego, a *Sporting News* correspondent could not resist commenting on his weaknesses, as well as his strengths: "Chances are that he will have a high old time instead of living an athletic life. Too bad that he does not take good care of himself in season and out of season, for he is one of the best natural ball players in the business."[47] While Donlin was in San Diego, a doctor operated on his face to "mend . . . a mighty scar, as if it had been made with a meat-ax."[48]

Sporting Life had a feature on its editorial page for many years titled "Wise Sayings of Great Men." Over the years a number were attributed to Mike Donlin, and many of them revolved around alcohol. One credited him with saying, "The fellow who swears off for a month doesn't cause the devil any anxiety."[49]

5
....

Donlin and McGraw Battle with American League Umpires

As the 1900 season unfolded, it was evident the National League's contraction to eight teams did not solve its problems. Frank F. Patterson wrote that such a move was like "the doctor who would amputate a patient's leg to cure him of Bright's disease or consumption." He called the owners "selfish, mercenary incompetents."[1] The league's attendance fell by more than 17 percent from 1899. Writers for the *Sporting News* were critical of the league's operation and hopeful a new league would facilitate improvement. An August editorial said, "The National League has been a failure in every sense of the word. . . . Competition is as necessary for the proper conduct of amusements as it is in any other line of business."[2]

Ban Johnson had operated his American League as a midwestern-based minor league in 1900 and was now prepared to challenge the National League. Patterson said of him, "He stands head and shoulders above all of them [National League owners] in brains, character, force, and as a man of affairs. With such a leader to oppose it, the National League would look like thirty cents."[3] The elimination of National League clubs in four cities gave Johnson his opening. As baseball historian John Thorn wrote, "The great consolidation, which had left many major leaguers suddenly unemployed, emboldened Johnson."[4] The upstart league's president also planned to plunder the National League for talent to stock his rosters and establish his league's credentials.[5]

Johnson said his American League would stand behind its umpires and curtail ruffianism. Early in the 1901 season he announced: "Clean ball is the main plank in the American League platform, and the clubs must stand by it religiously. There must be no profanity on the ball field. The umpires are agents of the League and must be treated with respect. . . .

Rowdyism and profanity have worked untold injury to baseball. To permit it would blight the future of the American League."[6]

Before Johnson finalized his choice of John McGraw as the manager and part-owner of the new Baltimore franchise, the men met for a frank exchange. "There is one thing I must make clear to you at the very outset: I am going to run the American League as a clean league," he told McGraw. "Many things have been going on in the National League that have disgusted patrons of the game. These things must stop. Furthermore, as a league president, I always back up my umpires." "I always play hard, and play to win," replied McGraw. "That is the way I run my teams."[7]

"Yes, John, I know you are an aggressive ball player and manager," added Johnson with less severity. "And, of your intense desire to win. I don't want to curb your zeal; it is desirable in a baseball man, but aggressiveness cannot be carried into rowdyism. You must understand now I will tolerate no rough stuff, nor the type of language you and your Oriole players have used in the past."[8]

In hindsight it seems puzzling that Johnson and McGraw thought they could coexist. Baseball historian Donald Honig called them "a couple locomotives started from opposite directions along the same track."[9] But at the time this partnership did not seem so odd. McGraw wanted to manage a team again, and what better place than back in his hometown and as a part-owner of the club?[10] From Johnson's perspective, what better way to show the sports world that his organization was a major league from the start than to sign one of the National's biggest stars?

McGraw's relatively disciplined demeanor during the 1900 season also suggested that he might be mellowing. On September 1 he was quoted in *Sporting Life* with some very out-of-character remarks. "I used to think that senseless kicking would get you something with the umpire, but experience has taught me differently. My crude ideas on that subject were responsible for my seeing many a game from the bench."[11]

McGraw began building his new team by signing Brooklyn's best pitcher, Joe McGinnity, who had won fifty-six games in the past two seasons, his first two in the National League. McGinnity had considered retiring after the 1900 season, embittered by the control that the National League teams had on their players. With the new league raiding the established one for personnel, salaries skyrocketed, and players experienced a rare opportunity of competition for their services. McGinnity signed for $3,000 with Baltimore, far more than his $1,900 salary with Brooklyn in 1900.[12] (McGraw also picked up a young utility man from Brooklyn, Roger Bresnahan, whom he would play primarily as a catcher.)

Cy Young, who won 286 games with Cleveland and St. Louis, jumped to the American League's Boston club and told Cardinals owner Frank Robison, "Your treatment of your players has been so inconsiderate that no self-respecting man would want to work for you if he could do anything else in the world."[13]

Mike Donlin was still playing in California in early March. One report that said he would play and manage a California club noted his "convivial soul" and in a careful choice of words said, "He is too good a fellow to be a good manager."[14] A *Sporting News* reporter reminded fans that Donlin "is to Santa Cruz what McGraw is to Baltimore."[15] There was lingering suspicion he was leveraging his California options to get a salary increase from Robison. Sure enough, in early March he told California reporters he would return to the Cardinals, where he had been offered a raise.[16]

Shortly thereafter Donlin met with John McGraw in Hot Springs, Arkansas, where players went to "boil" out in the natural spring-fed baths. He agreed to join McGraw's Orioles for a salary of around $2,500.[17] St. Louis papers attacked Donlin's "double-dealing," and one said "his Celtic proclivities and pugnacity" would not be missed.[18]

Donlin was about to see a vastly different McGraw from the relatively passive teammate he had been with the Cardinals. When she wrote *The Real McGraw* more than a half century later, Blanche McGraw (McGraw's second wife) captured the essence of the man on the ball field: "Defeat was his mortal enemy. He was a force that knew only one compromise: victory. All else was of minor importance, for without victory, without a team of fighting, hustling players to create that victory, baseball had no meaning for him. By the same token, life without baseball also had little meaning for him. It was his meat, his drink, his dream, his blood and breath, his reason for existence."[19]

Given another chance to show that Baltimore was a Major League city, more than ten thousand Orioles fans welcomed their new team on Opening Day. Donlin's two triples led the way to a 10–6 win over the Boston Americans. He tripled again and scored three times in another victory the following day, as Boston's Cy Young had one of his worst starts ever. In early May a

Washington sportswriter described Donlin as "the clever youngster who tramps around the local left patch of turf, stalking up to the plate with the swagger of an inborn appreciation of his prowess and in response to the numerous cries of his numerous admirers in the bleachers to 'kill it, Mike.'"[20]

On May 15 McGraw was at bat, arguing balls and strikes with umpire Joe Cantillon. When Philadelphia pitcher Wiley Piatt tried to sneak a quick pitch past him, McGraw quickly turned and hit a game-winning triple. But he continued with his verbal attacks on Cantillon from third base and was tossed from the game.[21]

Ban Johnson suspended McGraw two days later while expressing puzzlement: "I cannot understand how a man as intelligent as McGraw, and knowing, as he does, the high value of our trademark—clean baseball—can willfully jeopardize that reputation which we have worked so long to build up."[22] Baseball historian Joe Durso suggested that McGraw's behavior reflected "the forthright style of the day in personal relations, a style that seemed to follow a national mood embodied by the new President himself, Theodore Roosevelt. It was a kind of frontier style that had spilled over into the twentieth century."[23]

New York sportswriter Frank Graham pointed out that McGraw was a master at motivating his men: "McGraw was capable, of course, of hurtling into a violent rage in a split second, where he had been all sunshine and sweetness before. But many of his seemingly sudden charges on the field were carefully plotted and perfectly timed."[24] And the first-year league did have some below-average umpires. While Frank Patterson supported McGraw's suspension, he urged Johnson to address the "farcical umpiring" because "rotten umpiring will surely beget kicking."[25]

Donlin was having his own disputes with umpires. In Chicago near the end of May, with Johnson in the stands, he earned a $25 fine for rowdyism. One Chicago reporter wrote that "Mikemouth Donlin" used "hideous language" to the umpire.[26] Three days later in Detroit Donlin was again in the middle of a storm. "Oriole Hoodlums Ran Amuck," shouted the *Detroit Free Press* headline.[27] After veteran umpire Jack Sheridan ejected Orioles catcher Wilbert Robinson for disputing a call at the plate, Donlin threw a bat at the umpire. Johnson suspended him indefinitely and said, "Such a man as Donlin is an injury to us, and if he is to play in the American League, he must be taught to play American League baseball and improve his conduct from now on."[28]

McGraw was able to secure Donlin's reinstatement after only one game by sending a telegram to Johnson in which he guaranteed his young player would behave. "The next time Donlin breaks loose," said McGraw, "you can fire him out of the league altogether."[29] Both McGraw's promise and Johnson's response seem surprising in retrospect. It was a rare instance of Johnson's backing down in enforcing discipline and supporting his umpires. It would be a not-so-rare instance of Donlin getting another chance.

When the Tigers came to Baltimore for a four-game set in mid-June, Donlin pummeled Detroit pitching for twelve hits in eighteen at bats, as the Orioles swept the series. He pushed his batting average up to .339, and the Orioles moved into a tie for third place. On June 24 Donlin went 6-for-6 (including two doubles and two triples) and scored five runs in a 17–8 victory.[30] A Baltimore sportswriter spoke of Donlin's "fame as a destroyer of pitchers' self-esteem" in this "very saturnalia of slugging."[31] The next day, former Oriole Ducky Holmes robbed Donlin of a home run with a sensational, "seemingly impossible" catch. The Baltimore reporter noted it would have been Donlin's tenth consecutive hit over three games, "a feat that has not been equaled for many years, if ever."[32]

On July 12 McGraw tore cartilage in his knee, an injury that hastened the end of his playing career. He was leading the league with a .508 on-base percentage at the time. McGraw is not often recognized as the great batsman he was, "the best man in the game to get on first base," in the words of one reporter in 1900. "He gets there oftener than any of them."[33] Long before that statistic was fully recognized, McGraw understood the importance of getting on base. His career on-base percentage of .466 ranks all-time third highest, behind Ted Williams (.482) and Babe Ruth (.474).

On August 21 in Baltimore the Orioles' confrontation with umpire Tommy Connolly led to a forfeit of the game to the Tigers. The Orioles and their fans were already furious with his officiating during the homestand and asked that a substitute take his place.[34] When Connolly, a National League umpire the previous three seasons, entered the ballpark that day, the Orioles called the police department and requested fifty policemen.[35] In the fourth inning a close call at first base led Joe McGinnity to stomp on Connolly's foot with his spiked shoe and spit into the arbiter's face. Connolly forfeited the game to Detroit, and the scene quickly degenerated. Baltimore pitcher Harry Howell grabbed him, and Tigers shortstop Kid Elberfeld, no friend of umpires himself, tried to pull Connolly away to protect him. Donlin then entered the fray and knocked Elberfeld down. Various fights broke out, and the umpire was attacked by fans as he left the field.[36] Ban Johnson soon banned McGinnity, who already had won twenty-two games this season—for life.

The frightening nature of the incident and the danger umpires faced early in the century were conveyed in newspaper accounts across the country. The *Philadelphia Inquirer* put the story on its front page: "A first-class riot broke out during which Connolly was rushed by both players and spectators; and but for the energetic protection of a band of thirty-five policemen, he would have done well to have escaped with his life. As it is, Connolly has a swollen eye, and an enlarged jaw and many mementoes over his anatomy of body punches."[37]

Some sportswriters were critical of Connolly's ability. He had briefly retired the previous year because of the rowdyism of the New York Giants.[38] Frank Patterson wrote that he "never saw an umpire whose work was so openly partisan as to necessitate his being surrounded and protected by police for five games successively."[39] Connolly went on to a distinguished career and umpired until 1931, at which time he became the American League's umpire-in-chief. He officiated at eight World Series and, with Bill Klem, was the first umpire inducted into Baseball's Hall of Fame.[40]

Most observers were fed up with the continued rowdyism of John McGraw's club. One *Sporting News* reporter claimed many of the Orioles brought their "bad manners" over from the National League. "The Baltimores have no more place in the American League than a steamboat in Sahara or a bull-baiting at a May festival. They are in a class by themselves, or unclassified."[41]

A week later McGraw and McGinnity were subdued and contrite when they met with Johnson at his office in Chicago, and they persuaded the league's president to reduce the pitcher's suspension to twelve days.[42] McGraw "dropped his defiant air [and] ceased his talk of rebellion" in the meeting, wrote Hugh Fullerton.[43] Why Johnson backed down is unclear. Perhaps he was reminded how important a recruiter and loyal supporter of the new league McGinnity had been.[44] Perhaps he did not want to jeopardize his relationship with McGraw—at least not yet. It was a rare and fleeting reconciliation, possibly facilitated by McGraw's hobbling into Johnson's office on crutches, the result of his knee injury. "Mr. Johnson is a much better person than I had been led to believe," said McGraw when he returned from Chicago. "He seemed to be much more inclined to listen to our side than I had supposed, and anxious to do justice."[45]

On September 3 McGinnity was back on the mound and tossed a 10-0 shutout against Milwaukee in the first game of a doubleheader, helped by Donlin's two triples. He also pitched a complete game in the second game that day, albeit in a loss. This season, as in every one between 1901 and 1908 in which he played at least one hundred games, Donlin had at least ten triples and twenty stolen bases, indications of his speed.

Donlin finished the season with a .340 batting average, second best in the league but far behind that of Philadelphia A's second baseman Nap Lajoie's .426.[46] Years later former heavyweight boxing champion Jim Corbett, who had a syndicated column, wrote, "McGraw's judgment of Donlin was justified. Mike quickly learned the tricks of outfielding, and his arm, mighty in its power, cut off many runners going in from third."[47] He had twelve assists from left field, third most in the league.

Donlin sometimes worked in the coaching box during the season. To him it meant "saying mean and disagreeable things to the pitcher of the other team and showing off his own smartness," a *Sporting News* reporter said. "He does not aid the base runner at all, and words of 'advice' that he shouts to the men on the bases are so stereotyped and seldom timely."[48] The coaching tactic of trying to disconcert the opposing pitcher was a tool John McGraw often employed. The reality was that "skilled base-coaching" emerged only gradually in the first two decades of that century.[49]

The Orioles finished the season in fifth place with a 68-65 record. Six regulars batted over .300, and the club led the league in hitting with a .294 mark. Attendance in Baltimore was less than half that of pennant-winning Chicago and second-place Boston. Donlin then joined Lajoie's touring club, the All-Americans, which played exhibition games against the All-Nationals and independent teams across the country.[50] At the fairgrounds in Anderson, Indiana, Donlin hit the longest drive ever seen there.[51]

As the offseason continued, the war for players between the two leagues showed no signs of abating. One of the players much in demand was slugger Mike Donlin. One report said he might jump back to the Cardinals. Ban Johnson relocated the Milwaukee club to St. Louis, where it would go head-to-head against Frank Robison's Cardinals. "The scramble for star players is now in full blast, and from now until next spring there will be no let-up in scrapping, scheming and dickering by the magnates and adroit manipulation by the much-sought players."[52] For at least one more season players' pocketbooks would benefit from competition for their services.

Ban Johnson would continue his push to stamp out rowdyism in his league. An editorial in the *Sporting News* stated, "President Johnson declares that prompt punishment will be meted out to the anarchists of the diamond, and the umpires will be directed to enforce the rules to the letter. . . . The clemency that was extended to offenders in 1901 cannot be expected by the anarchists of the next season."[53]

6

....

A Brutal Assault

Despite reports he was headed to the new American League team in St. Louis, Mike Donlin was still a member of the Baltimore club when a drinking spree in March 1902 almost ended his career. Ernest M. Slayton, a Chicago businessman, had charged Donlin with committing an "atrocious and brutal assault" upon Miss Mamie Fields, a cast member of the *Ben-Hur* show playing at Baltimore's Academy of Music. The attack took place in front of the theater on March 13 at about 11:30 p.m. "The assault was all the more outrageous," wrote the *Baltimore Sun*, because Miss Fields was "physically frail and delicate and of petite figure."[1]

Charles F. Towle, the manager of the *Ben-Hur* company, said, "Miss Mamie Fields and Miss Margaret Kingston, chorus girls in our company . . . were approached by this man, Donlin, who attempted to take hold of one of the girls. Mr. E. M. Slayton . . . ran up and told Donlin to let the girls alone. Thereupon Donlin struck Slayton in the face, knocking him down. Miss Fields cried, 'Don't hit him!' and Donlin then turned and struck her. By this time several persons had gathered at the scene, and Donlin ran into a saloon in the vicinity."[2] This was Wilbert Robinson's and John McGraw's Diamond Cafe, which was rapidly becoming a Baltimore landmark.

Miss Fields was taken to a nearby doctor. Towle commented, "She vomited some blood and then lapsed into unconsciousness. One side of her face is badly bruised, and she will be unable to appear with us for some time."[3]

A man answering Donlin's description had to be removed from the lobby of the theater the night before the incident because of intoxication. Donlin was identified by the scar on his left cheek, the result of the slashing he received from the St. Louis bar incident in June 1900.

The general consensus was that the Orioles had no choice but to release or trade Donlin as he would no longer have the respect of the Baltimore fans. Manager McGraw, who was in Hot Springs, Arkansas, wrote in a wire to Orioles president John "Sonny" Mahon, "We are catering to the public of Baltimore and must meet their demands. Neither Donlin nor any other player can stand in the way. Anything you do will be satisfactory. Would advise indefinite suspension."[4]

The next day the officers of the Baltimore Baseball Association gave Donlin his unconditional release. The Orioles had advanced him $500 on his 1902 salary, money he was not obligated to repay. But there was a more significant potential loss to the club. Donlin was of great value to the Orioles, and at this point—before the trial—they might have gotten $2,000 or more for his sale.

The American League had from its inception made a strong stand against rowdy ball playing. Donlin's assault had not taken place on the ballfield, yet such an outrageous offense demanded strong action against the perpetrator. "The American League won't tolerate any rowdies, and certainly not the men of the Donlin stripe," Ban Johnson said. "I never met the boy personally, but his rotten conduct was reported to me several times last season by my umpires, and I was compelled to discipline him. It is with extreme pleasure that I declare him blacklisted from the American League for life, and I feel sure that the National League will follow suit."[5]

From the assault on March 13 to conviction and sentencing took less than a week. On March 17 Donlin appeared in criminal court, charged with two counts of night assault. Donlin's counsel waived an examination, and the case was sent to a grand jury.

Miss Fields and Mr. Slayton were the only prosecution witnesses to testify at the pre-sentencing hearing. The discoloration and bruises under each of Miss Fields's eyes became more apparent when she raised her veil at the state attorney's request. A large bruise under Mr. Slayton's right eye was also plainly evident. Miss Fields showed no animosity to Donlin. She smiled frequently and sometimes indulged in a little laugh. "Both my eyes were blackened, my teeth were loosened, and my nose was bruised," she said. "I don't know who did it. I fainted and afterward went to my home in Washington. I don't know Donlin," she added; "he must have crossed the street behind me."[6] Judge Albert Ritchie wanted to know what Donlin said before striking her. Miss Fields was reluctant to speak the words used by Donlin but agreed to whisper them to the state attorney, who communicated them to the judge.

Miss Fields said Donlin remarked to Slayton, "I recognize you," followed by a burst of abusive language. Slayton said he saw Donlin following the girls across the street, and his impression was that Donlin was trying to strike up an acquaintance with them. In addition to his discolored eye, Slayton complained of a cut in the back of his head, which he received in falling. He said he was a broker in Chicago and was in Baltimore on business. Slayton said he was talking to the ladies and had his back to Donlin when he heard Donlin say, "I can size you up," adding foul epithets before knocking him down.[7]

The crowded courtroom included many of Donlin's friends and fans. When the defense's turn came, it called the defendant as its first witness. Donlin said he was twenty-three years old, unmarried, and, added falsely, that he had no previous arrests. During his two seasons in St. Louis, wrote a *Sporting News* reporter, he dissipated and was often involved in street fights, in which he was the aggressor.[8]

When requested by his counsel to tell all he knew of "this unfortunate affair," Donlin replied, "I remember nothing at all of it. I was under the influence of liquor and lost my head. . . . I had not drunk liquor for four weeks before that day. I started to drink about noon. I don't remember seeing the ladies. The accident would never have happened had I been in my right mind."[9]

Donlin's attorneys asked for clemency. One said that the testimony showed a lack of premeditation or deliberation. The other said that a sober Donlin never would have committed such an act and asked the court not to put the stigma of imprisonment on him. Both reminded the court that Donlin already had been dismissed from the Baltimore baseball club and had thereby lost the balance of his salary of $2,800 for the season, and that he was the main source of support of a younger brother and sister. "It is possible that Donlin was too excited and too far gone in liquor to know that his assailant was no longer a man, but a woman," pitcher Joe McGinnity, Donlin's teammate, said.[10]

Donlin had been charged with two indictments for night assault, one against Fields and one against Slayton. As part of the agreement by which he avoided the need for a trial, Donlin pleaded guilty to the charges, which were downgraded to the less serious offenses of "common assault." In his ruling Judge Ritchie said, "Gentlemen, this young man seems to have borne a good reputation prior to this affair, but he nevertheless has committed a most aggravated assault. It is probably true that he would not have done so if not intoxicated. But the people, and particularly the women of our community, must be protected from drunken people as well as sober people. . . . I must pass a sentence which is somewhat commensurate with the act. I impose a sentence of six months in jail and a fine of $250."[11]

Donlin appeared stunned by the severity of the sentence. He had sat quietly through the proceedings, but he winced noticeably when he heard his fate. If the fine was paid, Donlin would be released in five months, after the usual commutation for good behavior.

"Of course, the American League is through with Mike Donlin," declared Ban Johnson after learning of the verdict. "His crime was a filthy one," he continued. "He is an illiterate cuss, they say, and he surely must be. . . . The officials of the Baltimore Club discharged him the moment the fact became public and wrote to me to have him blacklisted."[12]

"Drunkenness and debauchery can be forgiven in a ball player who becomes penitent and tries to reform, but the baseball public will never forget or condone an assault on a woman," wrote the *Sporting News*.[13] Detroit sportswriter Joe S. Jackson declared, "The day has passed when actions such as these may be overlooked as eccentricities of genius."[14] *Sporting Life*'s W. A. Phelon wrote after the sentencing, "Too bad, in one way—too bad that such a ball player could not control himself. I think Mike Donlin is one of the greatest ball players in the world. He has everything— the batting, the running, the fielding, the nerve, and the clever head. He was just beginning to show his speed, and another year would have seen him at the very top notch of perfection."[15]

Until this incident things had gone extremely well for the brash and colorful Donlin in Baltimore. His .340 batting average and thirty-three stolen bases in 1901 had catapulted him to baseball stardom. The *Sporting News* described him as a "jolly, generous whole-souled boy," while pointing out his "propensity to fight, especially when drinking."[16]

Within a month of Donlin's sentencing, a group of what the *Baltimore Sun* called "well-known citizens" was petitioning for him to be pardoned. The group claimed that when he pleaded guilty, it was in the belief that he only would be fined. The men said they were not attempting to minimize the seriousness of the offense but were suggesting that the punishment was disproportionate to the crime.

The confinement of jail life was torturous for the free-spirited Donlin. Ill much of the time, he nevertheless took part in regular exercise to stay in shape while also working in the boiler room. Moreover, he was struggling mentally as well as physically. The disgrace he had brought upon himself and the knowledge that his sister and brother missed his financial aid were making him a sick man. "He is suffering from several ailments, and looks a wreck of his former self," wrote a reporter for the *Cincinnati Enquirer*. "He weighs but 125 pounds, and his face is drawn and thin. He is at the present time in the jail hospital undergoing treatment."[17]

Donlin's belligerent style of play was a poor fit for the American League, which Ban Johnson sought to make the more gentlemanly league. However, no such culture was prevalent in the National League, and in one of baseball's more bizarre signings, that is where prisoner Donlin found a new home. On May 20, 1902, while still in the Baltimore City Jail, he signed a contract with the Cincinnati Reds, who were represented by a member of the clergy.[18] Following his release, scheduled for September, he would play for the Reds the rest of the 1902 season. The St. Louis Cardinals, the National League team for whom Donlin had played in 1899 and 1900, made no bid for him.

The correspondent for the *Enquirer* expressed some doubt as to how the rowdy and profane outfielder would be accepted by Reds fans. "Cincinnati has never cared particularly for the Donlin-McGraw school of manners," he wrote. "I wonder if he is in shape to play ball," was Reds manager Bid McPhee's reaction when he was told of the signing.[19]

Sporting Life reported that the Cincinnati club had decided to give Donlin a chance to rehabilitate himself. "In view of the fact that he is the sole support of his brother and sister," the paper wrote, "and that he has been sufficiently punished for his drunken folly, we trust the Maryland authorities will grant him a speedy pardon. He is by no means past redemption."[20] Because he had been punished as very few players before him had been, the newspaper thought it unlikely he would give the team any cause for criticism or discipline.

7

....

A Return to the National League

In the summer of 1902 the war over players and the bitter feelings between the leagues remained strong. The National League was determined to destroy Ban Johnson's new American League. Two of Johnson's most dedicated foes among NL owners were John Brush of the Cincinnati Reds and Andrew Freedman of the New York Giants.

Brush and Freedman, while difficult men in their own right, had "developed a harmonious working relationship," wrote historian Bill Lamb.[1] In July Freedman, working with Brush, surreptitiously gained controlling interest in the Orioles and effectively wrecked the Baltimore franchise by bringing six of its key members to New York. Among them was the club's manager–third baseman John McGraw, whom he made the Giants' new manager. After Freedman decided to retire from baseball, he transferred control of the Giants to Brush, who became the club's managing director on August 12, 1902.

Six weeks later Brush purchased Freedman's majority interest in the Giants' stock for $200,000. Brush, in turn, sold his Cincinnati Reds holdings for $150,000 to a group of local politicians, including Cincinnati mayor and yeast company magnate Julius Fleischmann and city water commissioner August "Garry" Herrmann.[2] Herrmann was named president and chief of baseball operations. While some owners disliked Herrmann's business decisions, few disliked him personally. "Garry was a walking delicatessen," wrote Lee Allen in his history of the Reds. "A connoisseur of sausage, he carried his everywhere he went."[3]

Herrmann's baseball acumen was questionable. George L. Moreland, in his 1914 history of baseball, wrote, "Since President Herrmann has been at the head of the Reds, that club has had probably more players—good players—on its roster than any other club in the National League. Had many of the players been retained instead of trading them off, Cincinnati would no doubt have had several pennants won."[4]

From the time John McGraw became the manager of the new Baltimore Orioles in 1901, he and league president Ban Johnson had feuded constantly over McGraw's behavior toward umpires. True to form, he continued his lifelong battles with them on Opening Day of 1902, when he was ejected by Tommy Connolly. Twelve days later Jack Sheridan ejected him when Sheridan refused to award him first base after he was hit by a pitch. (The umpire felt McGraw had made no effort to avoid the ball.) The Baltimore crowd was so incensed that "a lynching party was informally organized," in the words of a *New York Times* reporter. Had the police not assembled a "riot squad" of "twelve sturdy bluecoats," Sheridan would have been harmed.[5] The *Sporting News* reported that McGraw had encouraged the fans to go after Sheridan.[6]

On May 24 McGraw was seriously hurt when Detroit's Dick Harley spiked him in a play at third base and opened a deep gash on his knee. Before he was carried into the clubhouse, McGraw smashed Harley in the mouth.[7] When he returned to the lineup a month later, he forced another ejection by Connolly and then refused to leave the field. After that game was forfeited to Boston, Johnson suspended him indefinitely. Johnson's biographer, Eugene Murdock, wrote that McGraw may have deliberately triggered the incident to give him an excuse to leave the American League and jump to the National League's Giants.

The Baltimore club owed McGraw $7,000 for expenses he had paid out of his own pocket. McGraw was already concerned about rumors Johnson would not involve him with the proposed new American League club in New York. After Freedman offered him the Giants managerial job, he demanded the Orioles' board of directors pay him immediately. When it could not, it gave him his release.[8] McGraw always maintained he did not desert Baltimore, as Johnson charged, but merely gained his release when the club could not pay his debt.

Frank Patterson called McGraw's move "a great victory for the National League and a severe blow to the American organization."[9] But after McGraw made the move, a *Sporting News* editorial stated, "The same tactics which brought about his downfall in the American League will make his National League career brief."[10]

While Donlin was waiting for his release from prison, the Reds had undergone a major restructuring. In addition to the new ownership, they had signed star Baltimore outfielders Cy Seymour and Joe Kelley as free agents.[11] Kelley, a key member of the Orioles' dynasty of the 1890s, was named manager, replacing Frank Bancroft.

The changes in leadership and personnel brought great hope to Reds fans, who had long watched their team struggle. Kelley's leadership, it was predicted, would set an example for the other players to follow. And the addition of Seymour and Kelley, to go with holdover Sam Crawford, would give the Reds one of the fastest and hardest-hitting outfields in the league. Signing Donlin as a utility outfielder would further strengthen the team.

Donlin was released from jail on the morning of August 20. Thirty days of his six-month sentence had been taken off for good behavior. The fine of $250, which was part of his sentence, was raised from ballplayers and friends. The newly freed Donlin reunited with his sister, Mame, before going to Oriole Park, where he practiced with some of his former teammates.

Donlin reported to manager Kelley at the Palace of the Fans, Cincinnati's home park, on August 25. He made his debut for the fifth-place Reds on August 26, against the Giants. He pinch-hit in the ninth inning and was retired by Christy Mathewson. Donlin made his first start the following day. "The erstwhile Oriole was given a welcome that warmed his heart," reported Ren Mulford Jr. in *Sporting Life*. "No player ever received such a continuous expression of encouragement. . . . Donlin is battling to save himself. He has always been his own worst enemy."[12]

On August 29 Donlin had a triple, a single, and two runs scored against St. Louis, and he had two more hits and three runs scored against the Cardinals the next day. His time away from the game had not affected his batting eye. Donlin was Cincinnati's left fielder for the rest of the season, and with nine hits in his last eighteen at bats, he batted a respectable .287 and scored an impressive thirty runs in just thirty-four games.

Donlin explained his approach to batting in an interview with the *Sporting News* shortly after the season ended:

> It is batting which keeps a player on edge. . . . Batting, like everything else, requires a great deal of practice. During the season I put in an hour or so every morning hitting, particularly in the spring of the year, so as to get my eye accustomed to the distance and the ball. You

2. Mike Donlin batted .351 for the Reds in 1903 and was hitting .356 in the summer of 1904, when he was suspended and traded to the New York Giants. He said that when he came to bat, he had "'I'm going to do it' running through [his] mind" (*Buffalo Commercial*, October 6, 1908). SDN-001735, *Chicago Daily News* Collection, Chicago History Museum.

will notice that my position at the bat is peculiar, because I lean far over the plate. I do that so as to get a good start for first. By leaning, when I swing it throws me right into my stride, and that makes a difference of about a step, and many a ball is beaten out by just about that margin. . . . Furthermore, when you lean over the plate, it gives you a good look at the ball, and you can see a curve break better than when you stand back.[13]

Donlin had been well behaved since joining the club, but a disputed call in the Reds' final home game, against Pittsburgh, sent him, and eventually the crowd of eight thousand, into an ugly display of disorderly conduct.

He led off the seventh inning with a slow ground ball and appeared to easily have beaten the throw to first, but umpire Hank O'Day called him out. Donlin protested the call vehemently, and it led to O'Day ejecting him. The fans began screaming at O'Day, and when the game was over threatened him with bodily harm. An estimated three thousand fans gathered around the umpire, and when he came within twenty yards of the club's office, they began throwing seat cushions and other objects at him. A squad of policemen attempted to disperse the crowd with no success. When O'Day finally reappeared, it took protection from four policemen to get him to safety.

Cincinnati finished the season at 70-70, in fourth place. The field was muddy for the final game, which would have been postponed had it taken place earlier in the season. But the league-leading Pittsburgh Pirates (102-36) wanted to break a National League record by winning 103 games and insisted on playing. The Reds reacted by treating the game as a farce while losing, 11-2. The left-handed-throwing Donlin played shortstop before pitching the final inning. He succeeded two other non-pitchers on the mound, Jake Beckley and Cy Seymour.[14] Manager Kelley went to bat smoking a cigarette, and Seymour and Donlin also smoked while on the field. Pirates president Barney Dreyfuss refunded all money taken in at the gate and accused manager Kelley of unbecoming conduct on the field.[15]

That night Dreyfuss sent reports of the disgraceful conduct of the Cincinnati players to Chairman Brush of the Executive Committee of the National League and President Herrmann of the Cincinnati club. He cited the cigarette smoking of Kelley, Donlin, and Seymour, the Reds' ridiculous lineup, and other irregularities. Dreyfuss also sent Herrmann a check for the amount of money the Reds would have received if the admission fee had not been refunded to all the spectators.

Further investigation revealed that Frank Bancroft, now the Reds' business manager, was guilty of some chicanery of his own. He had directed the omnibus driver taking the Reds' players to Exposition Park to take a roundabout route to prevent the downtown crowd from learning that a game would be played, hoping that a small attendance would persuade the Pirates to not take the field. "Irregularities of this sort may go in the American League, which some of the Reds left recently, but they must not be repeated here," Dreyfuss said.[16]

The *Pittsburgh Press* excoriated the actions of the Reds for "one of the most reprehensible things that ever occurred on the ball field. . . . People who attend ball games don't go to see the contests turned into a farce, and the offense committed by these three players was an insult to every one of the 1,200 persons who paid their money to see the game." The *Press* wrote that as the manager, Kelley should have set a better example.[17]

A *Sporting News* editorial also criticized Kelley harshly, questioning whether his temperament made him fit to be a manager:

> Kelley has yet to prove that he is a manager. He is an umpire-baiter, and the Pittsburgh incident shows to what extremes he will go when he loses his temper. It is dangerous to give a man of his temperament complete control of a team. . . . The tactics which won games in the rowdy era now result in the banishment of players to the bench by the umpire and their suspension by the executive head of the league. Baltimore ball will not win a 1903 pennant for Cincinnati, and it is feared that Manager Kelley will sacrifice his club's interests in pursuing a policy that the rules forbid and patrons disapprove of.[18]

With Donlin signed for the 1903 season, Herrmann wanted to keep him in Cincinnati and out of trouble during the offseason. He secured a job for him in Covington, Kentucky, across the Ohio River. The job was in a poolroom, a setting with which Donlin was familiar. He also shared his residence with his younger brother, Joseph, who came from Erie to live with him.

Donlin kept in shape during the winter by playing indoor baseball, a game where the bats were slightly larger than broom handles and balls were twice as large as regulation baseballs.[19] Indoor baseball was a growing spectator sport in many cities. With Major League stars like Donlin and Seymour playing for a local team called the All-Cincinnatis, the sport was very popular in that city.

Off the field the war over the jumping of players was hurting both leagues. "Aside from all the financial considerations which promise eventual bankruptcy for one league or the other," wrote the *Chicago Tribune*, "if present conditions are continued, the national pastime itself will not stand much more war. While the sport has flourished in many cities this year, and the American League has stood the test best of all because of its remarkably close race, there is an element beginning to crop out that will work irreparable injury, if not checked."[20] The *Tribune* further lamented the ways in which many of the best players were acting in the matters of behavior and conditioning and in some cases acting in a criminal manner. It had been especially harsh toward Donlin, whom it had called "Stripes" Donlin in reference to his jail time.[21]

> Knowing well that they can get a contract for large money with almost any club, the star players whose heads are not strong enough to teach them better have scoffed at possible discipline this year, and the result has been deleterious to the standard of their play. When players like Mike Donlin, just out of jail after a six months' sentence for striking a woman, and Virgil Garvin of six-shooter fame, can get contracts to sign in any baseball league, it indicates desperate straits on the part of the club or league which will put these players before the public it is trying to propitiate.[22]

8

....

"A Manager Who Can't Control Himself"

At the December 1902 winter meetings the National League's major order of business was to choose a president capable of dealing with the American League's formidable president, Ban Johnson. Nick Young, who had served in the position for the previous eighteen years, had been no match for Johnson. The league's eight teams were unanimous in selecting thirty-three-year-old Harry Pulliam, a Pittsburgh Pirates executive who had been Barney Dreyfuss's right-hand man.

Over the past two years the American League had induced more than a hundred National League players to join it, including such standouts as Cy Young, Ed Delahanty, Nap Lajoie, and Willie Keeler. The influx of stars to the new league was being reflected at the gate, with the league's first-year attendance 30 percent greater than that of the established league. Realizing they had lost the "war" and their monopoly was over, the National League owners asked for peace.

On January 10, 1903, in a joint meeting in Cincinnati, representatives from the two leagues agreed to a peace treaty that included two major stipulations. The owners pledged to honor every contract hereafter entered into by the clubs of either league with players, managers, and umpires as valid and binding. Each league would also respect the other's territories and agreed (with a few exceptions) about which players belonged to which teams. Much of the credit for the end of hostilities belonged to Garry Herrmann, claimed a *Sporting News* editorial. "Garry Herrmann not only made peace possible, but he has prevented a resumption of the war between the major leagues and the extermination of one or both of them."[1] Herrmann, the Reds' owner, was chairman of the newly formed National Commission, whose role was to settle disputes. The other members were Johnson and Pulliam.

Among the most consequential provisions of the agreement was the acceptance of an American League team in New York to replace the disbanded Baltimore franchise. The American League, in turn, agreed not to place a club in Pittsburgh. John Brush and Charles Ebbets, owners of the Giants and Dodgers, voted against the settlement, mainly because they objected to the entrance of an American League team into New York City.

The Reds had not lost a significant player to the American League in the first two years of the war but had been fearful of losing outfielder Sam Crawford in 1903. In Crawford's three-plus seasons with Cincinnati, he had established himself as one of the National League's best hitters. In addition, he had led the league in home runs in 1901 and in triples in 1902.[2] Crawford received offers to switch leagues in 1901 and 1902 but stayed in Cincinnati because he was unsure if the new league would succeed. Shortly after the end of the 1902 season, confident the American League was here to stay, he signed a lucrative $3,500 contract for the 1903 season with the AL's Detroit Tigers.

Crawford's departure put a crimp in manager Joe Kelley's plans for his team's outfield. He had intended to play Crawford in right field, Cy Seymour in center, and Donlin in left, leaving himself free to fill any vacancy that arose. Kelley's revised plan was to play left field himself and shift the left-handed-throwing Donlin to right field.[3] Seymour would remain the center fielder.

On the last day of February Donlin left Cincinnati for Hot Springs, Arkansas, where he would get himself in shape before reporting to the Reds' training camp in Augusta, Georgia. He arrived suffering from boils on his neck and with a case of the flu, making regaining his health his first order of business.[4] "The Reds will have to hustle this year," he said. "I'll wager that any team which buckles up with us will know it has been playing baseball, and that doesn't bar the Pittsburgh team."[5]

Donlin was not alone in thinking the Reds could deny the Pirates a third consecutive pennant. Outfielder Willie Keeler of the new American League team in New York also thought so: "I look for Cincinnati to win the pennant this year," he said. "Kelley [his friend and former teammate with the National League's Baltimore and Brooklyn clubs] has a great ball team. . . . That outfield is, in my opinion, the greatest that ever stepped on a ball field."[6] Cleveland owner Charles Somers also had high praise for the new Reds' outfield, particularly Donlin: "To my mind, Donlin, when he is right, is one of the greatest players that ever wore spiked shoes."[7]

Donlin had split his time between first base and left field for the Orioles in 1901 and had played in left field for the Reds in 1902. Right field, which Crawford had mastered, was the sun field at the Palace of the Fans. Herrmann was confident Donlin would be a worthy replacement for Crawford: "I can't imagine that there is anything in the way of ball-playing that Sam Crawford could master that Mike Donlin could not learn," he said.[8]

Kelley was starting his first full season as manager of the Reds, and J. Ed Grillo of the *Sporting News* believed it would be to the team's advantage: "Kelley did not get the Reds to playing his kind of baseball last season," he wrote. "It was late in the year when he took hold. . . . This spring, however, he will start right to educate his team to play what was known as Baltimore ball. . . . I don't think scrappiness will be lacking in the Reds' world the coming season."[9]

Fans would get a quick read on the relative merits of the Reds and Pirates as the teams opened the season with four games at the Palace of the Fans. Barney Dreyfuss, some of his staff, and about fifty Pirates rooters traveled to Cincinnati for the series. They were thrilled when Deacon Phillippe held the Reds to two singles in a 7–1 win in the opener. The Pirates further delighted their hometown contingent when they swept the next three games to open a four-game lead on their purported challengers.

In the final game of the series Kelley and Donlin got into an argument with umpire Bob Emslie, leading to Kelley's ejection. That prompted a letter to Kelley from Pulliam concerning his and Donlin's conduct. Pulliam added that only an appeal for clemency from Emslie had prevented Kelley's suspension. He warned, however, that he would not put up with such behavior if the two men continued to conduct themselves in the rowdy way they had done with Baltimore.

Despite the warning, Kelley's antics continued. In 1904 the *Sporting News* said he was "fast losing his prestige because of his reckless disposition to take chances on crippling his team by making vigorous kicks against umpirical [*sic*] rulings. . . . There is a feeling that Kel's one failing—his bad control of temper—must eventually cost him his berth."[10] Ban Johnson had told Garry Herrmann, "You have a manager who can't control himself, let alone rule his men on a ball field, and that will be the weakest feature of the Cincinnati team."[11]

John Heydler, an umpire during that time and later president of the National League, said, "The Orioles were mean, vicious, ready at any time to maim a rival player or an umpire, if it helped their cause. The things they would say to an umpire were unbelievably vile."[12] Historian Noel Hynd wrote: "The Orioles were by their very nature a raucous, pugnacious crew, sort of an Irish street gang wearing baseball uniforms."[13]

Author Burt Solomon wrote about Kelley's personality and style:

Joe Kelley was liked, even admired, not only by the ladies but by his teammates, too. He was strong and swift and jaunty—a manly man, everything a boy could wish to be. He had self-confidence and a competitive fire. It was hard to say, for sure, what was missing. That he lacked Mac's [McGraw's] quick brilliance was not, in itself, disabling. It was more that there was something not quite responsible about him, at his core. It was not so much that he liked to drink, but that he gave the impression he drank less out of the pursuit of pleasure than out of need. He played in every game, but somehow, he could not be relied on. He was not quite a serious man.[14]

After nine games, eight of them losses, Donlin was batting .206, yet he retained his confidence. A twelve-game hitting streak, which included three two-hit games and a three-hit game, raised his batting average to .324. When the streak ended, the Reds' record had improved to 9-10. "Mike Donlin is more than filling [Sam Crawford's] shoes," wrote Grillo. "Not only is Mike getting hits, but he is getting them when they count most. He is also playing the game from start to finish. He bunts, runs bases well, and is putting up a star fielding game. Mike is truly playing the game of his life."[15]

On May 20 umpire Augie Moran ejected Kelley for too strenuously arguing a call at first base. The next day Bob Emslie ejected Kelley for the same reason, only this time there was no appeal for clemency, and Pulliam suspended him.[16] Several members of the press castigated Kelley for his pugnacious behavior. But Ren Mulford was puzzled: "It is absurd to think that Kel cannot conquer himself. In this world a man must be able to control himself before he can successfully direct others. The browbeating of umpires belongs to the tactics of a past era, and no one desires a revival." Conversely, he wrote, decidedly prematurely, "Donlin, once synonymous of unrest, has become a diamond model, and with that example in mind, all reforms are possible."[17]

Herrmann had predicted that Donlin would be able to master right field as well as Sam Crawford had. But that was not the case. "Donlin has not been playing good ball," Kelley said. "He is dropping flies that he is able to reach and failing to capture flies that should be easy for him."[18]

Aware of his poor play in the sun field, Donlin believed that if he was kept there much longer, it would shorten his career. He claimed it interfered not only with his fielding but also his hitting. He even offered to give back some of his salary if the Reds would move him out of right field. Kelley, who had been playing left field, said he would switch with Donlin if he could but believed that would be even worse for the team. "I am the worst sun fielder in the world," Kelley said. "I am satisfied that the sun is hurting Mike's work, but I can't make any change now, for Seymour would do no better there than Donlin."[19]

In a June 15 home game against St. Louis, Donlin made his eleventh error of the season. When the Reds moved on to Philadelphia, Kelley moved him to left field. Except for the six games he started at first base, Donlin would remain there for the rest of the season.

Donlin's batting spree after moving to left field seemed to validate his concern. After his last game in right, on June 15, his batting average was just .261. It climbed steadily from there, finally reaching the .300 mark on July 11. A week earlier Kelley had made Donlin his leadoff batter, and that too seemed to make a difference.

Donlin had hit safely in sixteen consecutive games when Phillies pitcher Chick Fraser hit him on the hand on July 19. The injury caused Donlin, "the man with the swagger strut," to miss two games.[20] In his first game back he had four singles and ran the hitting streak to nineteen games, during which he had forty hits in eighty-three at bats. Donlin's .482 batting average during those nineteen games raised his season's average to .333. Two days later he had three hits at Chicago, including his fifth home run, tying him for second most home runs in the league. July ended with the Reds in fourth place, twelve and a half games behind the Pirates.

Players of Irish descent, like Mike Donlin, had been a major presence in baseball since the founding of the National Association in 1871. "Ireland is there with the goods again in professional ball this season, and, if anything, is more in evidence than ever," claimed the *Pittsburgh Press.* "The Irishman, or, more correctly speaking, the Irish American, is a needful and essential component of baseball. His quick wit and ready head are the springs that move the game along. Who sasses the umpire?" the *Press* asked. "The Irishman," it answered. "And who is the umpire who runs the sassy ones off the field? Nearly always an Irishman." The *Press* suggested that Irishmen were involved in nearly all the fights and the vast majority of the comedy in baseball: "They play ball like fiends, love the game for the game's sake, and keep it stirred up all the time. Any game where as many as five Irishmen take part can be put down beforehand as a corker."[21]

The writer may have had Donlin's performance in the Reds' 4–2 win at St. Louis on August 7 in mind when he wrote those descriptions. Donlin led off the game with a long triple, but overslid third base and was tagged out. In the home half of the inning he dropped a fly ball for his twenty-second error of the season. He redeemed himself in the fourth inning by slugging his sixth home run. And in the eighth, after he was thrown out on a grounder to shortstop, he emphatically disagreed with the call by Irishman Hank O'Day. He persisted in his objection until O'Day, the game's lone umpire, ejected him. The St. Louis fans serenaded Donlin with cries of "rowdy" as he left the field.[22]

Donlin was not the only Reds outfielder causing problems for Kelley. In an August 2 home game against Chicago, Kelley noticed that "Seymour was under the influence of liquor." He removed an obviously inebriated Seymour from the game and took his place in center field. Herrmann and Kelley decided not to fine or suspend Seymour, but Ed Grillo voiced what he believed were the feelings of Reds fans: "Seymour is condemned by every lover of baseball here. His actions have been discussed everywhere where fans congregate, and he is stamped an ingrate. Even his fellow players are disgusted with him."[23]

On September 1 Donlin, out of the lineup but coaching at third base, went into full acting mode after umpire Jim Johnstone ejected him for complaining about a call. "I'll take my time about going too," he said. "And he did," reported the *Cincinnati Enquirer.* "He moseyed along with the speed of a spoony pair in lovers' lane on a moonlit night."[24] Chicago fans, upset at the delay he was causing, whistled the "Rogues March" and pounded the bleacher floor to keep pace with his slow exit.[25]

By winning thirteen of their final twenty-one games, the Reds held on

3. 1903 Cincinnati Reds. Mike Donlin is third from the left in the front row, playfully holding his bat in an unorthodox position. Player-manager Joe Kelley is in the back row, third from the right. Cy Seymour is third from the right in the front row. Dennis Goldstein Collection.

to fourth place while finishing sixteen and a half games behind the Pirates. Led by Donlin (.351), Seymour (.342), first baseman Jake Beckley (.327), third baseman Harry Steinfeldt (.312), and Kelley's .316, Cincinnati batters led the National League with a .288 average. Attendance under the new regime increased by 38 percent, to 351,680, third highest in the league.

Donlin had a sensational September, batting .467 (42-for-90), including two of the finest days of his career, both in front of the hometown fans. On September 18 he had five singles in five at bats against the Giants, and on September 22 he had the only three-triple game of his career.[26] For the afternoon he had six hits in seven at bats.

Donlin's .351 average was good for second place in the National League batting race, won by Pittsburgh's Honus Wagner's .355. He finished second in runs (110), home runs (7), and triples (18) and third in slugging (.516). Grillo called Donlin "the most improved fellow in disposition that can be imagined. Mike is traveling in good society these days, and he is behaving himself like a Chesterfield."[27]

9
....

"I Am Through with Donlin!"

In mid-December 1903 Donlin traveled to Hot Springs to prepare himself for the 1904 season. Visiting Hot Springs to "boil out" before the start of spring training had become popular over the years. "I took on weight very easily, and I can't get the kind of exercise I need here [in Cincinnati]," he said. "There are always lots of people who have to exercise, and I will have plenty of company. I have had a great deal of trouble with my legs every year, and I have come to the conclusion that I need a careful course in training during the winter."[1]

The supposedly reformed Donlin believed the Reds would be a much better team in 1904. He predicted Joe Kelley and the Reds would finish first or second in the 1904 league race.

Donlin sent a message to Frank Bancroft telling the Reds' business manager he had given up beer and whiskey and was drinking only water. "I am feeling fine," he wrote, "but am still a little overweight."[2] A week later the *Cincinnati Enquirer* reported that Donlin was taking four- or five-mile walks every day. Cincinnati sportswriter Ren Mulford Jr. predicted a great season for Donlin, calling him "one of the best-hearted boys that ever drew breath and one of the greatest ball players. With his whole heart on the game and the side issues smothered, he will come pretty near leading the National League in hitting and run-getting this season."[3]

Often under the influence of alcohol, a young and reckless Donlin was a frequent participant in violent confrontations. That was not the case in one encounter that took place in Hot Springs, where he was not a combatant but a peacemaker. In the early hours of March 3 a dispute between two young men over the attentions of a young woman erupted at the Majestic Hotel. As described by the *Cincinnati Enquirer*, "A wealthy young Texan arose from his chair and drawing a revolver pointed it toward the head of another young man. Donlin wrenched the revolver from the

Texan's hand and put it in his own pocket, after which the men were led away by friends."[4]

Manager Kelley was in the second season of his two-year contract, noted the *Sporting News*, "and he realizes that he must get better results than he did in the last race to secure its renewal."[5] By the end of spring training Kelley was expressing confidence in his 1904 club: "To me the Reds are stronger in every way than they were this time last year. We will escape all the harrowing mistakes of last spring in the right field, where Mike Donlin failed."[6] Donlin agreed. He believed the Reds would be a much better team in 1904 and predicted they would finish first or second in the 1904 league race.

In the second week of the regular season a controversy erupted centering on Donlin and the *Enquirer*, Cincinnati's major newspaper. In its coverage of the April 22 game at Pittsburgh, the *Pittsburgh Press* reported, "Mike Donlin didn't appear to be in very good shape. He didn't half try either in the field or when running the bases." In addition, he got picked off second base, "his third dopey play of the game."[7] Having seen enough, Kelley replaced him in the seventh inning with rookie Fred Odwell.

That night Kelley charged Donlin with having played the game with a hangover. Donlin denied the allegation; one bitter word led to another, and the men parted in anger. The next day Kelley again berated Donlin for going on a bender with three "sports" who had come to Pittsburgh to root for the Reds. Kelley told Donlin that unless he ended that kind of behavior, he would be "cut out of the game." The *Enquirer* reported that Donlin told Kelley he did not care whether he played ball or not. Kelley then sentenced him to sit on the bench for thirty days for using such careless expressions.[8]

A day later the *Enquirer* printed a lengthy retraction of the story that Kelley had suspended Donlin. Statements by Donlin, Kelley, Bancroft, umpire Jim Johnstone, and President Garry Herrmann were all to the effect that Donlin had neither been under the influence of liquor nor benched by Kelley for even thirty minutes. In the clubhouse after the game Kelley castigated the reporter who was responsible for the original story. "There is not a hue of truth in it," Kelley said. "Donlin has been doing the very best he can under the handicap of sore underpinnings, and Mr. Herrmann and I have nothing but praise for his efforts. He is heart and soul for his team, and that's what counts. . . . Stories of men drinking are bad, even if true. . . . Mike may make mistakes at times. We all do, but no one feels any worse about them than that same Mike."[9]

Kelley had played long enough and been around drinking men long enough to recognize whether alcohol or a hangover was influencing someone's play. And while the *Enquirer* printed a retraction the next day, the only statement it actually retracted was that Kelley had suspended Donlin.

As a leadoff batter lacking power, Reds rookie second baseman Miller Huggins had modeled himself after the scientific-hitting Willie Keeler, yet he still wished to be more productive and wistfully commented on Donlin, "I'd give anything if I could hit the ball like Mike Donlin. Donlin has the greatest swing at a ball of any player I have ever seen."[10] An unnamed member of the Giants also praised Donlin's offensive prowess: "I don't think that a greater batsman than Mike Donlin ever lived," he said. "He snaps at a ball, and when he meets it, it travels some . . . and it would not surprise me a bit to see him lead the league in hitting. . . . Young ballplayers would do well to watch Donlin bat, for he is an artist in that respect."[11]

An incident in a May 29 American League game between the Cleveland Naps and the Chicago White Sox drew Donlin's name back into controversy and set off a mini-war between the two leagues, at least in the press. In that game Cleveland's star second baseman Nap Lajoie threw a wad of tobacco in the face of umpire Frank Dwyer after a disputed call. League president Ban Johnson suspended Lajoie indefinitely, but the Naps were rained out the next two days, and Lajoie was back in the lineup for a home game against Boston on June 1.

According to Lajoie biographer David L. Fleitz, the local chapter of the Fraternal Order of Eagles had scheduled a presentation to fellow Eagle Lajoie that day and had reserved six hundred seats at League Park. The Eagles successfully prevailed upon Johnson to lift the suspension, and he instead fined the player $50.[12] Comments from the *Pittsburgh Press* and the *Washington (DC) Evening Star* showed the leagues' differing opinions on who was the greater ruffian, Lajoie or Donlin. "Had a National League player been guilty of doing what Lajoie did, it is a safe bet that he would have drawn a suspension of some definite period, and it would have been more than two days in duration, too," opined the *Press*. "In addition, he would probably have been compelled to pay a heavy fine. The policy of the National League is one that protects the umpires from dastardly assault. A man who will do what Lajoie did is no more of a gentleman than a man who would spit in a woman's face. But it all goes in the American League."[13] "People in glass houses, etc.," countered the *Evening Star*. "If the National League can stand for Mike Donlin, the American League can certainly put up with Lajoie. Larry assaulted a man, not a woman."[14]

"Lajoie's escape from serious sanctions shocked and angered many in the sporting press," wrote Fleitz. "Johnson had virtually driven John McGraw out of the American League two years earlier for constantly battling the umpires, but now the league's biggest star and leading gate attraction was hardly punished at all for something far worse than anything McGraw ever did."[15] Choosing gate receipts over principle in the Lajoie incident showed that Johnson's policy of zero tolerance was not really zero but one that depended on the situation.

Donlin, who rarely agreed when an umpire's close call went against him, had numerous opportunities to voice his disagreements in an early June series at Boston. He made disparaging comments to umpire Jim Johnstone in each of the first three games of a four-game series. Johnstone, the lone umpire in each game, ejected him during the third game after Donlin vociferously objected to a call at the plate. He continued to harass the umpire from the bench, calling him an "old bum" (Johnstone was thirty-one), in addition to more profane names. This led National League president Harry Pulliam to suspend him for three days. The absence did not hurt Donlin. In his first game back he went 3-for-4, raising his total hits for the season to a league-high sixty-four, and his batting average to .354, second only to Honus Wagner's .370.

The Reds, in a tight three-way race with New York and Chicago, had their best chance ever to win the championship this season, according to the *Boston Globe*. The *Globe* called them "aggressive players who fight for every point [and] have been altogether too strenuous in going after the umpires." It made particular note of Donlin: "Mike Donlin has been a mark for the fans here and has been jollied whenever there has been the smallest chance. He has more to say than the rest of the team combined and is one of the hardest men umpires have to handle. But he is a great ball player."[16]

On June 16 Cincinnati played an exhibition game in Erie, a day in which the city honored its native son by designating it Mike Donlin Day. When the Reds' train arrived in Erie that morning, more than a hundred people were there to welcome him home. The fans gave him a boisterous reception when he went to bat for the first time. The manager of the local team escorted Donlin to the grandstand, where he was presented with a diamond-studded Elks button.[17]

On July 4 in St. Louis, Donlin had two hits and two runs batted in in a 7–3 win and ended the day with a .356 batting average. He chose to celebrate the victory and American independence with a drinking spree that extended into the following day. The Cincinnati players were ready to leave for Robison Field on July 5, but Donlin was missing. Kelley discovered him navigating his way across Broadway with an uncertain gait and suspended him for drunkenness. The game was rained out, but Fred Odwell was in left field for the next day's doubleheader.[18]

Donlin returned home with the Reds, proclaiming he never again would wear a Cincinnati uniform. Kelley responded by declaring, "I am through with Donlin!"[19] Herrmann backed his manager and stated Donlin was undoubtedly guilty of drunkenness and reprehensible conduct. "The extent of his punishment rests with Manager Kelley, and I will do anything that he thinks will best serve the team."[20]

Kelley decided Donlin's drunkenness and disorderly conduct in St. Louis warranted a $25 fine and a thirty-day suspension. "Donlin was the hardest hitter in the league, but he was a temperamental cuss," Kelley recalled in 1918. "We had a good team that year, and I have always believed that if Donlin had not been suspended, we would have won the pennant."[21] (This was highly unlikely, considering the Reds were ten and a half games out of first place at the time.)

The majority of National League owners wanted Herrmann, in his role as the president of the National Commission, to banish Donlin from baseball permanently, but he remained steadfast in sticking to the thirty-day suspension: "I will not allow him to be driven out of baseball. I don't think that there is a chance for Donlin to wear a Cincinnati uniform again, but he shall have another chance in the League. As soon as his suspension has expired, I think we will find a berth for him with one of the teams."[22]

"Of course, Mike is a great ball player, and his hitting has been a tower of strength to the local club," wrote C. J. Bockley of the *Sporting News*. "The local club has been too lenient and is as much to blame as Donlin. Personally, I feel very sorry for Mike . . . [who] is more to be pitied than censured. . . . I have always found Mike a good fellow, and he has had more good traits than he has bad ones, but this particular one is certainly the

4. Hard-nosed Joe Kelley was Mike Donlin's manager in Cincinnati from 1902 to 1904. A clash between the two men, based in part on a misunderstanding, led to a breach in their relationship that lasted until a reconciliation at a 1918 dinner hosted by Yankees owner Jacob Ruppert. SDN-001730, *Chicago Daily News* Collection, Chicago History Museum.

worst that can hang onto a ball player, especially one of Mike's ability."[23] And from the *Cincinnati Enquirer*: "It isn't every man in this knock-about world of ours that has had as many chances as Donlin. He will never find another Garry Herrmann, and yet through the Red Chief he will get another opportunity, for the Cincinnati Club has refused to become a party to the movement to hang Donlin outside the breastworks of professional ball."[24]

10

....

Goodbye to Cincinnati;
Hello to Broadway

Donlin had stayed in shape during his 1904 suspension and supplemented his income by playing for semipro teams. C. J. Bockley of the *Sporting News* reported he played first base in a game in Middletown, Ohio, that brought out the biggest crowd ever in that city. "Donlin's batting was the feature of the game. Two home runs, two triples, and a double out of five times up . . . and if he would only take care of himself, he would be one of the greatest players."[1]

After Donlin's suspension ended on August 4, Garry Herrmann wanted to trade him to the St. Louis Browns for Jesse Burkett, but he had to obtain waivers from the other seven National League clubs. "Six managers, unwilling to be concerned with Mike's off-the-field adventures . . . agreed to waive," wrote historian Frank Graham.[2] All but Giants manager John McGraw. Three days of presidential telephone discussions culminated in a three-way trade on August 7. Cincinnati sent Donlin to the Giants, the Giants sent Harry "Moose" McCormick to Pittsburgh, and Pittsburgh sent outfielder Jimmy Sebring to Cincinnati. McGraw called Donlin "a great ballplayer" but acknowledged it would take him several days to get in shape. "Is he the best on the team?" reporter Robert Edgren asked. McGraw thought for a moment before coming up with a diplomatic answer. "Well, none of them is any better," he said.[3]

McGraw determined that with a few changes the Giants could make up the six and a half games they had finished behind Pittsburgh in 1903. His major addition was acquiring star shortstop Bill Dahlen from Brooklyn; Dahlen would respond by leading the league in runs batted in. McGraw also added three rookies: McCormick, left-handed pitcher George "Hooks" Wiltse, and third baseman Art Devlin. Wiltse and Devlin would emerge as two of the National League's best rookies in 1904. McCormick would benefit the club when the Giants traded him to Pittsburgh in the August deal that brought them Donlin.

The *New York Evening Journal* believed that "by securing Donlin, the New York club has made a ten-strike, always with the provision that the erratic Irishman can be controlled. Mike is a big-hearted, good-natured, hale fellow, something in the style of [1880s star] King Kelly."[4] The *Journal* added that if anyone could control Donlin, it was McGraw. "I feel absolutely sure that Donlin will work for me conscientiously and honorably," McGraw said. "If I did not think I could handle him, I surely would not have secured him."[5]

The *Sporting News*'s Timothy Sharp had a negative take on the Giants' signing of Donlin: "That old saying of birds of a feather flocking together is beautifully exemplified in the Donlin-McGraw-Brush coalition. This Donlin is a great ball player beyond all question, but in the face of his lurid career, there can be no doubt that the national pastime would be considerably improved by his elimination from it."[6]

On his arrival in New York, Donlin said, "I am glad to get the chance to play with McGraw's team. I always got along with him, I am sure that we will get along together in the future. . . . I would sooner play ball with the New York team than any other team in the business."[7] Yet according to the *Brooklyn Citizen*, Donlin had never gotten along with McGraw:

When McGraw jumped to the American League, many of the players who went over with him did so mainly because they had an idea that [with] McGraw, being one of the boys, their berths would be so much softer than elsewhere. . . . Mike Donlin, who is once more under McGraw's wing, was one player who never could get along with the scrappy little manager. McGraw and Donlin were not on the best terms even when the Donlin-Sebring-McCormick deal was put through. What McGraw will be able to accomplish with Mike this time remains to be seen.[8]

"Before I left Cincinnati," Donlin said, "President Herrmann called me into his office . . . and he wished me to make good. Mr. Herrmann has always treated me well. I wish I could say that about every man on the Cincinnati team."[9] No names were mentioned, but Donlin likely had Kelley at the top of that list.

Aided by an eighteen-game winning streak in June, the Giants were breezing with a ten-and-a-half-game lead over second-place Chicago when they acquired Donlin. The addition of his hitting and fielding ability practically clinched the pennant for them, wrote the *St. Louis Republic*: "Without question of doubt, Donlin is one of the most valuable players in baseball to-day. His hitting has always been his forte, but it must be remembered that he is now one of the most polished fielders in the business. He covers a vast amount of territory, and he is one of the most accurate throwers in the League."[10]

Donlin made his Giants debut as a pinch hitter at the Polo Grounds on August 8. He received a huge welcome before striking out. After a few more pinch-hitting appearances, he made his first start on August 15. Before the game some of Donlin's New York friends presented him with a large horseshoe of flowers. Donlin's play in center field was exemplary, and his two-run home run was responsible for half the Giants' runs in their 4–1 victory.

New York's lead was eleven games when they arrived in St. Louis in late August and swept a four-game series. The sweep began another long winning streak. Win number six included a near riot and was typical of the Giants' roughneck style of play. Chief Zimmer was the game's lone umpire, and the Giants began complaining about his decisions from the opening pitch.[11] When Zimmer called the Reds' Fred Odwell safe at second on a fourth-inning steal attempt, their anger exploded. Shortstop Dahlen, who had made the tag on Odwell, and first baseman Dan McGann loudly and profanely objected to the call. Zimmer ejected both men. League president Harry Pulliam suspended Dahlen for three days and McGann indefinitely. (He later limited McGann's suspension to three days.)

The Dahlen-McGann incident was a prelude to an even bigger blowup two innings later. Giants catcher Frank Bowerman was on the bench, where he had received a steady stream of abuse from fans sitting nearby. In the sixth inning Bowerman, one of the biggest and toughest players in the league, went into the stands, where he punched one of the offenders. Umpire Zimmer allowed Bowerman to return to the bench, a decision that did not please the city's acting mayor, who was at the game. He ordered the police to arrest Bowerman, but the man he hit decided not to prosecute.

The race for the pennant in the American League, between Boston and New York, would go down to the last day of the season, with Boston winning.

Hope had been high in New York for a Yankees' win and a world's championship series against the Giants.[12] But manager McGraw and owner Brush indicated early on that they considered winning the National League pennant sufficient to declare themselves world champions.

Despite the Boston Americans' stunning upset of Pittsburgh in the 1903 World Series—or perhaps because of it—McGraw and Brush had issued statements expressing their disdain for the new league. "Popular opinion will drive the Giants out of New York, should they show such a contemptible yellow streak as would certainly be the case should they refuse to play the post season series," predicted one New York newspaper. "Mr. [Ban] Johnson is emphatic that the only thing that prevents Mr. Brush from playing is the dread of defeat."[13]

In late July the American League president responded to the contempt coming from the Giants' leaders: "This is only the latest of a series of vicious attacks and unfriendly actions toward our organization by John T. Brush," he said. "There is a public demand for these tests of the strength of the rival major league teams, and we are content to submit to it."[14]

McGraw responded: "I have said all I am going to say about playing the Highlanders a series of games. There is no chance of the New York National League team ever playing the Highlanders, and that settles it."[15] Criticism directed at Brush and McGraw for refusing to play the AL winner was nearly unanimous. "Is John T. Brush stronger than the National League?" Timothy Sharp asked in the *Sporting News*. "One partner cannot hold out against seven by any law or part of any constitution that ever was or ever will be framed."[16]

Opinion among the fans of both teams and in the press was enthusiastically in favor of a championship series. Sportswriter Sam Crane gave four reasons why McGraw should agree to play the American League pennant winner (he referred to the Yankees, who had moved ahead of Boston that day, but his reasoning went for whichever team won the AL pennant):

He owes it to the National League to win back the title of world's champions lost by it last year.

He owes it to his players to play the series because if he does not, it deprives them of the fruits of victory.

He owes it to the public—the great public—for it paid his own princely salary and the salaries of his players.

McGraw owes it to himself, because the public will cry "coward" if he does not and can easily see through the thin veil of his protest.[17]

However, the *Brooklyn Citizen* gave a reasonable argument for the Giants' refusal, especially if the American League winner was the Yankees: "As it stands to-day the Giants, in popularity, have the Highlanders beat a block, and nobody is more fully aware of this than the owners of the American League team. The American League club would therefor stand to benefit more than the National League club, for if by any chance the Americans won, they would win over many of the admirers of the Giants, whereas a victory for the Giants would not do their club much good in that they are drawing as good now as if they were the world's champions."[18] While Crane's points are well taken, the *Citizen's* analysis rings true.

"We are determined to play the series. We want the money that will be in it for us," said one unidentified Giant. "We are not going to allow any personal differences Brush and McGraw might have with Ban Johnson to stop us from getting the money."[19] Donlin told a reporter the club's refusal to play a postseason series left a "sore bunch of ballplayers around the clubhouse."[20]

On September 19 the Giants held a team meeting in which the players announced they would play the American League winner. But it was not to be. Brush met privately with his three top pitchers, Joe McGinnity, Christy Mathewson, and Luther Taylor. He gave them each $1,000 and "presumably a near equal amount to each of their teammates." He also underwrote a theater event on October 2 where most of the proceeds went to the players.[21]

McGinnity's thirty-fourth win on September 22 was the team's one hundredth and the pennant clincher. McGinnity and Mathewson had combined to form the most productive one-two pitching duo of the twentieth century. The "Iron Man" finished this season with a league-leading thirty-five wins, while Mathewson was second with thirty-three.[22]

The Giants finished with a record of 106-47, thirteen games ahead of Chicago. There was a clear correlation between their accomplishments on the field and their aggressive style of play—and their profits at the box office. Their notoriety attracted record crowds wherever they played. Added to the more than six hundred thousand fans they drew to the Polo Grounds, fans in other National League cities turned out with the hope of seeing the rowdy New Yorkers get their comeuppance. The Giants estimated their profits for the season at $100,000, which was more than the two next most profitable teams combined. Yet despite their success and a chance to make even more money for the team and for the players, they refused to play the American League winner, Boston, in a championship series and proudly proclaimed themselves world champions.

In a letter to the baseball patrons of New York, McGraw absolved Brush and took full responsibility for not playing the American League champions: "I was never accused of being a coward. It is not in my nature to hide behind any man; I never yet did it, and I am not going to begin now. . . . If there is any just blame for criticism for the club's action in protecting that highly prized honor the blame should rest on my shoulders, not Mr. Brush's, for I, and I alone, am responsible for the club's action."[23]

McGraw may have absolved Bush of any responsibility, but the press did not: "No one takes Mr. Brush seriously when he speaks about the American League being a minor league."[24] In September Brush had given his reasons for bypassing a series against the American League champions: "There is nothing in the constitution or playing rules of the National League which requires its victorious club to submit its championship honors to a contest with a victorious club of a minor league. . . . Neither the players nor the manager of the Giants, nor myself, desire any greater glory than to win the pennant in the National League."[25]

While there has been much discussion over the years whether Brush or McGraw made the decision not to play in a World Series in 1904, there was a total alignment in their feelings on the matter. They both detested Johnson and the American League. What is perhaps surprising is that neither seriously considered the negative publicity their decision entailed. McGraw biographer Charles Alexander may have summed it up best: "The truth is that for both Brush and McGraw, disdain for the American League upstarts was mixed with fear of losing to them."[26]

There would be no World Series for Donlin in 1904, but in all it had been a successful year. Playing in forty-two games for the Giants, he batted

.280, bringing his season's average down to .329. Among National League players who appeared in one hundred games or more, only Honus Wagner, at .349, had a higher batting average. Donlin did, however, have trouble playing left field (the sun field) at the Polo Grounds, and his fielding average for the season was among the worst in the league for outfielders.[27]

11

....

"I Guess I Have Had My Share of Trouble"

After spending the first part of the winter in Cincinnati and Erie, Donlin returned to Hot Springs in the first week of January 1905. While there, he worked in the poolroom of a Cincinnati beer baron who also had a stable of thoroughbreds at Essex Park. "It don't make any difference whether I work or not, anyhow," said Donlin, who had noticeably lost the pot belly he had had with Cincinnati. "I can't pick a winner, and always leave my salary at the race track."[1]

John McGraw, along with much of the press, believed his 1905 Giants would be even stronger than his 1904 champions. For one thing, Donlin would be available for a full season. For another, the versatile Roger Bresnahan, mostly an outfielder in 1904, would become the first-string catcher.

New York sportswriter Bozeman Bulger predicted that Donlin, "one of the greatest hitters the game has ever known," would be the center fielder. Sam Mertes, whom Bulger called "another remarkable hitter," would play left, and George Browne, "a steady hitter and wonderful base runner, would be in right."[2] Bulger also reported that Archie Graham, a youngster who played with Manchester (New Hampshire) in the New England League in 1904, had been signed as a substitute outfielder. He was fast on his feet and a strong hitter, and McGraw believed he had a real find.

Donlin and teammate Dan McGann had often been cast as villains, on and off the field, but on February 25 at Hot Springs, they were real-life heroes. Early that Saturday morning, the two risked their lives to save an old woman from being burned to death in a conflagration at the Hotel Moody. They climbed a ladder to the second floor of the hotel and rescued the woman, who had been overcome by smoke and flames. Donlin escaped injury, but McGann was slightly burned on his face and hands.

President Brush of the Giants witnessed the rescue and said he was very proud of his players.[3]

The full contingent of Giants players, except for Graham, reported to Savannah in early March. The speedy outfielder wrote to McGraw asking to be allowed to finish his work at the Baltimore Medical College before he joined the team. Graham was taking his exams and would soon be awarded his medical degree. McGraw was not pleased with the request, but he did grant it.

Graham would play in just one game, on June 29—the only one in his Major League career. He played right field for the game's final two innings, with Donlin alongside him in center. Graham eventually became a physician in Minnesota. He later became a cult figure after his appearance as "Moonlight" Graham in the 1989 fantasy film *Field of Dreams*.

There was confidence in the Giants camp. "We all want to participate in a world's championship series and look forward to this with pleasure," said Christy Mathewson.[4] A *Baltimore Sun* article expected Mathewson would get his wish: "It is the consensus of opinion among baseball men that the New York Nationals will win their pennant again in easy style. They have by far the strongest team in the National League."[5]

The Giants had a successful spring training, including sixteen straight wins against various Minor League teams. There was, however, one negative incident involving Donlin and pitcher Leon Ames. While riding a train through Alabama, going from one spring training game to another, the two players were fined for helping pass the time by playing cards. Alabama law prohibited card playing on a passenger train.[6]

Donlin, who played consistently well all spring, was picked by the New York press as the likely winner of the National League's batting title. He confirmed that doing so was his ambition:

I'm not making any fool promises or rash statements, but I am going ahead determined to do my best and give the people in New York all the baseball that there is in me. I am in good physical condition, and I propose to remain that way. I guess I have had my share of trouble in this world, and I want to keep out of it for a while. . . . That Pittsburgh Dutchman [Honus Wagner] has had a monopoly of the batting in the National League for so long that I suppose he thinks he has got it copyrighted.[7]

Opening Day, against Boston, began with an automobile parade through the streets of Manhattan. Autos, liberally decorated with yellow bunting with the words "Champion Giants" written in black, carried the Giants players. When the Polo Grounds crowd spotted McGraw in the first auto carrying them onto the field, they let out a thunderous roar. Assisted by his players, McGraw raised the blue and gold championship pennant, which read "Giants, Champion Baseball Club of National League, 1904." The band struck up the "Star Spangled Banner," and Mayor George McClellan threw out the first ball.

As if setting the stage for what was to come, Donlin was the batting star of the game. He had three hits, scored three runs, and drove in three. He led off the first inning with a double and hit a three-run inside-the-park home run in the fourth. The *New York Sun*, in describing the home run, called Donlin "the demon slugger [who] tore around the highway like a racehorse."[8] Donlin further showed off his speed with a bunt single. The Giants won, 10–1, behind Joe McGinnity. The next day Mathewson shut out the Beaneaters, 15–0. Following the two wins over Boston, the Giants took four of five from Philadelphia. By then they were in sole possession of first place and would never relinquish the lead.

Donlin's quick start did not go unnoticed. Bozeman Bulger wrote that he and the Yankees' Willie Keeler had excellent chances to replace the 1904 batting champions in their respective leagues (Wagner and Cleveland's Nap Lajoie). "Both Donlin and Keeler started the season in the best of condition, and both are natural hitters."[9] Manager Jimmy Collins of the Boston Americans also had praise for Donlin: "If he can be kept right, he will be a tower of strength to the team and help the Giants to many a victory."[10]

The New Yorkers were proving not only that they were the best team in the National League but also that they were the most argumentative and belligerent, as they had been since McGraw became their manager. Already the most hated team—simply because they represented New York—McGraw's bullying and hooliganism had raised that hate to a new and often dangerous level. As a result, the 1905 season would have several dangerous confrontations, on and off the field.

The first occurred at Philadelphia on April 22. After being thrown out at the plate in the eighth inning, McGann punched Fred Abbott, the Phillies' catcher. Abbot retaliated, and a mini-riot ensued. One "almost brawl," at Brooklyn on the last day of April, was averted thanks to the peacemaking of Donlin. The *Brooklyn Eagle* described it: "Roger Bresnahan was called out on a close play at first and immediately made a dash for umpire Jim Johnstone. He was intercepted half way by Donlin and McGinnity, who held Bresnahan until he had cooled down."[11]

On May 4 Donlin had four hits off Boston's Vic Willis, including a triple, and two runs batted in. At day's end he was leading the National League in batting average, slugging percentage, runs, hits, and doubles. With a 12-3 record, the Giants had a three-game lead over the second-place Pirates.

Honus Wagner had been the best all-round player in the National League since the turn of the century, but was he the most valuable? Although a formal award for a league's most valuable player was still in the future, a writer for the *New York Evening World* made the claim that Donlin was more valuable:

Mike is a better man than the percentage shows, since he can drive men around the bases either with a long hit or short one. Although he played in only 96 games last year, he made only one less home run than Wagner. He is, in short, a mixture of the old-time slugger and the new scientific tapper, his especial value lying in his ability to hit the ball in some shape or manner both when bases are occupied or empty. Wagner will doubtless again lead Donlin in percentage this year, but will not contribute as much to his team's batting.[12]

One story that summer described the Giants' slugger at the bat: "Donlin is a heavily built man, with muscular arms like those of a veteran prize fighter. He uses a bat that is far too heavy for the average batsman, and when he hits the ball squarely 'on the nose,' the sound may well be compared to the explosion of a sixteen-inch shell."[13]

On May 22, following a Giants home game against Pittsburgh, Pirates owner Barney Dreyfuss wrote to National League president Harry Pulliam that McGraw had taunted and harassed him. Pulliam fined and suspended the Giants' manager. McGraw took the case to civil court, where two weeks later a judge nullified Pulliam's ruling.

In the weeks preceding June 15 Donlin's batting average had slipped more than fifty points and was hovering around the .300 mark. McGraw moved him out of the lead-off spot and batted him second. Donlin had one hit that day and went 15-for-28 over the next week to raise his average to .329 and extend his consecutive games hitting streak to thirteen.

Meanwhile, the Giants continued to be the target of spectator violence wherever they played. On June 18, in St. Louis, the police had to step in when the fans began throwing rocks at the Giants players as they left the field, and they continued to throw various things at the team's horse-drawn bus. The next day, in Cincinnati, fans threw bottles at first baseman McGann and right fielder George Browne. One bottle hit Browne, causing the game to be delayed for five minutes. Following the afternoon portion of a July 4 doubleheader, a few Giants players battled with a mob outside Philadelphia's National League Park. Donlin and Browne were arrested but were discharged at the police station.

When the Giants lost to Pittsburgh on July 19, their winning percentage dropped below .700, and their lead over the Pirates was reduced to five games. It was the hottest July 19 on record in New York City, causing sixty-three deaths, and the heat likely contributed to the foul mood of the home fans. In the fifth inning umpire Bill Klem ejected McGann and Donlin, a move that led the fans in the right-field bleachers to throw beer glasses onto the field. After the game police officers took the precautionary step of escorting Klem and fellow umpire Jim Johnstone from the field.

The Giants followed that loss with a thirteen-game winning streak that raised their lead to ten and a half games. Donlin continued his hot hitting all summer. Powered by hitting streaks of fifteen, eleven, and thirteen games, he raised his batting average from .322 on July 4 to .359 on September 12. From August 13 to September 12 he hit .500, going 46-for-92.

The New Yorkers needed one more win to clinch the pennant when they played the first game of a doubleheader at Cincinnati on October 1. The score was tied, 4–4, after nine innings. The Giants went ahead, 5–4, on Mertes's tenth-inning triple, which Reds center fielder Cy Seymour lost in the sun. Donlin, the Giants' center fielder, also had been struggling with the sun, so McGraw moved him to left field and Mertes to center for the bottom of the tenth. It was an inspired decision. With two outs and a man on second base, Harry Steinfeldt connected with a Joe McGinnity pitch and drove it to deep center field. Years later McGraw recalled Mertes's extraordinary play on the ball, calling his catch one of the best he had ever seen.[14]

Four days after clinching the pennant the club returned home to finish the season with five games against the Phillies. A large crowd gathered at Grand Central Station to greet the team's train when it arrived. The Giants, with a record of 105-48, had outdistanced Pittsburgh by a comfortable nine-game margin.

McGraw would later call his 1905 club the best he ever managed. Basically it was the same team that won the pennant in 1904, but this team had Mike Donlin for the entire season, and McGraw's best feat of managing may have been his ability to keep his star outfielder in check. Yet a few years later Donlin confessed he really had not been in check: "I drank enough amber-colored fluid that spring [1905] to float a battleship."[15]

The fast-living, hard-drinking Donlin batted .356 for the season, the highest average on the team and the third highest in the National League. He also stole thirty-three bases for the second time in his career; his speed is often overlooked. Donlin also led the Giants in runs (124), hits (216), and doubles (31), and he tied with Bill Dahlen in home runs (7).[16] Baseball analyst and historian Bill James called Donlin the third-best position player in the National League in 1905, behind Honus Wagner and Cy Seymour.[17] Seymour (.377) led the league in batting, and Wagner (.363) finished second. James had Donlin as an outfielder on his all-decade team for 1900–1909, along with Detroit Tigers teammates Ty Cobb and Sam Crawford.[18] "Next to the brilliancy of Mathewson's work last season," wrote William F. H. Koelsch, "the stick-work of Mike Donlin did more to bring another pennant here than any other individual factor in circumstance."[19]

Donlin, a good-looking man who combined a slightly sinister look with a winning smile, was the Giants' most popular player, more so than the cerebral and less demonstrative Mathewson. New York loved him, and he loved New York. According to sportswriter Harry Grayson, "Colorful Turkey Mike Donlin, a tremendous attraction at the Polo Grounds, was a man about Broadway, fitted [sic] right into the Big Stem, loved it. He hobnobbed with sports and actors, was one of the mob. He hung around the old Metropole, where everybody worthwhile hung out. . . . Donlin was the life of the party, held the center of the stage."[20]

"Donlin became a favorite of New York fans not only because of his hitting and outfielding, but because of his skills as a showman," wrote author Kevin Nelson. "He was a sharp-looking dude, eye candy to the ladies, and from his strut you could tell he knew it. Cocksure as a rooster, he liked to give the paying spectators their money's worth, give a show along with the game they came to see."[21]

Donlin was reportedly involved with a Broadway actress named Trixie Friganza that season. Trixie was known at the time as the "queen of the musical stage and the toast of Broadway." She would visit the Polo Grounds and flirt with Mike.[22] In a game against Chicago she shouted, "Mike, I'll give you a big kiss if you get a hit and score those runners." Mike hit a triple and after the game received his reward.[23]

Donlin had even crossed the cultural line from Broadway to classical music. Composer Charles Ives was a serious baseball fan, and music historian Timothy A. Johnson examined the heavy influence the game and some of its players had on his development as a composer. One who made an impression on the young musician was the flamboyant Donlin. An athlete by day and a playboy by night, Donlin's colorful character caught Ives's attention.[24]

Giants team members had been extremely upset with the decision by McGraw and Brush not to play in a World's Series in 1904. That criticism led Brush, along with the National Commission, to put into place a world's championship series for 1905 under rules devised by Brush. With minor modifications, the Brush rules govern World Series play to this day. The Giants would now play in their first postseason series since 1889.

12

....

Mathewson Pitches the Giants
to a World Series Title

On the day the Giants won the National League pennant the American League winner had yet to be decided. The race went down to the final week, with Connie Mack's Philadelphia Athletics finishing two games ahead of Fielder Jones's Chicago White Sox. In a year of overall weak hitting in the American League, the A's team batting average of .255 was good enough to lead the league. Led by Mike Donlin, Dan McGann, and Roger Bresnahan, the Giants' National League–leading batting average was eighteen points higher. They were also first in the National League in runs scored, on-base percentage, and slugging average.

Leading the pennant-winning teams were two men of Irish descent who could not have been more unalike. Connie Mack was the complete antithesis of John McGraw, in both physical appearance and his behavior on the field. Yet he was an equally capable manager, and, like McGraw, he realized it was typically pitching and not hitting that won championships.

While five pitchers had combined for the 105 Giants victories, "The only Giant twirler to be really dreaded is Mathewson (31-9)," predicted the *Baltimore Sun*. "The former Bucknell man is a wonderful pitcher, whose speed is likely to prove particularly baffling to a team that has never faced him before."[1]

Mack had put together a top-flight pitching staff very much the equal of New York's. And if Mathewson was the National League's outstanding pitcher, Rube Waddell (27-10) held that distinction in the American League.

Like Mathewson, who led the NL in games won, earned run average, and strikeouts to capture the pitching Triple Crown in his league, Waddell was the Triple Crown winner in his. Unfortunately for the A's, Mack would not have his best pitcher available to face the National Leaguers. Had a

74

face-to-face duel between Triple Crown winners Mathewson and Waddell taken place, it would have been the only one in World Series history.

In mid-September rumors began circulating that the unpredictable Waddell had injured his arm while engaged in some "horseplay" with fellow pitcher Andy Coakley and would be unavailable to pitch in the Series. Other rumors were spreading that gamblers had approached Waddell and told him to say his sore arm would continue to keep him out of action. Waddell denied those rumors and announced he was ready to take his regular turn despite his sore left shoulder. In a statement on September 22 he denied the gambling-related charge: "I have not been approached by anyone with a view to crippling my team. I want to help all I can to land the pennant."[2] The *Sporting News* believed Waddell's denial concerning the bribe offer.[3]

New York sportswriter Joe Vila also dismissed the rumors. "It is hard to believe that a baseball man would resort to such crooked methods. Even with the Rube an uncertainty, I still pick Mack's men to win, as they have a real ball team and are not bluffs or rowdies."[4]

The opinions of the *Sporting News* and Vila should be placed in the context of 1905. It was a time when the sporting press did not report such goings-on. Most would continue with this uncritical acceptance, if not partial cover-up, until 1920, when sportswriter Hugh Fullerton broke the story of the "fixed" 1919 World Series.

"It is unlikely we will ever know for certain whether Rube Waddell was bribed to sit out the last month of the 1905 season or that year's World Series," wrote historian Steven A. King. "However, there is a great deal of evidence to suggest that the whole story of his fight with Andy Coakley over a straw hat, and an injury resulting from it, can itself be knocked into another type of hat, the proverbial cocked one."[5]

Conversely Connie Mack dismissed the idea of Waddell's being involved with gamblers. Quoting Mack, his biographer Norman Macht wrote: "Knowing the Rube as I do, I'm positive that he would have shed his life's blood to be in the Series and duel with Mathewson. The Rube had his faults, but he was never a coward, and all the gold in Christendom could never buy him."[6] However, Mack, both the owner and manager of the Athletics, had the same vested interest as others in Organized Baseball to not expose any suspicions about fixed games.

When the Black Sox scandal broke in September 1920, Mack was asked about the 1905 rumors involving Waddell. He made a statement that suggested either extreme naiveté or a lack of forthrightness: "I don't think in those days the gamblers tried anything of the sort, or that players were reached. I think baseball has been clean up to the time the White Sox and Cincinnati met in the last World Series."[7]

Most Philadelphia writers picked the Athletics, while most New York writers, with the notable exception of Vila, went with the Giants. "Mr. Vila is persona non-grata at the Polo Grounds and hates everything that is in any way connected with them [the Giants]," wrote his colleague Timothy Sharp.[8]

McGraw, of course, picked the Giants. "I have not the slightest doubt about winning the world's championship," he said. "We can beat the Athletics at the bat and running bases. The only question left open to argument is the pitching."[9] McGraw's comment about pitching was part of a general consensus that the outcome would depend in large measure on the availability and effectiveness of Waddell. But after Waddell was ineffective in three games he pitched in the closing weeks of the regular season, Mack chose not to use him in the World Series.

After his refusal to let the Giants participate in the championship series in 1904, John Brush had taken the lead in arranging the format for the 1905 match. The teams would play a best-of-seven series, with the site of the games alternating daily. The teams would split 60 percent of the receipts from the first four games, with 75 percent going to the winners.

On Sunday night, October 8, a group of the Giants' loyal (and well-connected) supporters held a dinner in their honor in Manhattan. With every member of the team in the audience, a myriad of Broadway performers celebrated and entertained them late into the night. The next morning the entire Giants entourage boarded a train for Philadelphia. The players were accompanied by a legion of followers, including Jim Corbett, the former heavyweight champion, and George M. Cohan, Broadway's biggest star. Arriving at 10 a.m., they headed immediately to the Athletics' home field, where they would open the Series that afternoon.

Corbett, a big Giants fan, claimed he spent the night before Game One with Donlin, as a way to keep him from drinking. "Donlin always liked to go out with the boys for a good time, and there was no telling what he might pull off," Corbett said. "I grabbed Donlin and immediately got busy on him. . . . I kept him there [in my hotel room] playing pinochle all night, and he never had a chance to go out."[10]

The National Commission had no problem with gamblers or players betting on games. Gambling on games by players and managers was common and legal at the time and regularly reported in the press. A *New York Times* article on Game One noted that McGraw had wagered about $400 at even money and that some Giants players, including Donlin, had also gotten bets down.[11]

Every seat at Columbia Park was taken, and fans stood ten deep behind the ropes strung across the outfield. For the Series the Giants unveiled dramatic new uniforms. Whether playing at home or in Philadelphia, they dressed in black, with the "N" and "Y" lettering on their jerseys in white. It was an interesting psychological ploy by McGraw, one that had his team looking dynamic when contrasted with the A's, who were clad in their comparatively drab regular-season white home uniforms.

Mack chose left-hander Eddie Plank to pitch the opener. McGraw, as expected, went with Mathewson. If we take Corbett's story at face value, Donlin had little sleep the night before. Nevertheless, his fifth-inning single scored Bresnahan with the Giants first run; it was all Mathewson needed. He shut out the A's, 3–0, allowing just four widely scattered hits.

"When Mathewson is at his best, he is a pitching machine of comprehensive might," wrote the *New York Sun*. "Mathewson . . . unlimbered a service of such infinite and mystifying variety as to make the Quaker batters powerless and to wholly outshine Plank."[12] The next day in New York Philadelphia's Albert "Chief" Bender was equally dominating. He evened the Series by besting Joe McGinnity with his own four-hit, 3–0 shutout. Donlin, who had two hits in the opener, had two more in Game Two, including a double.

While sportswriters were reluctant to air "dirty laundry" in this era, they felt free to use stereotypical descriptions of Indigenous Americans. "Imperturbable at first, and even sullen in his moments of mildness, the big Indian went into transports of vindictive joy when he found his good right arm answering to his will," wrote the *New York Herald* about Bender, a highly intelligent graduate of the Carlisle Indian Industrial School.[13] The *Philadelphia Inquirer* wrote: "The big copper-skinned athlete had the speed of an arrow shot from the bow of a Chippewa marksman, he was cool as an Esquimaux in a snow hut, and his aim was as good as that of Davy Crockett when that hunter was wont to hit a squirrel in the eye. This combination was too much for the Giants."[14] Bender's masterpiece would be the only game the American Leaguers would win. In a Series where every game ended in a shutout, Giants pitchers won the next three.

The next day, in the only game that was one-sided, Mathewson, again allowing only four hits, defeated Coakley and the A's, 9–0. Donlin had a double and two walks (one intentional) and scored three runs. The intentional walk came in the fifth inning, when the Giants' lead was only 2–0. With runners at second and third Mack chose to load the bases rather than pitch to him. The move backfired as New York scored five runs in the inning.

In Game Four McGinnity topped Plank, 1–0, with the only run of the game unearned.[15] The *New York Sun* praised McGinnity in the florid reporting style of the time: "The Iron man was an avenging Phoenix arising from the ashes of last Tuesday's defeat. . . . He was as much master of his calling as Raphael was with the brush."[16]

McGraw came back with his ace for Game Five. Pitching on one day's rest, Mathewson ended the Series by outpitching Bender, 2–0, before a huge Saturday crowd at the Polo Grounds. After the game's final out the crowd broke through the police line and rushed for the players. Ten thousand fans surrounded the clubhouse and demanded to see their heroes. One by one the Giants appeared and were cheered.[17]

Commenting a few days later, McGraw continued to praise his best pitcher. "I knew he would be too much for the Athletics," he said. "In all my baseball career, I never saw such pitching as Matty did in that Series, and I don't think anybody else ever did."[18] To this day the twenty-five-year-old Mathewson's effort against Philadelphia remains the most dominating pitching performance in World Series history. In tossing three complete-game shutouts, he allowed just fourteen hits, struck out eighteen, and walked only one.

Roger Bresnahan, who caught and batted leadoff in each of the five games, led all hitters with a .313 average. Donlin (.263) had four hits in the first two games but only one in the final three. He led the team in runs scored with four. Dan McGann led in runs batted in, with four, one more run than the entire A's team scored in the Series.[19] Philadelphia batted a feeble .161 for the five games.

Each Giants player received a winner's share of $1,142, plus an additional $500 thanks to a generous gesture by Brush. Each Giants player also received a commemorative button valued at $50 from the National Commission.

A story that surfaced after the season helps magnify how much the game has changed off the field as well as on. Donlin confessed to having entered into an agreement with several members of the Athletics to split equally the money they would receive, no matter which team won.[20] More than a dozen other players were said to have made the same arrangement. "This simply illustrates that saying that is as old almost as baseball itself: 'The only way to reach a ballplayer is through his pocketbook.'"[21]

Joe Vila was gracious in acknowledging the Giants' victory:

It is a pill without a sugar coating, but down it goes with a grimace! . . . Truly Mathewson and Bresnahan were Giants in every sense of the word. . . . I must also give credit to Johnny McGraw. To him belongs the praise for moulding [sic] a good ball team together, for organizing a well-balanced, obedient combination that played the game up to the top of the handle. . . . The Athletics were severely handicapped by the absence of Waddell. The Rube was to the Philadelphia team exactly what Mathewson's was to New York.

Everything has broken the right way for McGraw since he came here from Baltimore. He has made good and has won a following which will not leave him for a long time. He has had magnificent support from the press and his employers and deserves all the praise that is his just now.[22]

Philadelphia fans were also ready to blame their team's defeat on not having Waddell available. Mathewson, however, questioned the overall effect Waddell's absence had on the outcome: "I would like some Quaker rooter to tell me how they would have won any of the four games in which we were successful with Waddell in the box. . . . It takes runs to win, and they were shut out in every contest."[23] Meanwhile, McGraw continued to praise his club: "I played on the old Baltimore team[s] of 1893, 1894, and 1895. In my opinion the Giants of 1905 can do anything the champion Orioles did and have a shade on them besides."[24]

Rather than returning to Cincinnati, Donlin spent the offseason in New York. Along with teammates Billy Gilbert and Art Devlin, he was one of three unmarried men on the Giants, but before the year was out, he would be the lone bachelor.

Donlin kept his batting eye sharp by playing a weekly indoor baseball game. On November 5 a team of professional players, headed by Donlin, defeated the army's Twelfth Regiment team at the regiment's armory by a score of 13–0. Donlin, who played first base, had three memorable at bats that day. In one the bat slipped from his hand and struck a youngster in the face, breaking his nose. In another he hit a high fly ball that hit and dropped a big glass chandelier. There was a wild scurry to get away from the falling glass and a ten-minute delay until the debris was cleared. Finally he hit one ball into the hanging balcony in left-center field for a home run.[25]

It was common practice in this era for big league teams, including the pennant winners, to keep playing after the regular season ended as a way to pick up extra money. Thus both the Giants and Athletics were in action the day after the Series ended. The Giants tour ended with a game in Trenton, New Jersey, on October 21. The game was uneventful, but a banquet that night was not. In an incident symbolic of the pugnacious 1905 Giants, Donlin, an equal-opportunity brawler, concluded the evening's celebration by getting into a fistfight with a group of Black waiters at the city's most fashionable hotel, the Sterling. As reported in the *Los Angeles Herald*, "The irrepressible Mike Donlin, the inevitable hero of many a hot scrap on and off the diamond, maintained his reputation as a rough-house artist early Sunday morning, October 22, when he whipped five waiters and an actor, created an uproar in a hotel dining room by his right and left leads for his opponents, started a panic among the guests, and raised such a disturbance that the fire department was hurried to the scene."[26]

After playing a local YMCA team that afternoon, the entire Giants team, together with prominent city and county politicians and officials, was given a dinner. "About one o'clock Sunday morning Donlin, Gilbert, and several others were in the main dining room opening wine at the rate of a bottle a minute."[27] Jim Jumble, a husky two-hundred-pound waiter, claimed one of the party had not paid for two quarts of wine. An argument ensued, and the waiter hit Donlin, who responded in kind. Other waiters jumped in and knocked Donlin to the floor. After he got to his feet, he started swinging, knocking down two of the waiters. An actor who claimed intimate friendship with Donlin tried to separate his friend and the waiter, but Donlin hit him with a right-hand smash that bloodied his face and sent him to the ground. Jumble was cut badly on his head. The crash of china and silverware made such an uproar that guests were awakened. Thinking the hotel was on fire, they ran through the corridors to the windows crying for help. "In the confusion someone turned on an alarm, and the fire department responded, thereby greatly adding to the excitement."[28]

A few days later, undeterred by what had happened in Trenton, 150 or so of "Mike Donlin's downtown friends," as they called themselves, gave him a dinner in Manhattan. It was a festive night, with many celebrities present, including almost the entire Giants team.[29] Once again, Mike had gotten away with behavior that was reprehensible and outrageous. But to New Yorkers, who loved him, Mike Donlin could do no wrong.

13

....

The New York Hoodlums

"With their obstructionism, overly aggressive style of play, unrelenting taunting of the opposition, and wide-ranging assault on authority, the Giants had become the most hated team in baseball, with McGraw as its most hated man. [Ban] Johnson went as far as to publicly denounce Brush and McGraw as more detrimental to baseball than the game's worst enemies."[1]

The raucous, disruptive behavior of the 1905 Giants exemplified John McGraw's methods and maneuvers. Throughout the season they created controversy and outrage. It was a season of many ugly incidents, which began during its first week, with Dan McGann as the instigator. McGraw and first baseman McGann had been teammates, friends, and drinking companions in St. Louis, Baltimore, and now in New York. "McGann helped McGraw bring to the Giants the rowdy brand of play for which the old Orioles had been famous."[2]

In an April 22 game at Philadelphia McGann was thrown out on a play at the plate. While the play was not close, McGann punched Phillies catcher Fred Abbott, who responded by throwing the ball at McGann, hitting him in the rear end. Plate umpire George Bausewine ejected both men. As McGann walked to the bench, the crowd began taunting him; several spectators threw cushions at him. A few of the Giants players responded by threatening to go into the stands.

The crowd grew even more infuriated when Christy Mathewson punched a young boy who had run onto the field carrying a lemonade tray. Mathewson had built a reputation as a courageous and clean-cut "Christian Gentleman." But one Philadelphia observer said Mathewson's punching the boy showed "that his association with the old Baltimore crowd had also made a hoodlum of him."[3] Timothy Sharp added that Mathewson "split [the boy's] lip and loosened a few of his teeth and, from what I can understand, simply beat up the youth."[4]

After the game thousands of spectators left the park to lay in wait for the Giants. A reporter for the *Philadelphia Inquirer* described what happened next:

> For a while the mob confined itself to hooting, then to throwing peanuts, paper balls, and small stones into the carriages. Finally, a half brick was thrown into one of the carriages, hitting a player. The players tried to pull down the hoods of their carriages to save themselves from the fusillade of missiles that was being hurled at them, but the angry crowd prevented them. One of the mob was hit over the head by a bat in the hands of a player, and another was locked up on the charge of rioting. The drivers of the wagons finally got their [horse] teams moving, but on their way down Broad Street at Dauphin they were again charged upon by thousands who had collected at that point. There was another volley of stones, but no one was injured.[5]

As would happen with disturbing regularity throughout the remainder of the season, the police were required to restore peace. A few days later there was more hooliganism after a Phillies-Giants game. "How long will the National League stand for the hoodlum tactics of this New York team both on and off the field?" railed one Philadelphia newspaper. "During a game McGraw and his men are fighting umpires all the time, questioning every decision against them, and resorting to all the dirty tactics known to baseball in order to win."[6] Joe Vila asked in the *Sporting News*, "What has John Tooth [*sic*] Brush got to say about these lovely methods, in view of his boasted preferences for clean sport and fair play?"[7]

The Giants' manager suffered his second ejection of the season on May 15. Rookie umpire Bill Klem was in his first game in the Polo Grounds and his first involving the Giants. He tossed McGraw in the sixth inning after McGraw asked him to call a balk on Chicago pitcher Mordecai Brown. When the rookie refused to be intimidated, McGraw continued to argue, and Klem ejected him.[8] "They fought after that for the rest of McGraw's life . . . at each other's throats," wrote author Joe Durso, "while in private they spoke highly of the other's abilities."[9]

When the Pirates played at the Polo Grounds on May 20, umpire Jim Johnstone ejected three Giants. The *New York Times* praised Johnstone for doing "very well to check the angry feelings of some of the players that were likely to cause much disorder."[10] Pirates owner Barney Dreyfuss wrote to league president Harry Pulliam, objecting to McGraw's constant taunting of him with calls of, "Hey Barney." He emphasized one remark in particular: "Hey Barney, I'll bet you $10,000 that the Giants win the [season] series against your club," McGraw allegedly said.[11] "[McGraw] then urged me to make a wager," Dreyfuss claimed. "With that he accused me of being crooked, of controlling the umpires, and made other false and malicious statements."[12]

"McGraw's vile epithets are still ringing in my ears," wrote Dreyfuss, "and I propose to see if an owner of a National League club must submit to such treatment at the hands of a thug."[13] McGraw likely used language far more vulgar, but it could not be published in the newspaper accounts.

Pulliam fined McGraw $150 and suspended him for fifteen days. Upset at the fine and suspension, McGraw said, "Why, there is no organization on the face of the earth, except the National League, that will convict an accused man without a hearing. We might as well be in Russia."[14]

McGraw had made the Giants a winning team again, and the New York fans were willing to overlook the damage he was causing the game. Ten thousand of them wrote to the board of directors with the claim that the Giants had no trouble with any other team except the Pirates. "We of New York admire the aggressive (not rowdy) sort given us by the New York club under the admirable and always gentlemanly methods of John J McGraw, and sincerely pray for the welfare of the game that you will treat him with the courtesy his grand work for the game in our city entitles him."[15]

The press was less mesmerized by McGraw. "There is no more foul-mouthed individual in the business than 'Muggs,'" wrote Pittsburgh-based Ralph Davis. "And McGraw has his underlings trained along the same lines."[16] The *Sporting News* continued in its editorializing against McGraw's vile tactics. "McGraw must mend his ways or get out of baseball. His Baltimore experience showed that he was too small mentally and morally to control a club, and his career in New York demonstrates that with a team that outclasses all others in its company, he has not sufficient sportsmanship to rely upon the Giants' playing strength to win their games. . . . The methods which made it impossible for him to remain in the American League have been followed by him as manager of the New York Club."[17]

Joe Vila's opinion of the McGraw-Pulliam case was as expected: "Aggressive ball is what some unsportsmanlike persons call it, but it is nothing

5. Intense and combative, John McGraw, seen here in 1905, turned the woeful New York Giants into champions just two years after he took over as manager. Often seen as a portly figure, he was slender in his playing and early managerial days. SDN-003763, *Chicago Daily News* Collection, Chicago History Museum.

short of thugism [*sic*] and low-down depravity. Does any man, who is a man, believe that it is necessary to go to the coaching lines and call a pitcher names that a moral degenerate could not invent?"[18] He later added, "They will continue to resort to bulldozing, obscenity, and terrorism to their own satisfaction."[19]

The Dreyfuss incident ended well for McGraw. On June 4 a Massachusetts Superior Court justice issued an injunction restraining Pulliam from enforcing the fine and suspension. "The ruling gave McGraw carte blanche to continue his tantrums," wrote Dennis and Jeanne Burke DeValeria in their biography of Honus Wagner.[20]

As the season wore on, the Giants' belligerent style of play continued to make them the target of fan violence and abuse wherever they played. On June 18, in St. Louis, the fans cursed at them as they left the field after their defeat. The crowd had been stirred up by McGraw's constant arguing with the umpires during the game and remarks he had made to some fans in response to their razzing. One fan hit McGraw on the head with an umbrella, while others threw stones and pebbles at the departing players. The police stepped in to prevent any further trouble, but objects of various kinds were thrown at the team's omnibus on its way back to the hotel.[21]

The next day the violence directed at the New Yorkers came from the crowd in Cincinnati. During the third inning a throw to first base by Giants pitcher Hooks Wiltse was wild and went down the right-field line. As first baseman McGann and right fielder George Browne chased the ball, several bottles were thrown at them from the stands, and one hit Browne.[22]

Following a July 4 doubleheader in Philadelphia, a crowd gathered around the carriages taking the Giants back to their hotel. According to the police, Donlin and Browne resented the attitude of the crowd and hurled several stones at those who were nearest to them. The players were then pelted with stones and tin cans. Donlin and Browne were arrested and charged with disorderly conduct. Following the arrest, the crowd started after the other carriages and began throwing objects at the players. Roger Bresnahan was hit on the head by a brick, and Joe McGinnity was struck in the face by a tin can. Donlin and Browne were discharged at the police station when the man who had asked the police to arrest them did not appear.[23]

In a home loss to the Pirates on July 19 McGann and Donlin were both ejected in the fifth inning by Klem, the base umpire. McGann's ejection came after Klem ruled Pittsburgh's Tommy Leach safe at first on his well-placed bunt. McGann grabbed the umpire's coat, but Giants second baseman Billy Gilbert grabbed McGann before he could do further damage. Later in the inning Donlin objected when Klem called Honus Wagner safe at third on a steal attempt. Like McGann, he used despicable language to Klem, although he did not touch him.

Fans in the right-field bleachers, upset that the Giants had lost two of their best players, started throwing beer bottles on the field. One hit Klem in the back, and several others came close. After the game a cordon of police officers escorted Klem and home plate umpire Jim Johnstone from the field.[24] "It was one of the most outrageous scenes ever enacted on a ball field in recent years," wrote *Pittsburgh Press* reporter L. M. Cadison. "Anything less than murdering an umpire in New York is considered 'a gentle man's game.' Baseball rooters throughout the country are up in arms against the thug tactics of the New York bunch."[25]

On August 5, after umpire George Bausewine called a Pirates player safe on a close play, "a few Giants jostled Bausewine before the umpire pulled a watch from his pocket and gave them one minute to resume play. McGraw threatened Bausewine, while 'Christian Gentleman' Mathewson tried to knock the watch from the umpire's hand. Several other Giants players carried on until Bausewine declared the game a forfeit."[26]

The hatred for the New Yorkers that had been building in Pittsburgh for the past few years exploded. About half of the eighteen thousand spectators rushed onto the field. They began punching McGraw and his players, who were huddled on their bench.

Although the rivalry between the teams was passionate, it did not extend to tolerating fan assaults. "Manager Fred Clarke and several of his players went into action. They helped shield their hated opponents from the angry fans until the police could lead them back to their horse-drawn carriages. And still it was not over. People began pulling the yellow blankets that read New York Champions off the horses."[27] The carriages were "bombarded by an assortment of fruits and vegetables as they passed the farmers' market en route to the team's quarters, the Monongahela House. Some players retaliated; others took whatever cover they could find. Shortstop Bill Dahlen was the only one hurt in the salvo when a well-aimed canta-loupe found his head."[28]

Meanwhile, everyone was wondering who had hit Donlin in the mix-up after the game was forfeited. Some claimed that umpire Bob Emslie did so after Donlin cursed at him. It remained a mystery, but whoever did it, hit him hard. Blood was still flowing when he reached the carriage that would take the players back to the hotel.[29]

While there were no more extreme incidents in the final two months of the season, the Giants continued to verbally, and sometimes physically, challenge nearly every umpire's call that went against them. McGraw himself was ejected three times in the four games from August 21 to 24, and he was ejected five times in a stretch of eleven games, four by umpire Johnstone. As a team, total ejections for the Giants went from seven in 1902 to twenty-one in 1903 to thirty in 1904 to thirty-six in 1905.[30]

In a post-career conversation with Sid Mercer of the *New York Globe*, Donlin spoke of the "good old days in baseball." "It required considerable agility to dodge the brickbats then," he said, "but we always managed to escape with our lives. McGraw's old championship team of 1904 and 1905 seldom got in or out of Chicago, St. Louis, Pittsburgh, or Philadelphia without a fight."[31]

Because of the Giants' success these past two seasons, New Yorkers adored them. But only the most unthinking partisans could have been completely proud of them. And even they had to think again when less than four months after the Giants won the World Series, Donlin made headlines across the country—for all the wrong reasons. On February 8, 1906, he was arrested for intoxication ("drunk and disorderly") and second-degree assault while traveling on a train in upstate New York. He was charged with beating up the conductor and, worse yet, pulling a gun on a porter.

Donlin and some Minor League and semipro ballplayers were on a train from New York City to Troy, New York, to play a game of indoor baseball against a team captained by Troy native Johnny Evers. They were drinking, "became frolicsome . . . and wanted to take possession of the [rail] car," according to the conductor's account. Donlin was also reported to have pointed a loaded revolver, which a diamond salesman on the train had lent him, at the head of the porter, who had refused to serve the party more alcohol.[32] One report said the players were throwing balls and paper wads throughout the car and that Donlin hit the conductor in the face when he tried to restrain the party.[33] The conductor telegraphed ahead to the chief of New York Central, and when the train reached Albany, Donlin and two others were arrested. When Donlin's identity was discovered, "a sensation" developed, with a large crowd following the party to the police station.[34]

Donlin's friend and Giants teammate Billy Gilbert arrived on a later train and, with the help of a New York state senator, arranged for the men's release after posting bail. They were arraigned the next morning. The porter charged that Donlin threatened to "let the sun shine through him." Donlin gave his version of the incident while making use of the racist language common at the time and blaming the porter for overreacting: "The story that coon tells about me threatening to kill him is a pipe dream pure and simple." He said that his party had been singing "coon songs," which the Black porter took as a personal affront. Donlin continued that he had borrowed a passenger's gun and "laughingly told the fellows I'd give Rufus Rastus a scare." When he told the porter he had a gun and showed him the handle in his pocket, the man took off. "I've seen baseball players get away from the plate in lively fashion, but nothing but lightning could pass that unbleached American as he beat it to the baggage car."[35] The case was adjourned until later in the month, when it was postponed again.

Donlin and his two co-defendants continued on to Troy, where he played that night. His "exploits" were widely reported that morning; a typical headline was "Ball Players on a Rampage," with Donlin's name prominent in the sub-headline.[36] Yet the "bad boy" got a big reception and was the "hero of the game throughout the evening."[37]

The Baltimore and Cincinnati ballclubs had given up on Donlin after they considered him uncontrollable and irredeemable. Now John McGraw of the Giants told reporters, "Well, if Donlin thinks the New York club will stand for any such nonsense as that, he is mistaken. I will go out and play center-field myself before I will tolerate it. Such actions are not only an injustice to the club, but also a blot on the game."[38] Had Donlin now made himself persona non grata with yet a third big-league team and perhaps all of Organized Baseball?

PART 2

Mabel

14

....

Vaudeville, America's Other
National Pastime

Baseball reigned supreme in the early 1900s as America's preeminent participatory and spectator sport. As historian Harold Seymour wrote, "Baseball was ingrained in the American psyche. Its importance in the first decades of the twentieth century was astonishing."[1] Attendance in the established National League grew by more than 42 percent from 1901 to 1905. Even more striking was the success of the new American League. Attendance rose by more than 85 percent in its first five seasons. The two leagues had a combined attendance of almost six million in 1905. Baseball was flourishing in America.

Yet another dominant form of entertainment in the country was vaudeville, and it too was flourishing. A medium that has now been gone from theaters for almost a century, it was uniquely American and enormously popular. Donald Travis Stewart, better known as Trav S. D., a show business historian, explained:

> The watchword of vaudeville was variety. The opposite of a variety show, you might say, is a "monotony show." Twelve hours of monks chanting the same mantra over and over again—that's monotony. Twelve *minutes* of monks chanting the same mantra, clad in fabulous silken outfits, accompanied by "mysterious" dry ice smoke and a very Chinese-sounding gong, preceded by a man who plays the vibes with his toes, and succeeded by a barbershop quartet . . . that's variety. . . . The common denominator was an aesthetic of constant surprise brought about through calculated novelty.[2]

In 1984 an elderly woman named Florence Sinow reminisced about her love of vaudeville decades earlier: "No one act was on long enough so that you lost interest—the evening shifted from excitement to excitement, but on different levels—high comedy, sophistication, slapstick, dancing, singing—sentimental—jazz—acrobats—animals—a panorama . . . a kind of entertainment audiences could lose themselves in, individually and collectively."[3]

Vaudeville had its roots in nineteenth-century minstrel troupes, traveling medicine shows and circuses, dime museums, music hall saloons, and burlesque. Among the memorable actors and singers who had their start in vaudeville were Fanny Brice, Joe E. Brown, Eddie Cantor, Jimmy Durante, W. C. Fields, Al Jolson, Buster Keaton, Will Rogers, Sophie Tucker, and Ed Wynn. Whether the acts were song, dance, comedy, or physical acts of dexterity, all vaudeville shows had one thing in common: variety, a succession of unrelated acts.

As vaudeville evolved in the late 1800s, the acts became more wholesome. When theater owner Tony Pastor opened his Fourteenth Street venue in 1881, he banned drinking, smoking, and vulgarity on stage.[4] Benjamin Keith and Edward Albee (whose partnership was known as Keith-Albee) were early vaudeville promoters who in the late nineteenth century built a chain of theaters. They too emphasized "clean vaudeville." They made vaudeville more respectable because they realized it was far more profitable: a "double audience" of women (and even children) as well as men.

The middle class was growing dramatically in the late nineteenth and early twentieth centuries, and it was driving the rising popularity of vaudeville. It was also demanding more sophisticated and wholesome performances in more attractive theaters. "Instead of a bar with a theater attached, it was a theater with a bar attached."[5] Trav noted that the times also had something to do with the move to more respectable shows. "A businessman with any instinct seeking to stay afloat in those years of high Victorianism must have been constantly mulling over the tirades of clergymen, temperance advocates, reformist politicians, and journalists railing against the saloon culture."[6]

The theaters were rarely dark; Keith offered shows from 10:30 a.m. to 10:30 p.m. "Continuous vaudeville," with the same acts repeated many times each day, made life difficult for performers but convenient for patrons (who could come and go as they pleased) and more profitable for promoters. The danger of a show's being a flop was not an issue; there was no front-end cost. And if an act was a failure, that performer could easily be dismissed and replaced. Trav wrote that there was a saying in vaudeville: "Don't send your laundry out until after the first performance." He described the theater manager's power over acts as "positively Dickensian."[7]

The audience had the ultimate power: its applause was the final arbiter. Eddie Cantor said, "The audience is never wrong. . . . If a performer failed to go across, it was either the fault of the material or manner of presentation."[8] Performers modified their acts based on audience feedback.

The next act would be different from the last and might be better. Sometimes the acts were surprising and even shocking. The most famous vaudeville promoter was William "Willie" Hammerstein, whose Times Square Victoria Theatre was the preeminent venue from 1904 to 1914.[9] He said that vaudeville was "just one damn thing after another."[10] He booked women who became celebrities for shooting their husbands, freak acts such as a man who was 9 feet, 2 inches tall and another man who had a seventeen-foot-long beard.[11] When an eager performer allegedly told Hammerstein that he would commit suicide on the stage for $2,500, the impresario was said to ask, "What would you do for an encore?"[12]

Hammerstein booked notorious people "on the strength of their fame alone," wrote Trav, "for he understood that although their acts might be incredibly lame, their drawing power wouldn't be."[13] Andrew Hammerstein, Willie's great-grandson, described the Victoria as a "National Enquirer for the theater."[14]

Comics, such as juggler W. C. Fields, "swarmed through vaudeville almost as a national symbol" in the first decade of the 1900s, wrote vaudeville historian Douglas Gilbert. They appealed to audiences because of the pathos they projected and the reminder, "There but for the Grace of God."[15] Onlookers looked favorably on an underdog, especially an amusing one. Charlie Chaplin later rose to fame in silent films with his persona as "the little tramp." Vaudevillian Ed Wynn once said, "A comedian is a man who doesn't do funny things but who does things funny."[16]

People of moderate income could relate to vaudeville, as opposed to what was known as "legitimate" theater. "Opera and drama held little appeal for this new stratum of theatregoers. That entertainment was too high-priced, too difficult to understand, too 'tony.'"[17] David Monod noted that vaudeville was revolutionary in its assault on nineteenth-century privilege;

it laid the foundation of the modern celebrity culture and linked success to "personality, pluck, and conspicuous consumption."[18] While nowadays we see vaudeville as somewhat tawdry, at its peak before World War I, "if you wanted to be up-to-date on the latest fads, you had to go to vaudeville."[19]

As the first decade of the new century progressed, vaudeville became so lucrative that even famous and well-respected dramatic actors, including John Barrymore, could not resist it. Vaudevillian Charles Ross, who performed with his wife Mabel Fenton, may have overstated the importance of his craft—but only somewhat—when he remarked in 1911 that the vaudeville artist "is no longer looked down upon as low variety. His position is assured. The social distinction between the variety and the legitimate stage is gone forever."[20]

In 1905 a new theater publication appeared. "The very fact of a newspaper named *Variety* reflected the new importance and growing professionalism of the business."[21] The name also reflected something that had not changed: vaudeville fans continued to expect novelty. The new weekly also became a vehicle for performers to hype themselves. Rising star Al Jolson once took out an ad that said simply, "Watch me—I'm a wow."[22]

New York was vaudeville's epicenter, with Chicago as its other hub. Vaudevillian Joe Frisco famously remarked, "Once you leave New York, every other town is Bridgeport."[23] New York City was undergoing dramatic growth and change at this time. In 1912 British author Arnold Bennett described Times Square with its brilliant lights as "an enfevered phantasmagoria."[24] A 1902 feature in *Harper's Weekly* pointed out that much more than those lights was dazzling in and about this city, which was "simply bursting its bonds. It is as if some mighty force were astir beneath the ground, hour by hour pushing up structures that a dozen years ago would have been inconceivable."[25]

The makeup of the city's population was also undergoing dramatic change. "The poor and disenfranchised poured in from abroad, making New York a city more variegated in its human splendor than any ever on earth."[26] These newcomers, as well as more established residents of the city, wanted and needed to be entertained. "There is little mirth in the every-day life of the busy New Yorker. . . . The public reaches out for the gay, the bright and the witty, as a child reaches for a blue and gold block in preference to a gray or black one."[27]

Vaudeville had some remarkable similarities to baseball. Travel was the essence of life for players in both arenas, though for different reasons. Baseball had its away games against teams in other cities, and vaudeville needed venues in other cities since Broadway could not absorb the multitude of available acts. The demand for variety also meant shows could not simply stay in New York City, nor did they stay in any one town for long.[28]

Neither ball players nor vaudevillians stayed in the best hotels or ate in the best restaurants. "Like vaudevillians, many [ballplayers] drank to excess, slept late, and ate cheap meals. They also played their ballgames around three in the afternoon, giving them a chance to visit the theatres in the evening."[29] And both were "playing the big, booming, rowdy, bustling American cities as well as the smallest, quietest, most God-fearing towns that could clear a diamond in the village square or erect a stage in a storefront," in the words of author Noel Hynd.[30]

Vaudevillian Will Rogers, who was signed by Hammerstein in 1905, endeared himself to the common man with his down-to-earth persona and act. His verbal humor, along with his lasso and horse, chewing gum, and Oklahoma-accented English, were "democratizing," said Trav.[31] In his 1949 book, *Not So Long Ago*, Lloyd Morris noted that Rogers's act "was directed at shattering shams and pretenses."[32] A year before his untimely death in 1935, Rogers wistfully looked back at the early days: "I wish there was a vaudeville like there was in those old days. No branch of entertainment was ever so satisfying to work in. Never was there such independence. It was your act. And you could do it like you wanted to, and it was your ingenuity that made it."[33]

Rogers was also an ardent baseball fan. One of his biographers, Ray Robinson, wrote, "When he had the opportunity on lazy sunny afternoons in cities around the big-league circuit . . . he took himself out to the ballpark, where he cheered for his baseball buddies."[34]

Like vaudeville, baseball was cleaning up its image by eliminating the rowdy aspects of the game. This change made attending a game more attractive to families, not just male audiences. The rising turnout of women certainly contributed to the sport's rising attendance.

Baseball and vaudeville were similar in another and more significant way. While fans of both came primarily from the middle class, performers of both came mainly from the working class. Their fields offered an escape from a menial and financially strapped existence. Both seemed to evince the American Dream that success did not require money, connections, or education. It was possible if the performer had talent and skill. When Minnie Marx, the mother of Groucho and his brothers, was asked why she put her children into show business, she replied, "Where else can people who don't know anything make so much money?"[35]

15

....

A Star Is Born

It was into this world of vaudeville that a young girl from Kansas City emerged and rose to stardom. Mabel Hite was born in Ashland, Kentucky, on May 30, 1883.[1] She spent her early years in Idaho before the family moved to Kansas City, Missouri, where her father, Lewis, was a druggist.[2] Mabel began singing in church and at business events before she was ten and surfaced in Kansas City newspapers as early as 1895. That fall twelve-year-old Mabel appeared in *The Fairies' Carnival*, described as *A Midsummer Night's Dream* for children. "The star of the attraction is Miss Mabel Hite," wrote a reporter for the *Kansas City Times*. "She is as pretty a little bit of femininity as ever stepped upon a stage, and her acting, instead of being the usual childish effort, is as finished and polished as though she had been upon the stage more years than she has ever seen. She is a natural actress, and her talents are far beyond the ordinary."[3]

A month later Mabel prepared for a leading role in Gilbert and Sullivan's *Iolanthe*. "I have always been crazy about the stage," Mabel told a Kansas City newspaper ten years later, "but my parents would not consent to my 'breaking' into the business."[4] Her father wanted her to become a schoolteacher, but her mother, Elsie, was more supportive of her theatrical interests. "We are the greatest pals. Mother is young, and it is so nice for me to have her with me," Mabel said in 1905.[5] The two would become constant companions.

Because she remained in Chicago, Mabel never graduated from high school. She gravitated to roles in comedy, many of which included singing; she was often described as a "soubrette," a description that stayed with her all her life. She was touring the Midwest in a farce-comedy in the fall of 1898 before her sixteenth birthday.

The authors found no detailed accounts of Hite's early vaudeville routines, but in 1910 prominent theater critic Amy Leslie referred to Hite's early success: "Mabel Hite is a name coupled with involuntary laughter, surprise, eccentric absurdities, and all that is unexpected and funny and audaciously comic. . . . People are so accustomed to greeting Mabel in clothes buttoned up on the wrong side, hats made like hay racks and shoes worse than a grand opera tenor's. . . . She is a constant bombardment of the unexpected in the broadest low comedy."[6] Leslie added, "Some time, perhaps, Miss Hite will stop ragging and clowning and exciting twenty new kinds of laughter in twenty new ways, but it will be a blow to sou-bretdom [*sic*]. . . . She flutters and capers and gyrates and burbles. She grins, fools, kicks, and stumbles with a peal of laughter following her every bit of mischief."[7]

Hite commented on her early career: "I don't even miss that first uproar-ious laugh that I used to get when my skirts hung askew, and my shoes weren't mates, and my hats were made out of assorted rag-bags and barn-yard feathers." She then explained the difference between vaudeville and theater in her own mind: "It [vaudeville] is much more difficult, and it requires much more brain-power to be able to talk and act like a clown than just to look like one."[8] The *Chicago News* described her meteoric rise: "She began as a child entertainer in variety houses and ran up the ladder of that kind of fame as if it had been made of electric batteries which shoved her to the top rung and left her laughing up there at the other dull stragglers below."[9]

Clara Lipman was a well-known actress who starred in a musical farce, *The Telephone Girl*, in 1898 and 1899. A revival of the show went on the road in 1900 with Hite in Lipman's starring role as Estelle, "the much-abused and overworked female, the telephone girl."[10] Chicago critics predicted a brilliant career for the young actress.[11]

Like many popular shows in this era, *The Telephone Girl* was a commer-cial, if not an artistic, success. Entertainment was more important than story, and elements of vaudeville were present. One early 1901 review of the show was positive, even though it stated that the "play" had no plot. The "skeleton" of a plot provided "a frame upon which to hang a glittering bunch of witty sayings and charming specialties."[12] This may have been theater, but it was not what would be called "legitimate theater."

In 1902 Hite, not yet twenty years old, was garnering rave reviews. One critic wrote, "Miss Mabel Hite is not only one of the youngest but one of the cleverest women on the American stage. She is really a girl with the

6. A unique comedic talent, Mabel Hite was described by critic Amy Leslie as an "eccentric, brilliant" performer with an "extraordinary sense of the ridiculous" (*Chicago Daily News*, May 12, 1910). Billy Rose Theatre Division, New York Public Library for the Performing Arts.

atmosphere of a woman, exceedingly bright and remarkably pretty, with large dreamy eyes. . . . She is one of the most original and graceful dancers on the American stage."[13]

But not every play is a success, and a new show is riskier than a proven box-office hit, even if it is written by a successful playwright. Hite's next role, in late 1902, was as the lead in the short-lived *The Burglar and the Waif*. It received savage reviews even in the smaller towns that welcomed shows with big-city connections. "Doubtless there are worse shows than *The Burglar and the Waif*, but doubtless not much worse," wrote a Topeka newspaper.[14] A Shreveport paper hoped Mabel would not "trifle with her audiences as she did last night. Some of her work was unworthy of a place even in a Mother Goose entertainment, exhibited exclusively before children."[15]

Early in 1903 theater impresario Frank Perley signed Mabel to play Phrosia in *The Chaperons*. This was a role in which Eva Tanguay, "the Queen of Vaudeville," had starred on Broadway. Tanguay was "the most outrageous star of vaudeville's golden age," wrote Amber Paranick of the Library of Congress.[16] Tanguay's biographer Andrew Erdman noted that she was discovering "the powerful appeal of freakish, kinesthetic energy," something that would also become central to Hite's appeal.[17] Mabel would be linked with and compared to Tanguay throughout her career.

In a 1911 interview Hite was asked, "When did you find out you were funny?" She replied, "I didn't. Eva Tanguay did. My mother met Miss Tanguay. It was in Kansas City, and I suppose there were the usual intimations to a visiting artist that there was local talent round waiting to be appreciated. I sang for Miss Tanguay . . . and she advised her [Hite's mother] to put me on the stage at once." The interviewer noted that though Hite had "marvelous eyes and at least ten degrees of featural superiority over most girls, she makes herself look a freak on the stage, and joys in it."[18] Tanguay took a similar joy in surprising, even shocking, her audiences and not taking herself too seriously.[19]

Like Tanguay, Hite understood that glamour and beauty had nothing to do with her success. "Why don't I try to play a part in swell dresses and try to look like Ethyl Barrymore?" she said in 1907. "It's because I'd make about 80 cents a week."[20] The 1908 *Who's Who on the Stage* wrote, "Miss Hite, unlike many other soubrettes, is not afraid to distort her features, assume ungainly attitudes and wear unattractive but laughter-inspiring apparel."[21]

While her role in *The Chaperons* gave Hite a proven vehicle, she also had the challenge of "big shoes" to fill. She did not disappoint. One critic wrote she earned her salary "by a ginger force that converts [a role] to irresistibility."[22] The play was described as "comedy opera," and one reviewer explained, "Plot and musical comedy have little in common."[23] First Tanguay and now Hite were able to use the show, not that far removed from vaudeville, as a vehicle for their talent, their flair for showmanship.

Just before her twenty-first birthday Mabel Hite made her New York City debut at the Knickerbocker Theatre. Perley had "discovered" Tanguay, and now he felt he had another rising star in Hite, whom he signed to a five-year contract.[24] *A Venetian Romance* opened on Broadway on May 2, 1904, with Mabel in the lead role. The show was not well received, though Hite was. "She had five recalls for her dance in the second act," noted the *New York Herald*.[25] The *New York Times* critic wrote that this "comedy opera" was "neither the one thing nor the other—and it is certainly not both. At best it is just continuous vaudeville from start to finish." The show was "at once loud and garish, and not infrequently vulgar."[26] It closed before the end of the month, but the production did go on the road later in the year.

Early in 1905 Perley cast Hite in *The Girl and the Bandit*. "All that Miss Hite does is queer and grotesque to the extreme," wrote the critic from the *Chicago Tribune*. "From her first appearance, every motion was a signal for laughter."[27]

Once again Hite was not performing in what was known as legitimate theater, though such shows were "more than" vaudeville. The lines between different types of stage shows were blurring. As late as 1916 New York theater critic Frank J. Price would write, "There was a time when those of us who professed some intimacy with stage terminology could easily differentiate between the operetta and the musical comedy, or the musical comedy and the comic opera, but that was in the long ago. . . . Today one must consult the program to learn whether he is enjoying a musical comedy or listening to an operetta."[28]

Playwrights and drama critics were not fans of vaudeville and were critical of these new forms of entertainment. Writing in *Cosmopolitan* magazine in 1905, British author Israel Zangwill said, "The artlessness of the public and the artfulness of the managers will long keep the present pabulum unaltered, save in increasing staleness." He called the musical comedy play "that mush of clotted nonsense." This hybrid form of entertainment interrupted acts with vaudeville, "comic songs or dancing dogs. To interrupt the continuity of the theme is as barbarous in itself as it must be bewildering to the casual spectator."[29]

In a remark that may resonate with modern-day concerns about social media, Zangwill (whose 1909 play *The Melting Pot* popularized the phrase) added, "The variety stage feeds and in turn aggravates that passion for snippets, which is the pest of our period, and which may end by depriving mankind of the capacity for sustained thought. . . . The incapacity for attention which is overtaking mankind has progressed too far."[30]

In spring 1905 Perley loaned Hite out for a Chicago production based on a Frank Baum book. Baum's 1900 children's book, *The Wonderful Wizard of Oz*, was immensely popular and led to a long-running Broadway musical in 1903 and 1904. His new production, *The Woggle-Bug*, was based on a sequel, *The Marvelous Land of Oz* (1904), but it closed in less than a month in Chicago and never reached Broadway. The *Chicago Tribune* called it "only a shabby and dull repetition of the cheapened *Wizard of Oz*."[31] The extravagant show had a loss of $45,000, a huge figure at the time.[32]

While the musical was a failure, Hite was one of its few redeeming features. Chicago's *Inter Ocean*'s said, "Miss Hite is the cleverest of the 'smart alecks' of the stage. . . . She has an appreciation of burlesque, and a sense of the ridiculous that will make her both famous and wealthy if she will but keep open her common-sense safety valves and occasionally place a chunk of ice upon her swelling bump of self-esteem."[33]

When Hite returned to the Chicago stage late in 1905 with *The Girl and the Bandit*, Amy Leslie expressed concern that she was falling into a rut. After watching the audience cheer "the wonderful little Mabel Hite [she was not much more than five feet tall], who is a whole parlor circus in herself," Leslie cautioned, "It is a pity she continues to drive on one line till her stunning style is becoming stultified. Sometimes a very young player may make too reverberating a hit to be of much use in a career . . . one vividly eccentric kind of clowning, rollicking, grotesque and all her own, but not a particularly lasting sort of sparkle."[34]

Early in 1906, when Frank Perley passed away, the show closed. With no immediate theater contract forthcoming, Hite returned to what she knew best, vaudeville. She teamed up with comedian Walter Jones, who was more than ten years her senior.

Mabel and Jones were returning to their previously successful field with "an eccentric comedy act" of "most amusing nonsense" that included singing, dancing, and conversations.[35] Critic Ludwig Lewisohn believed that musical comedy was bad art: "The music is thin and chirpy, the staging gorgeously vulgar, the fable calculated only to appeal to the meanest fancy. There is no touch of poetry or imagination."[36] Vaudeville, he felt, was more authentic and pure. Another writer explained Lewisohn's thinking: "Vaudeville is ancient and honest. It neither criticizes life nor attempts to tell a story."[37]

When Hite and Jones appeared in Indianapolis in late March 1906, the program provided a good sense of the variety of acts on a typical vaudeville bill. A trio of gymnasts and cyclists opened the show, followed by a group of performing dogs. Musical comedians performed, as did an opera trio that presented an entire scene from *Il Trovatore*. Two girls wearing black-face in minstrel style took their turn. A Tyrolean singer and a "monologist, mimic, and crayon artist" rounded out the program. A bonus was animated pictures shown with a new machine, the bioscope. The headliners were Jones and Hite, in a "Special Engagement of the Musical Comedy Stars" in a "bright farcical sketch."[38] The "high-class vaudeville" offered daily matiness for twenty-five cents.

The sketch had an extended tour, lasting much of the year. A Milwaukee reviewer noted that Jones seemed content to be in the background and was "willing to be eclipsed by his partner and shine along in her reflected favor." The critic then captured what made Hite such a special vaudevillian:

Mabel Hite's ability as an entertainer is in inverse ratio to her size. Every inch of her body is a dynamic force which brings forth laughter. Doing fearful stunts with her agile and supple body, she brings down the house with her every move. She moves above the stage seemingly without any plan, but the result is that she impresses her image indelibly on the minds of those who see her. Her act cannot be explained. It is *sui generis*. She may be imitated, but her imitators lack that personality which is a part of Mabel Hite that cannot be appropriated. She seemingly does not repeat herself, and yet every action seems of the minute born. She is a spontaneous funmaker, unctuously original, and with a mind attuned to humor.[39]

16

....

Mabel Meets Mike

Success came early and quickly for Mabel Hite. "I had often said to my mother, 'If I ever earn two hundred dollars a week, I shall not survive the shock. I'll pass away.'"[1] Mabel was appearing in *The Telephone Girl* in Denver in early 1901 when she drew the attention of a Chicago businessman, Edward Ellis Hamlin. To impress her he bought dinner for the theater company every night. Although Mabel resisted Hamlin's romantic overtures, he followed her to Salt Lake City. At the time, she was reportedly engaged to Raymond Hubbell, a young composer who was providing her with songs.[2]

An impressionable seventeen-year-old, Hite told reporters, "Ed's the dearest fellow in the world, and awfully rich, too." She explained how their sudden March wedding came about. "You see, I hadn't any idea of getting married till five minutes before it happened. Ed had been bothering me about it and saying he would take morphine and make away with himself and all that sort of o' thing, if I didn't take him."[3] Hamlin brought a minister to her hotel room, and her friend and a bellboy served as witnesses.

The new groom was spending money quite freely. "Already Hamlin has spent $6,000 within three weeks, fairly frightening hotel people, train porters, florists, and jewelers with his extravagant expenditures."[4]

Hamlin claimed that he came to Denver with $20,000 to look after his father's mining interests. His "immensely rich" father, he said, was an executive of the retail giant Marshall Field and Company.[5] The newlyweds traveled to San Francisco, where they stayed in the luxurious (original) Palace Hotel for $7.50 a day. Hamlin began spending much of his time and money at the racetrack and was drinking heavily.

Stories began to appear in newspapers across the country that the young Hamlin had been engaged to different wealthy women, in both Chicago and Denver.[6] Then came reports that his father was merely a salesman at Marshall Field and that Hamlin had borrowed the money he was spending and had done so under false pretenses. Now he was running out of money. At first Mabel refused to accept these reports and exclaimed, "These stories are just making me sick. . . . Ugh, such stories are enough to make a saint mad, and I do not claim to be a saint."[7]

But reality soon dawned on the young actress. She had to pay their Palace Hotel bill and even the train ticket for Hamlin to return to Chicago. They had been married for only three weeks. While some accounts said Hamlin's wealthy father insisted that the marriage be ended, the more likely account is that the family was not wealthy at all. Edward Hamlin was simply a con man.

In early June 1901, newspapers reported Hite would file for divorce. She claimed that Hamlin had pawned her jewelry and drank forty-seven whiskeys one day, to which he replied, "I may have drank [*sic*] twenty or twenty-five glasses in one sitting, but never forty-seven."[8] For some reason Mabel did not follow through with the divorce that year.

Two years later, when Hite was appearing in *The Chaperons*, she again filed for divorce. Hamlin told reporters, "I have suffered enough through my unfortunate infatuation with this woman. I saw Miss Hite on the stage one night in Denver, and her beauty and vivacity proved my immediate undoing. I haunted the theater every night." He added, "Miss Hite was only too willing to spend my money [$20,000 for a sealskin coat, a diamond necklace, and more, he said]. While the funds lasted, I was her adored one, but the trouble began when the money supply commenced to run low."[9]

In 1904 Mabel filed for divorce again, this time in Missouri. She told reporters, "I was a young girl in short dresses when I met him and wore my hair down my back. He bought me my first long dress. I was dazzled by the money and the rings he gave me, but my awakening was a rude one."[10]

The divorce was not made final until early 1905.[11] That year a Hite romance was back in the news: she reportedly was engaged to champion sprinter Arthur Duffy, who was known as "the world's fastest man."[12] Reports appeared that Duffy, who was competing in Australia in January 1905, would stop in Rome on his way home to get special dispensation from the Pope since Mabel was a divorcee.[13] Hite denied the engagement but admitted that Duffy was her friend.[14]

Hot Springs, Arkansas, was a popular vacation destination, famous for its thermal hot springs and for its gambling opportunities. Umpire and columnist Tim Murnane wrote in 1906, "The large number of ballplayers that journey to Hot Springs about February each year usually join their clubs later short of change as the result of trying to pick out the winning pony."[15]

It was probably in Hot Springs that Mabel Hite met Mike Donlin. It was the beginning of a loving relationship and a remarkable partnership. He was making his usual visit to Hot Springs to work off the excess weight he had gained in the offseason, and she was likely vacationing there with her mother.

In one account Mike explained their meeting as follows. One day in the early 1900s he noticed a young woman while sitting on the veranda of the Hotel Eastman. "Who is that young lady over yonder?" he asked an older local man. "She is way in advance of any one I've ever seen." The man replied, "That is Mabel Hite, a very clever soubrette." "Wish I knew her," said Donlin. "Can't you fix me an introduction?" A few minutes later, according to Donlin, Hite approached the same man and asked, "Who is that athletic-looking young man? He looks like a grand fellow to me." The old man told her that was Mike Donlin, the ballplayer, and added, "That's odd, Miss Hite, in view of the fact he was just expressing himself as wild to meet you." The man soon introduced them.[16]

Hite's account was slightly different. In early 1903 or 1904, she said, "I just met him casually at that time, but we got acquainted, and I didn't see much of him at all for a considerable time after that. Of course I met him occasionally the same as you would anyone and saw him play once in a while."[17]

A year or two later, when both were in New York City, Donlin asked her out to dinner. She recalled that evening:

I remember I was thinking he seemed like a real nice sort of chap, when he turned round and said sort of slow like, "Do you know I've been knocking around a good deal, and I've half decided that I'll get married, and I've picked out a little girl I think I'll ask." I never thought that I was the girl he was speaking of, but I remember I felt just a sudden lonesome sort of feeling all at once, and then that I didn't care anyway, so I just said in a careless tone, "Oh, well, it's just a matter between you and her, and I've got nothing to do with it." And I didn't find out until about six months later when we really became engaged that Mike had expected me to ask, "Who is she?" and then he'd have said, "Why, you're the girl."[18]

A 1906 article in the *New York Globe* gave yet another account of their meeting. Donlin first saw Hite in 1901, when she was performing in *The Telephone Girl*. This would have been around the time that Edward Hamlin met her. "At odd times since then the friendship between them was renewed, as they often met in their travels." When the Giants played in Chicago in 1905, the account added, they were frequently together. "The friendship gradually changed to a stronger feeling, and though Donlin never admitted it, it is believed that he has been engaged since last summer."[19] In 1912 Mabel told a reporter that she met Mike at a dance in Cincinnati, when she was performing there (likely some time between 1902 and 1904, when he was playing for the Reds).[20]

The midwestern entertainer, who had an unfortunate marriage in her past, and the eastern baseball star, who had suffered so many tragic losses in his immediate family, were drawn to each other. While she easily could have been attracted by his charm, she likely knew of his "history" of drinking, temper, and even violence. Perhaps, as young women sometimes do, she saw a troubled man she could redeem with affection and devotion.

Despite Donlin's drinking problem and violent outbursts, he was an authentic and kindhearted friend to those who knew him well. *Sporting Life* had a revealing article about the Giants' star early in 1906. People mistake "his jolly disposition, easy grace, and reckless accuracy for swagger and conceit. . . . Notwithstanding these opinions and paradoxical—to these people as it may seem—Mike Donlin is one of the most modest men playing professional ball today. . . . The worst enemy Donlin ever had won't accuse Mike of being a liar, for he was never known to be caught in one."[21]

Perhaps Donlin was drawn in turn to this woman because she would bring stability and love to his life, which had had so little of either. The *Dramatic Mirror*, a New York theatrical newspaper, later wrote of Mabel, "The eccentric comedienne was of large and generous soul. She used to give parties to her chorus and link arms with the humble human back drops while she was starring."[22]

On April 11, 1906, Mabel Hite and Mike Donlin were married at the home of a New York City alderman. Donlin's teammate Billy Gilbert and the alderman's daughter were the witnesses at the private event. Mabel had come from St. Louis, where she was performing vaudeville sketches with Walter Jones.

The wedding ceremony may have been small, but the event was big news in the city. The *New York Globe* stated, "Donlin is the idol of every small boy in New York, and of thousands of followers of the Giants. He is one of the greatest natural hitters in the history of baseball."[23] Many years later humorist and social commentator Will Rogers said, "Mike was the best-known baseball player of his generation. He it was who really introduced so-called 'color' into our national pastime. . . . He was the Babe Ruth of his time. When Mike and Mable [*sic*] were married, it was the most popular wedding New York ever had."[24]

On the first anniversary of their wedding Mabel revealed, "I guess I was cut out to marry a baseball man; anyway, I was nearly engaged to another one once before Mike. That was even before I met Mike. It was Billy Dineen [Dinneen, Boston pitching star of the 1903 World Series], if you really want to know, so there."[25]

It is not known how much Hite knew about Donlin's proclivity for alcohol. Whatever she did know, she probably saw past it and beyond the "swagger and conceit." This was a man who was described as a "generous, genial fellow, whose openness and honesty win and retain friendships."[26] This was the man "they wine and dine because he's Mike Donlin and not by reason of the fact that he is one of the most remarkable stickers of the age."[27] But as Mike was quoted in *Sporting Life* in 1907, "Many a man has more friends than are good for him."[28]

This was the man Mabel Hite fell in love with.

PART 3

Mike and Mabel

A Season Interrupted

Condemnation of Mike Donlin's February 1906 train escapade, which included raucous carousing and pointing a gun at a porter, dominated the Hot Stove League that month.[1] The disapproval was swift, harsh, and almost universal. Ralph S. Davis wrote in the *Sporting News*, "Donlin's case is one where the leopard cannot change his spots. Ever since Donlin has been in baseball, he has had a rowdy, ungovernable character, and his outbreaks were even more off the field than on it."[2] An editorial in that same February 17 issue went even further: "He has disgraced himself in every major league city in which he has played. . . . Donlin is a degenerate who, without the protection that his prominence as a ballplayer has afforded him, would have served more than one penal term. . . . He has never abstained from intoxicants during a season."[3]

Sports stars have often been able to deflect criticism of misbehavior, especially when they are performing well. But Donlin was considered a miscreant even against the standards of the rougher times of the early twentieth century. Syndicated columnist Heywood Broun wrote that early in his career Donlin walked into a Cincinnati bar and, hearing that a brawl was going on in a back room, asked the bartender, "Would you mind telling me, is that a private fight or can anyone join in?"[4]

There were still some who were willing to put up with Donlin's faults. Newspapers quoted "a leading manager" as saying, "I would rather have on my team a 'rummy' who can bat .350 than a Father Mathew who hits around the .100 mark." The same manager mentioned Abraham Lincoln's famous remark when told that Union General Ulysses S. Grant was a whiskey drinker: "I wish he would tell me where he gets his whiskey. I would like to have some to give to the other generals."[5]

During the 1905–6 offseason Donlin and his teammate and close friend Billy Gilbert opened a café-saloon in Harlem, with Donlin's name

7. Billy Gilbert was Mike Donlin's closest friend on the 1904–6 New York Giants. He served as a witness at Mike's marriage to Mabel Hite and was Mike's partner in a café-saloon in Harlem they opened after the 1905 championship season. Dennis Goldstein Collection.

"emblazoned in electric letters" outside. A Scranton reporter pointed out that Gilbert complemented Donlin because of his reputation for "the most even disposition" of any member of the Giants.[6] Joe Vila considered their venture another black mark against Donlin because he was having "one continuous round of festivities" at his new establishment.[7] Despite serving complimentary drinks to friends, the partners cleared $10,000 in their first year of operation.[8]

At spring training in Memphis John McGraw did not say why he now wanted Donlin on his club after declaring he would no longer tolerate his behavior. McGraw was likely thinking he would need Donlin's bat to defend the Giants' championship and felt he could control him. After all, he had kept Donlin in line the previous season. Also accounts surfaced that made light of the train incident, painting it as more of an innocent and misunderstood caper. One reporter concluded that "Donlin was playing the role of a 'game' fellow, and when found with the goods, had to suffer."[9] Once again his behavior was rationalized, and his transgressions were minimized.[10]

Problems between Donlin and McGraw quickly surfaced at Memphis. Donlin reported out of shape and was said to be the first player to tire during the team's drills.[11] One day he decided to end practice early by slugging a number of baseballs (only a limited supply was available) over the short right-field fence. McGraw fined him but later backed down, and Donlin abandoned that method of curtailing workouts.[12]

In mid-March McGraw suspended Donlin and fined him $10 for "misconduct [for drinking] and insubordination." This led to an "altercation which became very bitter."[13] After a couple days of "sulking," Donlin returned to the fold but only after he promised to behave.[14]

The relationship between Donlin and McGraw, only five years apart in age, was complex. Donlin had been quoted the previous summer poking fun at his manager. "He is a wonder," he said of McGraw. "He can start more fights—and win fewer—than anybody I ever saw."[15] McGraw surely saw those remarks. Like Donlin, McGraw's early life had been seared by tragedy. When he was a youngster, a diphtheria epidemic hit his hometown of Truxton, New York, near Syracuse. Within a few months McGraw lost his mother and three siblings to the disease. He left home before his thirteenth birthday, and baseball soon provided him with a path for advancement.[16] Charles Alexander aptly noted that this complicated man "was an amalgam of virtues and vices."[17]

Most sportswriters predicted the Giants would repeat as National League champions. They recognized that the Chicago Cubs were replacing the Pittsburgh Pirates as their main challenger. The Cubs' player-manager, first baseman Frank Chance, said of McGraw in 1906, "He is the most hated man in baseball. He has done more to injure the game than any other man at present engaged in it."[18]

In *The Irish in Baseball* historian David Fleitz pointed out that McGraw motivated his players by fanning ethnic rivalry. Irish players dominated his club (McGraw's father, like Donlin's, was an Irish immigrant), while the Cubs had a number of players of German origin. During the 1906 season the Giants' manager reportedly challenged his men not to let "a bunch of 'Dutchmen'" beat them for the pennant.[19] When the Giants raised their 1905 championship flag before their June 12 game, the Polo Grounds was decorated with both American and Irish flags.[20]

McGraw often would rally his men against the forces that wanted to deny the pennant to the Giants; he said these included not only opposing teams but also the umpires and the National League president, Harry Pulliam. A 1906 editorial in *Sporting Life* stated that McGraw was going too far with his conspiratorial rants: "No club wants to see New York, with its fine drawing capacity, lose the pennant for either personal, financial, or political reasons, but simply for sporting reasons and contrary assertion is a reflection upon the integrity of the sport and the honesty of the National League."[21]

Anti-McGraw sentiment was widespread. Timothy Sharp wrote, "No more despicable character than McGraw has ever been connected with the national pastime, and his success of late years has made many forget his shortcomings. However, I concede his transcendent managerial qualities. He 'gets there,' though all decent people deplore his bulldozing and browbeating methods."[22] McGraw's targets were the game's umpires, and his career would be intertwined with two of the best, Hank O'Day and Bill Klem. Sharp declared O'Day was the only "real umpire" in the National League because he would not let anyone push him around. He noted that Klem "puts up with a lot of abuse to avoid trouble" but that he was a promising comer.[23]

Now that the Giants were back-to-back champions, hatred of the club around the National League increased, and McGraw's behavior intensified that enmity. "McGraw loved playing the villain," wrote Frank Deford a century later.[24] Journalist Charles Fountain commented, "But if organized baseball beyond New York saw McGraw as the Antichrist, in New York he was the Messiah, for he had turned a moribund franchise into champions and put a sparkle and glitter into the city's signature attraction."[25]

Years later Donlin commented on the targets the Giants had on their backs from the start of that 1906 season: "I got so I could feel a brick coming when I couldn't see it."[26] With the Cubs now the rising power in the National League, he stated their fans were particularly boisterous: "They hated us in Chicago. The newspapers pointed out that we were as yellow as our horse blankets." He added that those blankets (which were emblazoned with "WORLD'S CHAMPIONS") were "perfect targets."[27]

As the season approached, Joe Vila cautioned that the Giants had to guard against "an attack of swelled head" and not take the pennant for granted. McGraw had designed new uniforms for his men, which also boldly shouted "World's Champions" across the jerseys. "Yet they tell me that some of the players think they own the world and that they can do as they please," Vila wrote.[28] Another concern Vila saw was that star pitcher Christy Mathewson was diagnosed with diphtheria and would miss the first few weeks of the season.

Sportswriters recognized Donlin's bat was a big reason the Giants were favored to repeat. In addition, his popularity in New York City was second to none, and that included Mathewson. One reporter wrote of Donlin just before the season began, "He is the idol of the American small boy."[29] His popularity with youngsters across the country was not reduced by his "bad boy" exploits, which may even have enhanced his image in their eyes. Sports fans have excused misconduct on the part of their teams' players as long as those players produced for their teams. "He's a scoundrel, but he's our scoundrel" has been a long-held fan reaction.

Such popularity may have added challenges to Donlin's predilection for alcohol since he was feted so often. As he himself observed, "Many a man has become sick from having too many other fellows say, 'Here's to your good health.'"[30] Yet Donlin maintained a remarkable modesty, despite projecting an image of swagger. Sipping on a lemon and seltzer drink in his Harlem café before spring training, he said, "When I get so that I can bat like little Willie Keeler, or Larry [Lajoie], or Big Cy [Seymour], then I'll commence to think that I'm going some."[31]

The day after Donlin's marriage to Mabel the Giants opened the season in Philadelphia, where they won two of the three games. Newlywed Mike started on a tear, going 7-for-15 in the series. Mabel was in the stands on Opening Day, with a bouquet of flowers sent by Billy Gilbert. One New York reporter wrote she wore "the becomingest [sic] of gowns, and smiled archly at her sturdy centerfielder, who, delirious with happiness, cavorted like a colt in the preliminary practice."[32]

When the Giants opened at home the following week against Brooklyn, Donlin was the hitting star. He drove in three runs with a single and a triple. On May 1 at Boston McGraw and two of his players, Roger Bresnahan and Dan McGann, were ejected (and later suspended) for arguing with umpire John Conway. Joe Vila again complained about the Giants' tendency to "bulldoze umpires . . . on the slightest provocation."[33] A *Sporting Life* reporter felt Donlin deserved the same fate but got off "scot free."[34]

8. A belligerent Mike Donlin in the 1906 Giants uniform John McGraw had designed to flaunt his club's 1905 championship. Library of Congress, Prints and Photographs Division, George Grantham Bain Collection.

Donlin's seventh hit in a May series in Cincinnati, a double, pushed his batting average up to .339.[35] In his trying to steal third base, newspapers reported he had badly wrenched his leg, an injury that would sideline him for a couple of weeks.[36] But X-rays revealed far worse news: he had fractured his ankle.[37] "His foot caught against the bag, and the force of his body driven against it snapped the bone," McGraw later explained.[38] Donlin was disconsolate, especially with the club headed to Pittsburgh and Chicago. His initial predicted absence of two weeks would become one of almost three months.

Syndicated columnist Hugh Fullerton pointed out that most of the top teams had one key clutch hitter: Wagner with the Pirates, Chance with the Cubs, "and without Donlin, New York has a hard time to keep going."[39] Vila, who had predicted the Giants would have trouble repeating as pennant winners, seemed to take pleasure in their misfortunes. With Donlin as their only "first-class hitter," he said, the Giants "have been unable to hit a flock of balloons with a common load of buckshot." He added that Mathewson, as he foresaw, "is all in. He is a sick man and has been put into the box totally against his will."[40]

The Cubs came to the Polo Grounds on June 7 and won three straight games. (The Giants got only eleven hits in the three games.) In one of his worst starts Mathewson lasted only one-third of an inning in the third game of the series. The Cubs scored eleven runs in that first frame, on their way to a 19–0 beating and a four-game lead over New York. Only seven thousand fans turned out for the game, and many of them booed the home team.

After convalescing in Cincinnati, Donlin returned to New York at the end of May and appeared at home games on crutches. He removed his cast in mid-June but was still six weeks away from his return.[41] Reduced to the role of a fan, he watched games from the porch of the outfield clubhouse. One report described his actions: "Leaning over the veranda, Donlin bawls out words of encouragement to his own pals. He stamps his good foot, claps his hands, and yells with all the glee of a kid."[42]

McGraw was concerned about the slow pace and extent of Donlin's recovery. He was still limping noticeably. The Giants were only five games out of first place and playing at a .630 pace. On July 12 they purchased Donlin's old Cincinnati teammate Cy Seymour for $12,000. Seymour had led the National League in many offensive categories in 1905, including batting average, with a .377 mark. He took over in center field, Mike's position.

9. Cy Seymour was a career .303 hitter (with five seasons in the top ten) who was Mike Donlin's teammate with the Orioles, Reds, and Giants. Like Donlin, he was a heavy drinker, and Mike served as a witness at his wedding before the two men had a falling out. Jim Chapman and the Chapman Deadball Collection.

On July 31 Donlin occupied the first-base coaching box and was greeted by umpire Bill Klem. "I'm back for keeps," said the recovering player. "'Perhaps,'" replied the umpire according to one account, "a sinister smile circling over the evil spirit which lurked beneath those muffled lips."[43] Before long, when Donlin disputed a close play at first base, Klem made his return brief. Years later Donlin told Jean Plannette what he had said to Klem to warrant the ejection: "If you're blind, just hang a sign around your neck and pass the hat! A thief is a school boy compared to you! Why don't you get a dark lantern and a jimmy and be a regular burglar?"[44]

On August 6 the Cubs won a hotly contested game at the Polo Grounds, 3–1, in which umpire Jim Johnstone called the Giants' Art Devlin out on a steal of home. McGraw and Devlin were ejected for "arguing." There is virtually no record of the language the foul-mouthed McGraw usually deployed. But Frank Deford quotes what McGraw said on this day. He called Johnstone "a damn dirty c**k-eating bastard, and a low-lived son of a bitch of a yellow cur hound."[45] The game ended in a near riot after Johnstone called out Bill Dahlen on strikes with two Giants on base.

The following day, almost certainly on orders from McGraw, Johnstone was not allowed to enter the ballpark; the umpire forfeited the game to Chicago, and the Giants were now six and a half games off the pace. Harry Pulliam, who had escorted Johnstone to the Polo Grounds for the final game of the series, upheld the forfeit, saying, "So long as I am president of the National League, I will sustain every forfeit when an umpire is refused admittance to any park, and if this doesn't suit the National League, it can have my resignation at a moment's notice."[46]

When Johnstone entered the Polo Grounds the day following the forfeit, "a most remarkable state of affairs" occurred, wrote the *New York Herald*: "Applause rolled from all parts of the stands and bleachers and continued for at least five minutes."[47] In addition, more and more reporters were getting disgusted with McGraw's tactics. A *Sporting News* editorial criticized "the anarchistic club owner and manager. . . . McGraw is making his baseball grave by persisting in rowdyism."[48]

Donlin returned to action on August 10, but he was out of shape and still hobbling. "Hog fat," in the words of one reporter; "when he attempts to run, the sight is pitiable," wrote another.[49] He would have only twelve at bats the remainder of the season, all but one as a pinch hitter, and hit safely only once. Despite Donlin's absence the Giants went on an eight-game win streak in early August, including a five-game sweep of the Pirates.

But when the club moved on to St. Louis, reporter John Sheridan observed, "The entire team is out of condition. Overfeeding and over-drinking are discernable in almost every man on the nine."[50] The Giants swept a doubleheader from the Cardinals on August 16. Donlin did not play but managed to get himself ejected from both games for arguing balls and strikes with Hank O'Day. In the meantime, as baseball historian Tom Ruane has pointed out, the Cubs went on "the greatest stretch in baseball history" as they lost only twice in six weeks. During that time they had win streaks of eleven, fourteen, and twelve games as they rolled on to 116 wins.[51] The Giants finished twenty games back.

Meanwhile, Mabel Hite continued to perform during the year. One Milwaukee reviewer saluted her as "one of the most eccentric and successful comediennes on the stage. Her queer poses, staccato form of speech, tricks of face, manner and makeup are as refreshing and winning as they are wholly ingenuous."[52] Another critic noted late that year that she was "almost too quick" with her humor because it often went over the heads of her audiences.[53] A St. Louis reviewer explained Hite's popularity this way: "She isn't multiplying the sum of human happiness by two, but she is adding a little to it all the time."[54] Hite continued to appear in sketches with Walter Jones until the end of 1906.

Before Donlin's marriage to Hite famous entertainers, including George M. Cohan, had repeatedly suggested to Donlin that he go on the stage in the offseason. One columnist made a prescient comment about Donlin: "He is a born comedian, and it is pretty safe to say that he could make as much of a success on the vaudeville stage as he has on the diamond in the past. Donlin is gifted with rare talent."[55]

18

....

Chicago, Their Kind of Town

Sports pages of early 1907 were dominated by a Mike Donlin story, one that would reappear in future years: would the Giants meet his contract demands? Unlike nearly every other ballplayer, Donlin had the large income of his wife to fall back on. And perhaps early on, with Mabel's encouragement, he began to see the possibility of parlaying his baseball success into a well-paying career on the stage. As journalist Elizabeth Yuko wrote in *The Atlantic* in 2017, "For some [baseball players]—given that they were the most popular figures at the time—the natural choice was to capitalize on that fame and join the vaudeville circuit."[1] Just before the New Year Donlin was quoted in the *Sporting News*: "I can act. I'll break the hearts of all the gals in the country."[2]

Donlin and Mabel spent the offseason in Chicago, the springboard to her theatrical success and where her mother was now living. Hite signed a lucrative long-term contract to star in a musical comedy, *A Knight for a Day*, at Chicago's Whitney Opera House. Beginning that spring, she and Mike likely began exploring alternatives to the peripatetic life of a ballplayer—sooner rather than later.

At the same time Donlin did his best to keep his baseball option alive. In January he told reporters his leg had healed and he would be "patrolling" the outfield again for the Giants in the 1907 season.[3] Joe Vila mocked McGraw's prediction that his club would "win in a walk" in 1907: "Has he lost his grip or is he conning the public? . . . If he stands pat, let me make the prediction that the poor old Giants will be lucky to finish in the first division next season."[4]

Sporting Life reported that while Donlin was in New York in early February, he and Billy Gilbert were helping train the Columbia University baseball team.[5] Donlin was in excellent shape, fifteen pounds lighter than before his injury, "with a face as pink and white as if he had been in daily training."[6] Which he had been. He trained at Billy Elmer's gym on West Forty-Second Street, where he played handball with his friend Kid McCoy, the former world middleweight champion, an alcoholic and inveterate gambler.[7] Donlin also worked out at the University of Chicago's Bartlett Gymnasium when he was in the Midwest.

Donlin came to New York for a Madison Square Garden benefit for his good friend, Terry McGovern, an Irish former boxing champion.[8] McGovern had lost his earnings of more than $200,000, "falling from the wayside from drink and dissipation."[9] Nat Fleisher, who founded *The Ring* magazine in 1922 and was its editor until his death fifty years later, noted, "American ring history from the middle of the nineteenth century through the early part of the twentieth is primarily a history of Irish supremacy."[10] The successful ones, like those of other immigrant groups that followed, became community heroes.

The press gave much of the credit for Donlin's good conditioning to the woman he had married. But some reports went further, suggesting he was a changed man. Typical was this from the *Sporting News*: "Marriage has made a man of Mike Donlin. . . . His appearance substantiates his statement that he is leading a temperate life and inspires his confidence in his resolution to continue in his straight and narrow path for the rest of his life."[11] He was sometimes seen with a walking stick now, which may have been not only a support for his leg but also an elegant accoutrement for the impeccably dressed Donlin.[12] A few years later an Erie newspaper called him the Beau Brummell of baseball, "dressed in the Hite of fashion."[13]

In mid-February Donlin revealed he had asked the Giants for his same 1906 salary of $3,300, plus a bonus of $600 if he stayed out of jail during the season. (His proposal did include the loss of $600 in salary if he was incarcerated.) Sam Crane, who played in the National League in the 1880s, wrote that no player in the country was indebted to McGraw more than Donlin, who got his second life after Cincinnati gave up on him.[14] An unnamed teammate of Donlin's on the Reds pointed out that his stage potential was limited: "Mike may think he can get more money as an actor than he can get playing baseball, but it will never happen. . . . About the only thing that Mike can do is be a good fellow with his friends and make a noise like a .350 batting average."[15]

The Giants held firm in negotiating with Donlin. After all, their 1905 star had not been a full-time player in almost a year, his limited return in

August was not impressive, and there was still concern about the extent of his broken ankle's recovery. Prominent comedian, actor, and Giants fan Richard Carle offered to pay half the $600 the Giants were refusing Donlin if the club would pay the other $300. Carle said, "I told Donlin that I was no philanthropist and would get my money back inside of a month by bets."[16]

Donlin surprisingly rejected Carle's offer before the Giants could do so. But a few days later he received a telegram from his anxious manager: "Dear Mike—Have just arrived here and received your letter. Will agree with you on that $600 proposition, so please report at once to the team in New Orleans. MAC."[17] McGraw explained: "It [is] a player's right to ask for as much as he thinks he is worth. There is no better nor more valuable player in the country. I probably will be reimbursed by the club, but if I am not, I will gladly pay the difference myself. I want a winner this year, and I am not going to allow any such small amount of money to interfere with my plans."[18]

Donlin reported to New Orleans and made an immediate impact. In a game against the Philadelphia Athletics, apparently before he had signed a contract, his pinch-hit triple was the winning blow. The next day the Giants resumed their ruffian ways as Donlin, McGraw, and Roger Bresnahan verbally attacked umpire Chief Zimmer for not calling a balk on A's pitcher Eddie Plank.[19] Zimmer ejected the men, and when McGraw did not leave the field, Zimmer forfeited the game to Philadelphia.

Vila quickly declared that McGraw's club was a disgrace. His disgust with McGraw's approach, which seemed like a vendetta, sometimes crossed into an exaggeration of those tactics: "If the umpires are not killed outright by some of the brave men who wear New York National League uniforms, it will be for the reason that the judges of play will carry firearms. It is a foregone conclusion that McGraw, with a team of four-flushers, intends to browbeat the umpires, terrorize and frighten them so that they will give him the best of it."[20]

Less than a week later Donlin left the club. Hite soon admitted Mike's contract dispute was really an act, a way for him to leave the game without seeming to reject it outright: "We couldn't see just how he was going to do it gracefully. So we decided that the best way was for Mike to ask for a big raise of pay, never thinking he would get it. Then to our great surprise, they promised to give it to him."[21] Donlin provided a different explanation, perhaps to minimize fan anger. His foot was giving him some trouble, and his doctor said it would not stand up to daily play.[22]

Mabel said fans should blame her, not her husband, for his leaving baseball: "Was it hard for Mike to do it? I guess it was. He tries to tell me sometimes that it wasn't, and I don't say anything, but don't I know that way down in his heart he longs to get out in the field again with the Giants." They were an inseparable couple, she said, and "if he went back with the team, I'd have him home just about twelve days during the season." She explained that if she went back to New York, her opportunities would be limited to vaudeville, while in Chicago she had offers for musical comedy.[23] Perhaps the elite New York theater scene had Mabel typecast as a vaudevillian.

Mabel's current contract paid her $1,400 a month, and the theater agreed to hire Mike as assistant manager at $50 a week.[24] Hite said the couple had acquired five lots on Long Island, had no debt, and had money in the bank. She pointed out that ballplayers had a hard time saving money, especially on the road: "You can't blame him if he gets lonesome at night, and being with a congenial bunch, spends it like they do."[25] And her husband's income was about to be supplemented enough to match the salary he would have earned playing baseball . . . by playing baseball.

If Chicago was America's number-two city in the world of theater, it could lay claim to being number one in baseball as 1907 began. The Chicago White Sox had upset the crosstown Chicago Cubs in the 1906 World Series, and there seemed to be an insatiable yearning for baseball in the area. Elizabeth Yuko explained: "This is what free agency looked like in the ragtime era: active major leaguers carving out niche opportunities in large cities such as Chicago, where the population's thirst for baseball far outstripped the ability of its two major league clubs to service it."[26]

At the end of 1906 the Chicago Intercity Association had almost four hundred clubs.[27] During the baseball season there were hundreds of games each weekend from which fans could choose to watch. Hugh Fullerton wrote, "If you really want to see baseball played, don't attend American or National League games. Go to the lots."[28]

As early as March 2 *Sporting Life* reported that Chicago semipro teams were offering Donlin "big wads of cash." It may have escaped notice that he had delayed his departure to New Orleans to join the Giants later that month in order to play a semipro game for Jimmy Callahan's Logan Squares against the University of Chicago.[29] Now that Donlin was back in Chicago, Callahan signed him to a lucrative $1,500 contract for weekend games. In fifty surviving box scores of the Logan Squares' 1907 season, Donlin played first base and batted .419.[30]

Jimmy "Nixey" Callahan was the rare two-way player, both a pitcher and a position player. In 1901, after four years with Chicago's National League team, he was one of the sensations of the new American League: he posted a 15-8 record and hit .331 for the White Sox. He briefly managed the club in 1903 and early 1904. By 1906 he had decided to become an owner: "I felt that I had given him [White Sox owner Charles Comiskey] five good years and that it was about time I began to work for James Callahan."[31]

Callahan bought property in the Logan Square section of north Chicago, built a ballpark there, and formed a team he called the Logan Squares. Logan Squares historian Brian McKenna wrote, "Callahan sought the best possible talent to fill his roster. . . . Callahan didn't actually raid major-league clubs, but he wasn't above fielding men who were suspended or otherwise available [playing under assumed names]. . . . For this, Callahan became known as the 'Anarchist of Baseball,' at least by major-league officials."[32]

The team not only won the city championship in 1906, but it also capped the season with a game against the Cubs and another against the White Sox in October, both of which it won. "My only regret," Callahan said after those triumphs, "is that Ban Johnson, August Herrmann, and Harry Pulliam were not sitting in the front row to learn how it happened."[33] Those wins gave Callahan's club the reputation as the best semipro team in the country.

While Donlin was playing weekends at first base for Callahan's team, the Giants started the season with a record of 24-3, including a seventeen-game win streak. Joe Vila admitted he had been wrong; he had predicted Christy Mathewson (6-0 at that point) would not regain his old form. "But in this I made a serious error and am only too willing to admit it."[34] However, the Cubs were only one game back at 23-4. After they hammered Mathewson in relief on May 23, the Giants' slide began. When the Cubs swept the Giants in Chicago in early June, they extended their lead to five and a half games. Vila wasted no time in resuming his criticism. He said that without great pitching, the Giants were now doomed. "McGraw realizes his goose is cooked."[35]

Donlin was smart enough not to burn any bridges. "Put this down and underline it," he told a reporter. "If I ever play in the big league again, it will be with the Giants. . . . McGraw is my friend always."[36] The Giants were still trying to get him back before the pennant slipped beyond their reach. "It is said that McGraw made his old outfielder an offer that would dazzle the eyes of a Rockefeller."[37] But Donlin was not moved.

After starting June only one game out of first place, the Giants finished the month eight games behind the Cubs. It was also a month in which they continued to have run-ins with umpires. Vila wrote, "It was proved beyond peradventure that he [McGraw] was not a good sportsman, that he was a cowardly, bulldozing bluffer; that he had a yellow streak a yard wide; that he did not know the first rudiments of clean baseball, and that as a user of vile language and personal abuse when safeguarded from a good beating at the hands of a real man, was in a class by himself."[38]

On Independence Day the Giants were eleven and a half games behind the Cubs, who were playing at a blistering .765 pace. McGraw was spending more and more time at the racetrack, and stories appeared that catcher Roger Bresnahan would manage the Giants in 1908.[39] McGraw still had his sense of humor, able to poke fun at himself. He said that summer: "They say the world is getting wiser, but you still find people who bet on the horse races."[40]

Mabel's show, *A Knight for a Day*, opened on March 31 to positive reviews and a packed house. The show would go on to an extended run at the Whitney Opera House for nine months. The Whitney promoted its venue as the only "ice-cooled theater in Chicago"; it claimed to use three tons of ice each day to keep its one-dollar-paying customers comfortable.[41]

The *Inter Ocean* critic wrote, "There are few eccentric comediennes in the country one-half as clever as Mabel Hite. She is decidedly original. . . . Her sense of humor is good, and her sense of the ridiculous is better."[42] Hite elaborated on her approach to comedy later that spring: "In being funny, one has to be serious too. The hardest thing in being funny is to be earnest. It is the earnestness which brings the laughs and makes the fun. . . . The comedian is serious in being funny."[43]

Mabel said she was content to remain in Chicago and did not care for the glory of Broadway. She confessed that stardom was frightening: "Of course, it looks good to see your name in big letters on the billboards, but when you stop to think that the people that come to the theater expect about nine times as much of you as they do when you've just got a leading part, it sort of scares you. No starring for mine [*sic*] yet awhile. I'd rather have my own little part in some good company, and the shorter the better for me."[44] This revealing statement suggests she felt pressure as a headliner; that stress may have affected her health.

Hite's part in *A Knight for a Day* was anything but little. She was one of the stars, as a lovelorn waitress on her honeymoon. The song "Because I'm Married Now" became a hit, and her fans knew that the title applied to the actress herself, as well as to the waitress. It included a verse that became popular, reflecting a young woman's betrothal impinging on her freedom: "I'd like to go with you to lunchin', / but I've got a hunchin' / that I'd get a punchin' / and I just hate to wear a veil. For I'm married now."

Mabel Tells Mike: Become a Changed Man—or Else

Mike Donlin's weekend heroics with the Logan Squares were a staple of the Chicago spring and summer of 1907. His three hits helped beat a South Side team in late June. A week later his three doubles led the club to victory over the White Rocks. On July 28 a huge crowd turned out to see Jimmy Callahan's club edge [former Washington Senators manager] Jake Stahl's South Chicagos. The crowd was also drawn to watch the umpire, former heavyweight boxing champion John L. Sullivan.[1] Sullivan explained how he dealt with Donlin when he "began to make a yelp about one of my decisions. . . . But I showed him the fist that used to deliver the goods, and Mike had a swift relapse in being just as good as anybody could expect." Sullivan suggested that National League owners and umpires follow his approach.[2]

While Major League baseball was segregated, the Chicago baseball scene was very different. There were approximately 40,000 Blacks in the city in the early twentieth century. That number would rise to 110,000 by 1920, as part of the great migration north.[3] Robert C. Cottrell wrote, "Multitudes were attracted to Chicago, a leading industrial center that was believed to be an open door to a brighter future."[4]

American League president Ban Johnson spoke out against Major League teams barnstorming in Cuba, saying, "It doesn't help the game to have our star teams beaten in Cuba by negroes and half-breeds."[5] But in Chicago Black teams were part of the baseball scene. Even former Chicago nineteenth-century star Cap Anson, who as a player often refused to play games against teams with any Black players, had his club, Anson's Colts, compete against Black teams. Perhaps financial considerations overrode prejudices: Black fans were a big part of the league's paying public.[6] In 1908, at age fifty-six, Anson played first base for his Colts, including late

August and early September games against the Leland Giants, a power-ful Black team.[7]

Urban sports historian Steven Riess has noted the Leland Giants were a great draw for both races, with crowds of fifteen thousand at their games not unusual.[8] Sunday baseball was legal in large midwestern cities such as Chicago but not in Eastern cities such as New York, Boston, and Phila-delphia. With most people working six days a week, semipro ball in these midwestern locales attracted better athletes and thus a higher quality of play.

With games primarily on weekends players could supplement their regular jobs. As historian Phil Dixon wrote, "Chicago's lure of increased wages for performing in a reduced number of games, an added incentive of limited travel and the assurance of mass newspaper exposure, was alluring from almost every angle. Earning so much for doing so little never seemed easier."[9] Semipro and amateur baseball was so popular in Chicago that a *Spalding Guide* devoted only to Chicago was published from 1906 to 1910.[10]

One of the leading Chicago clubs was Andrew "Rube" Foster's Leland Giants. Foster, who joined the Giants in 1907, was a talented pitcher as well as the club's manager.[11] A shrewd businessman, he increased the per-centage of revenue for the club when he took over bookings from owner Frank Leland. Frederic North Shorey wrote Foster had "all the speed of a [Amos] Rusie, the tricks of a [Hoss] Radbourn, and the heady coolness and deliberation of a Cy Young." Shorey, a Black man, went on to describe Foster as "almost the typical stage darky—husky, black as coal, with a halting stride, a head sunk between his shoulders, and without any ostensible neck."

Foster bemoaned his arbitrary exclusion from the Major Leagues. He told Shorey, "Five or six years ago, I think, I'd have been a first-class pitcher, but I found then I'd got as far as I could go and that there was no hope of getting into the big league, so I kind of let myself go."[12]

Foster understood that the best way to gain attention was by beating white teams. After he did so with regularity that spring, the white club owners decided to form a team of "All Professionals," whose players would be selected by Donlin and Callahan. The team, often referred to as "Mike Donlin's All-Stars," arranged for a three-game series against the Leland Giants in August.

The series was one of the highlights of Chicago baseball that summer. The first and third games were played at the White Sox's South Side Park, with the second at Logan Squares Park. David Wyatt, a reporter for the *Indianapolis Freeman*, a Black newspaper, described the scene at the games, in which there was "no color line drawn anywhere. . . . Whites and blacks, men and women, had congregated in the box seats and bleachers, readily discussing the relative merits of the two teams."[13]

When the Logan Squares beat Foster and his Giants in July, Mike Donlin was tossed for "kicking."[14] This time, as an All-Star, Donlin struck quickly with his bat and doubled in two runs off Foster in the first inning. But the Giants rallied for a 3-2 win, and the *Inter Ocean* reporter called the game a "revelation," praising Foster's "cool, deliberate pitching."[15] The All-Stars evened the series the next day, led by another Donlin double and two runs scored.

In the rubber match ten thousand fans, including many of Donlin's friends, swarmed to the park. As in the first two games, the races mingled as fans placed small bets throughout the ballpark. And Foster was even better than in the first game as he shut out the All-Stars, 1–0.

In a key at bat Foster preyed on a Donlin weakness: his impatience in the box. "Here, you pitch that ball, and pitch it quick," shouted Donlin, but Foster irritated him with dilatory tactics. "Donlin was nervously gripping his bat and glaring at Rube, Foster just stared into orbit, then stood on one foot and then on the other examining the sphere, glancing at the bases and driving the former New York Giant frantic," wrote Shorey. Foster then retired Donlin on a routine fly ball.[16] The game ended with an All-Star tagged out at home plate. White Sox owner Charles Comiskey said after the games that he would have signed at least three of the boys to contracts "if it were possible."[17]

Donlin showed respect for Foster when he called him the equal of Christy Mathewson and Mordecai Brown of the Cubs. "He is always outguessing the batter," said Donlin.[18] The *Sporting Life* reporter who covered the games wrote, "The white men admit this black whirlwind is as good as any white crackerjack and declare that he would be a star in any company."[19]

When the Black pitcher died more than two decades later, Donlin told a reporter, "Had Foster been white, he would have been the sensation of sensations. How that big-footed boy could toss the apple. He had everything—speed, curves, and control."[20] Donlin respected great athletes and competed against Blacks in 1897, 1907, and again in 1913–19.

When the two teams met again later in August, the result was the same: the Giants took two of three games, with Foster earning the wins. Respected

Chicago Tribune sportswriter Charles Dryden captured the scene at the American League ballpark for the first game: "While the combat raged, the yard presented shades of vivid color, done in black and white. Brothers of those colors rooted together in the bleachers, and the same scheme prevailed in the private boxes. There was no color line drawn anywhere."[21]

But Mike Donlin was not playing for his All-Stars in this later series; he was not even at the games. After a night of heavy drinking on August 23, an inebriated Donlin tried to see his wife backstage at the Whitney. Mabel's costar, John Slavin, intercepted him and put him in a taxi. By the time the cab reached his home, he had fallen asleep. When the driver woke him, Donlin started fighting and was soon hauled to the police station for both assault and refusing to pay the fare.[22] At around 4 a.m., Callahan, his manager and friend, bailed him out of jail.

Mabel was distraught. She said she had recently had to lock herself in her room when her husband tried to punch her. The next day she found him "dead drunk in a Russian bath house."[23] The day after the arrest she was in tears when she opened up to a reporter. She said she had sent Donlin to the bath "to boil out the remnants of the various liquids" he had consumed in a four-day drinking spree. While wiping away both tears and rouge from her cheeks, she continued:

> I can't stand it any longer. Now you don't think it's such a dreadful thing for a woman's husband to get drunk and in the newspapers, do you? But it means so much when you love a man, and he'd promised not to do it. And every time it happens, it's so much worse, and it worries me so I can't sleep, and I have to go out before the audience and act like a fool and make them laugh, and sing my songs and dance, and my heart is breaking. For he's good to me, except when he forgets himself.[24]

A now sober Donlin was contrite:

> I made a slip, and nobody's to blame but myself. There's the best little woman in the world down on the stage at this minute, and I know what it means for her to go through her lines. The only mistake she ever made was when she married me. But I'm going down to New York to sign with the Giants again, and the next time I see her, if she'll ever see me again, she'll have no cause to be ashamed of me.[25]

10. Before his marriage Mike Donlin was described as a "reckless, violent, husky-voiced swaggering brawler" (James Hopper, *Collier's*, September 19, 1908). Tom Hufford Collection.

Mabel told Mike to go to New York, join the Giants, and return a changed man—or else. Donlin did go to New York, where he met with John McGraw in early September. His former manager agreed to take him back for the 1908 season. Meanwhile, Mabel suddenly left her show in Chicago for a mystery trip, destination unknown.

11. Mabel Hite brought stability into Mike Donlin's life. While his nighttime carousing was notorious, he loved his wife dearly, and there were no indications he was a womanizer. When confronted with the possibility of losing Mabel, he gave up drinking. Billy Rose Theatre Division, New York Public Library for the Performing Arts.

Donlin told friends he was going to Europe but instead secretly checked himself into a facility in Dwight, Illinois, under an assumed name. Dwight was certainly not Europe. A town of about two thousand people, just under eighty miles southwest of Chicago, Dwight had gained fame late in the nineteenth century when Leslie Keeley (1836–1900) opened a clinic there. He had developed a "gold cure," or Keeley Cure, to treat alcoholics, for which he claimed a 95 percent cure rate. Keeley, a Civil War Union surgeon, opened Keeley Institute franchises across North America and Europe. While he was ahead of his time in viewing alcoholism as a disease and not a moral shortcoming, his controversial treatment was shrouded in mystery and condemned by mainstream medical groups.

As William L. White wrote in his history of America's response to alcoholism, "[Keeley] could cure it with a secret, specific formula, injected four times daily, about which all he would hint publicly was that it contained gold as one of its ingredients. . . . But everything else about Dr. Keeley's magic elixir was as secret as the ingredients in Coke."[26]

The atmosphere at Keeley's main sanatorium in Dwight was relaxed and informal, without the restraints that so many inebriate asylums of the time had.[27] When a patient arrived, he was gradually rationed off whiskey the first few days. The treatment took a month and consisted of four daily injections of a formula that was called bichloride of gold. Keeley's approach "carried an aura of scientific truth and all the emotional support and intensity of a revival meeting," White wrote.[28]

The proprietary tonic did not contain any gold, which had too many side effects. Analysis showed it contained alcohol, atropine, strychnine, apomorphine, and boric acid.[29] The extreme negative reactions to the treatment may have led patients to change their bad habits.

For obvious reasons of confidentiality, the Keeley Institute did not reveal the names of its patients, but it is likely several ballplayers of this era did go to Dwight for treatment. In early 1911 McGraw sent his alcoholic pitcher, Bugs Raymond, to the Institute, but Raymond "was expelled from the program for excessive horseplay."[30]

Mabel left her show in Chicago to spend some time with her husband in Dwight.[31] Neither of them ever talked publicly about the visit. Only a few newspapers reported Donlin had gone there and under an assumed name.[32] At least one prominent sportswriter elaborated. "Mike has in the past always had one great failing, but this winter he has taken the gold cure and is said to be entirely free from the appetite of drink," Ralph Davis of the *Pittsburgh Press* wrote that December. "He has reformed before, only to return to the forbidden paths of indulgence, and he may fall again."[33]

Mabel returned to *A Knight for a Day*, which was scheduled to open in New York City in December. But the producers decided that May Vokes, her understudy at the Whitney Opera House and better known in New York City, would take over her role. The news so upset Mabel that she quit the Chicago show in November. One Chicago critic wrote, "The longing for this beloved heaven [Broadway] for actresses took possession of her. Like them all, she longed for a New York engagement."[34]

Joe Vila was still criticizing McGraw's unruly behavior, though he admitted McGraw was "a gentle, quiet, well-behaved person off the field."[35] If McGraw would be the Giants' manager in 1908, he wrote, "there will be nothing but woe in joke baseball at the Polo Grounds," while McGraw would continue to spend a lot of time at the race track.[36] But McGraw was able to look past Vila's criticism and went to the Aqueduct race track that fall with the newspaperman. In doing so, he showed not only that he did not hold grudges but that he also had a remarkable kindness and generosity that rarely surfaced in the press.

At the track, Vila recounted, they saw an old trainer named Jim, "broken in health, with no overcoat, and looking ill enough to be in the hospital." When the man said he could not afford to winter in New Orleans, McGraw "peeled five $100 bills off a fat bankroll" and told Jim to send word if he needed more money. With tears running down his face, the trainer thanked McGraw for enabling him to get away from the cold winter and probably saving his life. McGraw told Vila that over the years Jim had given him many tips on which he had won money. He also told Vila not to put this story in the paper. "If you print a story about this, you and I will have another row, and surely we want to keep the peace for a little while, anyway, after the rumble which has kept us apart until we met on the way down here today."[37]

Vila recalled how McGraw "held court" in his hotel room each morning when the Giants were on the road. His "old friends" were "ex-boxers, broken-down jockeys, ancient ball players, old fans, unemployed bartenders, race track touts, and Heaven knows how many other strange characters who crowded in to shake his hand and receive words of encouragement and crisp bank notes." Vila revealed the story only after McGraw's death early in 1934. "McGraw gave away a fortune in that manner," he wrote.[38] A few weeks later, Vila himself was dead.

Earlier that year Mike Donlin revealed his own act of compassion and generosity. A man had greeted him on the streets of Chicago, saying, "You must be Mike Donlin, the great outfielder." When Donlin heard his hard-luck story, he bought the man a turkey dinner and invited the man to share his hotel room that night. "Old fellow, if you haven't a place to sleep, come up to my room and sleep with me. There is plenty of room, and I don't want to see a man walking the streets." When Donlin woke up the next morning, the old man was gone, as was Donlin's $500 diamond stud, and $500 in cash. The man was soon arrested. He had already pawned the stud for $100.[39]

Donlin returned to the Chicago baseball scene in October. He got three hits to help the Logan Squares beat the White Sox, 4–1, on October 13. His All-Stars then dropped a game to the Cubs, 2–0. He planned to stay in shape during the winter playing indoor baseball with the Lawndales, a Chicago semipro team.[40]

In late November Donlin told reporters McGraw had visited him in Champaign, south of Chicago, and "made me an offer I could not refuse." Donlin would be the field captain of the Giants in 1908, and his salary would be well over $5,000. He praised his manager, saying, "McGraw is the best man in the business, and he is a man from his feet up, despite the impression given out in the newspapers that he is a ruffian and a scoundrel. He is a fighter, and a fighter is the one who succeeds in baseball these days."[41] Various reports said the Giants hoped the captaincy would help Donlin take his work more seriously. His contract had a clause against drinking, sportswriter Ed Grillo said. He cautioned that "Mike is long on making promises and resolutions during the off season, only to break them when the season opens."[42]

As the Hot Stove League heated up in the holiday season of 1907, much of the focus was on whether the Giants could catch the two-time world champion Cubs in 1908. McGraw recognized the need for new blood. He realized he had misjudged his team's strength and lack of depth the past season. That summer he acquired two twenty-year-old players who would become key members of the Giants for years: second baseman Larry Doyle and outfielder Josh Devore. Late that year he made an eight-player trade with the Boston Doves.[43] It involved two former stars on the high side of thirty-five: first baseman Fred Tenney would come to the Giants, and shortstop Bill Dahlen would go to Boston.

And the Giants got back their slugging star from their last championship team, Mike Donlin. Two questions loomed about their new captain. First, could he regain his hitting and fielding form of 1905 as he approached the age of thirty? Second, could he keep his temper and drinking under control? The 1907 Giants had finished in fourth place, twenty-five and a half games behind the Cubs. Would these changes be enough for them to make up that deficit?

20

....

The Prodigal Returns

Even the New York press corps recognized the Chicago Cubs would be hard to beat in 1908. "Like a well-kept piece of machinery, [the Cubs] do not need repairing to any marked degree," reported the *New York Sun*.[1] Not so with the Giants. A week before Christmas 1907 the *New York American* wrote, "With nearly all of the Giant pitchers, greatness is a memory." Joe McGinnity was thirty-seven and coming off his least effective year as a Giant. As for Christy Mathewson, "no stretch of the imagination would place him as the best twirler in the league."[2] Yet before this season was over, the imagination would be stretched in numerous ways.

Joe Vila continued to be the Giants' most outspoken New York skeptic: "Take it from me, gents, that the Giants, in spite of their good hitters, will slide down pretty close to the second division this year. . . . After a few sound beatings at the hands of the Cubs, you'll see the interest in McGraw's team collapse like a punctured balloon."[3]

Those who saw Mike Donlin play with the Logan Squares in 1907 reported he hit well and moved around with ease. During the offseason he played handball almost every day.[4] "Donlin has made all sorts of good resolutions since then and says that he will 'play the game of his life.'"[5] Mike was quoted in February: "Strangely enough, many a man climbs up on the water wagon to get in out of the wet."[6] The question was whether he would stay on that wagon during the season.

In 1907 Donlin had played for a team Organized Baseball did not recognize, and there was a question whether the National Commission would allow him to return. American League president Ban Johnson said he was ineligible, but John McGraw said the matter was simply one between the player and his club. He explained that Donlin did not want to risk a full recovery by playing every day and added that National Commission president Garry Herrmann said Donlin was in good standing.[7] Even

Giants owner John Brush got involved, saying, "The calamity-howlers are making all the noise."[8] Donlin broke no contract, and Brush said he had no complaints against him.

However, the National Commission wanted to take a stand against players who were thinking of jumping to an outlaw team. Donlin paid a $100 fine and was reinstated. He was elated to be back. "Give me baseball all the time," he told reporters. "The game is simply born in me. Out in Chicago last summer, I played not for the money there was in it, but because I simply could not keep my hands off."[9]

Donlin traveled to spring training in Marlin Springs, Texas, with boxer Terry McGovern, who worked out with the Giants. About to turn twenty-eight, McGovern still harbored dreams of returning to stardom. But he continued to experience mental problems and was institutionalized for much of his remaining life.

The Pittsburgh Pirates, who finished second in 1907, suffered a devastating blow when their star shortstop, Honus Wagner, announced he would retire before the start of the season because of the wear and tear on his body.[10] But the thirty-four-year-old Wagner reconsidered when Pirates owner Barney Dreyfuss doubled his salary to $10,000.

Going into spring training, McGraw felt good about his club's chances. In addition to the trade that brought him veteran first baseman Fred Tenney, he had a group of promising youngsters: infielders Fred Merkle, Larry Doyle, and Buck Herzog and outfielder Fred Snodgrass. He declared the Giants had just one team to beat, the Cubs.[11] Like McGraw, Frank Chance, the Cubs' player-manager, also discounted the Pirates. Chance had taken over as manager in 1905 and ran his club as firmly as McGraw ran his. "Play it my way or meet me after the game," he was known to say.[12] Unlike McGraw, Chance was also a key contributor on the field as one of the game's best first basemen, both at the plate and in the field.

The Pirates' manager, Fred Clarke, was also one of his team's best players, covering left field. He had managed the club since 1900, the year star players from the eliminated Louisville franchise had come over to Pittsburgh.[13] In his history of the Pirates, Fred Lieb wrote that Clarke was "a fearless, intrepid, inspired player. He played ball much as did Ty Cobb some years later. A league race was a miniature war, and each ball game a battle."[14]

Veteran Giants pitcher George "Hooks" Wiltse had more concern about Pittsburgh than did his manager. He felt the Pirates were the team to beat: "Pittsburgh may be a one-man team, but that one man is a 'dilly.'"[15] A sportswriter for the *New York American* gave a vivid description of that "dilly" after the 1907 season:

No one ever saw anything graceful or picturesque about [Honus] Wagner on the diamond. His movements have been likened to the gambols of a caracoling elephant. He is ungainly and so bowlegged that when he runs, his limbs seem to be moving in a circle after the fashion of a propeller. But he can run like the wind. . . . His position of the bat is less awkward, and the muscular swing of his great arms and shoulders is strong enough to drive the ball further than most batters who hit from their toe spikes up. There is no question that Wagner is the greatest all-round ballplayer of this or any other season.[16]

The man who was expected to challenge Wagner for the batting title once again, Mike Donlin, was far smoother in his movement on the diamond. Sportswriters were not consistent in describing his hitting, and in an era long before the advent of video, we have no way of verifying which account is more accurate. One observed, "Donlin wields a rather heavy and long bat and depends on his natural batting eye to meet the ball squarely. He is of the old type of hitter, who believed in hitting them out all the time."[17] Another described him as a "vicious" swinger.[18] Yet another reporter gave a different perspective:

Donlin is one of the most natural hitters who ever handled a bat. . . . Donlin has a graceful, careless position at bat. He is never set. He places himself so as to either place the ball or pull it as the opportunity arises. . . . Donlin does not swing hard at the ball, only when he pulls to right field and when he thinks a long drive is the proper caper. Usually he just meets the ball, timing it perfectly, and with a little snappy wrist movement sends the sphere out like a shot.[19]

The Giants had a 5-1 record when they had their home opener on April 22 against Brooklyn, with Mathewson going for his third win. The large Polo Grounds crowd of thirty thousand spilled onto the outfield, behind ropes meant to keep them from the field of play. Marty McHale, who later pitched for the Red Sox and Yankees, was at that game and recalled a decade later, "Donlin's first appearance was the signal for one of the greatest ovations I ever witnessed. The prodigal son had returned to the fold, and the crowd was there to pay tribute to one of the best-loved ball players that ever ruined a pitcher's reputation."[20]

Donlin provided far more drama than by merely returning. With two outs (and two strikes) in the ninth inning and the Giants down 2–1, he hit a game-winning home run into the right-field bleachers, with Fred Tenney on base. "To say that the crowd went wild is putting it mildly. It went clean crazy," declared the *New-York Tribune* reporter. "Hats and cushions were tossed in the air; old men slapped their companions on the back and laughed and cheered like undergraduates. It was one of the greatest sights ever seen at an athletic contest in this country, and those who were present will never forget it."[21]

As he reached second base, the surging crowd picked Donlin up and carried him the rest of the way.[22] He had to sprint to the clubhouse to avoid the adoring fans from tearing the uniform off his body. Umpire Bob Emslie was calling balls and strikes that day and told a reporter what he saw (and did not see) after Donlin's last hit, his third of the day: "I watched Donlin round first base and then was swept off my feet by the crowd. . . . For the life of me, although I did my best, I couldn't see Donlin after he got halfway to second base, and I couldn't swear now that he completed the circuit of the bases."[23]

As he rounded the bases, Donlin stopped briefly at second base and waved to his wife. "I must give the Missus the shake every now and then," he said.[24] Mabel was quickly becoming hooked on the game. She had not followed baseball closely before she met Mike, and she confessed she had panicked when, early in their relationship, she read that he had "suicided" at the plate. "It flashed through my mind that he had failed to hit the ball and then, in a fit of disgust, had killed himself."[25] This season she would attend as many games as her schedule allowed and would be a recognized and vocal fan in the stands. She soon discovered that a Giants baseball game in which her husband was playing was "the most exciting experience that I ever encountered. It is awfully strenuous; I will have to confess that I am forced to take medicine for my nerves."[26]

A few days later Mabel opened as the star of a new show in New York, *The Merry-Go-Round*. She had been doing vaudeville earlier in the year, including a ventriloquist act with her mechanically operated dummy.[27] *Variety* pointed out that her subtle humor often went right over the heads of audiences outside of New York and Chicago. "[Yonkers audiences] passed up Mabel Hite's highly sophisticated witticisms in stony silence. . . . The fun of the 'bit' is the awfulness of the wit. Yonkers took it on its face value, however. The burlesque got past them completely."[28]

Chicago critic Amy Leslie lamented the fact that Mabel was not securing roles in legitimate theater: "She is one of the most talented young women America has ever produced, and it is a great pity some wise promoter cannot grab her away from the piles of money nonsense brings her and map out a splendid, lasting, and brilliant career for her, but they cannot."[29] Now, with *The Merry-Go-Round*, Mabel had moved beyond vaudeville but not by much.

A Philadelphia reviewer called the show "sheer crazy hilarity . . . [with Mabel Hite] now singing songs in falsetto, now giving imitations, now dancing, and always doing crazy little stunts on the side."[30] One commentator called the show "wholesome, though nonsensical" and felt that Hite was becoming "a caricature of herself."[31] A syndicated article noted that the ensemble had many show girls, "lightly clad, and an earnest effort is made by the management to display their massive curves to the best advantage."[32]

The show ran until mid-July, ninety-seven performances in all. When Mike was acknowledged in the audience one late April evening, the cheers for him rivaled those for the actors. Shouts of "Good for you, Mickey" and "Home Run Mike" resounded through the theater.[33]

On May 2 Donlin and McGraw were ejected from a game against the Phillies for arguing. Donlin would earn six ejections this season, and McGraw would garner eight. On May 29 Donlin scored the game's only run in Mathewson's shutout of Brooklyn, but he was not around at the end of the game after being ejected for arguing a close play at first base. The *New York Times* account was amusing and likely not as lighthearted as the actual incident. When Donlin complained to umpire Frank Rudderham, "Your eyesight appears defective," the arbiter replied, "Possibly you are right. I cannot see you for the rest of the game."[34]

McGraw prided himself in his ability to handle "rambunctious young rowdies other managers found too difficult to handle."[35] Frank Deford noted that McGraw "surely saw some of the worst of himself in these difficult types of players."[36] But umpire Bill Klem said McGraw and Donlin "fed off" each other: "Mike Donlin was a devil for stirring him, egging him on."[37]

Donlin was batting near .300 when the Giants went to Pittsburgh on May 11. In the first game he generated surprising cheers from the Pirates' crowd each time he came to bat, and he responded with a single, double, and triple.[38] Honus Wagner, who was still working his way into shape, was batting only .227 at the time. But he was the game's star, with fielding gems and an eighth-inning triple that broke a tie. Superlatives came even from the New York press: "The wonderful Teuton was everywhere, choking off sure hits and encouraging his comrades. . . . His large paws, the fingers of which seemed like tentacles of a devil fish, raked in everything that came within a mile of them."[39]

Joe Vila recognized the value of—and change in—the Giants outfielder. He was "trained to the minute and is behaving himself with marked decorum. He is on his toes all the time, is fielding and running the bases in grand style, and is practically the whole team. . . . I believe in giving credit to this great ball player, for he deserves all the praise in the world."[40] McGraw said, "Have you seen how much Mike Donlin improves our lineup? Mike is one of the greatest natural batsmen of the business."[41] By the end of June Donlin was hitting .351, and Wagner had raised his average to .314.

As Vila noted, Donlin's glovework did shine this season. When the Giants were in Cincinnati in early July, that city's Jack Ryder described one exceptional play. Reds slugger Hans Lobert hit a drive that appeared "was going to hit the fence untouched." Donlin "went back at great speed, did a few acrobatic stunts with his arms and legs, leaped seven feet [*sic*] into the sunshine and came down with the ball in his fin."[42]

Many articles during the 1908 season discussed the changes Donlin seemed to have undergone. His weight was down from 200 to 165 pounds.[43] One column, titled "How Mike Donlin Was Transformed," gave his wife much of the credit. Mike realized that "it was up to him to choose between wine and woman, and Mabel won out in a walk. The player is not henpecked. He would not stand for that. He has sense enough to appreciate affection and make himself worthy of it."[44]

In August Donlin wrote a letter to an old California baseball friend, Bill Devereaux: "I certainly have a darling wife. She is a dandy, and I wouldn't be single again for anything. Am taking great care of myself; have been on the water wagon for a year and intend to stay on it for good."[45] A Cincinnati sportswriter concluded, "The wild Turk is most effectually tamed."[46]

All three contending teams had tension in their clubhouses, and the resulting stress sometimes spilled over into public view. Two members of the Cubs' famous double play combination, Joe Tinker and Johnny Evers, had a long-running feud and had not spoken to each other for a few years. In early June Cubs outfielder Jimmy Sheckard got into a fight with rookie infielder Heinie Zimmerman. The youngster threw a bottle of ammonia at his veteran teammate that exploded when it hit him in the face. Sheckard was temporarily blinded, went to the hospital, and did not return to action until the end of the month. Manager Chance was so upset over the incident that he scuffled with his young player.[47]

Giants rookie Buck Herzog quit his team in mid-June after McGraw insisted he play in an exhibition game, despite Herzog's nursing a sore wrist. He did not rejoin the club until July 28. (He would raise his batting average from .227 to .300 and prove a crucial substitute when Larry Doyle was injured in September.) In Pittsburgh there were rumors that some of the players were drinking heavily. Where the stories emanated from was not clear, but Clarke was moved to say after the season, "Ball players are not angels. They are not expected to be. . . . One or two members of the Pittsburgh team have been accused of being drunkards and bums. The accusations have been basely false."[48]

When the Pirates won three of four games in the Polo Grounds in mid-June, Wagner reminded fans of his value in the field at the all-important shortstop position. "Honus was always in the way—that is, in the way of the Giants winning. The big Dutchman seems to take particular delight in robbing Captain Mike of base hits," acknowledged one New York reporter.[49] In the Pirates' 1–0 win on June 10 Wagner robbed Donlin of three hits. Yet the two men had a healthy mutual respect and sense of humor about their competition. During that game, after Wagner struck out, Donlin teasingly told him, "You may be handsome, but you ain't no Swat Milligan [sic] at the bat. . . . You may be a fair fielder, but you can't hit." The two men then grinned at each other.[50]

In six weeks, from May 29 through July 13, Joe McGinnity won seven games, and Christy Mathewson won eleven; each tossed three shutouts. But there were warning signs McGraw was overworking his ace: Mathewson had already pitched more than 180 innings. On July 13 the Giants, Cubs, and Pirates were bunched within one game of each other. They would remain so for the rest of the season.

The Most Popular Ballplayer in New York

On July 10, 1908, the Giants came to Pittsburgh trailing the Pirates by a half game and the Cubs by one and a half. With the score tied in the bottom of the ninth, the stage was set for heroics by the home team's little third baseman, 5-foot-6-inch Tommy Leach. His inside-the-park home run, past Mike Donlin in right field, won the game, 7–6. More than a half century later Leach told baseball historian Lawrence Ritter, "For sheer excitement, I don't think anything can beat [a triple or inside-the-park home run] when you see that guy go tearing around the bases and come sliding into third or into the plate."[1]

Five days later Mordecai Brown, the Cubs' ace, was knocked out in the fourth inning of a 11–0 home loss to New York. Two days after that he came back to beat New York and his great rival Christy Mathewson, 1–0, pushing his record to 15-2. Brown would have a combined 12-4 record against the Giants and the Pirates in 1908.[2] Once again the league's three contending teams were bunched within a game of each other.

During the past four seasons Brown had beaten Mathewson nine straight times. "It was just one of those things. It seemed I always was at my best against him," Brown said years later.[3] Brown had Johnny Kling on the receiving end. "I'm not ashamed to admit that I was just a so-so pitcher before I teamed up with Kling," Brown said. "A pitcher can always tell you how good a catcher is, and take my word, Johnny Kling was the best."[4]

As Mike Donlin turned thirty (on May 30), the age in that era at which many baseball careers are post-peak, he was hitting his prime. His batting average rose from .301 on his birthday to .356 on July 19. From June 27 to July 21 he had a twenty-four-game hitting streak, the longest in his career. A midsummer slump followed, when his batting average fell to .331. One reason for the slide, wrote a New York sportswriter, was anxiety: "[He wants] to get a hit and keep in front [of the batting race], with the result that he swings at any old ball that comes along."[5] In a late July game he was ejected for arguing balls and strikes—after he had gotten a base on balls![6]

When the Giants hosted the Pirates on July 24, Donlin was batting .352, well ahead of Wagner's .324 mark.[7] The DeValerias wrote that Donlin was taunting the Pittsburgh pitchers before the game. Wagner responded with an uncharacteristic display of emotion: "After his third, fourth, and fifth hits, he rounded first base and held up the appropriate number of fingers toward a fuming Donlin in right field."[8] Years later Wagner recalled that Donlin went after a heckling fan who said he was losing his grip on the batting title. "All you could see was Mike's feet," he chuckled.[9] The crowd of thirty thousand included spectators on the field, some of whom stood on chairs. One New York writer said, "It was a case of the survival of the tallest."[10]

What made Wagner's day even more impressive was that four of his hits came off Mathewson. In a remarkable show of class by New York fans, they tried to carry Wagner off the field after the game, but he resisted.[11] Ralph Davis wrote, "It is seldom, indeed, that New Yorkers can see any good in anything that does not bear the Gotham trademark, but Wagner's play was so great as to demand recognition anywhere."[12] Donlin managed only three hits in the four games.

In the final game of the series, Pirates ace Vic Willis and the Giants' Hooks Wiltse went the distance in a sixteen-inning game that was called because of darkness with the score tied at 2–2. The two men had already gone the distance in the first game of the series, a 2–1 New York win. Both are all but forgotten today. Willis is an eight-time twenty-game winner, and Wiltse became New York's second winningest pitcher in 1908, with twenty-three wins.

By the end of July New York was in second place, only a half game behind Pittsburgh. Donlin finished the month with a .339 batting average, with Wagner closing in with a .331 mark, though his slugging average was far ahead of Donlin's.[13] W. M. Rankin, the senior New York correspondent for the *Sporting News*, noted that the Giants were doing far better than so-called experts had predicted. He likely had Joe Vila in mind when he wrote in late July, "Fate is certainly very unkind to some prophets." And Rankin singled out one man for a lot of the club's success: "Mike Donlin is certainly playing the game of his existence, and his great work is being duly appreciated everywhere over the major league circuit."[14]

12. Donlin's fierce and aggressive nature as a player is conveyed in this image, in which he is wearing a rarely seen Giants sweater. As in 1905, he not only led the Giants in most offensive categories in 1908 but was also among the league leaders in many of them. SDN-003778, *Chicago Daily News* Collection, Chicago History Museum.

The summer of 1908 was the peak of Mike Donlin's popularity in New York. A local writer declared that Donlin had a "stranglehold on the Personal Popularity Stakes in this great big town of baseball enthusiasts."[15] In early August another New York reporter wrote that Donlin was "one of the best ball players who ever graced a New York uniform and without doubt the most popular player the city ever had."[16] A few days later a sportswriter for the *New York World* said, "No man who ever wore the uniform of the Giants was ever more popular in this city than Turkey Mike."[17]

What makes these statements striking to the modern reader is that this was the height of Christy Mathewson's career and a season in which he won thirty-seven games and the pitching Triple Crown. Kate Carew, a pioneering New York journalist who sketched the famous people she interviewed, wrote of the Giants' pitcher, "He's the greatest matinee idol of our time, his eyes ever so blue, and his hair ever so yellow, and his cheeks ever so red, and I thought of Phoebus, the sun god, and of a young Viking with a two-handed sword."[18] In the "Heroes" chapter of his Mathewson biography, Ray Robinson cautioned, "In assessing Matty's qualities one must avoid an excess of 'trolley car nostalgia,' as Martin Amis has written, for the endless superlatives led to his deification."[19]

After his premature death in 1925 Mathewson was elevated to near sainthood. Novelist and literary critic Robert Penn Warren wrote, "The dead hero is safe, more or less, from envy and detraction, and if in the first place, he had the heroic virtues, the distance of death, removing small blemishes and complicating factors, works to stylize the virtues, to give them a hieratic simplicity."[20] The reverence was so excessive that Mathewson's widow was moved to declare, "If Christy had been the way these people say, I don't believe I would have married him. He would have been too boring."[21] He gambled, smoked both cigarettes and a pipe, and sportswriter Frank Graham said, "Matty knew the difference between scotch and rye."[22]

Donald McKim has written about the two types of heroes, the "ideal" and the "flawed" ones.[23] Donlin has to be classified among the flawed. His frailties were very much on display, even before he joined the Giants. Richard Crepeau wrote, "The bad boy hero is a very appealing figure in America, in part, I think, because people can more easily identify with the flawed character than the perfect saintly figure. Donlin was perceived as a regular guy, not a high-toned gentleman."[24]

Jean Plannette spoke at length with Donlin in 1930 and wrote, "The quiet, taciturn 'Matty' was not the personality to appeal to the public. While Donlin's playing ability was sufficient to make him famous, it was his jaunty, fighting air which made him the idol of the sports world. When he strolled to the plate with that cock-of-the-walk stride which was responsible for his nickname of 'Turkey Mike,' the fans went wild. It finally became the custom of the bleachers crowd to keep time to Donlin's steps with a chant of 'Mike! Mike! Mike!'"[25]

Mathewson was aloof and did not welcome fan attention. "I owe everything I have to the fans when I'm out on the mound," he once said, "but I owe the fans nothing, and they owe me nothing, when I'm not pitching."[26] Donlin, by comparison, not only welcomed the spotlight, but he also reveled in it. His faults were well known and made him more relatable to fans.

When the city of New York held its first baseball parade in June 1906, to honor the 1905 World Series champions, McGraw, Mathewson, and Donlin were in the only white automobile, the lead car.[27] But while Mathewson's fame endured and his heroic status grew over the years, Donlin's acclaim proved transient. Ultimately he proved to be more of a celebrity than a hero. "Celebrity is, paradoxically and pathetically, the death warrant of *the* celebrity," historian Dixon Wecter wrote.[28]

Donlin's batting average was about one hundred points above the .239 league average in 1908, a significant achievement at the height of the Dead-ball Era. He walked only twenty-three times in 662 plate appearances. In early August Donlin commented on the vagaries of hitting: "There are weeks when the ball as it advances toward the plate looks as big as a toy balloon, no matter who's pitching. Then right atop of such a period comes a week when the ball looks to me like a mustard seed in a howling gale. . . . Explain it? You might as well ask me to explain an earthquake."[29]

Even Donlin was not beyond criticism from New York fans. When he struck out a second time in an August 12 home loss to Brooklyn, the fans booed. "It's pretty hard to be an idol at the Polo Grounds," wrote a Brooklyn reporter.[30] When Donlin hit a double and a triple the next day, one sportswriter spoke of the star's "recrudescence," surely a word most fans did not understand.[31] A week later Donlin showed that his recrudescence was real. He singled, doubled, and tripled in a win at Cincinnati.

One fan who never lost faith in Donlin was his wife. Mabel traveled with the team to the Midwest that summer and approached John McGraw at a newspaper stand in St. Louis's Union Station. She wanted to know how Honus Wagner had been doing. When McGraw told her the Pirates' star was still hitting well, she replied, "Oh, pshaw!" with a pucker of her lips.[32] Mabel told *Baseball Magazine* that year, "I used to think that an actress' life very nearly tested human endurance, but now I believe that a baseball player has more tiffs by far with unkind fate."[33]

The Giants had their season's most important stretch of road games in late August, with four in Pittsburgh followed by three in Chicago. Donlin's home run was the big blow in the first game. He drove the ball "with one of those half swings of his but met it on the nose, and it went whistling to left. [Left fielder Fred] Clarke tried to get in its path but could not steady himself in time to make the stop, and the ball headed to the left fence in leaps and bounds. Donlin never stopped running except to make a long slide for the plate."[34]

Before the big hit Mabel shouted from her box seat, "Mike, dear, if you don't make a hit, I will never speak to you again, and you can take back your old bracelet." After the blow, Mike got "smiles and a return to favor of his pretty better half."[35] Donlin had the key hit in the second game too, as Mathewson pushed his record to 26-7. In the third game, with the Giants down 3-1, Donlin led off the sixth inning with a bunt single that ignited a comeback rally and a 5-3 win.

In the ninth inning of the final game, with the Giants down 3-2 and Larry Doyle on second base and Roger Bresnahan on first, Mabel shouted to her husband as he approached the plate, "Hit it, Mike, hit it!" He blushed, threw a kiss her way, and shouted, "I'll soak it, girlie. Watch me! Never fear!" And Mike did soak it, a single to center field. "One minute later he was doing a pedestal clog on the first base bag, waving his cap like a big schoolboy at his wife."[36] Tears were rolling down her cheeks as she threw kisses his way. Doyle scored, and Bresnahan soon scored on Cy Seymour's sacrifice fly to secure the victory for the Giants.

After the Giants swept the Pirates, Joe Vila was magnanimous in his praise of the New York club: "The Giants have been the surprise of the year. I admire them for their pugnacity and earnestness. McGraw has the laugh on all of us who tried to show he erred in his trade with Boston. McGraw made a fine deal, and the results prove it."[37]

Fred Tenney was playing first base like a man younger than his thirty-six years and gave McGraw the luxury of not having to rush Fred Merkle along. In his groundbreaking 2011 book on evaluating fielders, Michael Humphreys called Tenney the greatest-fielding first baseman of the Dead-ball Era and "arguably the greatest ever."[38] Journalist James Hopper was traveling with the Giants that summer and called Tenney "the grand old man of the club," who was at the point of his career where "the curve of knowledge of the game, at its culmination, is bisecting the curve of physical skill, which is beginning to descend in a point which means mastery."[39]

Larry Doyle, who had just turned twenty-two, went 9-for-18 in the Pittsburgh series. "Doyle is the athlete. He is young; the world is before him, his to conquer with zest," Hopper wrote. "Two years ago he was in the coal mines."[40] The phrase "It's great to be young and a Giant" has been attributed to Doyle. It likely came from Hopper's article in *Collier's* that

September, when one section of the feature was headed, "To be young, and a Giant! Ah, me."[41]

W. M. Rankin wrote that summer, "Baseball is more fields [*sic*] than the Goddess of Fortune. Just when it looks as if she is going to smile on you, she gives you a cold stare and bestows her affection on the other fellows."[42] And just when the Giants seemed to have seized control of the pennant race, they were swept in Chicago. Brown beat Mathewson in the second of three games, 3–2; Donlin's two runs batted in were not enough. The game's play-by-play was posted on an "electric diamond" in Madison Square Garden, and ten thousand fans watched on the outdoor scoreboard set up by the *New-York Tribune*.[43] The Giants' three-and-a-half-game lead over its two rivals the morning of August 27 had all but vanished. At the end of the month the Cubs had pulled even with New York, and the Pirates were only a half game back.

22

....

A Pennant Race Like No Other

On September 4, 1908, Pittsburgh beat Chicago in ten innings, 1–0, in a game that would have far-reaching repercussions. With two outs Pirates outfielder Owen Wilson singled home Fred Clarke with what appeared to be the winning run. Rookie Warren Gill, who was on first base, ran directly to the clubhouse instead of going to second base, a common practice at the time. Cubs second baseman Johnny Evers retrieved the ball and stepped on second base for a force out of Gill. He then asked umpire Hank O'Day to call the inning's third out, which would have negated the winning run, and the game would have continued. O'Day refused, saying, "Cut it out, Johnny, the game is over."[1] The win allowed the Pirates to remain just a half game behind the Giants, while the Cubs dropped two games back.

Evers was known for his analytical mind. He told *Baseball Magazine*, "I would pick apart every play that was made, and then ponder myself whether the play was made right or whether it should have been played according to my ideas."[2] But Evers may have had some help with his thinking. On July 19 the *Chicago Tribune* had an inquiry in its "Inquisitive Fans" column asking about a similar play. The answer was, "No. Run cannot score when third out is made before [a runner's] reaching first base."[3] The Cubs were playing at home that day, and Evers likely read the column.

O'Day surely took note of the matter and realized Evers's understanding of the rule was correct. Nevertheless, the protest the Cubs filed with National League president Harry Pulliam was disallowed. In addition to the Chicago newspapers, both *Sporting Life* and the *Sporting News* commented on the incident, though very differently. An editorial in the former wrote that "mistake or neglect of that official [O'Day] must be accepted as philosophically as possible, as part of the fortunes of the game."[4] W. M. Rankin wrote in the latter, "It seems rather strange that if the facts were as above stated that O'Day would allow the run to count.

It is nothing for some newspaper men to make such stupid blunders, but an umpire should not do so."[5]

In the seventh inning of a September 16 game, with the Giants leading St. Louis, 4–1, O'Day called Donlin out at first base. It was a close play, but even some New York newspapers said O'Day got the call right. One reporter felt Donlin "made a spectacle of himself . . . bellowing like a maddened bull."[6] While he was ejected, the Giants' star was fortunate not to be suspended.

Donlin's temper was never far from the surface, and Evers was adept at exploiting any opening that would give his Cubs an edge. During a game with the Giants that season, when Donlin came in from the outfield between innings, the Cubs' captain asked him, "How's the Baltimore jailbird today?" Donlin, who was sensitive to tauntings over the 1902 incident, was furious and almost attacked Evers. But he was able to restrain himself, not wanting to earn a suspension, which was likely Evers's intent.[7]

On September 18 the Giants swept a doubleheader from Pittsburgh, their twenty-sixth win in their last thirty games. It pushed the Pirates five games back and seemingly out of the race. In the first game Mathewson tossed a shutout for his thirty-third win. Donlin's third hit of the game was a three-run home run that put New York up 6–0. Just before the big blow Mabel could be heard shouting to her husband, "Kill it; bring them home; win the game!"[8]

In the second game the Giants rallied from an early deficit, with Donlin's two-run single a key hit. With thirty-five thousand fans in attendance and many behind ropes on the field, there were fifteen doubles that day. The reporter for the *New York Press* gloated, "First position is New York's beyond the slightest shadow of a doubt."[9] Even a Pittsburgh sportswriter admitted, "The Giants have the National League pennant all but cinched."[10] The Cubs lost that day to fall four and a half games off the pace.

But it was another "hit" at the ballpark by Donlin that day that generated the most news. During the second game a fan in the bleachers shouted at him, "[Giants shortstop Buck] Herzog makes two base hits. Why can't you?" Donlin exploded and jumped into the right-field stands, as he yelled, "I'll show you what I can do!" and hit the spectator with a powerful blow under the eye that drew blood. When he kept up the attack, fans reacted in defense of the victim and turned on Donlin. He became a potential victim of the "infuriated mob" and had to be rescued by the police at his home ballpark.[11] Jeers and hisses from his usually adoring fans greeted Donlin when he came to the bench. The crowd cheered when he later struck out. Even Donlin could go too far. Surprisingly neither umpire, Bill Klem or Hank O'Day, ejected Donlin.

Ralph Davis complained that the Giants seemed to have the arbiters intimidated in their home ballpark.[12] Davis had long been critical of McGraw for his "reprehensible" behavior: "The opinion is general among the baseball writers that the sooner the National League decides that it can get along without McGraw and his hoodlumism, the sooner will the ideal state of affairs be realized."[13]

While most of the New York press did not look kindly on Donlin's rampage, there were strange exceptions. The *Evening Telegram* reporter denied Donlin had struck a fan but added, "He had reason to retaliate because some chap insulted him villainously."[14]

The Giants lost the final two games of the series. Perhaps reeling from the rebuke directed at him, Donlin managed only one hit in the two games. The first loss came in an extra-inning affair after Donlin fouled out in the ninth inning with the bases loaded and the game tied.

The repartee of Mike and his wife was a regular feature at Giants games. When he did not come through with the big hit, he was known to turn to the grandstand and shout to his wife, "Ain't it awful, Mabel?"[15]

After an off day on Sunday Mathewson gave up only three hits but was beaten, 2–1, by Vic Willis, who allowed but two. One sportswriter said that the two pitchers "made the ball talk and in a language that was Greek to most of the batters."[16] The game was played in just one hour and twenty minutes.

The Cubs followed the Pirates into the Polo Grounds and swept the Giants in a September 22 doubleheader. After picking up the win in the first game with three innings of relief, Mordecai Brown went the distance in the second one. "The chances are the Giants would have eaten supper out of his mangled [right] hand had he asked them," Chicago sportswriter Charles Dryden wrote.[17] (Mordecai was known as "Three-Finger Brown" because of the loss of digits in a childhood farming accident.) The Cubs climbed into a virtual first-place tie with New York, and the Pirates were now just one and a half games back. The lead had vanished in less than a week.

The next day, September 23, the two clubs played one of the most famous baseball games ever. In the fifth inning a Joe Tinker drive got past Donlin in right field, allowing Tinker to race around the bases for an inside-the-park home run. Hobbled by a nagging leg injury, Donlin, who appeared in all but two of the Giants' games that year, tried to stop the ball with his foot, but it rolled past him. He atoned for his misplay the following inning, when his single drove in the tying run.

With the score tied, 1–1, and with two outs in the bottom of the ninth inning, the Giants appeared to have won the game when, with Fred Merkle on first and Moose McCormick on third, Al Bridwell singled. Nineteen-year-old Merkle was playing only because regular first baseman Fred Tenney was out with a sore back (the only game Tenney missed all year). A month earlier *Sporting Life* had featured Merkle on the front page and wrote of his "good judgment on the bases."[18] But just as the Pirates' Warren Gill had done earlier in the month in Pittsburgh, Merkle did not run to second base and instead ran to the clubhouse as the celebrating fans poured onto the field.

John McGraw took pride in his thorough knowledge of the rules and in imparting the necessary information to his men. But it is not known if he reviewed the Gill incident with them. Only one New York newspaper mentioned it, and that was only to say that the Cubs had protested the result. Chicago sportswriter I. E. Sanborn mocked New York City's insularism and air of superiority: "If New York newspapers printed baseball news pertaining to anything outside Manhattan and Brooklyn, the Gotham fans might have understood from the Pittsburgh tangle what came off before their own eyes last Wednesday."[19]

As Johnny Evers waved frantically, trying to get the ball from the outfield, Donlin realized what Evers was trying to do. He ran to Merkle, to lead him to second, but Evers already had the ball and stepped on second base.[20] It was not the game ball since Joe McGinnity had grabbed it and thrown it into the crowd. O'Day, the home plate umpire, ran toward the pitcher's mound to better see the action but made no call. Base umpire Bob Emslie said he did not see what happened, but he told Mathewson, "It's all right. You've got the game."[21]

With so many fans on the field, the game could not be resumed. The Giants maintained they had won; the Cubs argued they should have been awarded the game by forfeit since the Giants did not clear the field and allow the game to continue. O'Day announced that the game was a tie.[22] McGraw was furious his Giants were not awarded the win.

In his book *Pitching in a Pinch*, Mathewson said of O'Day, "He is bull-headed. If a manager gets after him for a decision, he is likely to go up in the air and, not meaning to do it, call close ones against the club that has made the kick, for it must be remembered that umpires are only 'poor weak mortals after all.'"[23] But veteran sportswriter Sam Crane, who had played against O'Day in the 1880s, declared, "I can say that no squarer man lived."[24]

More than forty years later, in his serialized autobiography, Bill Klem called O'Day's ruling "the rottenest decision in the history of baseball."[25] He felt the rule was not meant for clear-cut game-winning hits. In the early 1960s Bridwell (who appeared to have had the game-winning hit) said wistfully to Lawrence Ritter, "I wish I'd never gotten that hit that set off the whole Merkle incident. I wish I'd struck out instead."[26]

The Giants salvaged the final game of the series, 5–4, when Donlin doubled and tripled, knocking in three runs. With two outs in the ninth inning and two Cubs on base, Tinker drove a ball toward the right-field bleachers, but Donlin made a game-saving catch. Mathewson won his thirty-fourth game, in relief, and the Giants moved one game ahead of both their pursuers. A few days later Donlin was honored at a pregame Polo Grounds ceremony as the most popular New York player, the result of a contest sponsored by the *New York Evening Journal*.

On September 28 the Giants were staring at defeat at the hands of the Phillies, 6–5. After already hitting safely twice in the game, Donlin tripled in the ninth inning to drive in Roger Bresnahan and tie the score. When pinch runner Shad Barry (Donlin's leg was still hampering him) later scored the winning run on Cy Seymour's single, Donlin ran out to home plate. He made Barry stand on it, as Mike asked umpire Bill Klem, "He is touching the plate, isn't he?" Klem said, "Yes," with a smile. "Just so nobody can protest it," added Mike.[27]

The final days of the season were a roller coaster for all three pennant-contending teams. The Giants lost three games in five days to young Philadelphia pitcher Harry Coveleski, who had won only two games previously in his career. In one of those games, a 6–2 loss on October 1, one New York sportswriter blamed the loss on Donlin's bad leg: "Rockets that ordinarily Donlin would make a pie of fell safe many feet from the crippled right-fielder."[28] Donlin was in the lineup because of his bat, and he did drive in the team's two runs. "Donlin's leg is so bad he ought to be on crutches," wrote another reporter.[29]

13. Mike Donlin had difficulty playing left field, the sun field, in Cincinnati, and he did not play left field, the sun field, at the Polo Grounds, either. Late in the 1908 season his leg injury hampered his ability to cover a lot of ground in the outfield. *Boston Herald-Traveler* Photo Morgue, Boston Public Library.

On Sunday, October 4, the Cubs (97-55) and Pirates (98-55) played their final game of the season in Chicago.[30] The Giants (95-55) still had a three-game series to play with Boston, starting the next day. A Pittsburgh win, after the Pirates had won thirteen of their last fourteen games, would be their ninety-ninth and would clinch the pennant for them. New Yorkers were in the strange position of rooting for their archenemy Cubs.

Large New York crowds followed the game on electronic scoreboards that some newspapers set up in front of their offices. Fifty thousand fans in Pittsburgh followed the game outside newspaper offices in that city. A West Side Park crowd of more than thirty thousand watched Honus Wagner make two errors, as Mordecai Brown won his twenty-eighth game for Chicago, 5–2. The Pirates (now 98-56, a half game behind the 98-55 Cubs), believing they had been eliminated, dispersed for the offseason. Wagner clinched the batting title, finishing at .354, but he was heartbroken: "I would gladly have given away every world's record I ever had or hope to have if we could only have pulled that game out of the fire yesterday."[31]

On Tuesday, October 6, the National League Board of Directors upheld President Pulliam's ruling (which had upheld the umpires of the "Merkle game") that the September 23 game was a tie. The board ordered the game to be replayed the day after the season ended. The decision had a strange and overlooked twist: the Merkle game would be replayed even if the Giants lost a game in their final series with Boston and finished the season a game behind Chicago. While John McGraw never forgave league president Harry Pulliam for not awarding the Merkle game to the Giants, this ruling gave the Giants an extra chance to win the pennant if they were to lose a game to Boston and finish a game behind the Cubs.

If the Giants lost one of those Boston games and then beat the Cubs in the replay of the Merkle game, the league's three top teams would all finish with identical records of 98-56.[32] It is not known how the pennant winner would have been determined, especially since the Pirates had already dispersed across the country. The Giants avoided what one Pittsburgh paper called "an awful muddle" by sweeping Boston.[33]

The following day, October 8, the Giants hosted the Cubs in a pennant-deciding game before a feverish crowd of about forty thousand. Mathewson, who had thrown almost four hundred innings that season, including more than one hundred since September 1, started for the Giants. Years later he said of that day, "I never had less on the ball in my life."[34] He was opposed by Chicago's Jack Pfiester, known as the "Giant Killer" for his success against New York. He had pitched brilliantly in the "Merkle game" a couple of weeks earlier. But he had elbow pain that made throwing a curve ball excruciating and did not get out of the first inning.

Donlin's double down the right-field line was the big blow, driving in leadoff hitter Fred Tenney, who had been hit by a pitch. (Ironically, five years later Donlin told a reporter that Pfiester was the one pitcher he had trouble hitting, one who "got my goat.")[35] The Cubs' manager–first baseman Frank Chance and catcher Johnny Kling were adamant in claiming the drive had gone foul but lost the argument after a lengthy dispute with umpires Jim Johnstone (who was behind the plate) and Bill Klem (who was on the bases). Donlin might have driven in two runs, but after Buck Herzog walked, he had been picked off first. When Seymour followed Donlin with a walk, Chance made a pitching change, and Brown replaced Pfiester.

The Cubs struck back in the third inning. Tinker, who hit Mathewson so well, tripled on a drive that center fielder Seymour would have caught had he backed up as Mathewson motioned him to do.[36] It led to a four-run inning, with Chance's double driving in two of them. The Giants rallied in the seventh inning when they loaded the bases with no outs. McGraw decided to pinch-hit for his star pitcher, who had settled down and shut out the Cubs the past four innings.

Who would bat for Mathewson? McGraw had a man on the bench he could have called on, perhaps giving him a chance for redemption, but the pressure might have been too much for Fred Merkle. McGraw instead tapped Larry Doyle, who was batting .308, second only to Donlin on the club. But Doyle had not appeared in a game for a month, after being spiked on September 8.[37] He fouled out. The next two batters were retired, though one run scored on Tenney's sacrifice fly. The Cubs held on to prevail, 4–2. The pennant was theirs for the third straight season.

In 1922 syndicated columnist Hugh Fullerton made a revealing, if not shocking, disclosure about what Donlin told him after the game, a story the columnist had "sat on" for fourteen years. To the veteran newspaperman it revealed that Donlin was "as square and straight a fellow as there ever was in the game." Mike told him, "Well, I'm glad they [the Cubs] won it after all. That ball I hit [in the first inning] was foul." The ball was curving, and the umpire missed the call, he said. That, asserted Fullerton, was "sportsmanship raised to the nth degree." Donlin did not want his comment revealed—certainly not in 1908 and not even in 1922—because "it showed a tenderness of nature under his veneer of toughness."[38]

The Giants had won sixteen more games than the previous year but fell one game short, as did the Pirates. After almost two seasons away from Major League action, Mike Donlin was second in the league in batting average (.334), runs batted in (106), and slugging average (.452).[39] *Baseball Magazine* named him the center fielder on its 1908 Major League all-star team.[40] He also showed that his ankle had healed by stealing thirty bases. Equally important was his focus on baseball and avoidance of trouble off the field.

Donlin's struggle for "redemption" with the help of the woman he loved made him an even more appealing figure. It had not been easy. Mark Roth and Sid Mercer noted that on western road trips Mike was offered beer or whiskey "fifty times a day." But they said Mike had "tasted nothing stronger than spring water since last fall."[41] In early September Mabel and a few of the couple's friends threw Mike a party to celebrate his one-year anniversary without alcohol. When presented with a cake with one candle, Mike said he would stay on the water wagon until the cake had twenty candles.[42]

While his public image was more accurate than that of Mathewson, even Donlin's image was idealized somewhat. James Hopper wrote the following in *Collier's* magazine late that summer:

> Two years ago Big Mike Donlin was a reckless, violent, husky-voiced, swaggering brawler. . . . Then he met Mabel Hite, who, discerning a chance for that redemption which woman so dearly loves, gently led him to the altar. Mike Donlin now is . . . a lithe, clean-hewed, supple athlete; his features, made firm through physical and moral health, have regained lines almost classical. It is a pleasure just to see him walk—with the light, elastic, and rapid tread of the man who has work to do in the world, who has regained his appetite for life, for the more subtle and exquisite joys which life reserved for those who do not try to gain happiness by assault and battery.[43]

23

....

Stealing Home

The August 1, 1908, issue of *Variety* announced that Mabel Hite and Mike Donlin would headline the bill at Willie Hammerstein's Victoria Theatre in Times Square, starting October 26.[1] The one-act sketch, *Stealing Home*, would be written by Vincent Bryan, who had composed the music and lyrics for the smash hit *The Wizard of Oz*. The couple would be paid $2,000 a week.[2] Donlin was one of baseball's highest paid players in 1908, but this theater contract was far more lucrative.[3]

Vaudeville had a voracious appetite for novelty, for a constant stream of new shows. Willie Hammerstein once said, "Every vaudeville manager must feel a dread at heart of that future . . . when novelty shall become tiredness, and there is no longer a new sensation left in vaudeville."[4] Willie found that "new sensation" in female wrestler Cora Livingston, at a time when female wrestling was an outlaw sport. "The buxom girl who nightly [ground] the faces of miscellaneous fair opponents into the mat" wowed crowds at Hammerstein's that summer.[5]

New York's theater season ran from Labor Day to Memorial Day. Most venues went dark during the summer; there was no air conditioning to cool customers. But Hammerstein's had a summer season on its roof garden. Because the acoustics up there were poor, summer acts were more action-oriented than dialogue-oriented. Cora was perfect for that.

It was not surprising that theatrical agents turned to the sporting world for acts. Baseball stars had made appearances as early as the late nineteenth century, when Boston's Mike "King" Kelly and Chicago's Cap Anson were headliners. Donlin was a trailblazer for a new wave of baseball personalities who would appear in vaudeville early in the 1910s. An October 1911 article in the *New York Times* featured the many ballplayers who were going on stage that offseason and noted, "Three years ago Mike Donlin was the only ball player of note whose name was flashed in blazing type over a playhouse entrance."[6] While some, such as John McGraw, did only monologues, others, including Rube Marquard and Joe Tinker, appeared in sketches. Hammerstein's would soon be known as baseball players' home plate.[7]

A joke in sporting circles was that when an athlete won or excelled at an athletic event, a business manager would tell him, "Hurry up, take a shower and put on a suit. You're booked at Hammerstein's this evening."[8] Even "Victory" Faust, the Giants' mascot, played in vaudeville.

The big vaudeville houses were already transitioning from acts to leading personalities. This focus on individuals helped create the celebrity culture that arose with moving pictures.[9] Mabel was among those performers who emerged from obscurity into stardom, and Mike was a celebrity before he stepped onto the stage. Together they would generate a powerful draw as vivid examples of the American Dream.

Stealing Home would open shortly after the baseball season ended, and it was premature to predict how Donlin would take to the stage and how audiences would take to him. A *Sporting News* columnist declared Donlin's baseball career was finished.[10] But Mike denied it: "If I divide my time between the diamond and the stage, my baseball career will help me get money in vaudeville, and I might as well get all that is coming to me."[11] He and Mabel were already well off economically, and this contract, along with the couple's continued investment in Long Island real estate, would likely secure financial independence for them.[12]

Donlin had appeared on stage the previous year but only in a bit part in Mabel's *A Knight for a Day*. The managing director of the Whitney Opera House in Chicago had given him a few tips, including never to cough or stammer on stage and not to kiss the girl (even if she was his wife) so as not to disturb her makeup.[13] Donlin engaged actor George McKay, who had appeared with Mabel in *The Merry-Go-Round*. "You big ham, you've got two left feet," he told Donlin. "Every lesson was an extra-inning battle."[14] During warm-ups in the latter part of the baseball season, Donlin was often seen kicking up dust in right field as he practiced his dance steps.[15] Mabel had a favorite reminder for him when his shoes slapped the floor too hard: "Try bunting, Mike, and you won't kick up so much dust."[16]

There was skepticism about Donlin's acting ability. "It will take a clever playsmith to blend Mabel Hite and husband, nee Mike Donlin, into an artistic and harmonious compound," wrote a Chicago sportswriter. "Esoterically speaking, when the sterner half of the sketch was here last summer, he was a mightily bad actor."[17] Donlin acknowledged his limitations: "I am not going to try to play Hamlet. . . . Mrs. Donlin is whipping our act into shape. She will be the real scream in it, and I am content to be a piece of scenery if she hands me the part."[18]

In *Stealing Home* the audience saw a fictional version of the private life of the Giants' star. Mike is ejected by his frequent antagonist, Hank O'Day, in a game against Pittsburgh. "You robber, why don't you get the dust out of your eyes. You big stiff," he tells the umpire, a rebuke that earns him an early exit.[19] When he comes home, his wife asks him how many hits he got. "Almost one," he sheepishly replies. When she hears that Honus Wagner had four hits that day, she explodes in anger: "I thought I had married a ball player, not a window trimmer who gets put out of the game and leaves the Dutchman to get four hits the same day."[20] The recriminations that follow threaten their marital harmony, but at the end they make up and close with a little dance as they sing a song.

As was often the case in such skits, the lyrics were gibberish, and the songs had a tenuous connection to the story, but they added variety to the sketch and gave the couple an opportunity to sing and dance together. "It took him all summer to learn this dance," Mabel said.[21] Entertainment historian David Monod wrote, "Modern celebrity involved the private being made public," and *Stealing Home* was an excellent example of a look "behind the curtain."[22]

Ticket prices ranged from twenty-five cents to one dollar, with matinees topping off at fifty cents.[23] While Mabel and Mike were headliners, their sketch was only twenty-four minutes long (most sketches were even shorter, under twenty minutes), and it was one of numerous acts that included acrobats, singers, musicians, and a blackface comedian. On opening night, reported the *New York Herald*, "a breathless throng of hero worshippers" gave Mike the biggest cheers.[24] The couple's unexpected song and dance at the end of the skit brought roars of approval. There were so many curtain calls that Mabel had to ask the audience to let the rest of the program go on.[25] After the sketch Mike was presented with two floral baseball bats, each more than seven feet tall.[26]

Will Rogers was at the premier performance of *Stealing Home*. "In my thirty years in all branches of show business," he recalled a quarter century later, "I never heard such a reception. It's always lingered in my memory."[27]

14. Twenty years before the arrival of sound in movies, Mike and Mabel made a "movie" with sound. Their 1908 sketch was filmed and synchronized to a recording of their dialogue and singing. Transcendental Graphics/The Rucker Archive.

Most sportswriters raved about the baseball star's work. Typical was Bozeman Bulger: "On the level, fellows, that was a real show. . . . When it comes to pulling the stuff that knocks the scales out of the old thorax, you want to see Mike get busy with his kicks."[28]

Many previously skeptical theater critics also were positive about Mike's performance. "Mike Donlin as a polite comedian is quite the most delightful vaudeville surprise you ever enjoyed, and if you miss him, you do yourself an injustice," wrote *Variety*'s reviewer.[29] The Victoria Theatre's account noted that Mike was surprisingly better on stage than most sports figures: "Public idols of the athletic field and fistic arena we have had without number. They are usually to be identified by a certain hang-dog sullenness mixed with a curious attitude of defiance toward their unaccustomed surroundings."[30] But not Mike.

Amy Leslie commented on this uniquely American phenomenon of star athletes being welcomed to the stage:

Mr. Donlin entered with a satisfied, friendly smile of modest assurance in his own celebrity, and upon that he calmly lay back, mostly silent, altogether agreeable, entirely happy and worshipped as a baseball magnet of a thousand candle power. Not that baseball has anything to do with the stage of America, but rabid hero worship runs the country. . . . Nowhere except in America have those who have triumphed and grown into notoriety or great favoritism elsewhere than the stage been given the opportunity to clinch their popularity by posing before their own reflection in another career for which they have talent. It was great to swim in the Donlin current of admiration last night.[31]

But it was Mabel who carried the show and "made a first-class light comedian out of a crack league batter."[32] Another reviewer pointed out, "She is doing more for Mike on the stage than a major league manager can do for a minor league recruit, for she is keeping his shortcomings so far in the background that the public doesn't see them."[33]

Mabel had been apprehensive that Mike might lose his nerve. When the idea of going on stage was first broached to him, he feared he'd be a "frost," a "lemon." But he warmed to the idea and overcame any jitters. "You see when a man's been playing baseball out in front of 30,000 people," he said, "and a lot of them of the critical sort, and mighty free with their remarks at that—well, it gives him a little assurance, enough, anyway, to let him get by when he faces an ordinary audience in a theater."[34]

Donlin later told New York theater critic Colgate Baker, "The principal difference between acting and baseball is that when you act, they wait until you get outside to tell you what they think of you, and when you play baseball, they tell you then and there."[35] Yet he later confessed to opening night stage fright: "If it hadn't been for those footlights, I'd have caved. As it was, I didn't see a soul in the black abyss across them, but then the house applauded."[36]

Several reviewers wrote of how fond Donlin seemed to be of his wife and that the show was the perfect vehicle to keep them together. Perhaps this explained why Mabel turned down a two-year contract offer from Florenz Ziegfeld that fall.[37] The only time Donlin showed any nervousness on stage was one night in December, when he noticed Cubs second baseman Johnny Evers in the audience. Since the Merkle game, relations between the two had cooled considerably. Mike became unnerved and forgot his lines; for a moment it seemed possible the show would have to end or at least take an intermission. But Mabel skillfully rescued him by improvising, and her husband regained his composure.[38]

The couple took their show on the road, where it would have life well into 1909. "When an actor gets a good sketch," wrote one reporter, "he hangs onto it like a shipwrecked sailor clinging to a floating spar."[39] Donlin said that if he were to return to the Giants in 1909, it would happen only if he received the highest salary any Giants player was ever paid: "For nine years the magnates had me and paid me little money. . . . I'll lose a lot of money if I stay in baseball, for this vaudeville stunt pays better than a major league contract. . . . It isn't hard work when you get going, and there is something about the footlights that always appealed to me."[40]

While Donlin had an alternative that few other ballplayers had, many sports columnists felt he was bluffing. "Nobody believes him," Joe Vila wrote at the end of the year.[41] And most of them felt his leverage would last only so long: "Donlin appears to think he is an actor. He isn't. He is a baseball player, and the moment he ceases to be a baseball player, he will lose all the power to attract on the stage which he now possesses as the husband of Mabel Hite."[42]

Late that year Mike and Mabel befriended Rogers and his wife, shortly after they were married. Rogers would rise to fame far greater and more enduring than that of Mike or Mabel, yet he never forgot an act of generosity the Donlins had shown the newlyweds. Twenty-five years later he recalled that special night: "It was the first time we had ever been in a swell apartment. It was the first time big actors had ever invited us out. . . . She [Mabel] showed her beautiful dresses, and a fur coat that cost I think it was maybe two thousand dollars. It was a fairyland night. . . . My wife will never forget her kindness to us, for you must remember there was 'Class' in vaudeville as well as in society, and for an 'Act' to visit a headliner was an event."[43]

24

....

Will He or Won't He?

So began a dance that would continue for the next few years. Would Mike Donlin return to the Giants? Would they be able to win the pennant without him? If he would not play baseball, would he continue to be a stage attraction? Finally, what did he really want to do? What did he want to be, a ballplayer or an actor? Love of the game, love for his wife, love of money: they were competing interests for the heart of Mike Donlin.

Donlin was threatening to sit out the 1909 season if the team did not satisfy his salary demands. The fans realized this was no idle threat: after the success of *Stealing Home*, he had a strong option for non-baseball employment.

In January 1909 Mike announced that he and Mabel had signed contracts that would keep them on the stage into April. "I can't afford to sacrifice a whole lot of time in Texas shaping up for next season," he said, "when Mrs. Donlin and I can be earning real money in large quantities making people laugh."[1] If Donlin was going to join the Giants, it would be on his terms and his timetable. He could not report until the start of the regular season at the earliest. Years later Damon Runyon wrote that Donlin was paid well to play baseball "because he always knew what he was worth."[2]

Donlin was demanding a salary of $8,000 from the Giants. John Brush was offering $6,000 while questioning Donlin's value as a ballplayer and his earning power on the stage. Entertainer George M. Cohan, a devoted Giants fan, offered to pay the $2,000 difference, but Brush was not interested.[3]

Giants fans followed the salary dispute with foreboding. Donlin gave them hope when he said he was staying in shape by playing handball two hours a day, with his weight down to a lean 160 pounds.[4] He said, "I'm willing to play with New York next season if they come up to my figure. If not, well I'll stay on the stage."[5] But in almost the same breath he reminded reporters, "I'll lose a lot of money if I stay in base ball for this vaudeville

168

stunt pays better than a major league contract. Mrs. Donlin and I have some very nice offers—nice in a monetary sense, you know, and very easy money at that."[6]

Manager McGraw appeared unperturbed: "I am glad he is doing well and getting the money. As I have said before, baseball is a good booster for theatrical folks, and his connection with the game has surely helped Mike in his vaudeville capacity. For that reason, I can't bring myself to believe he intends to forsake the game for the stage."[7] A writer for the *Pittsburgh Press* emphasized McGraw's point: "Mike has an idea that he is a big hit on the vaudeville stage . . . but if it weren't for his wife . . . and his own popularity, gained through his ranking in the baseball field, he would not draw flies."[8]

While they were in Cincinnati, Donlin and Mabel appeared in *Stealing Home*. "Both were received with much acclaim," wrote the critic from the *Cincinnati Enquirer*, who devoted much of his review to praising Mike. "The applause when he entered, attired in a swell Broadway costume, wearing a broad-brimmed straw hat and carrying a cane, was continued for five minutes, during which Mike was kept busy bowing and smiling in response to the hearty greeting of his Cincinnati friends."[9]

One example of the lucrative non-baseball options Donlin had was the report that the Donlins received a letter from Charles Frohman and William Harris, two of the biggest producers in the theater world. Mabel and Mike were being offered the privilege of selecting their own playwright and company for a production written as they wished. They would receive a large salary plus one-third of the gross receipts.[10] Another offer came from Florenz Ziegfeld.[11]

Vaudeville was at the zenith of its popularity in 1909. Even aspiring theater actors, including John Barrymore, could not resist the money to be made in vaudeville. While silent movies as we know them were still a few years away and talking films were even further into the future, a pioneering process made its appearance around this time. *Variety* magazine reported in 1909 that investors were developing devices for color photography for moving pictures that were accompanied by sound from Victrola records.[12]

Mike and Mabel were among the beneficiaries; the Cameraphone Theater Company, one of the leaders of this burgeoning industry, enabled them to appear in more than one place at one time. A newspaper ad in the small town of Sedalia, Missouri, for example, featured *Stealing Home* for ten cents. "People are wondering whether or not they are looking at real live performers. . . . You see people in vaudeville that you could never see in Sedalia."[13]

At the start of 1909 Mike and Mabel continued to appear in Chicago. Mabel explained that the continued popularity of *Stealing Home* reflected the public's desire "to get a view into domestic ties," and a Chicago reviewer noted that she bossed her husband around in the sketch like the acting coach she was for him.[14] One Chicago critic observed that Donlin was able to translate something from the ball field to the stage: "It often has been remarked at the West Side Park [the Cubs' home field] that all Donlin would have to do to make a hit in vaudeville would be to walk across the stage with the same swagger that he shows when walking to the outfield in a baseball game. They say Mike has gone one better on this swagger walk and has invented a swagger dance which is purely Mike Donlin."[15]

Other reviewers gave more balanced accounts. One wrote that Donlin does not try to be a great actor in the skit because, as "a popular idol," he does not have to be one. "Mike is required to be a big, loving, silent foil for his wife's abundant nervous energy, and that he does to perfection."[16] Another noted that the baseball star knew as much about real acting as he knew about Sanskrit and called his performance "a merry joke."[17] Reporters also recognized the key role Mabel played in Mike's stage success. Whenever he faltered on stage, she attracted attention to herself and allowed him to regain his poise.[18]

A mysterious illness struck Mike in Boston in late March. A typical headline read, "Mike Donlin Will Never Wear His Uniform Again."[19] He was suffering from serious blood hemorrhages from his nose or lungs that were alternately attributed to "the grip" and to burst blood vessels. Doctors told him it would be dangerous—even life-threatening—for him to return to baseball and that even his dancing on stage was risky.[20] Yet within months he was back to performing and working out with baseball teams in California.[21]

Mabel was also dealing with serious health issues. She told a Los Angeles reporter early that summer, "My head bothers me all the time. I think it's my eyes, and I wear dark glasses off-stage. There's no use in going to doctors all the time. . . . Sometimes my head hurts me, so I have to take hypo shots of morphine before I go on."[22] It is difficult to determine whether

15. Mabel Hite donned a Giants uniform to match that of her husband in promotional photos for *Stealing Home*, their 1908 smash vaudeville hit. Billy Rose Theatre Division, New York Public Library for the Performing Arts.

Mabel was suffering from a case of stress-related nerves or something more systemic.

Every week that went by without an announcement that Donlin had signed with the Giants made fans—and surely McGraw—increasingly uncomfortable. Joe Vila's comments reflected the emerging reality that the Giants would likely have to compete in 1909 without their star hitter. In January he wrote that Mike was bluffing. But by March he declared, "Mike Donlin, to all intents and purposes, has quit the Giants. He and his wife, Mabel Hite, have signed theatrical contracts which will keep them busy until July 5. This is not a fake move to force the New York Club to Mike's terms, but a cold-blooded fact."[23] But Vila cautioned the ballplayer-turned actor: "[Donlin] would lose practically all of his popularity in this city, because of his defection. New Yorkers are red-hot to have the Giants win the pennant this year. . . . That is why the fans are beginning to say hard things about Mr. Michael Donlin, actor and money-getter."[24]

Donlin likely sensed that he needed baseball notoriety to fuel his stage success. And perhaps he realized he would need another few seasons to perform at the high level he had in 1905 and 1908 to cement his place among baseball's all-time greats.

Colgate Baker summed up Donlin's dilemma and reminded readers that the stage offered one thing baseball could not provide: "He has traded the scepter of King of the Diamond for a stick of grease paint, the idolatry of the youth of the nation for the kid-gloved applause of Broadway theatregoers, the glory of the great game for what—well, for the light o' love in a woman's eyes."[25]

Mike did not want to be separated from his wife, who had been such a positive influence in his life. "She is Mike's moral trainer," wrote a Cincinnati reporter, "and she has him on a diet that includes nothing stronger than lithia water and billiards."[26] He had stopped drinking, carousing, and spending money so freely that he often had to borrow from the club or friends to tide him over. "What a wonderful ball player Donlin would have been from 1900 on if he had cut out dissipation and buckled down to business."[27]

As the Giants continued their spring training, the Donlins returned to the East Coast. They were headliners at Keith's in Boston, along with "the master juggling comedian," W. C. Fields. They then took *Stealing Home* to the West Coast, where one reviewer pointed out what made Mabel so special and successful. It was her "utter disregard for appearing languid and graceful—a disease affecting so many present-day actresses—her bubbling mirth and enjoyment of the situation."[28]

In early March a friend of Donlin's said Mike showed him his bankbook, which revealed a balance of $25,000. That friend told a reporter, "Donlin has got to get his while he can. I know that Mike has about $40,000 in sight in the next year. He can get it sure, and if he does can you blame him?"[29] Mike's $8,000 annual salary demand was far less than the $1,500 to $2,000 the couple was earning each week.[30] So what did Mike really want to do in 1909? If the Giants had accepted his offer, would he have walked away from all that stage money? Was all the back-and-forth posturing just an "act," perhaps to lessen the ire of fans by making the club appear to be the inflexible and unreasonable party?

More than a century later the conflicting reports make it difficult to know for certain. Even Mike himself was torn. He enjoyed giving interviews and answering reporters' questions. Yet it was Mabel who was "doing all the talking about hold-out stuff."[31] A scatterbrained ingenue on stage, twenty-five-year-old Mabel was a clearheaded and determined businesswoman off stage.[32] And while Mike was never at a loss for words, if Mabel was around when reporters brought up his plans for the 1909 season, it was she who usually jumped in with an answer.

When Mike was asked when he planned to sign with the Giants, it was Mabel who answered: "We'll not sign a contract until Mr. Brush agrees to Mike's terms. You know we think Mike is worth as much as two players, and more than five or six, and he will have to be paid accordingly."[33] After Mike said he and Brush were "the best of friends," Mabel stepped in and remarked, "But the best-of-friends thing doesn't buy any choice bits of Long Island real estate." When Mike started rambling about his love of the game, she interrupted him again and said, "But we are not considering our likes and dislikes in this connection."[34] Just a few days earlier Mabel had boiled the situation down to its essence: "Mike wants to play. Of course, if the New York club does not see fit to meet our demands, we will not be idle this summer."[35]

In the early weeks of 1909 Donlin would have joined the Giants had his salary demand been met. He and Mabel had firm contracts only into April at that point. The big East Coast theaters would be dark for the summer—for most of the baseball season anyway.[36] A successful baseball campaign

16. Mabel Hite had a goofy persona on stage, but she was an astute business-woman and a forceful presence when her husband had salary disputes with the New York Giants. When Mike's love of the game made him waver, Mabel provided the strength for him to hold firm. Billy Rose Theatre Division, New York Public Library for the Performing Arts.

would increase Mike's stage appeal come fall and would also secure his reputation as one of the game's all-time greats. Mabel understood the importance of these points. She said she would not let him quit the game: "Mike will be back again stronger than ever next year."[37]

Looking back at how 1909 played out, Mabel said Mike had expected to play that season. She encouraged him to ask for a good salary. Mike set his price at $8,000 and never expected the Giants to turn him down. He "was never dreaming but they'd [the Giants] agree, never dreaming they wouldn't, and then they didn't," she said. "Anyhow," Mike added, "I'm six seasons to the good now. Got six times as much money as I would if I'd played ball this sketch [*sic*]. So we're all right."[38] Financially, at least, it all worked out well for him.

25

....

I Play for the Money

When the Giants opened their 1909 season, Red Murray was in Mike Donlin's old spot in right field.[1] But just six weeks later the Giants were feeling the loss of their star outfielder. One sportswriter listed all the club had lost because of Mike's absence: "As a ball player Donlin has known very few equals and no superior. He is a falcon in the field, has an arm of steel, and as great a hitter as ever faced a pitcher. . . . Donlin is the true and ideal batsman. He can cut them to all fields, can drive them a mile or bunt with precision."[2]

Yet the loss went far beyond Donlin's baseball talent and fiery disposition, which so delighted New Yorkers. The sights and sounds of Mabel cheering or admonishing her husband from the stands had become a popular feature of watching the Giants play. "How are we going to get through a Polo Grounds afternoon without being given the opportunity to cry out in a loud voice: 'How's Mabel, Mike?' or 'Hello Mabel!' or 'Oh, you Mabel!'" asked sportswriter W. W. Aulick. "What are we going to do this year without our excellent, wit-inducing Donlin to greet as he steps proudly to the plate, after swinging two bats and shifting the chaw of honest long-cut from the port to the starboard cheek?"[3]

Asked if he had given up all idea of playing ball, Mike said, "Yes, I leave Saturday night with Mrs. Donlin for the West, and we will follow a long route which will end in California in the middle of summer. After that we expect to take a trip across the Atlantic for rest."[4]

With the approach of summer and the East Coast theater season coming to a close, Mike let it be known that he would return to the Giants for the remaining half a season for $4,000, half his original salary demand: "I have made all arrangements to sail for Europe in July, but if the fans, who have always been my friends, want me to stick and finish out the season with New York, I will feel that it is due to them that I stay."[5] He said it was all up to owner Brush: "If he meets my terms, I am willing to play at a day's notice."[6] Once again Brush was not interested in bringing Donlin back—perhaps because as July began, the Giants were already ten games back of the Pirates.

Mabel and Mike were planning to sail for Europe that summer for their oft-delayed honeymoon. It would be their first European visit, and Mabel was thrilled in anticipation of seeing London, Paris, Berlin, and Rome. Mike quickly added, "And Ireland."[7] Would he really have canceled the couple's belated honeymoon to play for the Giants?

After watching Donlin perform in *Stealing Home* on stage that spring, a San Francisco columnist described his contribution to the acting team: "Mrs. Mike is the big hit of the Donlin-Hite act. I don't mean to say that Mike doesn't do his share. He comes on. (Large applause.) He speaks. (Laughter.) He almost dances. (Great applause.) And he makes a speech. (Tremendous applause.) Honestly, now, Mike, was it ever that easy in the old ballplaying days?"[8] Another reporter saw a bright future for Donlin as a performer: "With his handsome face and excellent figure, we cannot see why Donlin should not make a very clever actor. . . . With these assets, and some hard work, there is not a reason in the world why Donlin should not make a better actor than the average."[9]

During an interview in Los Angeles Mabel admitted she was worn out, prompting Mike to suggest she needed a rest: "We had intended to sail for Europe next Saturday, but the doctors decided that my wife needed the country air more than salt air, so we have postponed the trip. . . . We shall depart for New York to-day, and then we will go out on a farm in Point Pleasant, New Jersey, for a week."[10]

Mike finally appeared on a New York baseball diamond in late July but not in the role fans were hoping for. A benefit for the New York Home for Destitute Crippled Children drew twelve thousand people to Hilltop Park (home of the American League Yankees) and raised $8,000. The girls from the Ziegfeld Follies played against vaudeville headliners in a baseball game, umpired by Mabel and actress Eva Tanguay. There were various contests, from those of strength and endurance to a pie-eating contest, which was refereed by Donlin.[11]

On July 31, 1909, tragedy again struck the Donlin family. Mike's brother, James, died in Cook County (Chicago) Hospital, a death attributed to alcoholism. A day earlier James, a thirty-four-year-old brakeman, was found unconscious in a shack at West Hammond, Illinois. He had lost his job after a foot injury and had started drinking heavily. Mike and his sister Mame attended the funeral.[12]

"Poor Mabel Hite" was the title of a feature story that appeared in the August 29, 1909, *St. Louis Post-Dispatch*. The subtitle read, "Six times she has started off on her honeymoon trip with Mike Donlin, and every blessed time she has 'got the hook.'" Whether it was a show or a return to baseball, the couple's long-awaited honeymoon had been in limbo. Now that it appeared certain Donlin would not be playing for the Giants, they prepared for a three-month tour of Europe. Then came yet another annoying interruption to the proposed honeymoon.

> "The Phillies want me for manager," Donlin said to his wife in July. "Felix Isman (a Philadelphia businessman) has been dickering for control of the club. He is going to discharge [Billy] Murray, the present manager, and put me in charge."
>
> "But that'll kill our honeymoon trip again," complained Mabel.
>
> "But it's the chance of a lifetime," Donlin answered. "There's a lot of money back of this club. They want me badly. They are willing to pay me $4,000 for the remainder of the season and make a handsome contract with me for next year. In a few years as manager, I could make enough to put us on Easy Street, without touching your earnings, and I'd like to do that if I could."[13]

Donlin was to go from the Giants to Philadelphia in exchange for outfielder Sherry Magee and a pitcher.[14] Murray was to be dismissed with a payoff for the balance of his three-year contract. But Murray disrupted Isman's plans by announcing that Isman had no stock in the Philadelphia club, that he was not an official of the club, and that he had no authority to either engage a manager or dismiss one. Ten days later Isman admitted that he had exceeded his authority, and Murray was correct on all counts. The deal fell through. Isman did not get his stock, Mike did not get his job, and, worst of all, Mabel did not get her honeymoon.[15]

Donlin was anxious to get back into the game again but was unable to make any plans while Brush and McGraw continued to ignore him. He and Mabel were scheduled to appear in *Stealing Home* for the last time

17. Mike Donlin and Mabel Hite were an immensely popular "power couple" in late 1908 and 1909. Shown here are autographed notes to fans. Hollywood Museum Collection, Margaret Herrick Library, Academy of Motion Picture Arts and Sciences.

on August 30, in Brooklyn, after which he would join with her in a new sketch, *Double Play*, in which Mabel would be the star.

The nineteen-minute *Double Play* featured Mabel as a maid who goes in disguise to test her husband's loyalty. Their biggest applause came for the following exchange: Mike tells her, "You can't be a baseball player. You're an actress." Mabel replies: "Well, you can't be an actor. You're a baseball player."[16] *Variety*'s critic wrote that the new skit was better than *Stealing Home* and would be a big hit. But the weekly noted that Mabel drew more applause than Mike and wrote, "Donlin is not the act; it is Mabel Hite all the way."[17] Other reviewers noted that after a year away from baseball, Mike was not "the lion among the fans he was in those days."[18]

There was also a desire among critics to see Mabel return to theater. But just as her husband was drawn away from baseball by the lure of money in theater, so too Mabel was drawn away from the "legitimate" theater by the lure of money in vaudeville. When asked by a San Francisco critic when she would return to theater, she replied, "No sir-ee. The money is in vaudeville. I could have been with [theatrical manager] Mr. [Charles] Frohman four years ago, but there was not sufficient money in it to tempt me away from vaudeville, and I'm still here. Then we had a chance to star together in farce, but we turned it down, too, because vaudeville pays better."[19]

Despite all the talk about the "reformed" Donlin, he remained quick-tempered and sensitive to any perceived slight or insult. On Saturday night, September 11, he exchanged blows with Edward N. Danforth, a New York lawyer. The confrontation took place in front of the Hotel Knickerbocker in Times Square. Reports said that just as Danforth reached the street in front of the hotel, Donlin, his wife, and another woman bumped into him after getting out of a car. He said that he complained to Donlin and Donlin struck him.[20]

Donlin, of course, had a different story: "We were driving up to the Knickerbocker in this machine when a fellow on the curb called out to my wife, 'Hello Dearie.' As soon as the car stopped, I ran back to him and said, 'What do you mean by insulting my wife?' He answered me with a blow on the nose, and I hit him back."[21]

Donlin was locked up on a charge of assault. Curiously it was Felix Isman who bailed him out. When Danforth did not appear in court the next day, Donlin was discharged. There was no doubt Donlin had been hit. He had the marks to prove it. Just the previous summer Mabel had garnered headlines when she punched a taxi driver in the jaw after a disputed fare.[22]

Donlin, an excellent billiards player, often frequented pool halls, "which were major gatherings for the sporting fraternity." Among the most famous of these establishments was Jack Doyle's Billiards Academy, located in the Times Square area.[23] It was at Doyle's, wrote Jay Polsky, "where the daily line [more or less official bookmakers' odds] was determined for every sporting event in New York City."[24] Donlin was a regular at Doyle's when he was in New York and played a well-attended match of three cushion billiards with Yankees first baseman Hal Chase there on October 26, a match won by Donlin. James J. Jeffries acted as the referee, and "the former heavyweight champion attracted as much attention as the players."[25]

Although he was still popular with the New York fans, Donlin felt the Giants' organization had mistreated him, and he seemed ready to move on. In early November he indicated that he hoped to play for Pittsburgh in 1910: "It is the greatest city in the country for the men who play the game. I would like to play here," he said. In addition to Pittsburgh's being—in Donlin's eyes—a great place to play, the Pirates were the defending world champions. "Now, look here," he replied when asked if he would go to any other club. "I am after one thing, and that is what everybody is after—the money."[26] In an era when players had little or no control over where they would play, Donlin summarized his plight: "When you sign a baseball contract, . . . you sign for life, and I am consequently in the hands of New York. . . . I am not a has-been; I am not down and out: but on the contrary, if I ever play ball again, I will show them that I was never in as fit condition as I am today."[27]

Before the year was out, Donlin announced he was quitting baseball for good. He said he and Mabel were making so much money in vaudeville that nothing could tempt him to return. *Sporting Life*'s E. H. Simmons was skeptical. "But this is the sort of thing Donlin was reported as saying last year," he wrote, "and then in the following spring it was announced he would be willing to play for an increase of salary." Simmons added, "[Donlin] would soon discover that he was physically unable to play Major League baseball, even if he so desired."[28]

Mabel later looked back at 1909 and said, "My word, had Mike accepted [his demand for $8,000 from Brush], do you know what he would have sacrificed? Just $45,000 in cash. For Mike and I made exactly $53,000 that year in cash. Wouldn't you jump your job for that?"[29]

26

....

Despite Health Concerns, Mabel's
Star Continues to Rise

While Mike Donlin's absence from baseball in 1909 allowed him to remain with his wife and earn an enormous amount of money, the New York Giants and their fans suffered that absence. As spring training 1910 approached, the *New York Morning Telegraph* pointed out the shortsightedness of both the former player and his former team: "The club has come to a painful realization [of] the fact that pennants can't be won when .330 batsmen are allowed to stay away through money differences."[1] It reported that Donlin and McGraw were negotiating their differences, and Mike would sign the papers in the next few hours. The reports amounted to nothing.

Other reports said Mike missed playing ball, and he figured his return to the diamond would earn him more attractive theatrical contracts for the fall.[2] "The applause one gets on the stage is artificial," he told a crowd of fans at New York's Waldorf Astoria Hotel. "The cheers one gets on the diamond are genuine. On the stage you are somebody else, repeating somebody else's line, living somebody else's life. On the diamond you are your own individual self, making your own plays and getting credit for your own ability."[3]

But only the most naïve could not recognize that Donlin's desire to play had always been tempered by the reality he could make more money on the stage than in baseball. He informed John Brush he would let the Giants' owner know his decision by early March. Brush said that if Donlin wanted to play for the Giants in 1910, it would have to be for the salary he received in 1908, and he would have to show that he was in condition to play.

Despite Donlin's outstanding 1908 season, the question remained whether he could regain his old playing form after sitting out a year. "Donlin was a wonderful ball player two years ago," reported the *St. Louis Star*. "But whether vaudeville engagements in stuffy theaters, with practically no outdoor recreation, have gradually dulled Sir Michael's qualities as a diamond star is a matter that cannot be cleared up until he has put on a uniform and taken part in a number of pennant contests." *St. Louis Post-Dispatch* columnist Ed Wray wrote that even if Donlin returned, he did not deserve the approval of the fans for the way he had let McGraw and his teammates down when they badly needed him in 1909.[4]

This year there would be no need for negotiations. On March 19, after the Donlins had secured theatrical contracts through June, Mike informed Brush he would not play in 1910.[5] Mabel certainly figured into the decision. Mike would not play ball this season, she declared, "as he does not care to be separated from me."[6]

Mike was a dutiful husband, but he missed baseball. "If I had my way about it, I would be back in right field, instead of treading the boards," he said. "Every time I go to a ball game my blood fairly boils in eagerness to get back into the fray. But what can I do? I can't jump my contract with Mabel, for she's the best little manager I ever had."[7]

Mike faced a classic conundrum—wanting to be in two different places at the same time. On the ballfield he was a star, one of the most talented in the game. On the stage his talent was indistinguishable from hundreds of other supporting players. But the stage offered far more money, and, more important, he would be with Mabel.

Quite often the couple appeared in newspaper and magazine features that usually included their photographs. They made a dapper fashion statement. While Mabel may have risen to fame outfitted in ridiculous and clownish costumes, she now presented a very different image, both on and off the stage. "There is, perhaps, no young woman in vaudeville today who wears prettier clothes and wears them better, than does Mabel Hite," wrote Washington DC fashion reporter Julia Murdock.[8]

Mike cut a dashing figure as well. He often was called the Beau Brummel of baseball; one paper used a play on words to call him "the Hite of fashion."[9] Another reported he changed his clothes three times a day.[10] While Mabel often spoke of saving money for real estate investments, she enjoyed spending money on expensive clothes, as did her husband. Mike was often seen at the theater wearing $350 suits, while Mabel would be adorned with a $500 bird-of-paradise hat.[11] In January Mabel was sued by a Broadway furrier when she stopped payment on a $185 check for a fur neckpiece she felt was not "the latest style."[12]

18. Mike Donlin was a stylish figure on Broadway. He often was called the Beau Brummel of baseball. He is seen here in 1910. Michael Mumby Collection.

Coincidentally the ballplayer known as Turkey Mike was connected to a dance known as the "turkey trot," which became a national craze around this time. Florenz Ziegfeld thought he had discovered it from Black dancers in San Francisco in 1910. But Mabel was reported to have beaten him by a few weeks when she paid those dancers $100 a week to teach it to her and Mike.[13] They introduced it into their new show, *A Certain Party*, which helped drive the dance's popularity. *Variety* reported that the "turkey trot" of Mabel and Mike was the show's biggest hit.[14]

With this three-act play Mabel had left vaudeville for musical comedy. Her constantly shifting interests now leaned toward legitimate theater. She said, "Vaudeville isn't in it with this. I'm mad about the legitimate, and my hope and prayer is that I'll succeed so well in it that I'll never have to go back to the two-a-day. Mikey likes it too."[15] Mike liked it because he had a role in the show as a secondary character. The show's producers planned to tour metropolitan cities with the goal of landing a New York contract at a Broadway theater.

In *A Certain Party* Hite plays a household maid. Donlin plays a policeman who is Mabel's sweetheart and the play's hero when he breaks up a gambling den. As with most of her roles and in keeping with the way musicals were structured at the time, Mabel sang songs that were unconnected to the story line but showcased her performance.[16] Her most popular song, "I'm on My Way to Reno," was about a girl who drops a nickel in a slot for a divorce and then gets back on the train and "shouts the battle cry for freedom."[17]

Theater critic Percy Hammond recognized the transition that Mabel was attempting: "She indicates her intelligence by abandoning her hitherto prevailing characteristic—the grotesque—and manages to present quite a bright, amusing, and real character."[18] Hammond also had some kind words for Mike: "He is easy, unaffected, natural, and he possesses an interesting amount of technical wisdom."[19]

Amy Leslie had followed Mabel's career for years and was one of her biggest fans. The Chicago critic raved about Mabel's "irresistible magnetism" on display in *A Certain Party*:

A sprite with delicious piquancy and originality, a creature whose delicate beauty would have lifted her into the dangerous flames of the emotional ingenues had not her extraordinary sense of the ridiculous, her buoyant wit and splendid humor given her a security which tethers her back close to the sane shore of versatility. . . . She is a fragile, intense, exquisite little genius, with hair like a storm cloud and beautiful eyes; eyes deep, poetic, and smoldering with tragedy. . . . She thrills, startles, delights, and entertains continually in *A Certain Party*.[20]

Yet *A Certain Party* was not considered a strong play. One reviewer wrote that Mabel would need a better vehicle to help her graduate to the legitimate and earn "enduring fame."[21] A Philadelphia critic wrote that the show was "just pretty good, that's all," with a weak score, not one that "we shall find ourselves whistling as we shave and dress mornings."[22]

As the baseball season approached, Mabel made some telling observations about ballplayers' lack of freedom: "Why, under the present system of organized baseball, a player has no more control of himself than a bundle of bats. . . . He plays not where he wants to, but where he is compelled to play."[23]

After four years of marriage the couple (accompanied by Mabel's mother) finally got their honeymoon when they sailed to Europe on June 10 aboard the steamer *St. Louis*. They planned to return in early August and open their show on Broadway later that month. But they cut their trip short and came back in mid-July because of Mabel's illness. Headlines shouted that she was going blind.[24] Papers quoted doctors as saying she was suffering from a partial paralysis of the optic nerve.[25] "I got up one day to discover I could scarcely see," she explained. "I believe I will recover. . . . It is a little hard, because we had been expecting to be such a hit in the new play."[26] There were expressions of sorrow from many quarters, both in theater and among the fans.

Mabel was staying at the couple's cottage at Sheepshead Bay in south Brooklyn, where she wore dark glasses, kept out of the sun, and did no reading.[27] The New York opening of *A Certain Party* was canceled. There were stories that Mike was considering a return to the Giants, but he denied it. "Tell McGraw I'm rooting [for his club]," he told reporters, and added that they ought to win the pennant.[28]

Mike stayed busy during the summer and fall playing baseball, usually as a first baseman. He played several Sunday games for the Sheepshead Bay A.C. at the neighborhood's race track. Unsurprisingly he was the center of attention and responded by playing well.[29] He also played for a team called the All-Leaguers in a game at Harlem's Olympic Field, against the All-Star Manhattans, managed by his 1904 Giants teammate Jack Warner. Manager McGraw and the entire Giants team attended the game.[30]

Two weeks after playing for the All-Leaguers, Donlin switched sides and played for the All-Star Manhattans in the second game of a doubleheader at Olympic Field. The opposition was the Leland Giants of

19. Mabel Hite is driving an Everitt auto from the Metzger Car Company in 1910, with husband Mike at her side. She was highlighted in a November *Leslie's Weekly* feature that year on the "feminine influence" on the motor-car industry. Lazarnick Collection, Detroit Public Library.

Chicago, the powerful Black team, who would play another white team in the opener. Bugs Raymond, still an active pitcher for the New York Giants, was scheduled to face Rube Foster in game two, and the *New York Times* predicted rough going for Warner's squad: "[Raymond], who will pitch for the Manhattans, will have a hard time to win over the colored champions, as Rube Foster, the greatest colored pitcher in the country, will be in the box for the Giants."[31]

The *New York Age*, a Black newspaper, gleefully told the story of the two games with this headline: "Leland Giants Have a Massacre." The Giants were ahead, 7–2, in the seventh inning when the first game was called, and ahead, 11–3, when the second was called on account of darkness. "Nearly ten thousand baseball fans turned out to see the games, and every window and roof in the vicinity was crowded with sightseers," wrote the *Age*, adding that "many were unable to obtain admission, as the grounds are small."[32]

We are forced to speculate as to what was really ailing Mabel. She already had revealed she was taking morphine for headaches. The *Brooklyn Eagle* reported that she had gone abroad after suffering a nervous breakdown.[33] Did nerves trigger the headaches and even the vision problems? She could have suffered from a rare high degree of nearsightedness called high myopia. Another possibility was that she had multiple sclerosis, which was not rare among young women. It is associated with inflammation of the optic nerve, optic neuritis. And the illness comes and goes, "notorious for getting better and worse."[34] By mid-October Mabel's eyesight was restored, and the couple moved back into Manhattan. Theater schedules had already been firmed up, and their musical comedy would not open until the following spring.

When Mabel and Mike headed out west on a vacation that fall, he relished the comfortable life he now had, one that would have been beyond his imagination a few years earlier.[35] "I'm a member of the leisure class now," Mike said. "The hardest work I do is paying hotel bills and wiring ahead for accommodations."[36] He and Mabel did a reprise of *Double Play* in California. *Variety* reported they would bring that sketch back to the Majestic in Chicago for a run that would pay them $2,000 a week.[37]

27

....

A Return to Baseball

When Mike and Mabel were not performing, they often spent the night at the theater. On one occasion in New York City in March 1911, they were sitting next to Pittsburgh Pirates owner Barney Dreyfuss. "Do you think Donlin will play again?" a Pittsburgh sportswriter had asked Dreyfuss that month. "Never," Dreyfuss responded. "He is not in good health. Thin, and scarcely anything like the athlete of 1908."[1] If Dreyfuss was speaking of Donlin's playing at the Major League level, he appeared to be correct when, for the third consecutive April, Mike was missing from the Giants' Opening Day lineup. However, he was still playing. Later that month he was at first base when Donlin's All-Stars played against the Lincoln Giants, "New York's newly-formed colored team" at Harlem's Olympic Field.[2]

Mike and Mabel continued to appear in *A Certain Party* on the road that spring, and the reviews were as mixed as they had been the previous fall. The *Washington Post* critic called the show a "hodge-podge" and a "crude conglomeration of farce and music."[3] But a Philadelphia reviewer captured the essence of Mabel's talent and appeal when he called her "an eccentric comedienne [with] the two qualities of personal charm and irresistible drollery."[4] Later in April Mabel made her Broadway debut, starring in *A Certain Party* at Wallack's Theatre in New York City. The critic from the *New York Times* wrote, "Mike bore away most of the honors. . . . What he lacks in histrionic ability, he makes up for in an expression of benign good nature."[5] But even Mabel could not save a weak story. *A Certain Party* closed after just twenty-four performances.

That summer Mike and Mabel took Giants pitcher Rube Marquard, who had emerged as a star, to see *The Hen Pecks* with actress Blossom Seeley at the Broadway Theater. After the show they went backstage, and Mabel introduced Rube to Blossom, who agreed to come to the Polo Grounds with Mabel to see a game.[6] A scandalous romance between the

Giants' star pitcher and the married actress soon developed, and after her divorce, they married. They also joined forces on the stage, following in the footsteps of Mike and Mabel. When Marquard would have a contract dispute with the Giants after the 1912 season, John McGraw said that he was "turning into another Mike Donlin. Mike would never have quit baseball if it hadn't been for Mabel Hite. I'm afraid Rube's dumb enough to pull the same thing."[7]

In May Mike applied to the National Commission for reinstatement. (His suspension had been based on a technicality—his failure to report.) "I haven't taken a drink in four years. . . . I feel as if I am as fast and can hit as well as ever," Donlin said. Mabel approved of Mike's decision to return to baseball: "Mickey's place is on the diamond in the summer time. He can go back on the stage, if he wants to, but not until the 1912 season."[8] While Mike was holding up his end in the act, both husband and wife realized that his baseball fame was an integral part of their drawing power.

The National Commission reinstated him on June 7, and Donlin signed with the Giants.[9] "McGraw always had a love-hate relationship with Donlin, liking him for his ability and his spirit and loathing him for the way he could drop in and out of baseball," wrote Giants historian Noel Hynd. McGraw once said, "Donlin was born on Memorial Day and has been parading around ever since."[10]

McGraw also had a love-hate relationship with the New York press. He had won over many sportswriters after building the Giants into a winner, but Heywood Broun was a significant dissenter. He found McGraw's constant arguing with umpires tedious and called him "the most fearful of all bores. . . . Very few spectators would complain if [National League] President [Thomas] Lynch suspended the tiresome little person for life."[11] By contrast, the editor of the *Sporting News* published a sympathetic editorial concerning the volatile Giants manager: "The game has advanced, and John McGraw has advanced with it. He has recently said that he would be willing to give anything—a pennant almost—if he could live down the nickname indicative of methods long since abandoned."[12]

Donlin made his long-awaited return on June 16 at St. Louis, grounding out as a pinch hitter for pitcher Bugs Raymond in the alcoholic pitcher's final game. He made two more appearances, as a pinch runner and a pinch hitter, before playing his first game before the home crowd.

The Giants played the first two games of the 1911 season in the Polo Grounds, but an overnight fire after the second game, on April 14, destroyed the grandstand. The Yankees allowed them to share Hilltop Park while the Polo Grounds was rebuilt. Only three months later, on June 28, the Polo Grounds reopened for baseball. A surprisingly small crowd of six thousand, perhaps limited by the scorching heat, saw Christy Mathewson of the first-place Giants shut out Boston, 3–0. The fans seemed to have forgotten, or forgiven, the back-and-forth bickering of the past few years between Donlin and the club. They welcomed him back as he made a grand entrance amid flower bearers in center field.

The fans got a glimpse of the old Donlin the next day. After replacing Fred Snodgrass in center field in the seventh inning, he singled in the eighth, went to second on Red Murray's single, stole third as part of a double steal, and scored on Al Bridwell's infield hit. Yet McGraw used him only sparingly.

A poem titled "Donlin's Return" appeared in some newspapers in early July:

> Time was when he fielded his job with ability—
> Time was when he peppered the pill with virility—
> But now he is listed as second utility—
> And Mike went back to the bench.[13]

At one point during the season Donlin berated *New York Times* beat reporter Harry Cross: "Don't you ever call me Turkey in your paper again," a nickname Donlin apparently hated, even though youngsters often imitated his cocky strut.[14]

Donlin appeared in thirteen games with New York, either as a pinch hitter, pinch runner, or defensive replacement. He had four hits in twelve at bats, including a home run. With an excellent young outfield of Josh Devore, Snodgrass, and Murray, McGraw had no place for the thirty-three-year-old Donlin. On August 1 McGraw sold him to the Boston Rustlers.[15]

Mike had not failed to deliver for the Giants when given the chance, which was not often. Still he was happy to leave. When he signed with the Giants, it was with the understanding he would play regularly. Yet there may have been some personal animosity in McGraw's disposing of his one-time star. They now barely spoke to one another, and that McGraw

20. A month after Mike Donlin was welcomed back to the 1911 Giants with great fanfare and ceremony, he was sold to the Boston Rustlers. Despite going from a pennant-contender to a tailender, he batted .315, including .414 the last month of the season. Dennis Goldstein Collection.

sold such a capable player in the midst of a fierce pennant race suggests McGraw had never forgiven Donlin for sitting out the 1907 season. In addition, Donlin joined new teammates Johnny Kling and Harry Stein-feldt as a candidate to replace Fred Tenney as the Rustlers' manager in 1912.[16] Nevertheless, he was going from a team in second place, one and a half games behind the Cubs, to one in last place.

Two years earlier, coming off his sensational 1908 season, Donlin had been among the game's biggest stars. If he had been sold or traded then, it would have been a major story and likely would have changed the for-tunes of the Giants and the team to which he went. But in those two years his star had dimmed. The New York and Boston newspapers, as well as those around the country, devoted little space to the news. The sale generated no great outcry among Giants fans and only muted optimism from Rustlers fans.

Mabel's fandom was directly affected by Mike's move to the lowly Rustlers. "I have decided that I am not going to take such a deep interest in the game," she said. "When Mike played his last season with the Giants in 1908, I simply rooted so much that I was almost a nervous wreck. I got so excited and fussed up that I only weighed 96 pounds, after that memorable game on the Polo Grounds. I can see the folly of rooting so much, now that he is a member of a team that is almost sure to lose more games than it wins."[17]

With Mike returning to baseball, Mabel returned to her roots, to vaudeville. In late August she appeared in *20 Minutes of Foolishness* in St. Louis. She was accompanied by only a pianist, Tom Kelly. Mabel wrote the skit herself and spent nearly $2,500 of her own money on costumes, which she changed often during the performance. One reviewer described her "of slender figure, delicate voice and much insouciance. . . . Miss Hite features her grotesque habiliments with a certain grace which cannot be defined."[18] And she was still drawing a big salary; one report estimated it at $1,000 a week.[19]

In October Mabel headlined at a Harlem vaudeville house with *20 Minutes of Foolishness*. Will Rogers was one of the other performers on the program, described as a "talker, singer, and roper," featured in a far smaller font than Mabel in the ads.[20] A bonus feature of Mabel's appearances was that Mike would join her on stage at the end of her performances, to cheers and applause from the audience, and talk about the just-concluded World Series.[21]

The Philadelphia Athletics beat the Giants in that Series, four games to two. A few months later Christy Mathewson bemoaned the fact that Donlin was not in the Giants' lineup when they faced the Athletics—not so much because of Mike's hitting but "because of his pepper-spilling qualities and the toning influence he has on his team-mates and the rattling effect he frequently has on some weak point in the opposition."[22]

Donlin made his Rustlers debut at St. Louis on August 3, batting cleanup and playing center field. The large crowd gave him a warm welcome when he batted in the second inning. He responded with a hard-hit double and, in the top of the fourth, a line single. Unfortunately for Mike and the Rustlers, heavy rains drenched Robison Field in the bottom of the fourth, and the game was called before becoming official. Mabel was at the game and greeted her husband afterward as though he had just won the World

Series. "You're back with both feet," she said, "and maybe McGraw won't [*sic*] start to thinking when he sees those two hits and run. We'll make him sorry he traded you, won't we Mickey?"[23]

Two days later Donlin made his first official appearance. After his first seven games he was hitting a microscopic .107. "The signing of Mike Donlin has not caused any great amount of enthusiasm so far," wrote Tim Murnane; "there is doubt expressed as to his ability to get into the game at the old plant, but Boston fans will withhold judgment until he proves that he has really 'come back' to the game because he means to play it, or that he is just looking for advertising."[24] None of the accounts mentioned that Mike was now thirty-three, an age at which most ballplayers' skills were eroding.

On August 11 Donlin played his first home game after five on the road and received a warm welcome from the crowd. As the season wore on, the fans in the center-field bleachers often gave him a ribbing, but he took it well. "Mike keeps up his end of the joshing, too, failing to take the testy comments of the crowd seriously."[25]

Donlin's bat finally came to life on August 17, when he had two singles and an out-of-the-park home run in the Rustlers' 12–8 win over the Cubs. Seven days later he had a three-hit game against the Cardinals, moving his batting average above .200, and from then on the trajectory of his average rose almost daily.

The long layoff had not affected Donlin's penchant for arguing with umpires. As a member of the Giants, he had been ejected by Bill Brennan on July 6 for bench-jockeying. He would add three more ejections as a Rustler. Brennan tossed him again on September 7, this time for disputing an out call at second base. Jim Johnstone, the home plate umpire, was the ejector in the other two games. The cause in both cases was Donlin's complaints over ball and strike calls, though his language included his calling Johnstone a "drunkard."[26]

Mabel was appearing in Cincinnati when the Rustlers played there in September. She said she and Mike would soon retire to their Long Island country place. They had accumulated close to $100,000, at which point Mabel said, "It's us to the easy life until the orchestra plays the exit march."[27]

The Rustlers would continue their season-long swoon and finish fifty-four games behind New York. Donlin was a rare bright light on the team. He played in fifty-six games, all in center field and mostly as the cleanup hitter. His sensational September and early October raised his season's batting average to .315. In 106 at bats between September 7 and the end of the season, he batted .406. It was one of his greatest months ever, but it went little noticed on a last-place team that won only forty-four games. During that stretch the Boston newspapers were suggesting that Donlin was biding his time with the woeful Rustlers. He was aching to show the pennant-bound Giants that he had made a full comeback from his long layoff in the hope that McGraw would bring him back to New York.

Nevertheless, Donlin had become a big favorite with the bleacher fans. A reporter for the *Sporting News* commented, "It's worth the price of admission to sit in the Boston bleachers and hear the talk that passes between Donlin and his admirers in the 25-cent section. . . . Some ball players make the mistake of trying to fight the bleacher boys. . . . I think he [Donlin] is the most popular ball player who has ever donned a Boston uniform since the days of Jimmy Collins."[28]

In late September a reporter asked Donlin if he intended to go on the stage again when the baseball season ended. His answer was definitive: "I am through with the footlights forever," he said. "I am going to stick to baseball in the future. . . . And next season will be the best that I have ever had during my career. . . . I will give all my attention to the Spring training next year, and then watch the difference both in my playing and batting."[29]

In November Mabel and Mike prepared for a pleasure trip to the West Coast. The couple spent Christmas in Hot Springs, where Mabel performed at the Princess Theater.[30] They bought a cottage that winter in Oaklawn, a residential neighborhood of the Arkansas resort town.[31] Mabel saw one she liked, and after a long negotiation told the realtor he could accept her price or lose the sale. He promptly took her check. "Mike, this little home is for you and me. No more expensive hotel bills for yours truly. . . . We must provide for the rainy day," she told her husband. "That's right, dear," Mike answered. "You have a great business head, girlie."[32]

For those who did not realize how difficult it was to combine a baseball career with a stage career, Ty Cobb's experience is worth recalling. Cobb, the game's reigning superstar, tried it following the 1911 season and decided that continuing his stage career would contribute to shortening his baseball career. "Walking on the stage every night and playing a part has been a whole lot harder on me than playing an entire game of ball," he said. "For a week I was so nervous that I thought a breakdown would come."[33]

Donlin, perhaps missing New York, had hoped to impress McGraw and did so with his strong finish. McGraw, perhaps wondering if he had given up on Donlin too quickly, added him to the Giants' roster for a postseason visit to Cuba. Each player was guaranteed $500 for the trip.[34] Mike responded by leading the Giants in batting with a .353 average.[35] He was impressed by the talent he saw on the island: "Cuba is crowded with some mighty good ballplayers. They are good naturally, but none of them know much, and that is why we beat them. You ought to see those black chaps throw. . . . The 'Black Matty' [pitcher Jose Mendez] is a wonder."[36] W. A. Phelon wrote of the dark-skinned pitcher, "We can't help thinking what a sensation Mendez would be if it was not for his color. But, alas, that is a handicap he can't outgrow."[37]

But by doing so well, Donlin may have harmed his chances of returning to New York. "Any chance that the New York Giants had of securing Mike Donlin of the Braves for next spring was stopped when the Braves' new president, John Montgomery Ward, announced that after Donlin's exhibition in the closing day of last season, together with the excellent work in performing as a member of the Giants on the Cuban trip, there is not a club that could secure him. Ward considers Donlin one of the strongest assets of the club."[38]

But Ward would reconsider. A month later he traded Donlin to Pittsburgh.

28

....

A Trade to Pittsburgh

In addition to club president John Montgomery Ward's assurance that Mike Donlin would remain in Boston in 1912, one reporter suggested he had an excellent chance of replacing Fred Tenney as the team's manager. "Mike stopped drinking and is now smart enough to be considered a managerial eligible," he wrote.[1]

Ward, the famed pitcher-infielder of the late nineteenth century, was appointed president by James E. Gaffney, who had bought the club after the death of William Russell in December 1911. Gaffney renamed the club the Braves. Shortly after the new year Ward, who was also a part owner, asked Donlin to come to Boston for a discussion about Mike's 1912 contract.

Donlin's departure from Hot Springs refueled speculation that he had gone to New York at the request of John McGraw to discuss signing a contract with the Giants. When Ward was asked if he would permit Donlin to return to New York, he replied, "Not so I can see it. We are anxious to get Boston as far away from the bottom of the league as possible, and Donlin appears to me as if he will do us more good than he will do for the Giants."[2]

While Donlin did not secure that managerial position, even new manager Johnny Kling said there was no chance he would trade Donlin to the Giants. Professions by Ward and Kling as to how important Donlin was to the Boston club began to fade when contract negotiations stalled. Donlin wanted a substantial raise while Ward was offering him his same salary.

Meanwhile, the Pirates' Vin Campbell, a promising young outfielder, was threatening to forego baseball to go into business in Pittsburgh. "It is to be hoped that Campbell will fall into line," wrote Ralph S. Davis, the sports editor at the *Pittsburgh Press*. "He is one of the speediest men in the business and a natural batsman."[3]

Gaffney and Ward wanted Campbell and offered to buy him. However, Pirates owner Barney Dreyfuss did not want money in exchange for

Campbell; he wanted Donlin.[4] While the teams continued to discuss a Donlin-for-Campbell trade, Donlin turned down a contract offer from the Braves for $5,000. The *Boston Globe*'s Tim Murnane called the offer "rather a good salary for a man passing into the 'has-been' class." Donlin would turn thirty-four early in the 1912 season but felt his play at the close of 1911 had been anything but that of a "has-been." He had made his disappointment known when Ward named Kling as manager. He considered it a big mistake and said that he was the man for the job. "I consider it a big joke to offer me any such money," Donlin said, "for I believe that I am worth more than any outfielder playing ball." Ward responded that "Boston is offering Mr. Donlin as much money as any outfielder is getting in the National League."[5] Murnane hypothesized that Donlin, disappointed at not getting the managerial position, might not give his best effort in the upcoming season, another reason why Ward might be willing to trade him for Campbell.

On February 17 Dreyfuss announced that the Pirates had traded Campbell for Donlin, "one of the real kingpins among the outer gardeners."[6] Kling, who was now much in favor of the deal, planned to play Campbell in center field. He presumed Campbell would be around for another ten or twelve years, while Donlin had only about two years left.[7] Murnane called the Campbell-Donlin trade "pleasant news to the Boston fans. . . . [Campbell] is young and coming, while Donlin must naturally be going back." And, added Murnane, Ward "was not pleased with the way Donlin acted when he talked business."[8] It is not surprising that the well-educated Ward, raised in comfortable surroundings, would have trouble negotiating with the rough-hewn Donlin.

In the view of the *Pittsburgh Post* the trade was made to add spark to the team: "The veterans of the Pittsburgh team are noted for being quiet on the field," while "Donlin belongs to the rare class of players, never beaten until the last man is out, and he should be one of [manager Fred] Clarke's most able lieutenants this year." Donlin said he was overjoyed to be in Pittsburgh: "I have always regarded Pittsburgh as a great town in which to play ball, and you can tell the fans that I will give them my best efforts."[9] He accepted Dreyfuss's salary offer without any fuss and told him to rush the contract. Perhaps after assessing his options, he signed for the same $5,000 he had rejected from Ward.

"The Pirates get a player who once was regarded as one of the three royal outfielders of the country," wrote Philadelphia sportswriter James C.

Isaminger. "Donlin is getting along in years but is a magnificent specimen of humanity and may last as long as Lajoie or Wagner. If he is as brilliant for the Pirates as he was with New York, his presence on Dreyfuss' team makes a pennant possibility out of the Corsairs."[10] Grantland Rice argued against those who thought Donlin was through. He called Donlin "one of the game's greatest natural hitters, and like Wagner, Lajoie, Delahanty, and Anson, [he] will hit around .300 as long as he is able to carry a war club up to the plate."[11]

Wagner had a combined .337 batting average in the past four seasons (1908–11), since turning thirty-four, while leading the National League in batting three of those seasons. Lajoie would have a combined average of .361, with one batting championship, in the four seasons (1909–12) after he turned thirty-four.

"I think the presence of Mike Donlin will help us a great deal," said manager Clarke. "Mike will take my old position in the outfield. . . . With Donlin on the job, I can now take things easier."[12] The veteran would also help Clarke "keep the other fellows on their toes all the time," wrote Davis. "Clarke and Mike are inseparable companions at the training camp. There is no doubt that Fred is delighted over having the star slugger on the team."[13]

Delight could not begin to describe the way Mabel felt after uniting with Mike in Hot Springs in their newly purchased home. "Gee, but it's good to see the only man you care for in the world, after being separated from him for three long weeks," she said upon arriving by train from St. Louis. The feeling of mutual love was obvious. "Mike's every look showed that he fairly worships the ground on which the fascinating Mabel Hite walks," wrote W. B. McVicker. "While his wife was talking, Mike was walking by her side, clinging to every word. This couple has any pair of turtle doves in the world backed to the wall when it comes to showing affection for each other."[14]

"You know, this is the place I met Mickey," Mabel explained. "That was just eight years ago. It doesn't seem that long, does it, dear?" she asked Mike. "I should say it doesn't. Babe," he answered, "but there are many more as happy years in store for us, I think." Mabel said she would keep an eye on Mike's eating and conditioning habits, while acknowledging he was doing a good job of that himself. "Mike isn't more than eight pounds overweight now, and under my guidance he will soon take that off. . . . Another reason for my coming here is that I need a rest very badly myself.

21. Mike Donlin was traded to the Pittsburgh Pirates before the start of the 1912 season and batted .316 at the age of thirty-four. Note how he "choked up" on his bat despite being known as a power hitter. This was a common batter's hand position during the Deadball Era. William Trefts Collection, Missouri Historical Society, St. Louis.

I have been writing for some time, and now I truly believe that I have a good vehicle [theater sketch] for the two of us next winter. Mike thinks it's great, but Mike's judgment on stage things isn't quite as good as it is on baseball. Why, do you know, Mike thinks I'm the greatest actress that ever lived, honest he does."[15]

Mabel's saying "I need a rest" suggests she was not well. She did not travel to Boston in late January, though she was booked to appear at Keith's Theatre there.[16] She said the weather was too cold in the Northeast and wanted to stay in Arkansas with her mother and husband.

At the end of March Clarke announced that his outfield for 1912 would be Owen Wilson in center, Donlin in right, and Max Carey in left. "We'll beat the Giants out of the pennant," said an optimistic Donlin a few days before the April 11 opener. April 11 was also Mike and Mabel's sixth wedding anniversary, and this was the first year the two would not be together to celebrate since Mabel had returned to the stage in late March. "Mike

22. Opening Day 1912 in St. Louis. Mike Donlin was pleased to be on a team where he could get more playing time. In seventy-seven games with the Pirates he responded with a sparkling .316 batting average. William Trefts Collection, Missouri Historical Society, St. Louis.

is unable to hide his lonesomeness," McVicker wrote. "Mike acted this morning as if he had lost his best friend. He refused to be comforted."[17]

The opener was in St. Louis, where a huge crowd greeted the new season with high hopes. The Cardinals had stayed in the 1911 pennant race until August before fading to fifth. Still, led by player-manager Roger Bresnahan, they had topped the .500 mark for the first season since 1901. Bob Harmon, a twenty-three-game winner in 1911, shut out the Pirates, 7–0, limiting them to four singles, two each by Donlin and Wagner. Mike went hitless in five at bats in Pittsburgh's next game, dropping his batting average to .250. It would be the only day of the 1912 season his average was below .300.

Mike made his home debut on April 18, an appearance that impressed McVicker for the way the fans greeted their longtime opponent: "Never before has a player on his first appearance with the team, jumped right into the warm places in the hearts of Pittsburgh fans as did one Mike Donlin." He had "no sooner reached the diamond yesterday than he waved his hand to the crowd, and from that moment the fans knew that Mike was theirs, and Donlin knew the fans were his friends."[18] The debut was cut short when he stepped on a pebble rounding first base, tearing a toe ligament. In addition, he was undergoing special electric treatment for the severe cold that had settled in his back and had proved very painful.

Clarke instructed Donlin to make the sixty-six-mile trip to Youngstown, Ohio, to see John D. "Bonesetter" Reese, the famous muscle and ligament specialist. Reese found the toe had been dislocated; he "fixed" it and told Mike not to play until the toe healed.[19] Donlin returned to Pittsburgh and later the same night left for New York to join Mabel, who was appearing in a vaudeville show in Waterbury, Connecticut.

In all Donlin missed a week, returning to the club in Cincinnati on April 28 as a pinch hitter. He also pinch-hit on May 3 at home against the Cubs. That was after he had been ejected by umpire Bill Brennan for bench-jockeying.[20] Yet neither Brennan nor Cubs manager Frank Chance objected when Clarke sent Donlin up to bat for George Gibson in the seventh inning. He drew a walk and was removed for a pinch runner.

Mabel's new show took elements from vaudeville and musicals, incorporating music, song, and dance (usually with attractive female dancers) in dazzling spectacles, often built around a story, with the Ziegfeld Follies perhaps the most famous and most lavish. *Mabel Hite and Her Clowns*, also called *The Café Cabaret*, involved at least fifteen singers and dancers. Willie Hammerstein expressed interest in the show but felt the $2,000 a week salary her agent was asking was "a trifle high."[21]

Mabel Hite and Her Clowns was a one-hour show that again blurred the lines of entertainment categories. Mabel brought the show to audiences in a refreshing and engaging way. At the end she led her cast through the theater, singing a ragtime tune and handing out party hats to the patrons. She brought her show to New York and Brooklyn in May. When Mike was in the audience one night, the cast "kidnapped" him and marched him onto the stage.[22] One reviewer called her "grotesque humor . . . the epitome of many of the best features of contemporaneous musical farces."[23] New York theater critic Vanderheyden Fyles saluted Mabel as one of the "Queens of Broadway," a leader of the new wave of cabaret shows.[24]

23. In her last role Mabel Hite headlined a 1912 revue, *Mabel Hite and Her Clowns.* Descriptions of the comedienne's performances often included the word "ridiculous" but also the word "genius." Mabel collapsed on stage in Harlem in June, and doctors discovered she had a fatal illness. Billy Rose Theatre Division, New York Public Library for the Performing Arts.

Around this time Mike and Mabel learned that their attempt to secure custody of two young children rescued from the sinking of the *Titanic* had failed. They had used their many connections in New York to request temporary custody of the children, with an intent to adopt. "I'm glad that the proper custodians of the little ones have been found, but they would have been a grand blessing to us," said Mike, who himself had been orphaned as a youngster. "Kiddies are the grandest blessings that can come to man, and had those two been bereft of parents by that terrible disaster, Mabel and I would have spent the rest of our lifetimes trying to make them happy."[25]

Donlin did not start another game until May 9. He went 3-for-4, including a double and a triple, scored two runs, and made a fine running catch in right field. The May 10 return of Honus Wagner from the injured list put the Pirates back at full strength for the first time in a week. Donlin had three hits in an 8–4 thumping of the Phillies, including a double and a triple. Two more hits against Philadelphia the next day raised his batting average to .429 for the season. The return of Donlin and Wagner and the two wins against the Phillies gave the Pirates hope that they were ready to improve on their 9-11 record as the first-place Giants (17-4) came to Forbes Field for a highly anticipated four-game series.

No player on either team awaited the Pirates-Giants series more than Donlin. A friend told Mike he wished he had saved those eight hits he had made the previous week for New York. "Gee, I got a whole collection of those bingles to uncork this week," Donlin replied. "Take it from me. . . . We'll make those Giants wish they had never seen Pittsburgh. Why, we'll eat 'em alive!"[26]

But that is far from what happened. The first two games were rained out, and the Giants won the May 14 and May 15 games, dropping Pittsburgh nine and a half games behind New York and Cincinnati. In the May 15 game Donlin's error was responsible for the winning run in the Giants' 4–3 victory. The next day the Pirates managed only four hits against Rube Marquard in losing, 4–1. It was Marquard's seventh straight win on his way to a record-setting nineteen.

No one, least of all the fans, was blaming Donlin for the Pirates' losing ways. His hitting had been the sensation of the team's play. According to Ralph Davis, "The very fans who used to roast him when he was with the Giants are now his best boosters. . . . He is the life of the outfit and does more chattering in one game than some of his mates do in a whole season."[27] But his toe continued to bother him, and he was forced to run on his heel. He had a special shoe made, and it helped somewhat.

On May 25 Clarke announced that because of his injured toe, Donlin would be unable to play in the upcoming games and sent him to New York to see a foot specialist. Donlin did not make another start until June 4 at Philadelphia. He was noticeably limping yet went 6-for-16 in the next three games.

On May 17 Mike had gotten word that his oldest brother, John, had died unexpectedly at the age of forty. The Pirates let him leave for the funeral in Cleveland, and Mike would appear in only one game the last two weeks of the month. On June 1 Mike's maternal uncle, William Cayton, passed away in Erie. Death had once again shadowed the ballplayer who had lost so many close to him when he was young.

29

....

Tragic End of a Loving Partnership

"Brittle days come to every man in the diamond game," observed a Pittsburgh writer in early June. "Veterans know the sign seldom fails. When an old boy is idle now and then disabled by whips, kicks, toes, and such like, those signals mean that back number hours are in the offing. Eventually all must obey Time's demands."[1] He was referring, as his readers recognized, to Pirates outfielder Mike Donlin while mentioning an exchange between a fan and John McGraw when the Giants were in town: "You made a bull in letting Mike go," said the fan to McGraw "Perhaps," replied McGraw, "but wait until the sun bakes the soil for about three weeks. Donlin's legs will break off at the knee."[2]

"Brittle days" did come to Donlin in 1912 but not only from the inevitable aging of an athlete's body. On June 10 Mabel collapsed on the stage during a performance at the Alhambra Theater in Harlem.[3] Thought to be suffering from appendicitis, she was rushed to Dr. William Bull's Sanatorium in Manhattan, where family doctor James T. Hunt called in prominent surgeon John F. Erdman to perform an operation the following day.[4] But when Dr. Erdman began the surgery, he quickly discovered her condition was far more serious than appendicitis. One account said he removed cancerous tissue to prolong her life.[5] Whether it was intestinal cancer, as later reports said, is not clear; this was long before the existence of CAT and MRI scans. Within a day peritonitis set in, and her physicians announced there was "very little hope for her recovery."[6]

Mike was devastated by the news and stayed at his wife's bedside though she was unconscious much of the time. The Pirates came into New York on June 14, and he was able to focus on baseball enough to tell reporters, "The Giants [37-8 and twelve games up on the Pirates] can't keep up their fast pacemaking [sic]. Marquard is the only pitcher they have, and he's bound to blow up soon.[7] We'll put the rollers under the Giants in at least two games and maybe three."[8] Pittsburgh took three of the four games though a distracted Donlin appeared in only one of them.

According to the *Pittsburgh Post-Gazette*, Mike would not have played in that one game had his wife not assured him she was improving and that he had nothing to worry about. He had a great day at the plate in a 5–4 win: four hits, including a double and a triple, to push his batting average up to .420. Mabel was delighted when word of his performance was relayed to her.[9] In twelve games against McGraw's Giants in 1912, Mike would bat .419, with a .558 slugging percentage and thirteen runs batted in.

A New York reporter faulted Mike for his slow running: "If Donlin hadn't that turkey style of transportation, he would also have had a home run and another three-bagger to his credit. . . . Any other runner except Mike would have made them both in a canter."[10]

Mabel was moved to the hospital sanatorium of Dr. John B. Walker to recuperate, if not recover. The prognosis was grim. Mike's telegram to Mabel's father in Kansas City read, "Mabel very low. . . . Be prepared for the worst at any time."[11] But there were glimmers of hope. Mike appeared in "a jubilant mood" a few days later and sent a positive message to his teammates in a June 22 telegram to Barney Dreyfuss that Fred Clarke read to the team. The message read: "Mrs. Donlin improving slowly but steadily. Have great hope now. Hope to join the boys in Chicago or sooner. Thanks for the inquiry."[12]

"The doctors tell me my wife has made a wonderful fight," Donlin said, "and while, of course, she will have to remain in the sanatorium for some days, there is every reason to believe that she is now on the mend."[13] His comments on his wife's illness ignored the doctors' assessments. Perhaps he was in denial and could not accept the looming reality. Perhaps he saw this as yet another challenge in his life he had to overcome as he had done so often in the past.

Clarke told Donlin to stay in New York and take as much time as he needed with his wife. "The ball player realizes that he owes all that he is today to the clever little woman, who changed him from a rollicking care-free sport to a man who took some interest in life other than getting rid as quickly as possible of every cent he could earn," Ralph S. Davis wrote. "Mike Donlin makes no bones about telling his friends that Mabel Hite has been a real angel to him, and he doesn't try to conceal his feelings for her. More power to the man and to the power of a good woman over him."[14]

Donlin returned to action on June 28 in Chicago. He went a combined 1-for-19 over the next six games, dropping his batting average down to .341. In early July Mabel was well enough to get away with Mike for a few days in the Adirondacks and then went home to their apartment at West Ninety-Seventh Street and Broadway.[15] Clarke did not start him in the big four-game home series against the Giants (July 17–20), thinking that rookie Ed Mensor's superior speed and defense would offset the loss of Donlin's hitting. The series was a chance for the third-place Pirates to close the gap on the league-leading New Yorkers, but they lost three of four and fell thirteen and a half games behind.

In August the Pirates made their move. They won fifteen of eighteen games and picked up five games on New York. But they were still in third place, nine games back. Included in that streak were three wins over the Giants, with Donlin going 6-for-14 with six runs batted in. He also had three hits and added several fine running catches in a 3–1 win at Brooklyn on August 13.

While Mabel was foremost on Mike's mind, he was becoming more aware that his baseball career might soon be over. On August 18 Clarke announced he was benching Donlin. Mensor would replace him in center field. "Donlin is a fine hitter, but he knows his limitations in other departments as well as I do," said Clarke. "Mike is slow, and he can't help it. He cannot cover a large amount of ground, and he cannot make speed on the bases. He is a fine emergency hitter, and it is in that role I intend to use him hereafter."[16]

The *Pittsburgh Press* offered another reason to support Clarke's move: "There is no discounting Donlin's weakness on fly balls hit in front of him. He absolutely refuses to play close to the diamond, for fear of being unable to get long flies, and for this reason is often unable to reach short flies, which go as hits whereas they would be easy picking for a man who can cover more ground."[17]

St. Louis sportswriter Ed Wray believed that Donlin would not be content as a benchwarmer and would soon retire as an active player. In looking back, Wray, who had covered Donlin during his 1899 and 1900 seasons with the Cardinals, marveled at the change in the man from the "uncouth rowdy" he had been when he broke in to "the polished, affable, clever and likable fellow" he had become. "Mike was a boozer, a bruiser and all-round champion bad actor, in his day," he wrote. Wray gave the credit for Mike's transformation to Mabel: "In five or six years the change in Donlin was so marked as to be almost unbelievable."[18]

Wray was hasty in thinking Donlin's career was over. When Mensor failed to hit, Mike returned to his starting position and remained there for the rest of the season. "Mike Donlin, by his fine work with the willow, has been a tower of strength, and toward the latter part of the season his performance in the field has been almost a revelation," wrote Pittsburgh reporter Ed F. Ballinger.[19]

From September 11 to 14 Donlin had ten hits in sixteen at bats in a four-game stretch. He finished the season with a respectable .316 batting average in seventy-seven games. However, Clarke's decision to have speed in his everyday lineup, a decision he reaffirmed near the end of the season, was an ominous sign for Mike's future in Pittsburgh.[20]

Donlin skipped the last few games to return to New York and be with Mabel. The Pirates had been out of the race since late August, trailing the Cubs and the first-place Giants. They eventually would pass Chicago to finish second, still a distant ten games behind New York.

Mabel's mother had been interested in Christian Science for a long time. As her daughter's health declined, she tried to convince her to give up the surgeons and physicians and all medicines.[21] Mabel refused but changed her mind after the doctors told her that her illness was fatal. She left the sanatorium, moved back to her apartment, and replaced the doctors and nurses with a Christian Science nurse, a Miss Sayford.

Mrs. Hite had asked Dr. Erdman if Christian Science would do any harm once traditional medicine could do no more. He later recalled what he told her: "No, go ahead. It may relieve her mind and kill the suspense. I have no doubt it buoyed her up and made the remnant of her life happy. I guess people would snatch at any hope if they thought that they were doomed. Of course, in surgical cases Christian Science cannot be expected to work a cure. Her benefit must be purely mental and moral."[22]

One summer day, Mabel recalled, her doctors told her that she had only a short time to live. "So I turned to God, just as I suppose I hope we all do," she said. "For almost two months I haven't taken any medicine, and I haven't let a doctor come near me."[23] Many converts come to Christian Science after traditional medicine offers no hope. It is grounded in the belief that prayer and thought can heal the sick more than medicine.

24. Despite her "grotesque" performances Mabel was an attractive woman who loved her husband dearly, helped him stop drinking, and paved the way for his long career as an actor. Billy Rose Theatre Division, New York Public Library for the Performing Arts.

The Christian Science aspect of Mabel's improvement made a big impression on Mike. One night Mabel seemed very low; all sensed the end was near. A woman whom none of them knew came in quietly. She sat all night at Mabel's bedside, and toward morning the patient slept soundly. For several days the woman devoted herself to Mabel, talking quietly with the sick woman. The essentials of Christian Science were explained. Mabel improved rapidly, and only one nurse (Nurse Sayford)—really what that faith calls a "practitioner"—was retained. Mike watched and listened. The change in his wife was wonderful. That was enough for him.[24] "Christian Science saved my wife's life," said Mike. "I don't know much about it, but I'm learning, and I'm for it."[25]

On September 21 the Pirates came to New York to make up a rainout game. There was a surprise fan in attendance: Mabel watched the game from her electric car, which was situated near President Brush's automobile in right field.[26] Brush, who had invited her to attend, was seriously ill himself and viewed his team's games from his vehicle nearby.[27] Mabel cheered her husband enthusiastically when he batted in the first inning, imploring him to hit a home run. She had to settle for a single as the Giants won, 2–1. Some newspapers carried a picture of her at the game, kindling hopes a remarkable recovery was at hand. The illness had left Mabel emaciated. But after the game she said she had regained her appetite and had been gaining weight and for the past two weeks had been eating her meals at table while seated in a wheelchair. She hoped that before long the wheelchair would no longer be necessary.[28]

Mike believed in his wife's improvement, if not recovery, enough to leave her and travel to the Midwest for vaudeville appearances after the baseball season. He joined the George Evans "Honey Boy Minstrels," a blackfaced band.[29]

Mabel was living with her mother at West 111th Street in Manhattan when she began to weaken suddenly early in the afternoon of October 22. Within an hour twenty-nine-year-old Mabel Hite was dead. At her bedside were her mother, Mike's sister Mame, the family physician (Dr. Hunt), and Nurse Sayford. All said that she suffered no pain, and her sudden death had been wholly unexpected.[30] Mike was in Youngstown, Ohio, about to appear on stage when word reached him that his wife was dying. He left immediately; a reporter caught up with him nervously pacing at Pittsburgh's Union Station. "I hope and pray her condition is not so serious as I fear, and that she will rally again as she so often [has done] since first afflicted," he said.[31] He arrived too late. So too did Mabel's father.

Mike's absence from his wife's bedside at the end is somewhat surprising. Their bond seemed so strong. After refusing to return to baseball in recent years at least in part because he wanted to be with Mabel and after missing much of the current season to be with her, why did he leave her now? Was he truly convinced Christian Science was curing her? Or was he unable to cope with her inevitable slide to death? Were they experiencing such financial pressures that he needed to replace her income? This lapse of love and loyalty remains puzzling.

Mabel had battled illnesses the past three years, severely limiting her career. Still she was a very popular entertainer, with fans throughout the country. "To the end," wrote the *Evening Sun* of Baltimore, "Mabel

Hite, whose cheerfulness and merry spirit had delighted thousands of theatregoers everywhere in the United States, refused to believe she was dying."[32] Funeral services were held on October 25 at the Frank Campbell Funeral Chapel, on West Twenty-Third Street, led by a Christian Science reader. Mame Donlin sat by the side of her grieving brother. An overflow crowd of hundreds stood outside.[33] Per her wishes, Mike had her body cremated.[34]

While Mabel was reported to have died of intestinal cancer, diagnoses in 1912 were rudimentary. It is more likely she died of colon cancer, which was more common among young women, or even ovarian cancer, which is hard to diagnose, even today.[35] One New York newspaper reported her June 11 surgery was for an "obstruction of the intestines."[36] But it is also possible she died of something else. Abdominal pain could also have been a symptom of abdominal tuberculosis, which was not rare in the early 1900s.[37]

In Mabel's last theater role, in *A Certain Party*, one reviewer described her unique talent: "Miss Hite is an entertainer of pronounced and unusual gifts. Her mimetic sense is extraordinary, and she has a fund of personal droileries [*sic*] which are piquantly irresistible. She is indefatigable, too, and carries the burden of the entertainment with unwavering vivacity."[38] Plaudits rolled in for the lovable entertainer from the entertainment world upon her passing. Singer and actress Cathryn Howe Palmer said, "She was immeasurably the best of all of us. I have seen them all of my own day, and . . . Mabel Hite flashed on us, with her sheer genius for grotesque fun."[39]

A reporter for the prominent trade weekly *Dramatic Mirror* wrote, "The maker of genuine laughter blesses herself and others. The eccentric young comedienne was of large, generous soul. She used to give parties to her chorus and link arms with the humble human back drops while she was starring. . . . 'A girl who has a mother and husband like mine, needn't fear anything,' she said to me."[40] Mabel's hometown newspaper, the *Kansas City Times*, wrote, "Miss Hite had pathos, too—a distinct and profound sincerity."[41]

PART 4

Mike after Mabel

30

....

Life Goes On

When he was an old man, the poet Robert Frost said he could sum up everything he had learned about life in three words: "It goes on." And so it went on for Mike. He had lost the great love of his life but found solace in returning to the stage, the alternative career Mabel had nurtured for him. As a performer he was following the theater tradition that demands "the show must go on." But now his anchor, the woman who helped him turn his life around, was gone.

Mike was back on the stage soon after the funeral. He performed in Akron, Ohio, a week later and followed with an engagement in New York. In addition to needing the income, he was better able to cope with Mabel's loss by throwing himself back into work. While her death was a devastating blow, it did not come as a sudden shock. She had been dealing with different, perhaps undiagnosed, maladies for three years.

It was a reflection of Mike's ability to bounce back from adversity that he was able to return to the stage so soon after Mabel's passing. It was also a reflection of his ability as an actor and his staying power as a celebrity that he teamed up with two of the most respected entertainers in America in the ensuing months: noted comedian Tom Lewis and his friend Charles Ellsworth Grapewin. In *The Ballplayer and the Unknown* Donlin played the straight man, reading letters on baseball, and Lewis carried the comedy with impersonations. They finished their act with the oversized Lewis sitting on Donlin's knee as the "dummy" to Mike's ventriloquist. A New York critic called the eighteen-minute sketch "a screamingly laughable and varied talking act. . . . There never was a comedian so uniformly original as Tom Lewis, nor was there ever a straight so debonairly individual as Mike Donlin."[1]

Other baseball figures were appearing on the stage that winter of 1912–13, but a Pittsburgh columnist noted that it was Donlin who had started

25. After Mabel's death Mike toured with Tom Lewis, a famous comic. One New York writer described the veteran actor as "the heavyweight funny man" who was "unexcelled as an all-around funmaker" (*New York Sun*, November 12, 1916). David Eskenazi Collection.

it all.[2] And Mike was getting more comfortable with his alternate career: "I am delighted with the actor game. . . . It is easier money than ball playing, and old age doesn't creep upon one nearly so fast as it does on the diamond."[3]

Donlin had seen and heard it before—that some team or other was considering hiring him as its next manager. Now, according to press reports in November 1912, the New York Yankees were considering him, along with Roger Bresnahan and Frank Chance, as possible successors to Harry Wolverton in 1913. The 1912 Yankees, under Wolverton, were coming off what is still their worst season ever, finishing in last place. "Everybody in baseball would like to see Mike get a job as a manager, and it is believed that a majority of the magnates would go in to help him."[4]

Before the Yankees made their selection of Frank Chance, Mike was in Pittsburgh, performing with Lewis. "Probably never before on baseball field or in a theater, has he been accorded a reception similar to that yesterday afternoon and evening," James Jerpe commented on Donlin's November 11 performances at Pittsburgh's Grand Opera Theater. He wrote that Donlin looked well and that "he is the same cheerful, rollicking Mike, and though that characteristic breeziness lacks the genuine qualities, he shows that he has borne up well under the ordeal occasioned by his recent sad bereavement."[5]

Just before Christmas, in keeping with manager Fred Clarke's desire to make his club younger and faster, the Pirates asked for waivers on Donlin. Charley "Red" Dooin, the Philadelphia Phillies' manager and part-time catcher, claimed Mike for the $1,500 waiver price. "While Donlin is far past his prime, he ought to be a big help to Dooin if he only plays the role of a pinch hitter," noted the *Philadelphia Inquirer*. "There is no more harder or feared batter in the National League than Donlin."[6]

Ralph S. Davis, who had long been a critic of Donlin's actions on and off the field, was kinder to Mike on his parting. "The passing waiver of 'Mike the Biffer' was genuinely regretted by thousands of friends Donlin made among the fans during his brief career as a Buccaneer," he wrote. "There is no belittling Mike's defects. His slowness and poor fielding were handicaps to him when he was in his prime, but they became more evident as time passed. Nevertheless, he was a hitter, par excellence, and is a hitter still. Moreover, he possessed those great qualities: ginger, aggressiveness and earnestness which endear any ball player to the fans and cause them to overlook a multitude of weaknesses."[7]

Just a few weeks earlier an article had appeared in another Pittsburgh paper that referred to Donlin's intense competitiveness: "Mike's fighting spirit came through, whatever the game and the stakes. Even when he played a card game for eighty cents, he played hard and was upset if he lost. Mike plays everything to win whether it be baseball, cards, billiards, or argument."[8]

In the early weeks of the new year an unsigned Donlin announced that his theatrical engagements would prevent him from attending spring training with the Phillies. Moreover, he was again talking of devoting all his time to his stage career. It was a familiar scenario with Mike, who insisted he had not closed the door to playing in 1913. When he was asked to name the salary he would demand, he did not hesitate in replying: "Seven thousand, and not one cent less."[9] His asking for a 40 percent increase in salary suggests that Mike was going to stay on the stage unless Philadelphia was desperate enough to meet his terms.

Donlin voiced hope that the move to Philadelphia would bring him a less traumatic season. "The year 1912 was certainly a bad luck one for me," he said. "Early in the spring I broke one of my toes. This held me back in my efforts to get a regular place in Pittsburgh's outfield. Then my brother died. Next an uncle, who had raised me, was taken ill, and he also died. Finally, my wife's illness became very grave. Every time that I had an opportunity, I jumped a train and rode to New York in order to be at her bedside."[10]

In addition to the trauma that the death of a spouse brings, there were many administrative tasks with which to deal. For example, Mike had to go to court to settle Mabel's debt of $1,700 owed to a furrier. In his defense he explained that Mabel had no estate and left neither real nor personal property.[11] The couple had made a great deal of money during the last six years and owned real estate. Where did it all go? How had they managed to dissipate all their real and personal property? Mabel's medical bills, her limited income these past three years, Mike's ongoing support of two siblings (Mame and Joe), and their Manhattan housing expenditures had cost him dearly, not only personally but also professionally and financially.

On a train from Pittsburgh to New York in December 1912, Mike had discussed his current money problems with Christy Mathewson. "I would have a lot of money today if things had not broken against me lately," he told Matty. "I had to spend $54,000 in the last two years, not foolishly, but for absolute necessities arising from ill fortune." And as if to assure his former teammate that alcohol had not contributed to his financial woes, he said, "Matty, I have not had a drink in five years but I can lay off it for five more and still have a pretty fair average, one that few fellows can tie."[12]

Donlin was touring with Grapewin and Grapewin's wife, Anna Chance, in a show called *Between Showers* in 1913. Grapewin was a respected veteran of the stage from Long Branch, New Jersey.[13] "Mr. Grapewin has a great show, and he and I enjoy working together," Donlin said. "I am anxious to make good behind the footlights, and my friends have been kind enough to say very nice things about my work on the stage. As far as baseball is concerned, I am merely a fan and always will be a loyal one."[14]

Donlin and Grapewin made an interesting pair. Grapewin was a big baseball fan who built a ballfield on his property and operated a semipro team based there. He and Mike met on Broadway and became close friends. One reporter said, "Grapewin is an actor who wishes he had been born a ball player, and Mike is a ball player who would gladly have surrendered his baseball prestige and honors for Grapewin's success before the footlights."[15] Mike played first base on Grapewin's Long Branch Nationals team that summer.

When Grapewin was asked why he hired Donlin to support him in his comedy, he said, "For the reason, that is he is as good an actor as he is a ball player. When he first went on the stage, he attracted attention simply because he was a member of the New York Giants, but he has studied hard and is today a better performer than a great many on the American stage."[16] One reviewer said, "If you did not know [Donlin] as the hero of the ball field, you would readily accept him as a decidedly clever comedian."[17]

Donlin had another advantage as a performer: his rugged good looks appealed to the women in the audience. Dolly Dalrymple, a female reporter who knew little if anything about baseball, wrote, "Mr. Donlin is a 'star' looker—real Irish type—big gray eyes, long lashes, and as courtly as a prince, and he's very kind; because what I didn't know about baseball, he didn't let worry him at all, but went serenely on his way, just as if I did. You'd never pick Mr. Donlin out for a ball player if you met him in a church choir on a Sunday morning."[18]

Donlin continued touring with Grapewin. When he arrived in New York in mid-May, he looked fit and said he had been playing ball in his leisure moments: "I think I could help the Giants in the outfield," he said with a confident smile, "for I certainly can hit the ball, and I'm not as slow as some people think. If McGraw wants me, he can pay the Philadelphia club $1,500 for my release. If not, I'll look for a job somewhere else. But I'd like to wear a Giant uniform once more."[19] Despite Donlin's success on the stage, he still had the desire to again play for McGraw and the National League champions before the adoring crowds at the Polo Grounds.

But with the Giants seemingly not interested, Donlin kept in baseball shape by performing with the Grapewin All-Stars. Grapewin lived near the Ross-Fenton Farm in New Jersey's Ocean Township, near Asbury Park and Long Branch. Actor Charles Ross and his wife, Mabel Fenton, a popular vaudeville team, bought the property in 1898 and rebuilt it after a 1902 fire.[20] The farm was also a resort, with a hotel, nightclub, and two casinos. The Ross-Fenton act was built around the comic relations between the sexes and their domestic issues, not unlike *Stealing Home*. They raised their two nieces on the farm. One was Rita Ross, born Marguerite in 1887, who worked for the Ross-Fenton musical comedy troupe and now appeared in *Between Showers* as the girl in love with Donlin's character.[21] Soon the couple had a budding real-life romance, and Mike probably stayed at the Grapewin mansion that summer, where he was able to court Rita.

In mid-October several newspapers reported the couple would be married in Chicago within a week. That city's *Inter Ocean* reported Arthur Sell, stage manager for the Ross and Fenton company, said he did not know exactly when the ceremony would take place, "but Miss Ross and Mr. Donlin will be married soon." The announcement did not go over well with Miss Ross. "I don't know who authorized Arthur to make this statement," she said. "I will not say yes or no. I do not care to discuss it. I will say, however, that Mike is a very dear friend, and I hope he has not been talking ahead of time at the other end of the line."[22]

On August 14 the Phillies, who finally had tired of waiting for Mike, released him outright. Rumors arose immediately that he would join manager Frank Chance's Yankees as a way to spark the offense and the spirit of that moribund team. Another rumor had him succeeding manager Lou Ritter of the New York State League's Elmira Colonels. When neither of those possibilities materialized, he signed to play for the Jersey City Skeeters of the International League. Donlin made his Skeeters debut on August 16, going hitless in four at bats. But playing with Grapewin's team all summer had kept his batting eye sharp (and his girlfriend Rita nearby). The next day he had a single and a double, stole two bases, and scored three runs.

Overall Mike appeared in thirty-six games for Jersey City, batting .272. At the advanced baseball age of thirty-five, he showed surprising speed, with five triples and nine stolen bases. The woeful Skeeters finished last, forty-three games behind their pennant-winning neighbors, the Newark Indians.

During the summer of 1913 Charles Comiskey, the owner of the Chicago White Sox, and John McGraw developed a plan to take their teams on a world tour. The teams would play a series of games as they traveled to the West Coast, from where they would travel to the Far East to begin the "world" part of the tour.

When the group's train left New York City, McGraw said, "It's just a little treat for the boys and it will give us a chance we may never get again to see the world."[23] He asked Donlin to join the tour, perhaps to have a drinking buddy and perhaps out of empathy for his still-bereaved and struggling former player. Recognizing his declining ability with age and reflecting his intense desire to return to baseball, Donlin was no longer driving a hard bargain. He would be taking the trip as a member of the Giants and would be on the team's payroll when he returned.[24] He left the salary issue to McGraw.

The U.S. leg of the tour began in Cincinnati on October 18 and ended in Portland, Oregon, on November 18. Donlin played golf when he could, sometimes with Mathewson. He even got himself thrown out of a game by Bill Klem in Houston. He thought Klem was kidding and let loose "blunt words" that "shocked the female patronage." But Klem was not kidding, and he would not allow the game to resume until Mike left the field.[25] Two weeks later, in a game at Oakland, Klem tossed both Donlin and McGraw after Mike came to McGraw's aid.[26]

The Giants and the White Sox each won fifteen games with one ending in a tie. The domestic portion of the trip was an artistic and financial success. The teams embarked for Japan from Victoria, British Columbia, aboard the liner *Empress of Japan*.[27] They played in numerous countries on the tour, highlighted by having audiences with Pope Pius X at the

Vatican and King George V in London, seeing the pyramids in Egypt, and being entertained by America's Cup yachtsman Sir Thomas Lipton on his tea plantation in Ceylon. In Melbourne, Australia, Donlin twisted his ankle while trying to stretch a single into a double. The injury limited his playing time for the rest of the trip.

In November a possible stumbling block to Donlin's joining the Giants in 1914 was removed when Jersey City gave him his unconditional release. When the touring ballplayers returned to the United States, McGraw told reporters that based on Mike's strong performance on the tour, he would be the best "emergency" outfielder and pinch hitter in the National League in 1914.[28] At the same time Mike would be able to fulfill his wife's wish that he return to baseball if anything were to happen to her.[29] As early as February 1912 one newspaper had reported Mabel had told Mike to get back to baseball and make another reputation for himself.[30]

31

....

Remarriage and a Final Return
to the Major Leagues

On March 6, 1914, the British liner RMS *Lusitania* arrived in a snowy New York City harbor, where the touring ballplayers were greeted by a large crowd. One New York newspaper called it "one of the noisiest ovations ever witnessed in New York City . . . no conquering warrior of the old days was ever accorded a more genuinely enthusiastic greeting upon his return."[1] Adding to the tumult was the presence of representatives from the new Federal League, who were trying to lure players from Organized Baseball with lucrative salary offers and even immediate cash for signing contracts. The war with the new league, which would drive salaries up and profits down, was on.

John McGraw was not worried about losing any of his players to the new league: "Can you imagine any player wanting to leave a championship team—an established quantity—to take a chance with such an uncertainty as the Federal League? . . . No, I cannot see any of the boys leaving the team. They are quite content to remain with a winner."[2]

The *New York World* trumpeted Donlin's return by declaring, "The Apollo of the whackstick is back with the Giants."[3] One reporter saluted his ability to bounce back from tragedy. "If it weren't for Mike Donlin's incomparable grit, his history wouldn't be worth writing."[4] As the regular season approached, syndicated columnist Grantland Rice wrote a poem that ended with, "Each dog has his day in the spinning of glory that youth makes a cinch—BUT show me a pitcher that's grinning when Michael strolls up in a pinch."[5]

Variety noted that the Giants now had two major ballplayers-entertainers, with Donlin and Rube Marquard on the team. The weekly wrote that when others heard they were in show business, they commented on one of three matters: "I'll bet you know a lot of swell dames"; "Do the actors

26. Mike Donlin joined the 1913–14 world tour at John McGraw's behest. He is seen here on the *Lusitania* returning from Europe with ballplayers (*left to right*) Sam Crawford, Tris Speaker, and Larry Doyle. Donlin first used a cane during his rehabilitation from his 1906 leg injury and incorporated it into his fashionable wardrobe. Jim Chapman and the Chapman Deadball Collection.

get sore at the critics?"; and "It's pretty soft for you guys the way you make your money."[6]

Before the Giants' home opener on April 23 the club presented Donlin with a gold-gilded bat and a glass ball. His good friend boxing announcer Joe Humphreys made the presentation. The names of two hundred of Mike's "faithful followers" were engraved on the bat, and the ball said "Welcome Home, Mike Donlin." When Rita Ross brought the bat to the Warner Brothers studio in 1936, the *Los Angeles Times* reported that among the names engraved on the bat were those of gambler Arnold Rothstein, future New York governor Al Smith, and sportsman Harry Payne Whitney.[7]

On May 26 in Chicago Donlin's three-run inside-the-park home run helped beat the Cubs, 10–7. The *New York Sun* gave a dramatic account of Mike's race around the bases, with the headline "Mike Nearly Dies

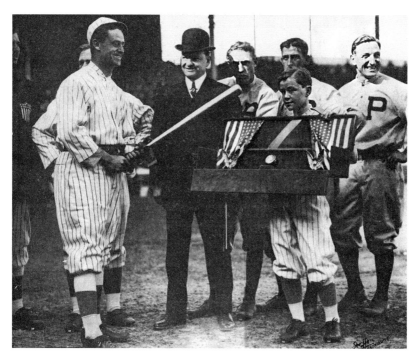

27. As in 1911, Mike Donlin's return to the New York Giants was marked by a ceremony presided over by famous boxing announcer and manager—and Donlin friend—Joe Humphreys. At the 1914 home opener Mike was awarded a gilded bat and ball with the names of two hundred of his friends engraved on the bat. National Baseball Hall of Fame Library, Cooperstown, New York.

Running Out Homer": "He was puffing and blowing as he rounded third, and he fairly staggered the remainder of the way. He tossed away his cap as excess baggage."[8]

When the Giants played an exhibition game in Mike's hometown of Erie in late May, he managed the club in McGraw's absence. In his first appearance on an Erie diamond in more than a decade, Mike's friends presented him with a walrus leather traveling bag.[9]

A Boston reporter noted that Donlin was "Muggs McGraw's right hand."[10] Yet when McGraw was suspended for five days in early August, Doyle—and not Donlin—became the acting manager.[11] (McGraw was ejected from four games in eight days.) And Mike the player was being used only sparingly. First, there were not a lot of pinch-hitting opportunities. Second, Mike was not hitting well. At the start of August he was batting .227, and his average would fall to .161 by the end of the season.[12] Like that of many thirty-six-year-old athletes, his performance had declined significantly.

Damon Runyon devoted a column to Donlin's discussing his batting slumps: "A bat has its periods of staleness, just like a person. Many a time I've had a favorite stick suddenly sour on me, until I wouldn't be able to get a foul with it. The wood apparently loses all its life temporarily, all its body and substance, as you might say. You can almost feel it grow soft and spongy and stale in your hands. Then you've got to lay it aside for a while until it sweetens up again."[13]

What had not softened was Mike's fierce temper. While he was ejected at least five times in 1914, none of the ejections came at the hands of an old nemesis, Bill Klem. Heywood Broun explained how, in a game against the Cubs, the stern-faced umpire "disarmed" Donlin without tossing him out of a game: "There seems to be something gorgon-like about Bill Klem. Under his gaze, the stoutest ballplayer turns to stone."[14] Donlin had argued, and after Klem's stare-down, went back to the bench.

Mike's fiery personality was on display even as the Giants faded from the pennant race. He was ejected from two late-season games and had another run-in with Johnny Evers, who was in his first season with the Braves. When he taunted Evers, the little second baseman shot back, "I have been in a few more world's series than you."[15] In another clash between the two men that year, when Evers was called out on strikes, Donlin shouted, "What was [sic] you waiting for?" The quick-witted Evers replied, "I wasn't waiting for the first and fifteenth of the month so as to get rent money, anyway."[16]

In October the Giants and the Yankees met in a postseason City Series for the championship of New York, only the second (and what would be the final) time they met in such a series. In his only appearance and his final at bat against a Major League team, Donlin's pinch-hit triple scored two runs in the 6–5 win in the third game.[17] When Donlin got his unconditional release from the Giants in December, one sportswriter noted his passing by saluting "one of the most picturesque, most written about, and most likable athletes that ever cut his mark on the big circuit."[18]

Heywood Broun put it this way: "As a player Mike's loss means little now; as a personality much. His departure will rob the game here of color, both local and linguistic. To see Mike on the Polo Grounds, striding away from an umpire, was to get the impression that the man was a consummate

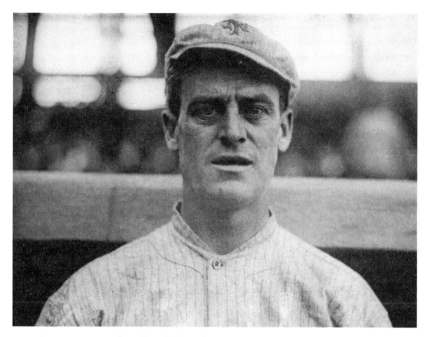

28. After a year away from baseball Mike Donlin made yet another comeback, with the 1914 New York Giants. John McGraw brought him back in part because of Mike's hitting on the recently concluded world tour and in part because McGraw wanted to help him after the death of his wife. But at age thirty-six, the magic was gone from his bat. In thirty-one at bats Mike hit only .161. Andrew Aronstein Collection.

actor. Yet in vaudeville Donlin was every inch a ball player. Once a truly great outfielder, Mike has tarried in the big leagues long beyond the days of his playing worth."[19]

Stories surfaced during the summer that Donlin wanted to be released so he could land a Minor League managerial position.[20] Nothing materialized from such reports. When Yankees manager Frank Chance quit in frustration before the end of the season, there were reports that Donlin might take over the club.[21] But Harry Cole, writing in *Sporting Life*, poked fun at the stream of unsubstantiated rumors: "We have positive assurances from at least a score of sources that the 1915 leader [of the Yankees] will be Mike Donlin, Heinie Wagner, Charley Herzog, or somebody else. Even [Giants mascot] Charley Faust has emphatically denied he ever refused the management of the New York team."[22] Nothing came of the rumors; the Yankees would hire former Detroit Tigers star pitcher Bill Donovan.

Then came reports that Mike would manage the Venice, California, Pacific Coast League (PCL) team.[23] Once again nothing came of these accounts. He was also said to have turned down the job as manager of the San Francisco Seals because "San Francisco is too far from New York" and "Mike has several irons in the fire and will remain closer to Broadway."[24] Still *St. Louis Star* sports editor Billy Murphy wrote in December, "Among newspaper men, Donlin is known as one of the most appreciative ball players in the game. . . . There is still a good future for him as coach or manager."[25]

But like many ballplayers who have a hard time accepting that their playing careers had come to an end, Mike felt he could still compete. And the Federal League, which would conduct its second Major League season in 1915, seemed to be a good place to continue since the level of play there was a step below that of the established Major Leagues. "I'm not through by a long way," said Mike. "They have mighty few southpaws in that league, and I'll bet a suit of clothes I can get into the .350 circle with the Feds."[26] Donlin made overtures to both Phil Ball, owner of the St. Louis Terriers, and James Gilmore, the league's president.[27] But no offer came from any Federal League team.

Following a two-year courtship, Mike Donlin and Rita Ross were married in the Catholic Church of the Holy Spirit in Asbury Park on October 20, 1914. Actor Fred Mace, who appeared in more than 150 films between 1909 and 1916, was his best man. Rita's sister Blanche was the bridesmaid. Rube Marquard and his wife, Blossom Seeley, were among the three hundred guests. After the wedding they held a reception at Price's Hotel in Long Branch, with John McGraw in attendance. The couple planned to reside in the Bristol Hotel in Manhattan.[28]

Will Rogers wrote of Donlin almost twenty years later, "He was tremendously fortunate in his next marriage. A girl much younger, beautiful girl. Daughter [*sic*; Rita was a niece] of one of the stage's shining lights of their day, a great vaudeville team, Ross and Fenton."[29]

Time can be a great healer of tragedy. Yet in Donlin's case the death of his first wife came back to haunt him just a few weeks after his marriage to Rita. The incident was almost comical, had it not revolved around Mabel's remains. Her ashes had remained at the Campbell Funeral Home because Mike had not designated a final repository.[30] When that company was moving uptown to a new location, the employee transporting her ashes stopped for dinner with his wife at Murray's restaurant in Times Square, one of Manhattan's most famous eateries. When he gave the coatroom boy the box containing the urn, to ensure better handling, he said, "Don't drop this package; if you do, it's liable to blow your head off."[31]

The coatroom employee notified the manager, who saw wire extruding from the box, feared it might be a bomb, and submerged it in a pail of water. The police and the Bureau of Combustibles were notified, and once the contents were identified, the wet package was returned to the Campbell's employee. Donlin sued him in a case one New York newspaper called "one of the most grewsome [*sic*] cases." Donlin testified, "I don't want to sue anybody, but when someone tampers with something that is sacred to me, I can't stand for that."[32] The case was dismissed.[33]

In November Donlin returned to the stage in a vaudeville routine with Yankees pitcher Marty McHale. McHale had been a member of a singing quartet when he was on the Boston Red Sox in 1910–11. When he was interviewed by baseball historian Lawrence Ritter in the early 1960s, McHale said, "Now, you may not remember Mike, but he was—well, he was the Babe Ruth of his day."[34] McHale told Ritter they performed together for five years and recalled they did a song, "When You're a Long, Long Way from Home," after which they would explain, "When you're on third base alone, you're still a long, long way from home."[35] After World War I McHale wrote Saturday sports columns for the *New York Evening Sun* and drew on "inside information" that Donlin gave him.

Donlin and McHale opened in New York's Palace Theatre, which was becoming the flagship showcase of vaudeville. In December *Variety* called the Palace "the greatest vaudeville theater in America, if not the world."[36] Mike and Marty then headed out on the Keith-Albee circuit, which controlled theaters across the country and booked only first-line acts.[37] In St. Louis, just before Christmas, they followed "[Harry] Houdini, the handcuff king" at the Columbia theater.[38]

Variety gave the Donlin-McHale show positive reviews: "Mr. Donlin has greatly improved as a vaudevillian. He slips over dialog like a veteran. Mr. McHale needs to get a bit more easy in his bearing, but this will come with a few more appearances. The two work well together."[39] A week later a different *Variety* critic went into more detail: "Mike Donlin and Marty

McHale are a bit beyond the freak classification, despite that another profession is responsible for their vaudeville appearance. McHale has a corking good voice, delivers a song with the best, and looks good. Mike fits in perfectly, reputation notwithstanding, and with a neatly constructed routine of talk and numbers, they present one of the best baseball specialties of this or other seasons. They were a popular hit, but beyond sentimentality, their effort deserves a great section of the reception tendered them."[40]

Their tour continued into 1915, until McHale reported to spring training with the Yankees. Later in the year Donlin teamed up with blackface actor Ben Deeley in a skit called "The Right Hitter and the Hit Writer," what one reviewer called "a merry dialogue of repartee" and "a snappy comedy act."[41]

Mike still wanted to remain in the game he loved. In early 1915, with no managerial offer forthcoming, he became a more active campaigner for a Minor League position, and there was almost a sense of desperation to his search. "I'm foot-free and consider myself a candidate for the job of playing manager in any minor company," he said in February.[42] His friends were "plugging" him for vacancies in the International League. A month later he wired the owner of his hometown Erie club for a position.[43] With no job offer in sight, in April Donlin assisted former pitcher Andy Coakley to coach the Columbia University team.[44]

Mike then assembled Donlin's All-Stars, a club that played weekend games against semipro teams, including Black teams, that spring and summer. Donlin's club did not have any stars other than Coakley, his starting pitcher. He spoke highly of Coakley, who "has everything that he ever had and knows exactly how to use it. But he must have at least six days' rest between times."[45]

On April 25 Donlin got two hits off "Cyclone" Joe Williams and the Lincoln Giants, but his All-Stars lost, 1–0.[46] In June his team faced another talented black pitcher, Dick "Cannonball" Redding. Again Donlin got two hits, but again his team was beaten.[47] These games did not generate big gates. *Variety* reported that Donlin's team received $180 when it beat the Cuban Giants in June.[48]

It must have been difficult, if not humiliating, for the proud former star to be so insignificant in the baseball world. In July a San Francisco newspaper headline announced, "Mike Donlin a Busher; [Weekly] Salary Limit Is $90." When the semipro Lehigh Valley League was formed, Donlin was hired to manage the Phillipsburg team, and Coakley the Easton one.[49] But he continued with his All-Stars, who were back in the news when Redding again beat them, for his twentieth win in his past twenty-one games.[50]

It is understandable that teams were not interested in a ballplayer who turned thirty-seven in March 1915. But Donlin's inability to land even a low Minor League managerial job is more puzzling. James Jerpe addressed this subject later that year: "The wonder of it all is that so few opportunities have presented themselves to Mike Donlin in recent years. A great ball player in his day, smart fellow and a likeable character, the former biffer would seem to be the ideal man for a manager in major or minor. . . . Donlin should have a standard value with some strong club somewhere. Picturesque managers are passing, and a pepper-box like Donlin ought to prove valuable somewhere."[51]

A few explanations can be considered. Mike was often unable to control his temper during a game, when he was driven by an intense desire to win. He was also aggressive with his salary demands, though they may have diminished as time away from stardom went on. Finally, after Mabel's death, Mike may have returned to drinking.

On a train from Pittsburgh to New York shortly after Mabel died, Donlin encountered Giants pitcher Christy Mathewson. "Matty, I have not had a drink in five years," he told his former teammate, "but I can lay off it for five more and still have a pretty fair average, one that few fellows can tie."[52] But perhaps he could not.

While there were no reports in the press of drunken binges or arrests, Donlin was no longer a star, and such reports were no longer good copy. After 1912 there were references to and hints of his drinking, if not specific incidents. Consider just two. After writing years later about how fortunate Mike was to have found and married Rita, Will Rogers continued: "She stuck with Mike through many ups and downs, and an awful lot of downs among the few ups."[53] Sid Grauman opened his Chinese Theatre in Hollywood in 1927, and his movie house website features Donlin among its many personalities. His biography notes that after his baseball career, "Donlin's alcohol use was getting the better of him."[54]

32

....

Mike Enters the New World
of Motion Pictures

Moving picture photography emerged as early as the 1890s. Thomas Edison, in 1895, explained that his interest in this new technology was "to devise an instrument which should do for the eye what the phonograph does for the ear."[1] The first rudimentary motion pictures appeared in New York amusement arcades. "People were amazed by even mundane images— because they were moving."[2] Though the kinetoscope ("peep hole") could play for only one customer at a time, it alerted inventors and investors to the commercial potential of moving pictures. Now the focus shifted to creating a projector that would allow for longer lengths of films.

While early projected movies (1895–1905) appeared mostly in penny arcades and traveling shows, they also found a home in vaudeville as one more novelty act. *Variety* reminded patrons that if they stayed for the moving pictures at the end of the shows, they would see "some real excitement." The magazine predicted "the picture machine is here to stay."[3] The weekly was assuming film would remain an adjunct to vaudeville and did not foresee that the former would eventually hasten the death of the latter. *Theatre* magazine had a more realistic view of the rising threat to the entertainment form it covered. In October 1908 it wrote, "The scientific brains are at work improving it [the kinetoscope], so that the slightest facial expression may soon be caught. . . . The [theater] actor has a for-midable rival in the kinetoscope."[4] Less than five years later the periodical was lamenting the "feverish leaps and bounds" by which moving pictures were rising in popularity.[5]

By 1910 films were longer than a minute or two in length, and stories could be introduced and developed. (Even vaudeville sketches, which ran fifteen to twenty minutes in length, could not build plots and characters the way films could.) Drama and emotion could be conveyed. Nickelodeons gave the budding industry a home for this new entertainment. The synergy of rising attendance and more theaters fueled "nickel madness," a growth that seemed inconceivable a few years earlier.[6]

Many of the motion picture theaters were former vaudeville houses. Who could blame managers for booking such "automatic vaudeville"?[7] Movies did not argue about conditions or get sick, and they were easy to move from one theater to another. Films of longer length meant less turnover of patrons each day, a development that led to the building of bigger and more lavish theaters. When the Strand Theatre, dedicated to movies, opened in Times Square in 1914, with a capacity of three thousand, *Moving Picture World* described the prosperous-looking patrons as an "animated edition of 'Who's Who in Society.'"[8] Vaudeville was also feeling the impact of another rising competitor, lavish Broadway revues, exemplified by Florenz Ziegfeld's *Follies*. These shows raided vaudeville of talent, and performers who moved on to this new entertainment earned better pay and working conditions.[9]

Vaudeville and film had now come full circle: competing movie theaters often added vaudeville acts to their showing of films to boost attendance. But motion pictures had limitations. Unlike the stage, they could not utilize dialogue. They could not talk. Not yet.

In the years 1913–19 film companies began leaving the East Coast for southern California, where property was cheap, locales were exotic (desert and ocean), sunlight was plentiful, and unions were not. Actors were no longer nameless, and the industry's "star system" began to emerge.[10] Universal Film Company bought a 230-acre ranch in Los Angeles in 1914, and the city of Hollywood was quickly becoming the nation's film capital. The devastation caused by World War I in Europe helped Hollywood gain worldwide ascendancy. In 1925 screenwriter Herman Mankiewicz made his first visit to Hollywood and telegraphed his friend, journalist and playwright Ben Hecht, "Millions to be grabbed out here, and your only competition is idiots. Don't let this get around."[11]

Early attempts to synch sight and sound were primitive. Some attempts took existing phonograph records and then had performers "faking" the dialogue. An editorial in *Moving Picture World* in March 1909 stated, "We have no hesitation in prophesying that before long, hardly a moving picture theatre in the country will be without the talking or singing phonograph as part of its entertainment."[12] But it would be two decades before Warner

Brothers' strong capitalization and Vitaphone's standardization of synching for audio and video brought sound films to the masses.[13]

Major studios did not pursue "talkies" at first; they already had a profitable business with silent films. William Fox of Fox Film Corporation said, "I don't think that there will ever be the much-dreamed-of talking pictures on a big scale. To have conversation would strain the eyesight and the sense of hearing at once, taking away the restfulness one gets from viewing pictures alone."[14] James Quick argued in *Photoplay* in the mid-1920s for the beauty and importance of silence: "The value of silence in art is its stimulation to the imagination. . . . The talking picture will be made practical, but it will never supercede [*sic*] the motion picture without sound. It will lack the subtlety and suggestion of vision—that vision which, deprived of voice, to ears of flesh, intones undisturbed symphonies of the soul."[15]

Film, as best represented by star Charlie Chaplin, was a mime art. Sound would change it to a theatrical art. With the rise and spread of radio in the 1920s (which trained listeners to the sound of dialogue), film needed a novelty. Sam Warner and his brothers took the financial risk in 1926 when they were offered the Vitaphone sound system, synchronized sound on phonograph records with video on film projectors, which quickly paid off after they produced *The Jazz Singer* with Al Jolson in 1927. Films could now be synched with sound, but this required many changes in the production process. By 1928 Hollywood had $300 million of financing from Wall Street banks for "the sound revolution that nothing could stop."[16]

Lloyd Morris wrote of the personal tragedies that resulted from that dramatic change. It ended the careers of "visually lovely girls who talked through their noses, silent heroines with adenoids or squeaky, tinny voices . . . [and] splendid young heroes whose enunciation was lingual goulash."[17] Jeanine Basinger explained that the voices of the actors and actresses of those silent films "had already been 'heard' in the heads of the moviegoing public who had met them in the silence. . . . To hear them speak without the voices that had been mentally supplied for them wasn't acceptable."[18]

Many movies of that era have not survived to the modern day since cellulose nitrate film was very unstable and deteriorated over time.[19] Many films were simply discarded. They were not considered works of art, and once they finished their theater runs, they were viewed as no more valuable than old newspapers. Even if there had been a demand by collectors among the growing number of fans, there was no way to market the films.

John Barrymore, whose stage performances were legendary (most famous was his *Hamlet* in 1922–23), made a dozen movies between 1914 and 1919. With the emergence of sound on film in the late 1920s, Vitaphone promoted his first "talkie," *General Crack*. "John Barrymore[:] Yesterday a speechless shadow," read the ad. "Today a vivid, living person—thanks to Vitaphone. Until you've heard him in 'General Crack,' you can but guess at the full force of the flaming personality that is the *real* John Barrymore."[20]

Mike Donlin was searching for income streams after his baseball-playing career had come to an end. It is not surprising that film would be an option he would pursue. When columnist Hype Igoe looked back at Mike's life in 1945, he headlined his article "Donlin Own Press Agent in Turkey Trot to Top." Donlin's first opportunity in movies would be a showcase for his outsized personality and enduring popularity.[21]

In the early summer of 1915 *Variety* wrote that Mike Donlin would appear in a film about his life in which Donlin, "undoubtedly the best known and most popular ball player in the world, will be pictured from infancy to manhood."[22] *Moving Picture World* referred to him as the "famous son of Swat."[23] The five-reeler was shot in Winsted, Connecticut, in the Berkshires, for a cost of $20,000. It was coupled with a one-reel prologue of his baseball career.

Donlin had appeared in a movie years earlier, one with sound, though it was a primitive precursor of the motion pictures that followed and the talkies of the late 1920s. With Cameraphone technology *Stealing Home* was filmed and synchronized with sound back in 1908. When Mike was appearing in Joseph von Sternberg's *Thunderbolt* in 1929, a cast member recalled that when he was a child, he saw Donlin in that movie. Actor Robert Elliott, then a young baseball fan with theatrical ambitions, said he saw that 1908 baseball movie every day and knew the dialogue by heart. Donlin then explained that he and Mabel did their songs and dances and read their lines for the phonograph records, with no cameras rolling.[24] After they practiced their actions to perfect the timing, the cameras filmed them, and the audio and video were synched.

After the traveling ballplayers returned from their world tour, Donlin and former teammate Larry Doyle appeared in the tenth segment of *Our*

Mutual Girl. This weekly series ran from early 1914 to early 1915, with fifty-two one-reel episodes in which actress Norma Phillips outwitted villains, saw New York's sites, and met celebrities who made cameo appearances. Donlin was also in a documentary film about the 1913–14 world tour. Like *Right Off the Bat* and so many other early twentieth-century movies, it has not survived.

In *Right Off the Bat* a young Donlin saves his sweetheart, Viola, from drowning when her canoe almost goes over a dam. After his father's death Mike supports his mother and gets a job as a machinist for the company owned by Viola's father and stars on the firm's baseball team. But her parents do not approve of her marrying such a lower-class man. Mike saves Viola a second time when a horse leading her carriage bolts. He joins the Connecticut League's Winsted team, which is in a fierce race for the pennant. After he refuses a request to "throw" the championship game, the gambler (who first tries, unsuccessfully, to get Mike drunk) kidnaps him, but Viola helps Mike escape. He gets to the ballpark late in the penultimate game and hits a triple to tie the score. He then steals home to give Winsted the title, and a New York Giants scout (played by John McGraw) signs him to the Major League club. Mike is then welcomed into Viola's family and gets his sweetheart at the end.

As was often the case with biopics, the story had little similarity to Mike's actual life. A *Sporting Life* reporter noted that the story was "made over by an imaginative director."[25] Viola was not at all like Mabel Hite, Mike's drinking and temper were not covered, and Winsted in the Berkshires was not Erie. Mike's wife, Rita, had a small role, and a *Variety* critic suggested she would have made a better Viola since she was so full of "pep." That reviewer hailed Mike's performance: "Mike was a distinct surprise, and contrary to custom, could pass as a film lead on ability alone . . . displaying emotion, joy, and disappointment with a perfected ease that even suggests a sequel to his early life."[26]

The film was significant for many reasons. It was the first feature-length baseball film and began the messaging that players of the national pastime were model citizens in a growing industrial society. As Marshall Most presented in a Cooperstown Symposium, "The relationship of baseball and film was not just synchronous, it was symbiotic as well. Even as baseball constructed and promoted its ideology of an ideal game for an exceptional American nation, the emerging medium of moving pictures

29. Mike Donlin starred in a 1915 movie, *Right Off the Bat*, the first baseball biopic, which took liberties with his life story. Though he was a few years past baseball stardom, *Variety* called him "undoubtedly the best known and most popular ball player in the world" (July 16, 1915). CineMaterial.

became perhaps its most ardent proponent."[27] The film also was revealing about the danger to the game from gambling, four years before the Black Sox scandal of the 1919 World Series. The script suggests that the "ideal game" could be (and likely was) compromised by a very different relationship.

The movie had "situations which will tug at the heartstrings of all who have had to fight the daily struggle . . . a pleasing combination of comedy, melodrama, and romance," wrote *Moving Picture World*.[28] In his paper on prototypical baseball films author Robert Repici noted that they emphasized "veracity, tenacity, and morality" as means to attaining "social mobility and personal meaning."[29] Baseball was the national pastime, and its stars were legitimate national heroes, long before the age of celebrities, the 1920s. While mythology has two kinds of heroes, the "good guy" and the "outlaw" or "bad boy," in this movie Mike is the former, even though early in real life (before Mabel) he was the latter.

33
....

Memphis Blues

In January 1916 Mike Donlin played and lost a publicized billiard match at Doyle's pool hall in Manhattan against Yankees manager Bill Donovan. One newspaper wrote, "With the possible exception of Johnny Kling, these two are probably the most expert three-cushion players who ever performed in big league baseball."[1] Shortly thereafter Honus Wagner's serialized biography appeared and included a chapter titled "Hard Losers," in which he featured Donlin and Johnny Evers. Wagner noted that while Donlin fought intensely and was a hard loser even in a card game with minimal stakes, he would take the other players out to dinner after he lost.[2]

Meanwhile, Mike's money woes continued. The Baseball Hall of Fame Library in Cooperstown, New York, has a 1916 letter on a Fenton-Ross Farm letterhead in which he writes to someone named Joe, asking for a loan of $100: "I was all in financially. . . . Do what you can for me as I am broke at present." Donlin offers to handle the Long Branch baseball grounds on Sundays in return and says he has "a couple of things in sight and could hand it back this summer."

Donlin was once again reportedly being considered for a Minor League managerial job. Early in the year the Newark and Rochester clubs of the International League were mentioned.[3] During the summer he was said to be in line for the position with the Columbus, Ohio, American Association team, based on John McGraw's recommendation, and then for the Wilkes-Barre New York State League team.[4] As had happened so often, all these reports came to naught. Donlin again managed (and played first base for) his semipro team in Long Branch. It played at the Horse Show Grounds, where a grandstand was erected. John McGraw brought his New York Giants there for the semipro league opener, and a couple of weeks later the Giants returned for another game.[5] The league's games were played on Sundays, and Donlin and his pitcher, Andy Coakley, were in the news in July when they were arrested and fined one dollar each for violating the New Jersey Blue Law. The source of the complaint was a local theater owner who felt his entertainment should not be the only spectator recreation shut down on Sundays.[6]

The Jersey shore was a popular summer resort; President Woodrow Wilson made Long Branch his summer home. In early July five people were attacked by sharks; four of them died. The incidents set off a nationwide panic and devastated tourism along the coastline.[7]

After the baseball season ended, Donlin and Marty McHale again teamed up and appeared in a new sketch at the Palace in New York. Their appearances were combined with silent movie shorts, often starring Charlie Chaplin. The films, about thirty minutes long, added to the appeal of a theater's combination entertainment: live sketches and cutting-edge moving pictures.

Late in 1916 Donlin parlayed his love of boxing and his connections to many top fighters into a promotional role with millionaire Grant Hugh Brown. The wealthy sportsman had built a thoroughbred racetrack, ballpark, and arena in Havana, Cuba, and turned to Donlin to arrange a big fight there. Mike wanted to bring together Freddie Welsh, the world's lightweight champion, and Johnny Kilbane, the featherweight titleholder, for a forty-round match.[8] He also approached Australian sensation Les Darcy, that nation's middleweight and heavyweight champion, who had just turned twenty-one.[9] But he was unable to bring any of these bouts to fruition.

Donlin's matchmaking efforts had been unproductive, but as John McGraw's widow Blanche wrote, "Mike had become a promoter of sorts, and suddenly emerged with a barnstorming scheme. He lined up several players from National League teams other than the Giants for a trip to Cuba. He completed his barnstorming group with all the young Giant players John wanted to see."[10] McGraw was in Cuba at the time and had Donlin send the ones who looked promising to New York's training site in Marlin, Texas.

Mike also achieved a goal that had long eluded him. In that first week of the new year he signed to manage (and play for) the Memphis Chicks of the Southern League for the 1917 season.[11] He was highly recommended by several big leaguers and was given a special boost by McGraw, his former manager.[12] Mike's new position would not interfere with his Cuban barnstorming plan. The traveling party included McGraw, Hughie Jennings, and Christy Mathewson.

"How do you like the idea of going to the minors?" Mike was asked after agreeing to the Memphis position. "Like it?" he said. "I'm tickled to death. The greatest opportunity in baseball lies in the minor leagues. It is the acid test for any fellow who wants to become a manager. I have many ideas that I want to work out, and I confidently believe they will go a long way toward helping me pilot Memphis into a championship."[13] Donlin also had the backing of columnist Damon Runyon. "We had always been of the opinion that the old-time slugger would make a good manager," Runyon wrote. "He was the beau ideal of the big league ball player with the fans on down to the very day that he turned in his uniform for the last time."[14]

Long an admirer of Donlin, Runyon had witnessed him progress from a hard-drinking, brawling youngster into a polished man about town. He concluded one column on Mike with the following little yarn:

He was a great dresser in his baseball days, with a weakness for all the fancy sartorial doo-dads of the hour. One day when he was with the Boston club he ran into Sid Mercer, the New York baseball writer, in the lobby of a Philadelphia hotel, and Sid noted that Michael was a plate of fashion. He wore a carefully tailored suit of gray; his haberdashery was just so; his hair was combed back in a long sweep from his alabaster brow in the very latest college boy fashion, and in one hand he twirled a nifty little bamboo stick. "Say, Mike," said Sid, who remembered the slugger from Michael's rough-house era, "what would you have done a few years ago if you had met a guy made up the way you are?" Mike blushed slightly, then went over to a mirror and carefully surveyed himself. Then he came back to report. "Sid," he said, earnestly, "I'd a-busted him right in the nose."[15]

Of course neither being a "great dresser" nor "the beau ideal of the big league ball player" were indications of managerial success. The *Chattanooga Times* pointed to another McGraw protégé, Moose McCormick, who was let go in his second season as manager of the local club, the Lookouts, also in the Southern Association. "McCormick knew baseball if given long enough time to think it out but had little or no fighting spirit. He knew nothing about how to play 'according to the book' and lacked totally in resourcefulness to meet critical situations. He knew the McGraw theory thoroughly but he couldn't apply it." Critics, the paper reported, were saying that Donlin was much like McCormick in that he had secured his job strictly on his slugging ability: "He is a quicker thinker than McCormick, but be lacks the latter's evenness of temper and splendid habits."[16]

When Donlin arrived in Memphis in February, he confirmed that he would be a playing manager and expected to play first base. He believed that being in the game, and particularly in the infield, would make him more valuable to the team. He could play full time, alternate with another first baseman, or be strictly a pinch hitter. The *Chattanooga Times* wondered if his two years away may have set Mike back further than he thought.[17]

In addition to winning games, Minor League managers were expected to aid in the development of young players. Donlin would have one in particular that baseball people would be watching: pitcher Waite Hoyt. "Today I looked over one of the most remarkable, if not the most remarkable boys who has ever broken into baseball, Wade [*sic*] Hoyt, of Brooklyn," reported Knoxville sportswriter Paul Purman from the Giants' training site in Marlin. "Old-time players . . . I talked to are enthusiastic about Hoyt. He is only 17, the youngest ballplayer ever taken seriously by a major league ball club." Purman added that "Hoyt would be sent to Memphis where Mike Donlin, an old Giant, will look after him."[18] Hoyt lacked only "experience in shrewd baseball company," wrote H. C. Hamilton of the *Buffalo Times*: "In going to Mike Donlin, he is accepting service under a tutor who knows all the ins and outs and the dark corners in the national pastime."[19]

As the league's only new manager, Donlin was cautious in making a prediction for the upcoming season. "Not being familiar with the strength of the Southern League, I am unable to make a statement," he said, "but I am very much pleased with my club and look for a big season."[20]

Donlin was not in the lineup for Memphis's opener, a 3–2 loss at Little Rock in which Hoyt pitched a complete game. He got his first managerial win the next day and his first ejection in the team's fifth game. Umpire Charlie Moran threw him out for arguing too vigorously when a New Orleans runner was called safe at home. In the following game Mike put himself in the lineup for the first time—not at first base but as the center fielder.[21] He batted leadoff and was hitless in three at bats.

After watching the Chicks get off to a mediocre 3-4 start, a reporter for the *Chattanooga News* claimed to know the source of the problem: "The trouble with the Chicks is an ailment which was also anticipated during the training season—Mike Donlin has underestimated the strength of the Southern League."[22]

Meanwhile, on the other side of the state of Tennessee, in Chattanooga, the fiery Kid Elberfeld was back as the manager of the Lookouts. "Fiery" is a kind word. Elberfeld has been called "the dirtiest, scrappiest, most pestiferous, most rantankerous [*sic*], most rambunctious ball player that ever stood on spikes" for his vicious arguments on the field.[23] After one over-the-top outburst in a game against the Birmingham Barons at Rickwood Field, league president Robert H. Baugh fined Elberfeld $15. Elberfeld refused to pay. "What President Baugh wants in this league," said the Kid "is a ladylike game of parlor golf instead of a real man's game of baseball with fight and pep in it."[24] Not to be outdone, Donlin continued being Donlin, and it led to several confrontations of his own with umpires. "Rowdy tactics in the Southern League must be brought to a halt," Baugh said, "and if Donlin and Elberfeld insist on staging the rough stuff, they will be banished from the league. . . . I am astonished that Donlin should employ such methods in that he is just breaking into this league."[25] Baugh wrote scorching letters to both managers, telling them that their umpire-baiting must cease.

Memphis continued to play at a .500 level (22-22) before dropping below that mark in a mud-soaked home loss to Birmingham on May 27. Heavy rains had turned the Russwood Park basepaths into a quagmire by the fifth inning, when the umpires halted play. But after a wait of thirty minutes and despite seemingly unplayable conditions, they decided the game should continue. Many years later Waite Hoyt recalled that rainy Sunday afternoon in Memphis. "Donlin's best pitcher [Roy Fentress] was out there, but despite the rain the umpires would not call the game," he told author Eugene Murdock. "So, Mike called his best pitcher out of there. And to show up the umpires, he went in and pitched. . . . The stands were very close, and Mike was a profane guy, and he had a profane argument with one of the umpires, and he was let go the next day."[26]

Donlin was surely under a terrific strain at the time. He had already lost the best man at his second wedding, actor Fred Mace, in February. Mace was found dead in his New York City hotel room at age thirty-eight.

Then came a double loss days before the rain-soaked game in which he had acted out. His maternal aunt, Julia Cayton, passed away in Erie, and on May 24 his friend, boxer Les Darcy, died from septicemia and subsequent pneumonia. Darcy was in Memphis, where he was scheduled to fight, and Donlin likely visited with the young man he had befriended in Australia on the world tour as his health declined.

As Hoyt remembered, Mike was indeed gone the day following his farcical May 27 performance. Either he resigned or was fired, with the evidence strongly pointing to the latter. The *Nashville Banner* wrote that Donlin had "resigned owing to illness in his family in New York" and that pitcher Cy Barger would replace him.[27] The illness, and it was a serious one, was that of his wife's uncle, Charles Ross, who had raised her. Ross had had his spleen removed, a very delicate operation. He survived and left the hospital on August 1 but died the following June.[28] However, the "resignation" followed a storm of protests filed with the team over Donlin's actions in the previous day's game.

Within two weeks it was clear Donlin had lost favor with the Memphis owners and had been summarily dismissed. Donlin, no stranger to the legal system, filed suit against the Memphis Baseball Association, seeking to recover the remainder of the salary called for by his contract. Donlin's contractual salary for the year was for $3,000, and he was asking for $1,600.[29]

"A managerial berth in the minor leagues is no sinecure," Donlin said in summing up his brief stint in that role. "In order to be a first-class minor league pilot," according to Mike, "one must have the patience of Job, the hypnotic powers of Herb Flint, and the mental and physical ability to play every role from president of the club to third assistant groundkeeper."[30] Evidently not realizing he had contributed to his own downfall, he said "his troubles began when the club lost something like fifteen games by one run. Then the umpires commenced to make life miserable for Mike, who is a hard loser, and finally he was blamed for everything that went wrong."[31]

Several years later Philadelphia A's manager Connie Mack supported Mike's complaints about being a Minor League manager: "I think Donlin hit the tack right on the head when he said a minor league managerial berth was the surest way to take the joy out of a guy's life."[32] That manager had no scouts and no money to acquire players, Mack explained.

Donlin returned to Broadway, where he teamed up with comedian and acrobat Stan Stanley.[33] But he soon left the act because he was not being paid the money he wanted.[34] He also returned to appearing in movies. On December 15, 1917, the motion picture *Raffles, the Amateur Cracksman* was released. The star of the film was Donlin's friend John Barrymore, who helped him get the role of Crawshay, a stickup man, and shared several minutes of screen time with him. From this point on Mike Donlin's primary profession for the rest of his life would be as an actor, both in motion pictures and on the stage.

34

....

Back on Broadway and Hollywood Calls

In his biography of John Barrymore Gene Fowler wrote that Barrymore liked to find roles for his friends—including Mike Donlin—in his movies: "He said that these familiar although somewhat wizened pals 'brought good luck.' Besides, he was at ease among friends."[1] Barrymore's long friendship with Donlin was based at least in part on the predilection both men had for alcohol. Simply put, they were "drinking buddies."[2]

Donlin's film following *Right Off the Bat* was *Raffles, the Amateur Cracksman* (1917), in which he appears as a professional crook. By playing a character other than himself, Donlin took the step of establishing his bona fides as a legitimate actor, a solid character actor. One film columnist wrote, "Mike Donlin as a burglar proved that he didn't die when he quit playing baseball. Mike got away with the burglar thing very satisfactorily. I don't want Mike to take offense when I say that he 'looked the part.'"[3]

Donlin later explained how he got the role of a pickpocket in *Raffles*. "I'll put the cards on the table," he said. "I needed a job, and I happened to walk into the manager of this show [producer John Golden]." "You look like a pickpocket," Golden said. "I feel like one," Mike answered. "I must say I like the part. After battling umpires all my life, I seem to fall into pickpocket life with ease and precision."[4]

Barrymore starred in *Raffles*, and perhaps it was here their friendship developed. In 1926 he would get Mike a role in his epic *Sea Beast*, based on the novel *Moby Dick*.

In the next few years Mike's name was most often before the public in connection with a movie or show in which he appeared. The parts were usually small, and in many films he was not even credited.[5] He appeared in at least four movies between 1918 and 1922 and at least eleven in the next three years. In only a few did he have roles large enough that he could be called a character actor. He was more often a bit player.

In *Extras of Early Hollywood* Kerry Segrave wrote that the entry point to the world of acting in Hollywood was as an extra. But many "struggled for far too few jobs that were available."[6] Abel Green and Joe Laurie wrote, "Life on the West Coast in the 1920s was . . . precarious for the thousands who battered vainly at its shiny circumference, hoping daily for the 'break' that never came."[7] Steady work was rare, and rags-to-riches stories were even rarer.

Yet Donlin was not just any "extra." He became a beloved figure on the lots of Hollywood, drawing on the same warmth and decency that sportswriters had come to know. Casting directors found spots for him. Will Rogers later said of Mike, "He had been out here in pictures for years. Everybody liked him. Everybody used him when they had a chance. . . . Here he was. Looking for no sympathy, offering no alibis, not sore at the world, not sore at anybody. Just a kindly soul."[8]

Mike's personality gave him an edge in nurturing relationships. One reporter noted that he had "the sort of smile that makes you like him the first time you see him."[9] Another pointed out that "there is nothing mean in his nature. He was always big-hearted and ready to help the man who was not getting the breaks."[10]

Donlin continued to appear on stage following the war. He had much more meaningful roles than his usual bit parts in Hollywood. Playwright Winchell Smith's *Turn to the Right* went on the road in 1919 after a successful run on Broadway in 1916. Mike played the pickpocket, Muggs, with much of the original Broadway cast. A St. Louis critic wrote that Donlin was a "glad surprise" in the play: "He has humor of his own and a way of presenting it that puts it across regularly."[11] With this role, wrote a columnist, finally Donlin's "stage work matched his prominence as a diamond star. Lack of opportunity . . . had kept him in comparative obscurity."[12] He and Rita flew in a biplane from Dayton to Cincinnati and tossed out flyers advertising the show, a marketing "first" in the world of theater.[13]

Mike continued to be a big boxing fan. "I think boxing is the greatest game in the world," he told a reporter early in 1920.[14] When Jack Dempsey met champion Jess Willard for the heavyweight title, most people picked the far bigger champion to win because of his height and weight advantage. But Mike bet heavily on his friend Dempsey for the July 4, 1919, fight. One newspaper said a "reliable estimate" of Donlin's winnings on Dempsey's third-round knockout was $17,000.[15] Donlin also told people he won $2,000 on the Cincinnati Reds in their victory in the 1919 World Series over the Chicago White Sox.[16]

In 1921 Mike appeared as a criminal in *Smooth as Silk*, which ran on Broadway for fifty performances and then toured the country. When he was appearing in that production, he told a reporter, "I enjoy the show business, and I believe that I have finally signed up with a real show."[17]

In 1922 Donlin appeared in the Midwest in a vaudeville sketch as an ex-boxer in *The Kid Drops In*. It was a romantic comedy in which Rita also appeared.[18] New York syndicated columnist O. O. McIntyre wrote, "Never was an actor finer over success. Donlin simply could not believe that he was destined to become a real star. He took the whole thing as a joke."[19]

Yet Donlin's activities that year suggest a man who was searching for an anchor in his life. He sold cars and trucks in Chicago for a while that year.[20] That stability may have come when Donlin visited the Louis B. Mayer Studios in Los Angeles that fall, as the guest of actor Ben Deeley. Mike liked the climate so well that he took an option on a residence near the city. This move likely facilitated his landing roles in so many films, starting with 1923 releases (some filmed in 1922).

In many ways Donlin had not changed much. In a 1919 interview a sportswriter wrote that his voice had "not lost the brogue of the bogs inherited by his father."[21] In early 1920 a reporter said that Donlin had not aged noticeably since he had retired as an active player in 1914: "Yes, girls, he does look rather young; if it wasn't for that slight tinge of grey around the edges of his voluptuous head of hair."[22] In that interview Mike maintained that he had not had a drink in thirteen years—since Mabel had sent him away in the summer of 1907. If that was indeed the case, at least for a while, he had managed to overcome his grief over losing her and the end of his baseball career without returning to alcohol. But there are hints of that sobriety not being permanent.

With Mike fading from public view, Rita was hardly ever mentioned in the press. She did have a small part in *Turn to the Right*, and while it was only a minor role as a maid, she was "one of the most valued members of the company," wrote the *Philadelphia Inquirer*, as she was the main understudy to each of the four major female roles.[23] One critic wrote of the youthful Rita that she was "as fresh to look upon as dew-sprinkled violets on a summer's morn."[24] After the death of her uncle Charles, Rita began helping her aunt run the New Jersey family farm and resort. In

30. Mike Donlin was active both on the stage and in films in the early 1920s. This photo of him at age forty-three was released in conjunction with his appearance on Broadway in *Smooth as Silk* in 1921. *Boston Herald-Traveler* Photo Morgue, Boston Public Library.

afternoons and evenings, wrote one newspaper, "She radiates beauty and good nature as a hostess."[25]

There was no mention of what role Rita played in making family decisions—on what her husband should do or where they should live. She seemed a more passive, yet equally supportive, spouse than the more dominant and headstrong Mabel had been. Asked in 1919 about her "managerial skills" when it came to handling her husband, she made a revealing comment. "'Oh, yes, Mike still loses his temper once in a while. . . . He would hardly be Mike if he did not. But we have studied him so carefully that a cure is effected almost instantly.' She patted her husband on the cheek, and he beamed like a groom. 'We have been married quite a while now,' Donlin said, 'but we are still on our honeymoon.'"[26]

At the end of 1921 *Variety* had an article titled "Athletes as Entertainers." The writer pointed out that unlike a decade earlier, athletes were not drawing well when they appeared on stage. Babe Ruth appeared at the Palace Theatre, for example, without a bump in attendance, and Yankees pitcher Waite Hoyt drew poorly in his hometown of Brooklyn. "Unless the athlete can entertain them and 'draw' them simultaneously, he is no more entitled to a vaudeville engagement than the champion checker player." The writer pointed out there was a notable exception: Mike Donlin. "Donlin elected to follow the stage as a career and developed into a first-class actor."[27]

Donlin had put his athletic ability to good use in 1918 when he saved his friend and movie star George Walsh from serious injury on the set. He prevented some falling scenery from landing on Walsh.[28] Donlin often did his own stunts, and in 1924, during the filming of *Oh, Doctor!*, he was in a motorcycle accident and suffered serious bruises. He badly wrenched his back and was unconscious for an hour. "That slide off the motorcycle was lots worse than any I ever took on the diamond," he said.[29]

Donlin had one of his larger roles in *Oh, Doctor!*, which starred Reginald Denny as a hypochondriac who suddenly decides to live dangerously to impress a nurse. Donlin is Denny's chauffeur, Buzz Titus, and the two are riding the cycle when the crash occurs. The website *Movies, Silently* noted the film's many crashes, which were "handled with panache" and had to be done with stuntmen. But not this one; the actual accident with Donlin on the bike was used in the film.[30]

In his early movies Mike often played a "bad guy." Even Buzz Titus in *Oh, Doctor!* was known as a "speed maniac" whose driving had resulted in fatalities. Perhaps his persona fit the roles, but Donlin expressed unhappiness with such typecasting. "They're trying to make a crook out of me!" he complained. He said he had been cast as an underworld character so often that he would soon "have fingers sensitive to combination locks and eyes that can see everything in the dark."[31]

31. This 1925 cartoon highlights Mike Donlin's career, though it softens the harsher parts of his past. The most critical vignette, his run-ins with umpires, is portrayed humorously. *San Francisco Examiner*, February 7, 1925.

Whether he later became more selective with his roles or had more opportunities offered to him, starting in the mid-1920s Donlin appeared in several baseball movies, often as a scout. They included *Hit and Run* (1924), *Warming Up* (1928), *Hot Curves* (1930; an early talkie), and *Swellhead* (1935). He would also be a consultant for other baseball movies, including *Slide, Kelly, Slide* (1926) and *Fast Company*, the first baseball talkie (1929).

Syndicated sportswriter John Lardner wrote, "Critics used to say that Mike played ball like an actor and acted like a ballplayer."[32] Yet many accounts belie that retrospective comment. "The real fact is that Donlin has shown himself to be a finished stage star," was a critic's typical comment.[33] Mike garnered many positive reviews during his long film career, and—unlike many athletes—he made a successful transition from one career to another.

At the end of 1925 Donlin looked back on his film career to date in a humorous vein with syndicated columnist Frank Menke: "I've been a better bandit than Jesse James, a locomotive fireman, a taxicab chauffeur, a great lover, a thief, beggar, banker, athlete, the little Childe Harold, a couple of railroad presidents, a gun-totin' gambler, a villain, lots of heroes[;] I've been wounded, dead, buried, resurrected, married 89 times—or maybe 90—and all that stuff, y'know, that happens in the films." Donlin wistfully added, "I'd risk one year's pay that if I had my old black bat back again and could just go out there and swing it at those one-speed curve ball pitchers that I'd bust lil' ol' Babe Ruth's 59 homers record." Menke added, "Baseball was his first love—his real love—and it will always be just so with 'Adonis Mique.'"[34]

35

....

"The Very Breath of Life"

Mike remained close to the game he loved. He even managed to mend a longtime enmity from his baseball days. The fourteen years of hostility that had existed between Donlin and Joe Kelley, his manager in Cincinnati, finally ended in March 1918 at a steakhouse in New York City. It was at an impromptu dinner given by Yankees co-owner Jacob Ruppert, and it was attended by some of the biggest names in the game. The spirit of good fellowship in the room prompted Red Sox manager Ed Barrow to attempt a reconciliation between Donlin and Kelley. "You fellows haven't known each other for 14 years," said Barrow, "and it's time you got acquainted. Life is too short to carry baseball grievances to the end." Kelley, now a Yankees scout, and Donlin shook hands and recounted the story of their estrangement. "Back in 1904, when I managed the Cincinnati Reds, Donlin was the hardest hitter in the league, but he was a temperamental cuss," Kelley said.[1]

At this point Donlin spoke up: "I am not trying to excuse myself, for I know I was a hard guy to handle in those days, but I still maintain that [Kelley] had me wrong the day we split." Donlin claimed he had gone to bed early the night before but that about three in the morning two of his roommates came home feeling "very jolly" and insisted that Donlin and another sleeping player wake up and join them in a card game. "We did so," said Donlin, "and none of us went to bed after that."[2]

Donlin remembered that Kelley made some inquiries the next morning, and as a result, he fined and suspended Donlin. "We were both to blame, Mike," said Kelley. "I was too hasty, and you were so sore that you never even attempted to explain the situation." "That's right, Joe," Donlin replied. "Let's forget it." Yankees manager Miller Huggins had the final word: "I was a member of that Cincinnati team, and I remember well how the boys hated to see Mike leave. We needed his hits. And now, after all these years, I am a witness to the reconciliation."[3]

For Donlin the specter of death was never far away. In May 1918 his first Major League manager, Patsy Tebeau, committed suicide at age fifty-three. A month later Mike's wife's uncle, Charles Ross, passed away. Later that year Frank Arellanes, a friend and teammate from the late 1890s in California and the first Latin ballplayer for the Boston Red Sox, died at thirty-six. In 1920 George Browne died at forty-four. Not only had he been Donlin's teammate on the New York Giants, but he had also played for Mike's semipro team based in Long Branch. In 1924 Donlin's vaudeville friend, noted blackface performer Ben Deeley, died at forty-six.[4] And of course the death of pitcher Christy Mathewson from tuberculosis at forty-five made national headlines in 1925.

When Donlin registered for the draft in the summer of 1918, his home address was still the Hotel Bristol in Manhattan.[5] Mike's name appeared in a Major League box score that year. When the umpires did not show up for the July 22 game between the Yankees and the Browns, he served as the first-base umpire for the game, which went fifteen innings.[6] Almost a year later his old nemesis, Johnny Evers, umpired a game between theater actors (whom Donlin managed) and songwriters at the Polo Grounds before the start of the 1919 season.[7] The actors won with the help of two long drives by Donlin.

Donlin gave an interview that year in which he discussed what he thought was wrong with baseball, particularly in the way players were treated:

> Theatrical people take more interest in actors and actresses who have helped the profession, given their life to entertaining the public. They provide homes for them. Only a couple of weeks ago I saw the game at the Polo Grounds between actors and song writers where was raised $17,000 for the actors' fund. . . . In baseball there is no such sentiment. Honus Wagner was the greatest of all ball players. Why does not some big-league club employ this wonderful old fellow as an attraction; he would be worth a good salary, and the very fact of his being taken up would cheer the heart of this hero and gratify the millions of fans, many of whom would gladly pay just to see Honus in spangles on the diamond.[8] There is more sentiment and feeling among theatrical people than among baseball folks. This goes for everyone I ever came in contact with excepting John McGraw, who

32. As ballplayers, the fiercely competitive Mike Donlin and Johnny Evers had run-ins and did not like each other. But in April 1919 they appeared at the Polo Grounds in a benefit game between New York actors and songwriters. Donlin captained the actors and led them to victory with his hitting. Evers was one of the umpires. Library of Congress, Prints and Photographs Division, George Grantham Bain Collection.

is to-day the backbone of the National League and by all odds the man with more baseball vision than anybody alive or dead.

Donlin then added, "The game has greatly improved since I got into it. I remember when women were mighty few at a ball game. . . . The men were rough in their talk. Now the stands show 50-50 in the sex attendance. Ball players are a mighty sight more decent than they used to be. What the game needs is sentiment particularly for the men who gave much of their lives to establishing the great pastime in this country."[9]

Unlike many players of his era who said they were better than the current players of the early 1920s, Donlin saluted the current performers: "It's all wrong to say the old-timer was better than the modern player."[10] During 1920, Babe Ruth's first season with the Yankees, Donlin told sportswriter Sid Mercer that Ruth was the hardest hitter ever: "This bird gets more into a punch than anybody I ever saw."[11] But he did find fault in what he felt was excessive friendliness among players of opposing teams nowadays. "They don't sharpen their spikes on the bench anymore, and there are too many handshakes," he complained.[12] In the old days, he said, "if you couldn't fight, you couldn't play ball."[13]

When asked why he did not remain in baseball, Mike gave an interesting answer. He said that as he grew older, "sooner or later I would be done," while in acting, he could continue "as long as I am able to totter across the boards."[14] But Donlin showed remarkable insight into a concern about the game that would be a major topic of discussion a century later: the pace of the game. "I believe that the people of today are fed up on excitement," he said. "The fan of today sees auto races at terrible speeds, sees aviators do all kinds of thrilling stunts, drives his automobile at a speed too great for the safety of himself and others, and otherwise carries on at a pace that makes the best sort of ball game a mere incident in his sight."[15]

Yet Donlin did remain connected to baseball. He appeared in benefit and exhibition games, such as one between the Los Angeles Angels and the Vernon Tigers of the PCL in 1920. He played the entire game at first base for Vernon, while Frank Chance did the same for Los Angeles.[16] Mike told a reporter that he always traveled with a baseball uniform and joined a game whenever the opportunity arose. He said that shouts from the bleachers were "the very breath of life."[17]

When Jesse Burkett, Mike's former St. Louis teammate of 1899 and 1900, left the College of Holy Cross in 1921 to join John McGraw's Giants, he recommended Donlin to replace him.[18] When the job went instead to former infielder Jack Barry, Mike signed with the semipro Bronx Giants, which prepared young players for a professional career.[19] But he did not stay in one place for long. In September 1921, while his theatrical company was in Kalamazoo, Michigan, Mike accepted an invitation to play first base for the Class B Central League's Kalamazoo Celery Pickers. He had a single in four at bats and made one error in a 3–1 loss.[20]

In May 1922 Donlin accepted manager Hugh Duffy's offer to scout for the lowly Boston Red Sox.[21] It was in that capacity he attended an early August weekend series in Rock Island, Illinois, between the hometown Islanders and the Ottumwa (Iowa) Cardinals of the Class D Mississippi Valley League. Mike agreed to put on a uniform and play for the Islanders in their Sunday doubleheader on August 6. Playing right field in both games, he had one hit in seven at bats. The second game was his final appearance as a professional ball player, at age forty-four.[22]

When Duffy was replaced as manager by Frank Chance at the end of the year, the former Chicago Cubs great was reported to have signed Donlin as a coach for the 1923 season, but there is no evidence Mike ever appeared with the club.[23] Instead, that summer he told an Oakland reporter he would manage the San Francisco Seals of the PCL if offered the job.[24] That winter he managed the Glendale White Sox of the semipro California Winter League, an integrated league with Black teams.[25]

Early in 1924 Donlin was featured in a "What They're Doing Now" column. The article said he was living in Los Angeles and appearing in movies and doing an occasional vaudeville sketch. "It's a great life, he opines, though he does miss the thrill of the old baseball days occasionally."[26]

Syndicated columnist Hugh Fullerton gave confirmation to the impact Mike's relocation had on his career choices. When they met in Chicago early in 1922, the former ballplayer told him, "Bring my regards to Broadway, and tell them I don't care if I never see it again."[27] While Fullerton shed no light on why Donlin was done with theater despite some real success there, he did give a penetrating overview of this complicated man and the qualities that endeared him in Hollywood. Fullerton began by describing how Mike had started out: "There was probably not a tougher, wilder kid in the game," one who felt it was "necessary to fight his way to success. His idea was to whip everyone who stood in his path. He achieved a bad reputation before he really got started."[28]

Then Fullerton continued:

I discovered even in those days that Donlin was a man of entire honesty, of sincere friendship, and that underneath that swaggering toughness was one of the kindest hearts in the world. I discovered this when I found that he had done one of the prettiest, most tender acts ever known [admitting he was glad the Cubs beat his Giants in the final game of the 1908 season because he felt his first-inning double was actually a foul ball], and it was funny, for when I spoke to him about it, he wanted to hit me on the nose. He was ashamed of being soft-hearted.[29]

36

....

Acting Success and a Mysterious Illness

Mike Donlin's movie career gathered momentum in the mid-1920s (in the number of films, if not the prominence of his roles) but was interrupted by a mysterious life-threatening illness. His Hollywood friends rallied to his support, and he too rallied for an improbable recovery and ended up appearing in about twenty films in the second half of the decade. Yet through it all he remained connected to baseball.

In 1926 Mike had small parts in two famous silent films starring now legendary actors John Barrymore and Buster Keaton. One was hailed as a hit when it appeared, and the other was rediscovered and even venerated decades later. Barrymore secured a role for Mike in his epic *Sea Beast*, based on the novel *Moby Dick*. Warner Brothers added a love story and changed the ending to an implausibly happy one. The film was hailed by critics and fans and was a financial success. One New York reviewer praised the scenes at sea as "beyond question the finest ever done."[1] Newspaper reviews did not mention Donlin in his minor role as Flask, the young and scrappy deck hand.

The second film was Keaton's *The General*, released just after New Year's Day 1927. Keaton's friendship with Donlin revolved around baseball, for which both men had a passion. In his autobiography Keaton wrote, "As far back as I can remember, baseball has been my favorite sport."[2] To be a member of his production team, it was a requirement that one could play baseball. One of Keaton's friends, actor Harold Goodwin, called his crew "an ever-ready baseball team, prepared to start a game on a moment's notice."[3] When making a film, if the crew reached a difficult stage in production, Keaton would call for a break, and the group would go to a nearby ballfield for a game. In Cottage Grove, Oregon, where *The General* was filmed, Keaton had the local Kelly Field improved, with leveling of the turf and construction of a new backstop.[4]

Two Major League players other than Donlin were members of Keaton's movie team, one after his baseball career, like Donlin, and the other before his career on the diamond. Byron Houck was the former, and Ernie Orsatti was the latter. Houck had been a pitcher for Connie Mack's Philadelphia Athletics from 1912 to 1914.[5] He started working as a cameraman in 1919, the year he won nineteen games for Vernon of the PCL. He became a regular on Keaton's crew a few years later. Orsatti was a member of Keaton's crew and a bit player in his movies. He so impressed Donlin with his baseball ability in the early 1920s that Mike persuaded Keaton to sign him to a contract with the Vernon team in 1925, of which Keaton was a part owner.[6] St. Louis Cardinals president Branch Rickey signed him later that year, and Orsatti played nine seasons in St. Louis, where he hit .306 and appeared in four World Series.

While *The General* was a financial and critical failure, it is now considered Keaton's best film. The American Film Institute ranks it as the eighteenth greatest movie ever.[7] Donlin has a small role as a Union general. But he was in a film destined for greatness, one directed by his drinking pal. While Keaton would descend into alcohol binges when he was chafing under MGM's control in the late 1920s and 1930s, he was already an alcoholic as early as 1925.[8]

Shortly after the release of *The General* in March 1927, the baseball film *Slide, Kelly, Slide* premiered. William Haines, a rising star in Hollywood, plays a cocky but talented member of the Yankees.[9] A number of ballplayers appear in the film, including Donlin, the Yankees' Tony Lazzeri and Bob Meusel, and Meusel's brother, Irish. Donlin was also the movie's "technical director" (who hired ballplayers for the film and ensured the baseball scenes were realistic), a role that brought him to St. Louis for the 1926 World Series.

Damon Runyon visited with Donlin during that Series. "The years have thinned him down to some extent and put a few streaks of gray in his hair," Runyon wrote. "He was always a wiry, dapper fellow. The dapperness came in the later years of his baseball career, however. Before that he was a rough-and-tumble, devil-may-care sort, a rootin', tootin', cuttin', shootin' sun-of-a gun."[10] Runyon said that "Sunny Jim" Bottomley, the colorful first baseman for the Cardinals, reminded older fans of "some old-timer by his walk and manner, and I can now tell them the name of the old-timer they are trying to recall. It is 'Turkey Mike' Donlin."[11]

Donlin had not seen a Major League game for a few years, and this was surely a joyous visit for him. Runyon noted that he was "pounded almost out of shape . . . by the backslapping of old friends" and greeted effusively by the young sportswriters too.[12] The movie included footage from that Series between the Yankees and the Cardinals.

The film's director was Edward Sedgwick, and the story of Donlin's connection to "Eddie" appeared in newspapers across the country.[13] Sedgwick grew up in Texas and served as a Giants batboy when the team trained in Marlin Springs. "One fat and sassy home-town urchin pestered McGraw to be his bat boy," said one account.[14] "I took a fancy to the kid," said Donlin. The moral of the story, he said, was "Be kind to the small boy—he may be your boss some day!"[15]

Another Giants batboy from Donlin's years with the club connected with him years later in a different context. Al Watrous was now a professional golfer, and in the 1931 Los Angeles Open Donlin told him, "You carried my bats years ago. I'll carry your clubs now, and we'll be even."[16]

In the mid-1920s Donlin lost considerable weight, and in 1927 he had a serious, and mysterious, illness. Accounts are both confusing and contradictory. The illness was described as either cancer or a heart ailment. It was even attributed to a serious bout of influenza or tuberculosis.[17] Whatever the cause, Donlin's limited finances were preventing him from getting the treatment he needed.

There were periodic newspaper articles in this era about the many athletes who starred in their sport but failed with their finances. One column at this time said that "gambling helped to reduce Donlin to his present state," as it had done with many other stars.[18] (This is the only mention of a gambling problem the authors came across.) A more general column about athletes' poor money management appeared in 1931. It mentioned Donlin's situation in 1927 and Olympics star Jim Thorpe's digging ditches: "The best time to think about the future is the present. Very few athletes do this."[19]

Mike's many friends in the worlds of entertainment and baseball came to his support. Runyon framed the matter to his readers nationwide in mid-May: "He is ill at his home in Hollywood and, as only too often happens when a fellow encounters illness, the exchequer is a trifle short. One of the proudest men you ever saw and sensitive, Mike kept his troubles to himself until one of his friends recently became apprised of the true state of affairs. . . . He never asked the world for anything but an even break in his life. He was always helping someone else in his heyday, but he never intimated he might need help himself."[20]

John Barrymore, "one of 'Turkey Mike's' oldest friends and admirers," was the chairman of a committee that was organizing a huge benefit event at the Los Angeles Philharmonic Auditorium on June 9, 1927. The *Los Angeles Times* reported Mike's friends (including John McGraw, Charles Comiskey, and George M. Cohan) had already raised $10,000 to help him fight "a malignant cancer in the stomach."[21] Another California newspaper reported he had been suffering from cancer for several years.[22]

Donlin was to be treated at the Mayo Clinic in Rochester, Minnesota.[23] He had gone there in early April but was unable to pay for the operation he needed to save his life. Tests showed he had intestinal cancer, the disease that may have killed Mabel.[24] At least initially he was unaware of the money-raising efforts on his behalf.

Among the entertainers at the gala event were actors George Jessel and Tom Mix and Mike's old vaudeville partner, Tom Lewis. Barrymore delivered his famous soliloquy from *Hamlet*. Mike received the money for his operation and in early August was reported to be "recovering nicely" in Minnesota. He also had his tonsils and some teeth removed and was hoping to avoid another operation. "Imagine me weighing 136 now with my clothes on!" he told one reporter.[25] A few days later he learned that Billy Gilbert, his old teammate, business partner, and witness at his wedding, had died suddenly of a stroke. He was only fifty-one. Mike returned to California in early September, just as *Slide, Kelly, Slide* premiered in New York.

Post-surgery reports surfaced that Mike's ailment was not cancer but rather a heart ailment, an athletic heart. The condition is seen in people who engage in intense and strenuous exercise. Their resting heart rate drops, and their heart increases in size. Nowadays the condition is not considered serious; the physiological changes do not cause cardiac damage. But in the mid-1920s the condition was debated in medical circles and on the sports pages. There was no medical consensus on the relationship between athletics and heart disease. Many considered it a life-threatening disease for former athletes, and it was attributed as the cause of early deaths.

Veteran sportswriter Hype Igoe had covered Donlin in California as a San Francisco reporter in the late 1890s. He ran into Donlin, whom he had not seen for many years, in 1927. He barely recognized the former

33. These images show the dramatic aging in Mike Donlin's appearance after his serious 1927 illness. On the left he is with actor Lloyd Hughes when they appeared in the 1926 film *Ella Cinders*. The scar on the left side of his face is still visible. On the right he is with actress Mary Brian when they appeared in the 1928 movie *Partners in Crime*. National Baseball Hall of Fame Library, Cooperstown, New York.

ballplayer. Igoe described him as "a bent, shriveled character. . . . Time and the dreaded white plague [tuberculosis] had jackknifed his face and body horribly."[26]

Donlin went to New York for treatment in January 1928 and returned to the Mayo Clinic in April.[27] On April 7 a Pittsburgh paper cited cancer, and a Minneapolis paper mentioned heart trouble as Donlin's disease.[28] Yet he bounced back from his illness with remarkable productivity. In 1928 and 1929 he appeared in at least ten films, including two by directors who would later be acclaimed as among the greatest ever: William Wellman and John Ford. In *Beggars of Life*, directed by Wellman and starring Wallace Beery and Louise Brooks, Donlin had a small role. The movie is significant because it was Paramount's first movie with spoken dialogue, and film historian Kevin Brownlow felt it was "brilliantly thought out and superbly made."[29] It was also released in a silent version.

In *Riley the Cop* (a silent movie with sound effects and music), directed by Ford, Donlin is unbilled and simply referenced as "Crook." In one scene, after Riley fouls off a ball that breaks a nearby window in an at bat with city kids, and they all scatter, Donlin appears in a cameo, looking up and smiling with a cigarette hanging from his lips. In their book on baseball players who became actors, Rob Edelman and Michael Betzold noted the charm of this "fleeting" scene, "perhaps Donlin's most memorable screen appearance." Whether Ford realized it or not, the scene "serves as an homage to Donlin's past and a wink of an eye to anyone who recognizes him as an ex–major leaguer."[30]

That same year Donlin again appeared in a baseball film in a small role (as the "veteran") and was also the film's technical director. *Warming Up*, starring Richard Dix as a small-town pitcher who gets a chance to try out for a Major League team, was also released by Paramount with silent and sound versions. This time the latter had no dialogue, but it did have music and sound effects.

The introduction of sound into movies turned the industry upside down. In the early 1920s James Quirk, president and editor of *Photoplay* magazine, maintained that the "talking picture" would never replace the silent film: "It will lack the subtlety and suggestion of vision—that vision which, deprived of voice to ears of flesh intones undisturbed the symphonies of the soul."[31] The Vitaphone sound system delivered the knockout blow to silent films with *The Jazz Singer* in October 1927.

"[Movie] producers now realized that it was a case of sound or sink."[32] Even the fame of actor Charlie Chaplin could not save the medium he loved. "A good talking picture is inferior to a good stage play," he said, "while a good silent picture is superior to a good stage play."[33]

In 1929 moviegoers were told that Mike Donlin may have appeared in the first movie ever made with sound, with both music and dialogue, two decades earlier. In the movie version of *Stealing Home* he and Mabel Hite spoke their words and did their singing and dancing for phonograph recordings, which were distributed to theaters with the film, and "[the] perfect timing of the start of picture and phonograph resulted in fairly accurate synchronization."[34]

It is not surprising that actors were now playing baseball stars because the decade of the 1920s saw the rise of movie celebrities as well. In the early years of motion pictures actors were not identified by name; studios wanted to keep wages low by not creating stars. In his 1915 film Donlin was the lead actor. Ballplayers like him were already known and generated box-office appeal. In 1920 Babe Ruth starred in the comedy *Headin' Home*. But as moviegoers demanded to know about the leading ladies and men they were watching, producers realized they could capitalize on

34. The 1920s saw the rise of celebrities, both in sports and in motion pictures. Three of the biggest movie stars of that era were Douglas Fairbanks; his wife, Mary Pickford; and Charlie Chaplin, seen here boarding the White Star liner *Olympic* on their way to Europe in 1921. Steve Steinberg Collection.

the emergence of stars. By the early 1920s there were more than a dozen movie fan magazines.

In the 1920s movie stars (led by Mary Pickford, Douglas Fairbanks, and Charlie Chaplin) joined sports stars (from Ruth to Jack Dempsey, from golfer Bobby Jones to tennis player Bill Tilden) as icons for a venerating public. By the mid-1920s screen favorites such as Haines and Dix (and Hoot Gibson in an early Sedgwick film, *Hit and Run*, in which Donlin plays a baseball scout) were cast as baseball stars. The transition had come full circle, from ballplayers as actors to actors as ballplayers.

Donlin's 1928 performances would not have been complete without a gangster film (or two). He appeared uncredited in *Partners in Crime*, starring Wallace Beery, a film that one reviewer called "a savage feud between two underworld gangs."[35] Donlin also was not credited for his role as a con man in a Raoul Walsh movie, *Me, Gangster*.[36] He told a reporter that summer, "I'll take baseball, even in the old days, over the real-life gangster's job, though. I'd rather face baseballs than police machine gun bullets."[37]

In the fall of 1928 Donlin returned to the stage, in Los Angeles, for the first time since playing Muggs in *Turn to the Right* a decade earlier. He played a crook named Blake in *Nightsticks*, a show that had a brief run on Broadway in late 1927 and early 1928. He had been in several baseball films in recent years, playing a scout or veteran player and working behind the scenes as the technical advisor. Syndicated columnist James T. Long wrote that Donlin had developed a reputation for expertise: "Mike's counsel is sought [by Hollywood film execs], and his advice acted upon to assure that all baseball scenes are absolutely correct from a technical standpoint."[38] But Donlin wanted variety in his work and told a reporter, "I jumped at the chance of playing a lawbreaker" since he had been in so many baseball films recently.[39] Yet a couple of weeks later he told another newspaperman that he longed for a role as a regular guy, "a good-natured chap."[40]

Two years later Donlin returned to Broadway in a meaningful role in *This One Man*, starring Paul Muni. He said that his doctors advised him not to make the cross-country trip and leave the warmth of southern California for the harsh New York winter. After the show, when Donlin returned to California, he lightheartedly said he had gained six pounds while on the stage.[41]

Donlin's write-up in *Playbill*'s "Who's Who in the Cast" followed that of Muni, where he was described as "one of the best known baseball players in the history of the game."[42] A Brooklyn critic praised Muni's acting, which "ranks high among the major events of the modern theatre." He also noted Donlin's "fine performance." But the reviewer warned that the drama's high quality "may stand in the way of extended success as popular entertainment."[43]

Mark Barron, the Associated Press (AP) theater critic, rated Muni's performance one of the greatest on Broadway since John Barrymore played *Hamlet*. He called the play both depressing and thought-provoking.[44] The show lasted only thirty-nine performances. Donlin explained its short run. "Nowadays the public cares little for the legitimate play," he said. "What people want is plenty of fun, and I'm going back to Hollywood shortly and return to the comedy game."[45]

Ed Sullivan, who would become a successful television personality, began his career as a sportswriter in the early 1920s. By 1930 he was a

35. Mike Donlin returned to the stage in 1930 with a key role in the critically acclaimed play *This One Man*, starring Paul Muni. Columnist Ed Sullivan featured and saluted Donlin for his performance. Billy Rose Theatre Division, New York Public Library for the Performing Arts.

syndicated theater and gossip columnist for the *New York Daily News*. After sitting down with Donlin during *This One Man*'s Broadway run, he wrote, "Never have I heard a sporting personage talk so interestingly as Donlin reminisced under the spur of memory." After noting that Donlin's first love still was baseball, he saluted the baseball great:

You see him eating dinner at the Tavern, or you see him knife his way through crowded Broadway, and the sharp eyes in the thin face would make you turn and look at him a second time, even though you were not aware that this was the famous Mike Donlin. . . . Yessir, Turkey Mike is back on Broadway, and the old street that once echoed with his praises when Donlin co-starred with Matty on the Giants, is glad to see him again. Even though Donlin is no longer 190 pounds of hellcat, it is not difficult to picture him as the stormy petrel of a rough league. . . . Today he is an actor, and a good one. His performance as Jiggs, an underworld character, in Paul Muni's hit show, "This One Man," is a remarkable tribute to Donlin's facility in adapting himself to conditions as he finds them.[46]

Sullivan noted that Donlin's admiration for his former manager with the Giants had not waned: "John McGraw is still his idol."[47] The years had not been kind to either man; neither had reached the age of sixty, yet both looked like they were seventy. When Donlin bounced back from "his victorious battle with death" in 1927, a St. Louis drama critic noted that he was continuing in "his life-long work of proving [sic] entertainment for the public."[48] After many years in show business Donlin understood that the baseball diamond, as well as the stage and movie theater, provided entertainment.

Donlin also understood that while McGraw was a great leader of men and baseball tactician, he was also a master entertainer. He once said of McGraw, "He shows what personality means in the game, and he has no illusions. Baseball is a show business, just like this play I am in. But it is the greatest of all games, and you cannot blame a manager for using some theatrical stunts at times to keep the public jazzed up. McGraw, himself, is the greatest attraction for the fans. If he is absent a couple days without uniform, the attendance drops off."[49]

Yet Donlin himself had towered over the game, if for a shorter period of time. When Damon Runyon featured the former Giants star in his October 1926 column, he wrote, "'Turkey Mike' was the most picturesque, colorful baseball player I ever saw. He had more color than that mighty man, George Herman Babe Ruth. It is a sure thing that Mike had the greatest acquaintance and following of any player the game has ever known."[50]

37

....

"Lights, Camera, Action"
Continues to the End

Despite Mike Donlin's physical ailments and gaunt appearance, he continued to stay active in motion pictures and connected to the game he loved. Throughout his life he had been touched by tragedy, and after his brush with death in 1927 he likely realized how severely his health had declined. All he had to do was look in the mirror and see the emaciated face that looked back at him. But as he had done so often in the past, he pushed ahead and remained both relevant and engaged.

In 1931 Mike lost yet another sibling as brother Joe died in New Jersey of tuberculosis and abdominal complications. As an infant, Joe had survived the train crash that killed his mother, and as a young man, he played semipro baseball in Chicago. He had been in poor health and poverty-stricken for two years and had been estranged from Mike for nine years.[1] As the end drew near, Joe wanted to reconcile with his brother, but Mike could not be located. While reports said he "doubtless" would have come to his brother's bedside, it seems odd that a well-known actor could not be located in Hollywood.

Mike's image as a ballplayer had softened in recent years. Brooklyn sportswriter Harold C. Burr wrote in his "And Do You Know That—" column in June 1932 that Donlin had become "the mildest and frailest of men."[2] A Pittsburgh sportswriter who had covered him during his career recalled his friendly side when his teams visited the Pirates. Whenever Donlin walked to or from the outfield, a band mockingly played the "Rogue's March." Yet Mike was always good-natured about it and kidded with the Pittsburgh fans.[3]

But the other side of Mike's personality was not forgotten. Damon Runyon wrote that Donlin would have been the best fighter of all ballplayers had he turned to boxing.[4] Giants secretary Eddie Brannick, while reminiscing with sportswriter Jimmy Powers, called Donlin "the toughest scrapper" on the early Giants teams: "He could fight like hell."[5] What emerged from these contrasting accounts of past and present was a man who had mellowed.

Though he had a steady stream of acting roles, Mike seemed to need baseball in his life, even if it was at a level far less lofty than the Major Leagues. Walter Winchell, syndicated gossip columnist, wrote in 1933 that Donlin wanted a job of broadcasting baseball games on the radio, but he doubted it would pay the $35.50 daily he was getting from acting.[6] If Winchell's figure was accurate, it would have been compensation equivalent to almost $800 a day in 2022. But Donlin did not work exclusively for one studio for any length of time. He appeared in a similar number of films made by five large studios: Fox, MGM, Paramount, Universal, and Warner.

MGM leased a ballfield in Culver City (California) in the summer of 1929 for games against Paramount and announced that Donlin would be the umpire.[7] He had just finished appearing (uncredited) in another Eddie Sedgwick movie, *Spite Marriage*, with Buster Keaton. During the filming Donlin and Keaton pitched in to spruce up the field. In September Keaton's MGM team played a group of former players led by Donlin and Jim Thorpe.[8]

In September 1929 the first baseball talkie, *Fast Company*, based on a play by Ring Lardner and George M. Cohan, appeared. Donlin did not appear in the movie but was its technical director. The following week he was at Sid Grauman's Chinese Theatre for the gala farewell party of the MGM film *Hollywood Review of 1929*. The midnight matinee included appearances in person by Donlin and other old-time ballplayers, as well as Stan Laurel and Oliver Hardy, Roscoe "Fatty" Arbuckle, Jack Benny, and others.[9]

Mike also helped organize and play in annual benefit games for needy players, in which other old-timers participated.[10] He never forgot the destitute ballplayers of earlier years, even as he himself faced financial difficulties. There were periodic reports of his interest in establishing a permanent home for needy former ballplayers.[11]

Late in 1932 Donlin and some other California former players formed a traveling club that planned to play semipro teams across the country and to present baseball clinics for youths in the towns in which they appeared. They ran a "Games Wanted" ad in the *Sporting News* in January 1933,

36. Mike Donlin was a familiar figure at benefit baseball games in the Los Angeles area, often events that raised money for destitute former ballplayers. He is seen here in a 1925 game with the bat girl, actress Virginia Castleman. Steve Steinberg Collection.

looking for teams to compete against "the Old Timers Baseball Club."[12] A Brooklyn newspaper predicted success: "Mike will be well remembered by those who were gay blades when he was in his prime. Mike was the toast of New York from 1904 to 1908."[13] It is not clear how many games, if any, they played.

Mike inquired about the managerial opening for the San Francisco Seals of the PCL in late 1931 and, in the summer of 1932, a scouting job with the Boston Red Sox, for whom he had scouted a decade earlier.[14] Neither materialized. He continued to admire the skills of modern-day ballplayers, lauding the power of pitchers, as well as hitters such as Babe Ruth: "I like to watch pitchers who can make 'em smoke. This [Lefty] Grove can."[15] But he also showed disdain for some current players: "Today big-league pitchers are prima donnas. They are nursed and pampered, and their precious arms are massaged with lavender water."[16]

Donlin had reunited briefly with Major League baseball in 1926, when he visited St. Louis during the World Series to film *Slide, Kelly, Slide*. In 1932 Major League Baseball came to him when the Giants moved their spring training site from Texas to Los Angeles. John McGraw hosted a dinner for his friends in Beverly Hills that spring. Donlin was at his table, along with Will Rogers, former jockey Tod Sloan, former heavyweight boxing champion Jim Jeffries, and race car driver Barney Oldfield.[17] In a letter to the editor to the *New York Times* Rogers wrote of the gathering, "All [former stars] passing over the horizon of popular clamor, but never forgotten by McGraw."[18]

Just a few months later an ailing McGraw resigned, after seven pennant-less seasons. With McGraw gone, Donlin no longer had a direct channel of communication to his old club. When he explored a return to the Giants as a scout or coach, he used veteran sportswriter Joe Vila as his conduit.[19]

In the early 1930s Donlin's film appearances were so numerous that the pace must have put a strain on his body. Between 1930 and 1932, the early years of the Great Depression when salaries were being slashed, he was in at least thirty motion pictures. He was in films with some current and future leading men of Hollywood, from Spencer Tracy and Humphrey Bogart to William Powell and Edward G. Robinson. The female leads, from Jean Harlow and Ginger Rogers to Barbara Stanwyck and Bette Davis, would go on to glamorous careers.

Two of Donlin's films that premiered late in 1932 warrant interest. In *Madison Square Garden* he plays a referee in a boxing film that includes many sports figures (including former boxers Jack Johnson and Tom Sharkey and former jockey Sloan) and sportswriters (including Damon Runyon, Grantland Rice, and Paul Gallico). In *One Way Passage*, a romantic comedy starring William Powell and Kay Francis, Donlin plays a bartender. He has an extended clip, perhaps the longest continuous scene in his film career since *Right Off the Bat*, as he expertly prepares the perfect cocktail for Powell. The clip can still be viewed online.[20] The screenplay for *Right Off the Bat* won the Academy Award for best original story, and the film is still highly regarded. Director Tay Garnett, who was a big Donlin fan as a boy, told reporters, "My cherished admiration for Mike is not the only reason for his presence in my pictures. No matter what role is assigned to him, Mike can be depended upon to give a fine, sincere characterization."[21]

On September 20, 1933, Donlin was reported to be looking for a Minor League managerial position yet again.[22] Two days later *Dr. Bull*, a movie directed by John Ford and starring Will Rogers, was released. Donlin has an uncredited role as a supporter of the small-town doctor. On that same day, he saw his own doctor, Hiram Farnham, in Los Angeles; we can only surmise the reason. The following evening the cast of *The Chief*, led by Ed Wynn, had a "wrap party" to mark the completion of filming. Once again Mike was a bad guy in the movie, an uncredited "henchman." He went back to his West Hollywood home at 1216 North Vista Street and went to sleep.

He never woke up. Rita found him in bed the next morning, dead of an apparent heart attack. Dr. Farnham signed the death certificate, based on a physical exam only. He noted "the principal cause of death and related causes of importance in order of onset: Aortic Insufficiency (10 years) and Myocarditis (2 years)."[23] There was no mention of cancer. Mike was fifty-five years old. Rita said he died of an athletic heart after his "strenuous years" in baseball.[24] A ballplayer to the end, Mike was scheduled to manage and play in another old-timers' benefit in Wrigley Field in Los Angeles on October 6.[25]

The *Los Angeles Times* of September 25 reported Mike's funeral service would be held the following day at the Hollywood Cemetery Chapel, with cremation to follow. The eulogy was delivered by Harry English, the president of the National Vaudeville Association, and 350 people attended. More than sixty of them were honorary pallbearers, including people from the motion picture world (Will Rogers, Sid Grauman, Ed Wynn, and Joe E. Brown) and the sporting world (the Meusel brothers, Sam Crawford, and Chief Meyers, and former heavyweight champions Jim Jeffries and Jack Dempsey).[26]

Donlin appeared in at least seventeen films released in 1933 or later. (Four came out after his death.) His final appearance was in *Swellhead* (released in May 1935), in which he plays a baseball manager, Brick Baldwin. One of his last motion pictures was *The Mad Game* with Spencer Tracy. Donlin plays an assistant prison gardener, again uncredited. When he misses trimming a rose bush, his boss, Tracy, tells him, "You miss another, and you'll be missing a lot of fresh air." An Oakland film critic said that such "prophetic last lines" made actors superstitious. It was the last scene Donlin ever filmed, he wrote.[27]

When Eddie Sedgwick's *Death on the Diamond* was released in 1934, it was the first baseball film in many years in which Donlin was not involved. Sedgwick commented on his absence: "Everyone idolized him. Mike died recently. You know how Notre Dame fights for the memory of Knute Rockne. Well—it was like that with our picture. Every time the boys went in for a play, the world [*sic*] went around—'Let's make this a good one—for Mike.'"[28]

38

....

A Life Well Lived

The outpouring of grief and praise for Mike was immediate, widespread, and heartfelt.

"There is echoing today in the old Polo Grounds in New York—for ears not attuned to hear them—repercussions of a mighty shout: *Oh, you Mabel's Mike*. It was the most familiar cry of baseball 25 years ago, when Mike Donlin, the Babe Ruth of his day, the mightiest slugger of the National League, was the star of John McGraw's Giants. It was dedicated to his little wisp of a wife who was known on the stage as Mabel Hite."[1]

An Oakland columnist wrote, "An umpire baiter on the diamond, Mike was a friendly fellow out of uniform and a beloved character in the motion picture colony."[2] Will Rogers related that during the filming of *Dr. Bull*, he recalled Mike and Mabel's opening night at Hammerstein's in October 1908. The audience cheers were the greatest Rogers had ever heard: "When dear old Mike was playing with me in my last picture, *Dr. Bull*, I used to tell him about it."[3]

When Mike was so ill in the spring of 1927, Damon Runyon had put his baseball career in perspective: "I have never seen another ballplayer of Mike's color and personality. Babe Ruth may be able to hit more home runs, but Babe never had quite the appeal to me as a showman that Mike did. No one who ever saw him will forget that walk of Mike's moving to the plate."[4] Sportswriter Roundy Coughlin wrote, "Strutting to the plate with his big bat handled like a toothpick, he would shoot a stream of tobacco juice from the big plug in his mouth, kid the opposing catcher or pitcher, battle with the umpire and lace out a base hit. And the fans would roar as they do today when Ruth parks one in the stands."[5]

Just a few months before Donlin's passing, sportswriter Grantland Rice listed the ten most colorful players he had seen, and Mike was on his list, along with Babe Ruth, Ty Cobb, Honus Wagner, Joe Jackson, and

Johnny Evers.[6] After Donlin's death Rice recalled his "swagger and easy, careless grace" and lamented there were not a few more Mike Donlins in the game. "But Turkey Mikes are born, not made. You can't fake the stuff he had," he wrote.[7]

Mike's post-playing career in baseball had few successes. His repeated attempts to land a Minor League managerial job (with the exception of his brief stint with Memphis) were rebuffed. Was he unsuccessful, possibly even blackballed, because of a drinking problem? Because of his belligerence on the ballfield? Because he demanded too much money? Perhaps owners felt Mike was simply more trouble than he was worth.

Almost twenty years before Donlin's death, St. Louis sportswriter Billy Murphy described him as "a man of inherent virility and vigor" who was loved by many "despite the perversity of a reckless nature that strung Mike to curious electric tension at times and was responsible for many outbreaks of a kind that netted him much trouble."[8] Throughout his life Mike wiggled out of that trouble and got repeated "second chances"—the result of his talent on the ballfield and perhaps a little luck.

Mike was also fortunate to have married two women who provided stability and support to his life. He was married to Mabel Hite only six years before her tragic death. Her loving yet firm hand may have saved him from a downward spiral of alcoholism. He was able to control his drinking because he could not chance losing her; he loved her so much. Before Mike and Mabel were married, Amy Leslie wrote of the character of this woman who helped Mike stay on top of his game in his original field and showed him the possibilities in her field. Hite was "so magnetic, so genuine, so brainy and full of quick wit, fine humor and courage without impertinence that she is irresistible."[9] Irresistible to her husband as well as to her fans.

While Mabel performed exclusively in comedy, in different venues, from vaudeville to the legitimate theater, Mike appeared in dramas as well, a broader range than his wife's. One can only wonder what she would have accomplished in motion pictures, which were taking off when she died. Just before she and Mike were married, she was described as "a spontaneous funmaker, unctuously original, and with a mind attuned to humor."[10] Years later famed actress Gloria Swanson said, "I hated comedy, because I thought it was ruining my chance for dramatic parts. I didn't realize that comedy is the highest expression of the theatrical art and the best

Actress Runs Fine Farm in Vacation

RITA ROSS

37. Actress Rita Ross was married to Mike for the last nineteen years of his life. She acted only occasionally and rarely appeared in the press. *El Paso Herald*, March 20, 1920.

training in the world for other roles. . . . The mark of an accomplished actor is timing, and it can be acquired only in comedy."[11]

Donlin's second marriage lasted almost twenty years, but Rita Ross is an almost invisible part of this story. Little is known about their marriage; perhaps the most revealing comment came from Will Rogers, who wrote after Mike's death, "She stuck with Mike through many ups and downs, and an awful lot of downs among the few ups."[12]

Some of Mike's obituaries were fairly critical of his acting career. New York theater critic Ward Morehouse wrote, "Mike Donlin was never the actor he thought he was, or wanted to be."[13] John Lardner, Ring's son, noted, "Critics used to say that Mike played ball like an actor and acted like a ballplayer."[14] Those evaluations have carried over to articles of more recent vintage. In 2001 Rob Edelman wrote, "Make no mistake, Mike Donlin was no movie star. Nor was he movie star material."[15]

But such accounts are both unfair and inaccurate. As we have seen, Donlin garnered many positive reviews; he was a good, if not a great, actor. Will Rogers said, "He did some splendid things on the stage."[16] And Frank Jackson wrote in *Hardball Times*, "To achieve star quality in any human endeavor is a status bestowed on a chosen few; to attempt to achieve it in two endeavors is to defy the odds as well as the gods."[17]

From a statistical standpoint Mike's baseball numbers are outstanding. We can only wonder how great a ballplayer he could have been and how he would be viewed today had his "attention" not been diverted by a second career. A natural hitter, his departure from baseball was driven at least as much by his love of his wife as by economic inducements. Mike played more than eighty games in only five seasons, and his offensive numbers were dominant in all five. Sabermetrician David Kaiser has written that a season of 4.0 or more wins above average (WAA) is a superstar season; only 142 ballplayers have done it twice (out of more than 22,000). Donlin is one of them.[18] The more traditional marker, career batting average, has Mike thirty-second all-time, with a .333 mark in 1,049 games, almost all in the pitching-dominated Deadball Era. In on-base percentage, slugging percentage, and on-base plus slugging, as well as batting average and home runs, he was in his league's top ten in all five of those seasons. He had three seasons in which he finished second in batting average and two in which he finished third.

Donlin's popularity in New York was unparalleled, though it has since faded from view.[19] Runyon remarked that while many people "wanted" New York, the city he called "the end of the rainbow," the city seldom "wanted" them. Yet Mike was a rare exception: "He somehow belonged to the big town. . . . Turkey Mike was one of the big white line [Broadway] as much as he was of the baseball diamond."[20] Mike and Mabel were at the height of their fame in their respective entertainment fields during their marriage and truly one of the great "power couples" of the early twentieth century. As early as 1906 one New York sportswriter recognized Mike was "the idol of every small boy in New York."[21] He was such an idol more than a decade before sportswriters created celebrities in their columns. While he was "a little too stormy for one of the stormiest periods of the pastime," said Runyon, that he overcame that "shows his real calibre."[22] And two decades after Mike practically "owned" New York, Runyon—as well-connected as any journalist—said he never knew anyone who had more friends.[23]

Donlin's longtime manager, John McGraw, weighed in: "What a man he was. . . . He was something of a headache but more often a joy to me, and always a headache to opposing pitchers. . . . Donlin was a natural-born player . . . a fighter, the kind that used to make for winning teams in the days I played the game."[24] And when Will Rogers died tragically less than two years after Mike did, a newspaper columnist recalled what the humorist told McGraw shortly before McGraw's death in 1934: "There ain't enough fellows in the game like you and [former Washington Senators player-manager] Bucky Harris, and Mike Donlin. Why, I can remember when Mike was playing, if he couldn't hit what the pitcher throwed at him, he'd go out and lick the pitcher. What baseball needs is more fellows with more intestinal fortitude."[25] A year later New York syndicated columnist O. O. McIntyre expanded on Rogers's remarks: "Mike was swathed in exciting glamour. He had a cocky walk every boy tried to imitate, was handsome, wide-shouldered and booming with Blarney of the Irish."[26]

Mike craved attention and success. He achieved both, perhaps because of what one sportswriter termed a combination of "his intense eagerness to win" and "his cold nerve."[27] He projected bravado and swagger, but those who knew him realized it was just a veneer, perhaps overcompensating for the insecurities that tragedy had generated in his tumultuous life. Veteran sportswriter Joe Vila, who criticized Babe Ruth for the slugger's showmanship, admired Donlin and called him "one of the finest characters I ever met in baseball."[28] Despite Donlin's drinking and occasional violent outbursts, many people saw him as a kind and decent man, and those traits explain why he was so beloved. Will Rogers described him as "just a kindly soul."[29] Mike Donlin was a public figure of whom it truly could be said, "To know him is to love him."

Postscript: Mike's surviving sibling, sister Mame, died in Ohio in 1944. Mike's second wife, Rita, died in Boca Raton, Florida, in December 1979 and is interred at the Ross-Fenton burial plot in West Long Branch, New Jersey. Mike's ashes are beside her.

NOTES

1. Growing Up with Tragedy

1. Damon Runyon, *Milwaukee Sentinel*, May 14, 1927.
2. Will Rogers, *San Bernardino (CA) Sun*, October 8, 1933.
3. Damon Runyon, *New York American*, May 12, 1927.
4. Donlin ranked in the top three in batting average all these seasons and in the top three in slugging percentage in all but one of them. During those years he played fewer than forty games in two seasons and completely missed another season. Yet he bounced back to be among the league leaders in those categories.
5. Donlin's headstone at his New Jersey burial site says 1877, but both his Peoria County birth registration and his World War I draft registration say 1878.
6. The Irish Penal Laws, repressive measures against Catholics, reflected the power of the Protestant Church of England.
7. McCusker, "A Panoply of the Ambitious."
8. Kenny, *The American Irish*, 91.
9. Dolan, *The Irish Americans*, 73.
10. Daniles, *Coming to America*, 126–27.
11. M. A. Jones, *American Immigration*, 121–22.
12. Maguire, *The Irish in America*, 281.
13. Kenny, *The American Irish*, 201.
14. Dolan, *The Irish Americans*, 122.
15. Kenny, *The American Irish*, 200–202.
16. *Pittsburgh Daily Commercial*, March 17, 1875.
17. Excel spreadsheet of Donlin family researcher Judy Cash.
18. *Conneautville (PA) Courier*, July 3, 1885.
19. *Weekly Wisconsin*, July 8, 1885.
20. *Owensboro (KY) Messenger*, January 10, 1894.
21. *Erie Times-News*, April 18, 1892.
22. *Erie Dispatch*, January 8, 1894.

23. Excel spreadsheet of Donlin family researcher Judy Cash.

24. "Trinity Cemetery," Find a Grave, accessed May 2021, www.findagrave.com /cemetery/46488/trinity-cemetery.

25. *Daily Times*, January 8, 1894.

26. Quoted in *Akron Beacon Journal*, February 17, 1908.

27. Sid Keener, *St. Louis Star and Times*, September 26, 1933.

2. "I'm Going to Be a Sensation"

1. One writer said he suffered from a "concave chest due to consumption." Betzold, "Turkey Mike Donlin," 80.

2. Quoted in Joe Fitzgerald, *Erie Times-News*, July 14, 1908.

3. *Erie Times-News*, April 9, 1910, and June 4, 1907.

4. *St. Louis Globe-Democrat*, January 14, 1901. A "tragic train cigar" was a cheap cigar of poor quality.

5. Quoted in *Akron Beacon Journal*, February 17, 1908.

6. *St. Louis Globe-Democrat*, January 14, 1901.

7. John P. Brady, *Buffalo Courier*, August 2, 1908.

8. *St. Louis Globe-Democrat*, January 14, 1901.

9. Kelly coached the Santa Clara College team before coming to the University of Oregon. *Eugene Guard*, March 26, 1909.

10. *Bisbee (AZ) Review*, June 8, 1909.

11. Dolly Dalrymple, *Birmingham Age-Herald*, April 22, 1913. See also *St. Louis Post-Dispatch*, August 13, 1899.

12. Mike Donlin, *Los Angeles Herald*, March 13, 1920.

13. Plannette, *Two Centuries of Baseball*, 2–3.

14. *Los Angeles Herald*, November 22, 1897.

15. Spalding, *Always on Sunday*, 68.

16. Spalding, *Always on Sunday*, 69. The new league resulted from the merger of two new leagues that had started the season.

17. *Santa Cruz Surf*, April 13, 1898, and March 24, 1898.

18. *Santa Cruz Evening Sentinel*, August 10, 1898.

19. *San Francisco Call*, July 11, 1898.

20. Quoted in *Williamsport (PA) Sun-Gazette*, January 29, 1910.

21. Joe Corbett, *San Francisco Call*, July 31, 1898.

22. *Santa Cruz Evening Sentinel*, September 9, 1898.

23. Quoted in *Santa Cruz Evening Sentinel*, September 6, 1898.

24. *San Francisco Call*, August 22, 1898. "John Barleycorn" was the fictional personification of alcohol.

25. *San Francisco Call*, August 22, 1898.

26. *San Francisco Examiner*, August 25, 1898.

27. *Santa Cruz Evening Sentinel*, October 4, 1898.

28. *Santa Cruz Surf*, October 31, 1898.

29. *Santa Cruz Evening Sentinel*, November 8, 1898.

30. *San Francisco Call*, November 19, 1898.

31. Quoted in *San Francisco Chronicle*, November 20, 1913.

32. *San Francisco Call*, April 23, 1899.

33. *San Francisco Examiner*, May 29, 1899.

34. *Santa Cruz Surf*, May 22, 1899. Keeler had won the National League batting title in each of the previous two seasons.

35. *Sacramento Record-Union*, June 16, 1899.

36. Forest D. Lowry, *Sporting Life*, June 24, 1899; and *San Francisco Call*, June 8, 1899.

37. Quoted in *Buffalo Enquirer*, March 28, 1900.

38. A. H. Noyes, *Sporting News*, January 5, 1907.

39. The charges were intoxication and indecent exposure. *Santa Cruz Evening Sentinel*, March 28, 1899.

40. *Buffalo Enquirer*, March 28, 1900.

41. McKenna, "Reluctant Ballplayer"; and Phil Luciano, *Peoria Journal Star*, April 2, 2016.

42. *Santa Cruz Evening Sentinel*, June 24, 1899.

43. *San Francisco Examiner*, June 25, 1899.

44. *St. Louis Post-Dispatch*, August 13, 1899.

45. Quoted in *Santa Cruz Evening Sentinel*, October 11, 1899.

46. Spalding, *Always on Sunday*, 75; and McKenna, "Reluctant Ballplayer."

47. "Hype" Igoe's nickname came from his "extreme slimness," which prompted people to compare him to a hypodermic needle. *New York Times*, February 12, 1945.

48. Quoted in *Sporting News*, January 25, 1945.

49. Quoted in *New York Times*, February 12, 1945. Igoe attended a Giants-Cubs game with cartoonist Tad Dorgan.

3. The Making of Mike Donlin

1. Sid Keener, *St. Louis Star and Times*, September 26, 1933.

2. Keener, *St. Louis Star and Times*, September 26, 1933. For Donlin's name, intimates used the more casual and endearing "Mickey" and sometimes "Mikey."

3. Keener, *St. Louis Star and Times*, September 26, 1933.

4. Quoted in H. W. Lanigan, *Indianapolis Star*, January 7, 1912.

5. Quoted in H. W. Lanigan, *New York Morning Telegraph*, December 30, 1911, dateline.

6. Spink, *Judge Landis and Twenty-Five Years of Baseball*, 257.

7. *St. Louis Post-Dispatch*, August 13, 1899. *Baseball-Reference* lists Donlin as 5 feet 9 inches.

8. *St. Louis Republic*, February 2, 1901. This prescient and insightful quote was likely written by the *Republic*'s baseball scribe, John B. Sheridan. A soubrette is a female performer playing a lively, flirtatious role in a play or opera.

9. In 1900 St. Louis was the fourth largest city in the United States, with a population of just over 575,000. Cleveland was the seventh largest, with just over 380,000 people.

10. No team has ever lost more games in a season.

11. *Sporting News*, July 1, 1899.

12. Hetrick, *Misfits!*, 65.

13. *St. Louis Post-Dispatch*, July 29, 1899.

14. *St. Louis Globe-Democrat*, July 29, 1899.

15. He made only one more appearance as a pitcher, throwing one inning in 1902.

16. *Washington (DC) Times*, August 30, 1899.

17. *St. Louis Post-Dispatch*, July 31, 1899.

18. In 1899 Donlin made fifteen errors in the outfield and had an .873 fielding percentage as an outfielder. The league's fielding percentage in 1899 was .942.

19. D. Jones, "Jesse Burkett."

20. Quoted in Lane, *Batting*, 19.

21. Quoted in "How Mike Donlin Became a Big Leaguer," 79–80.

22. Lane, *Batting*, 19.

23. Quoted in *Sporting News*, August 12, 1899.

24. Quoted in *Nebraska State Journal*, February 24, 1907.

25. *Sporting News*, July 29, 1899.

26. *St. Louis Globe-Democrat*, August 8, 1899; and *Washington (DC) Evening Star*, August 11, 1899.

27. *Sporting News*, August 12, 1899.

28. Quoted in Plannette, *Two Centuries of Baseball*, 37.

29. Quoted in *Sporting News*, January 5, 1907.

30. *Baltimore Sun*, September 2, 1899.

31. Frank F. Patterson, *Sporting News*, September 9, 1899.

32. Minnie McGraw died of a ruptured appendix two days later, on August 31.

33. *St. Louis Post-Dispatch*, September 8, 1899.

34. *Sporting News*, September 16, 1899.

35. *Sporting News*, September 16, 1899.

36. Redmond, *The Irish and the Making of American Sport*, 10–11.

37. *Sporting News*, October 21, 1899.

4. "Provided He Takes Care of Himself"

1. Quoted in Seymour, *Baseball: The Early Years*, 304.
2. Seymour, *Baseball: The Early Years*, 302 and 304.
3. Editorial, *Sporting News*, July 1, 1899. McGraw led the National League in runs, walks, and on-base percentage in 1898 and 1899.
4. H. G. Merrill, *Sporting News*, October 21, 1899.
5. Quoted in Lieb, *The St. Louis Cardinals*, 27.
6. Quoted in Klein, *Stealing Games*, 14.
7. Alexander, *John McGraw*, 70.
8. Frank F. Patterson, *Sporting News*, September 8, 1900.
9. Frank F. Patterson, *Sporting News*, March 17, 1900.
10. *Sporting News*, March 17, 1900; and *Sporting Life*, March 24, 1900.
11. *St. Louis Republic*, May 9, 1900. "Rubbered" likely means the ball bounced out of his mitt.
12. *Brooklyn Times-Union*, May 16, 1900.
13. *St. Louis Globe-Democrat*, May 21, 1900.
14. *St. Louis Republic*, May 21, 1900.
15. *St. Louis Republic*, May 21, 1900.
16. *Sporting News*, May 26, 1899.
17. *St. Louis Globe-Democrat*, June 4, 1900.
18. Seymour, *Baseball: The Early Years*, 290.
19. *St. Louis Post-Dispatch*, June 18, 1900.
20. Editorial, *Sporting News*, June 23, 1900.
21. Seymour, *Baseball: The Early Years*, 341–42.
22. *Sporting Life*, April 28, 1900.
23. *Santa Cruz Evening Sentinel*, June 26, 1900.
24. Retmus, *Sporting Life*, June 30, 1900.
25. Frank F. Patterson, *Sporting News*, August 4, 1900.
26. Retmus, *Sporting Life*, August 4, 1900.
27. Quoted in *St. Louis Republic*, August 5, 1900.
28. Quoted in Frank F. Patterson, *Sporting News*, August 4, 1900.
29. Quoted in *St. Louis Republic*, August 20, 1900.
30. Retmus, *Sporting Life*, September 1, 1900. A cereus is a plant with large, funnel-shaped flowers.
31. Quoted in Frank F. Patterson, *Sporting News*, September 8, 1900.
32. Quoted in Lieb, *The St. Louis Cardinals*, 28.
33. Editorial, *Sporting News*, August 25, 1900.
34. *Sporting News*, November 10, 1900.
35. Patsy Donovan took over as manager the following season.

36. Lieb, *The St. Louis Cardinals*, 28.

37. Quoted in *Kansas City (MO) Star*, January 30, 1914. The fine was likely far less, perhaps $10.

38. Quoted in Smith, *Baseball's Famous Outfielders*, 73.

39. *Sporting News*, October 20, 1900.

40. Quoted in John J. Sumpter, *Sporting Life*, October 27, 1900.

41. *San Diego Union and Daily Bee*, October 15, 1900; and *Los Angeles Herald*, March 13, 1920.

42. *San Francisco Call*, January 26, 1901.

43. *Santa Cruz Surf*, January 28, 1901.

44. *St. Louis Globe-Democrat*, November 9, 1900.

45. *Los Angeles Times*, January 28, 1901.

46. *Sporting Life*, December 8, 1900; *Santa Cruz Evening Sentinel*, January 8, 1901.

47. *Sporting News*, October 27, 1900.

48. *St. Louis Globe-Democrat*, November 9, 1900.

49. *Sporting Life*, October 28, 1905.

5. Donlin and McGraw Battle with Umpires

1. Frank F. Patterson, *Sporting News*, August 18, 1900.

2. Editorial, *Sporting News*, August 25, 1900.

3. Frank F. Patterson, *Sporting News*, August 18, 1900.

4. Thorn, "The House That McGraw Built," 116.

5. Thorn, "The House That McGraw Built," 116.

6. Quoted in Mrs. John J. McGraw with Mann, *The Real McGraw*, 151.

7. Quoted in Lieb, *The Baltimore Orioles*, 92–93.

8. Lieb, *The Baltimore Orioles*, 93.

9. Honig, *Baseball America*, 19.

10. McGraw had a minority share in the new Orioles. Graham, *McGraw of the Giants*, 18.

11. Quoted in *Sporting Life*, September 1, 1900.

12. *Baseball-Reference*. This was far more than McGinnity could have earned working in the family foundry. Doxie, *Iron Man McGinnity*, 57.

13. Quoted in Burk, *Never Just a Game*, 150.

14. *St. Louis Republic*, February 2, 1901.

15. *Sporting News*, December 29, 1900.

16. *Santa Cruz Surf*, February 28 and March 12, 1901.

17. *Pittsburgh Press*, April 27, 1901.

18. *St. Louis Post-Dispatch*, March 26 and 28, 1901.

19. Mrs. John J. McGraw with Mann, *The Real McGraw*, 190.

20. *Washington (DC) Times*, May 9, 1901.

21. *Philadelphia Times*, May 16, 1901.

22. Quoted in *Chicago Tribune*, May 18, 1901.

23. Durso, *Casey & Mr. McGraw*, 42.

24. Graham, *The New York Giants*, 51.

25. Frank F. Patterson, *Sporting News*, May 25, 1901.

26. *Inter Ocean* (Chicago), May 28, 1901.

27. *Detroit Free Press*, June 1, 1901.

28. Quoted in *Chicago Tribune*, June 2, 1901.

29. Quoted in *Detroit Free Press*, June 9, 1901.

30. Donlin was the first American Leaguer to hit safely six times in a game.

31. *Baltimore Sun*, June 25, 1901. Donlin had gone 5-for-5 on June 2, 1900, and would again go 5-for-5 on September 18, 1903.

32. *Baltimore Sun*, June 26, 1901.

33. *Topeka State Journal*, March 20, 1900.

34. Connolly had ejected McGraw, as well as McGinnity and Bresnahan, in recent days.

35. Nemec and Miklich, *Forfeits and Successfully Protested Games*, 104–5.

36. *Sporting Life*, August 31, 1901.

37. *Philadelphia Inquirer*, August 22, 1901.

38. Editorial, *Sporting News*, May 19, 1900.

39. Frank F. Patterson, *Sporting News*, August 31, 1901.

40. Anderson, "Bonesetter Reese."

41. B. F. Wright, *Sporting News*, August 31, 1901.

42. Doxie, *Iron Man McGinnity*, 61.

43. H. S. Fullerton, *Sporting News*, September 7, 1901.

44. Frank F. Patterson, *Sporting News*, September 7, 1901.

45. Quoted in *Sporting Life*, September 7, 1901.

46. This is the largest gap ever between first and second place for the batting title, more than 20 percent.

47. James J. Corbett, *Binghamton (NY) Press and Sun*, March 1, 1919.

48. *Sporting News*, March 16, 1901.

49. P. Morris, *A Game of Inches*, 361–62.

50. Fleitz, *Napoleon Lajoie*, 76.

51. *Indianapolis Journal*, October 12, 1901.

52. *Sporting Life*, November 9, 1901.

53. Editorial, *Sporting News*, February 8, 1902.

6. A Brutal Assault

1. *Baltimore Sun*, March 14, 1902.

2. Quoted in *Baltimore Sun*, March 14, 1902.

3. Quoted in *Baltimore Sun*, March 14, 1902.

4. Quoted in *Baltimore Sun*, March 15, 1902.

5. Quoted in *Dayton (OH) Herald*, March 22, 1902.

6. Quoted in *Baltimore Sun*, March 20, 1902.

7. *Baltimore Sun*, March 20, 1902.

8. Frank F. Patterson, *Sporting News*, March 29, 1902.

9. Quoted in *Baltimore Sun*, March 20, 1902. That Donlin had not drunk liquor for four weeks was likely not true.

10. Quoted in Frank F. Patterson, *Sporting News*, March 29, 1902.

11. Quoted in *Evening Star* (Washington DC), March 20, 1902.

12. Quoted in *Santa Cruz Evening Sentinel*, March 27, 1902; and *Dayton (OH) Herald*, March 22, 1902.

13. *Sporting News*, March 22, 1902.

14. Joe S. Jackson, *Detroit Free Press*, March 14, 1902.

15. W. A. Phelon, *Sporting Life*, March 22, 1902.

16. Frank F. Patterson, *Sporting News*, March 29, 1902.

17. *Cincinnati Enquirer*, June 23, 1902.

18. *Pittsburgh Press*, May 23, 1902.

19. *Cincinnati Enquirer*, May 21, 1902.

20. *Sporting Life*, June 7, 1902.

7. A Return to the National League

1. Lamb, "New York Giants Team Ownership History."

2. Lamb, "New York Giants Team Ownership History."

3. Allen, *The Cincinnati Reds*, 75.

4. Moreland, *Balldom*, 71.

5. *New York Times*, May 2, 1902.

6. *Sporting News*, May 10 and 17, 1902; as cited in Murdock, *Ban Johnson*, 55.

7. *Boston Globe*, May 25, 1902.

8. Graham, *McGraw of the Giants*, 19–21.

9. Frank F. Patterson, *Sporting News*, July 12, 1902.

10. *Sporting News*, July 12, 1902.

11. Since 1893 only Babe Ruth has combined to have more pitching victories and more hits than Seymour. Kirwin, "Cy Seymour."

12. Ren Mulford Jr., *Sporting Life*, September 6, 1902.

13. Quoted in *Sporting News*, October 25, 1902.

14. Cy Seymour won sixty-one games for the Giants from 1896 to 1900, including twenty-five in 1898. This was Jake Beckley's lone career pitching appearance.

15. *Baltimore Sun*, October 5, 1902.

16. Quoted in *Pittsburgh Press*, October 5, 1902.

17. *Pittsburgh Press*, October 7, 1902.

18. *Sporting News*, October 18, 1902.

19. When Indoor Baseball moved outside, it was renamed softball.

20. *Chicago Tribune*, September 14, 1902.

21. *Chicago Tribune*, September 16, 1902.

22. *Chicago Tribune*, September 14, 1902. In August 1902 Garvin, a pitcher for the Chicago White Sox, became intoxicated and shot a Chicago bar owner and also pistol-whipped a policeman during the incident.

8. "A Manager Who Can't Control Himself"

1. *Sporting News*, September 5, 1903.

2. In his nineteen-year Major League career Crawford would lead his league in triples six times, and his 309 career triples are still the Major League record.

3. Even though Kelley was a twelve-year veteran, he was only thirty years old.

4. Donlin was suffering from "*la grippe*," a name often given to the flu in those years.

5. Quoted in *Sporting News*, March 7, 1903.

6. Quoted in *Pittsburgh Press*, March 25, 1903.

7. Quoted in *Pittsburgh Press*, January 11, 1903.

8. Quoted in Ren Mulford Jr., *Sporting Life*, February 21, 1903.

9. J. Ed Grillo, *Sporting News*, March 7, 1903.

10. *Sporting News*, August 27, 1904.

11. Quoted in *Sporting News*, August 27, 1904.

12. Quoted in Lieb, *The Baltimore Orioles*, 68.

13. Hynd, *The Giants of the Polo Grounds*, 83.

14. Solomon, *Where They Ain't*, 104.

15. J. Ed Grillo, *Sporting News*, May 23, 1903.

16. Kelley was ejected six times in the 1903 season.

17. Ren Mulford Jr., *Cincinnati Enquirer*, May 24, 1903.

18. Quoted in *Fall River (MA) Globe*, June 30,1903.

19. Quoted in *Pittsburgh Press*, June 13, 1903.

20. *Cincinnati Post*, July 9, 1903.

21. *Pittsburgh Press*, August 29, 1903.

22. "Rowdy" was most likely the tamest thing the St. Louis fans called Donlin.

23. J. Ed Grillo, *Sporting News*, August 8, 1903.

24. *Cincinnati Enquirer*, September 2, 1903.

25. The melody of "The Rogue's March" was a well-known tune used by the American army during the Revolutionary War. The tune was played when military or civil rogues, criminals, offenders, and various undesirable characters were drummed out of camps.

26. The three triples came in his first three at bats and followed a triple in his final at bat of the first game to tie the Major League record for tripling in four consecutive at bats.

27. J. Ed Grillo, *Sporting News*, December 5, 1903. "Chesterfield," as Grillo used it here, was what the ideal eighteenth-century British gentleman was called.

9. "I Am Through with Donlin!"

1. Quoted in *Sporting News*, December 19, 1903.
2. Quoted in *Cincinnati Enquirer*, February 12, 1904.
3. Ren Mulford Jr., *Sporting Life*, February 20, 1904.
4. *Cincinnati Enquirer*, March 4, 1904.
5. *Sporting News*, February 6, 1904.
6. Quoted in "Tips by the Managers," *Sporting News*, April 9, 1904.
7. *Pittsburgh Press*, April 23, 1904.
8. *Cincinnati Enquirer*, April 24, 1904.
9. Quoted in *Cincinnati Enquirer*, April 25, 1904.
10. Quoted in *Cincinnati Commercial Tribune*, June 5, 1904.
11. Quoted in *News-Journal* (Mansfield OH), June 1, 1904.
12. Fleitz, *Napoleon Lajoie*, 115.
13. Quoted in *Wilkes-Barre (PA) Leader*, June 4, 1904.
14. Quoted in *Wilkes-Barre (PA) Leader*, June 4, 1904.
15. Fleitz, *Napoleon Lajoie*, 115.
16. *Boston Globe*, June 9, 1904.
17. *Cincinnati Enquirer*, June 17, 1904.
18. Odwell would become the Reds' full-time left fielder after the Reds traded Donlin to the Giants on August 7.
19. Quoted in *Chillicothe (OH) Gazette*, July 8, 1904.
20. Quoted in *Cincinnati Enquirer*, July 8, 1904.
21. *Sporting News*, March 7, 1918, as quoted in Waldo, *Characters from the Diamond*, 45.
22. Quoted in *New York Evening World*, July 15, 1904.
23. C. J. Bockley, *Sporting News*, July 16, 1904.
24. *Cincinnati Enquirer*, July 17, 1904.

10. Goodbye to Cincinnati

1. C. J. Bockley, *Sporting News*, July 30, 1904.
2. Graham, *McGraw of the Giants*, 27.
3. Quoted in Robert Edgren, *New York Evening World*, August 5, 1904.
4. *New York Evening Journal*, August 6, 1904.
5. Quoted in *New York Evening Journal*, August 6, 1904.

6. Quoted in Stark, *The Year They Called Off the World Series*, 143.

7. Quoted in *New York Evening World*, August 8, 1904.

8. *Brooklyn Citizen*, August 21, 1904.

9. Quoted in *New York Evening World*, August 8, 1904.

10. *St. Louis Republic*, August 28, 1904.

11. Zimmer was a rookie umpire who had just retired as a player after a nineteen-year career.

12. Some New York newspapers had started calling the team the Yankees this season rather than the Highlanders.

13. *New York Evening Journal*, July 24, 1904.

14. Quoted in *New York Herald*, August 1, 1904.

15. Quoted in *New York Evening World*, August 2, 1904.

16. Timothy Sharp, *Sporting News*, August 20, 1904.

17. Sam Crane, *New York Evening Journal*, September 19, 1904.

18. *Brooklyn Citizen*, August 14, 1904.

19. Quoted in *New York Evening Journal*, September 11, 1904.

20. Klein, *Stealing Games*, 45; as quoted in Alexander, *John McGraw*, 109.

21. Hernandez, *Manager of Giants*, 37.

22. In the five years from 1903 to 1907 the two would produce 272 victories for McGraw's Giants: 140 by Mathewson and 132 by McGinnity.

23. Quoted in *New York Press*, October 7, 1904.

24. W. M. Rankin, *Sporting News*, October 8, 1904.

25. Quoted in *New York Evening World*, September 26, 1904.

26. Alexander, *John McGraw*, 109.

27. *Brooklyn Citizen*, September 30, 1904. Donlin's fielding percentage was .885. He never again had a mark lower than .900.

11. "I Have Had My Share of Trouble"

1. Quoted in *Buffalo Times*, January 23, 1905.

2. Bozeman Bulger, *New York Evening World*, February 18, 1905.

3. *Brooklyn Eagle*, February 27, 1905.

4. Quoted in *Star-Gazette* (Elmira NY), March 4, 1905.

5. *Baltimore Sun*, March 7, 1905.

6. *Wilkes-Barre (PA) Times*, March 24, 1905.

7. Quoted in *Kansas City Star*, April 15, 1905.

8. *New York Sun*, April 15, 1905.

9. Bozeman Bulger, *New York Evening World*, April 18, 1905.

10. Quoted in *New York Times*, April 19, 1905.

11. *Brooklyn Eagle*, May 1, 1905.

12. *New York Evening World*, May 22, 1905.

13. *Miami News*, July 14, 1905.

14. *Los Angeles Times*, February 9, 1923.

15. Quoted in *St. Louis Republic*, April 13, 1912.

16. Donlin's 124 runs scored led both Major Leagues.

17. James, *The New Bill James Historical Baseball Abstract*, 756.

18. James, *The New Bill James Historical Baseball Abstract*, 82.

19. William F. H. Koelsch, *Sporting Life*, November 18, 1905.

20. Grayson, *They Played the Game*, 80.

21. Nelson, *The Golden Game*, 171.

22. James, *The New Bill James Historical Baseball Abstract*, 756.

23. Smith, *Baseball's Famous Outfielders*, 70–71.

24. Johnson, *Baseball and the Music of Charles Ives*, 99.

12. Mathewson Pitches to a Title

1. *Baltimore Sun*, October 9, 1905.

2. Quoted in *New York Evening Mail*, September 22, 1905.

3. *Sporting News*, October 7, 1905.

4. Joe Vila, *Sporting News*, October 7, 1905.

5. King, "The Strangest Month in the Strange Career of Rube Waddell," 45–52.

6. Macht, *Connie Mack and the Early Years of Baseball*, 349.

7. Quoted in *Philadelphia Inquirer*, September 30, 1920; and *New York Evening World*, October 1, 1920.

8. Timothy Sharp, *Sporting News*, September 30, 1905.

9. Quoted in *Evening Star* (Washington DC), October 6, 1905.

10. Quoted in *Chicago Eagle*, July 12, 1913.

11. *New York Times*, October 10, 1905.

12. *New York Sun*, October 10, 1905.

13. *New York Herald*, October 11, 1905.

14. *Philadelphia Inquirer*, October 11, 1905.

15. Eddie Plank was one of the toughest-luck World Series pitchers ever. He lost five of his seven postseason games despite a 1.32 earned run average.

16. *New York Sun*, October 14, 1905.

17. *New York Times*, October 15, 1905.

18. Quoted in *New York Times*, October 17, 1905.

19. This has happened only one time since. In 1966 Frank Robinson drove in three runs for the winning Baltimore Orioles while the losing Los Angeles Dodgers scored only two.

20. This practice, dating back to the Temple Cup Series of the 1890s, was not uncommon.

21. *Buffalo Enquirer*, November 8, 1905.

22. Joe Vila, *Sporting News*, October 21, 1905.

23. Christy Mathewson, *Sporting News*, October 28, 1905.

24. Quoted in *Baltimore Sun*, October 16, 1905.

25. *New York Times*, November 5, 1905.

26. *Los Angeles Herald*, October 29, 1905.

27. *Los Angeles Herald*, October 29, 1905.

28. *Los Angeles Herald*, October 29, 1905.

29. *Washington Post*, October 26, 1905.

13. The New York Hoodlums

1. Spatz, *Bad Bill Dahlen*, 133.

2. Jensen. "Dan McGann."

3. Joe Vila, *Sporting News*, April 29,1905.

4. Timothy Sharp, *Sporting News*, May 6, 1905.

5. *Philadelphia Inquirer*, April 23, 1905.

6. Quoted in Jensen, "Dan McGann."

7. Joe Vila, *Sporting News*, April 29, 1905.

8. Klem would hand out a league-leading twenty-six ejections his rookie season.

9. Durso, *Casey & Mr. McGraw*, 59.

10. *New York Times*, May 21, 1905.

11. Quoted in *New York Evening Mail*, May 23, 1905.

12. Quoted in Hernandez, *Manager of Giants*, 38.

13. Quoted in DeValeria and DeValeria, *Honus Wagner*, 154.

14. Quoted in Hittner, *Honus Wagner*, 80.

15. Quoted in Arthur James, *New York Evening Mail*, May 30, 1905.

16. Ralph S. Davis, *Sporting News*, May 27, 1905.

17. *Sporting News*, June 3, 1905.

18. Joe Vila, *Sporting News*, June 3, 1905.

19. Joe Vila, *Sporting News*, June 17, 1905.

20. DeValeria and DeValeria, *Honus Wagner*, 154.

21. *New York Herald*, June 19, 1905. A horse-drawn vehicle used for passenger transport was referred to as an omnibus.

22. *New York Herald*, June 20, 1905.

23. *Philadelphia Inquirer*, July 6, 1905; Francis C. Richter, *Philadelphia News*, as noted in *Sporting Life*, July 15, 1905.

24. *New York Times*, July 20, 1905.

25. L. M. Cadison, "Pirates to Receive Reception on Return," *Pittsburgh Press*, July 23, 1905.

26. DeValeria and DeValeria, *Honus Wagner*, 156.

27. Spatz, *Bad Bill Dahlen*, 143.

28. DeValeria and DeValeria, *Honus Wagner*, 154–55.

29. *Washington (DC) Times*, August 7, 1905.

30. Ejection totals come from *Retrosheet*, where they are still a work in progress.

31. Quoted in Mercer, "Clippings and Cartoons," 426.

32. *Sporting News*, February 17, 1906.

33. *Washington Post*, February 9, 1906.

34. *Buffalo Evening News*, February 9, 1906.

35. Quoted in *Buffalo Times*, February 10, 1906.

36. *Buffalo Evening News*, February 9, 1906.

37. *Sporting News*, February 17, 1906.

38. Quoted in *Washington Post*, February 19, 1906.

14. Vaudeville

1. Seymour, *Baseball: The Golden Age*, 4.

2. Trav, *No Applause—Just Throw Money*, 5 and 7.

3. Quoted in Snyder, *The Voice of the City*, 129.

4. Gilbert, *American Vaudeville*, 124.

5. Trav, *No Applause—Just Throw Money*, 67.

6. Trav, *No Applause—Just Throw Money*, 66.

7. Trav, *No Applause—Just Throw Money*, 223 and 122.

8. Quoted in Trav, *No Applause—Just Throw Money*, 89.

9. Hammerstein was the son of opera theater owner Oscar Hammerstein and the father of lyricist Oscar Hammerstein II. The Victoria, at Forty-Second Street and Broadway, was demolished in 1916 after Willie's death.

10. Quoted in Mansch, *Rube Marquard*, 97.

11. Seib, *The Player*, 72.

12. Quoted in Gilbert, *American Vaudeville*, 249.

13. Trav, *No Applause—Just Throw Money*, 129.

14. Andrew Hammerstein phone conversation with Steve Steinberg, October 27, 2021.

15. Gilbert, *American Vaudeville*, 269.

16. Quoted in "Disney Legends, Ed Wynn," Walt Disney Archives, accessed July 2021, https://d23.com/walt-disney-legend-ed-wynn/.

17. Green and Laurie, *Show Biz*, 83–84.

18. Monod, *Vaudeville and the Making of Modern Entertainment*, 11.

19. Monod, *Vaudeville and the Making of Modern Entertainment*, 10–11.

20. Quoted in Staples, *Male-Female Comedy Teams in American Vaudeville*, 2–3.

21. Staples, *Male-Female Comedy Teams in American Vaudeville*, 121.

22. Trav, *No Applause—Just Throw Money*, 141.

23. Quoted in Trav, *No Applause—Just Throw Money*, 218.

24. Quoted in M. Wallace, *Greater Gotham*, 429.

25. Quoted in M. Wallace, *Greater Gotham*, 497.

26. Deford, *The Old Ball Game*, 96.

27. *Leslie's Weekly*, October 24, 1907, 300.

28. Vaudevillians had a more difficult travel routine than ballplayers. The former traveled all over the country, while Major League baseball did not have a team west of St. Louis.

29. Robinson, *American Original*, 88.

30. Hynd, *Marquard & Seeley*, 5.

31. Trav, *No Applause—Just Throw Money*, 139.

32. Morris, *Not So Long Ago*, 202.

33. Quoted in Yagoda, *Will Rogers*, 89.

34. Robinson, *American Original*, 88.

35. Quoted in Snyder, *The Voice of the City*, 46.

15. A Star Is Born

1. Some accounts list her year of birth as 1884 or 1885. Since Mabel was cremated and there is no grave site and since the 1890 U.S. census records were destroyed in a 1921 fire, evidence is lacking.

2. Mabel said she lived in Pocatello from ages four to twelve; March 8, 1901, dateline, Robinson Locke Collection.

3. *Kansas City Times*, October 10, 1895.

4. Quoted in *Kansas City Star*, March 24, 1905.

5. Quoted in *Des Moines Register*, March 14, 1905.

6. Amy Leslie, *Chicago News*, May 12, 1910, Robinson Locke Collection. Leslie was an American actress, opera singer, and drama critic. She was one of the few female critics of that era.

7. Amy Leslie, *Chicago News*, May 12, 1910, Robinson Locke Collection.

8. Mabel Hite, unsourced in Robinson Locke Collection.

9. *Chicago News*, no date, Robinson Locke Collection.

10. *Los Angeles Evening Express*, March 23, 1901.

11. *Chicago Tribune*, March 4, 1901.

12. *Fort Smith (AR) Times*, January 9, 1901.

13. *Herald Press* (St. Joseph MI), July 23, 1902.

14. *Topeka Daily Herald*, September 17, 1902.

15. *Times* (Shreveport), October 14, 1902.

16. Paranick, "Eva Tanguay."

17. Erdman, *Queen of Vaudeville*, 55.

18. Quoted in Ada Patterson, *The Theatre*, July 1911, Robinson Locke Collection.

19. Tanguay did use sexual innuendo in her dialogue and suggestive routines, something Hite never did.

20. Quoted in Frederic North Shorey, *Inter Ocean* (Chicago), April 14, 1907. Shorey was the pseudonym of a Black writer for the *Indianapolis Freeman*.

21. Brown and Koch, *Who's Who on the Stage, 1908*, 238.

22. Will Fischer, Amusements, *Spokane Press*, September 4, 1903.

23. *Minneapolis Journal*, December 28, 1903.

24. *News-Journal* (Mansfield OH), June 20, 1904.

25. *New York Herald*, May 3, 1904.

26. *New York Times*, May 3, 1904.

27. *Chicago Tribune*, January 12, 1905.

28. Frank J. Price, unsourced 1916 article, Robinson Locke Collection.

29. Zangwill, "The Future of Vaudeville in America," 639, 642, and 643.

30. Zangwill, "The Future of Vaudeville in America," 642.

31. Quoted in K. M. Rogers, *L. Frank Baum, Creator of Oz*, 130.

32. *Kansas City Times*, July 14, 1905.

33. Burns Mantle, *Inter Ocean* (Chicago), June 20, 1905.

34. Amy Leslie, *Chicago Daily News*, October 20, 1905.

35. *New-York Tribune*, October 14, 1906; and *Washington Post*, September 11, 1906; Brown and Koch, *Who's Who on the Stage, 1908*, 238.

36. Quoted in "The Golden Age of Vaudeville."

37. Quoted in "The Golden Age of Vaudeville."

38. *Indianapolis Star*, March 25, 1906.

39. *Milwaukee Sentinel*, May 7, 1906, Robinson Locke Collection.

16. Mabel Meets Mike

1. Quoted in Ada Patterson, *The Theatre*, July 1911, Robinson Locke Collection.

2. *Springfield (MO) Leader and Press*, June 15, 1901.

3. March 8, 1901, dateline, Robinson Locke Collection.

4. March 8, 1901, dateline, Robinson Locke Collection.

5. *San Francisco Call*, March 9 and 10, 1901.

6. *Los Angeles Evening Express*, March 4, 1901.

7. Quoted in *Los Angeles Evening Express*, March 28, 1901.

8. Quoted in *San Francisco Chronicle*, June 25, 1901.

9. Quoted in *San Francisco Call*, September 17, 1903.

10. Quoted in *Evening Chronicle* (Spokane), July 25, 1904.

11. *Kansas City Star*, March 24, 1905.

12. In 1902 Duffy set a world's record for the 100-yard dash.

13. *Rochester Democrat and Herald*, January 22, 1905.

14. *Kansas City Star*, March 24, 1905.

15. Tim Murnane, *Minneapolis Journal*, April 1, 1906.

16. Quoted in *Cincinnati Enquirer*, November 27, 1909.

17. Quoted in Frederic North Shorey, *Inter Ocean* (Chicago), April 14, 1907.

18. Quoted in Frederic North Shorey, *Inter Ocean* (Chicago), April 14, 1907.

19. *New York Globe*, April 11, 1906, Robinson Locke Collection.

20. *Vanity Fair*, October 19, 1912, Robinson Locke Collection.

21. *Sporting Life*, February 3, 1906.

22. *New York Dramatic Mirror*, October 30, 1912, Robinson Locke Collection.

23. *New York Globe*, April 11, 1906, Robinson Locke Collection.

24. Quoted in B. Rogers, *Will Rogers*, 115.

25. Quoted in Frederic North Shorey, *Inter Ocean* (Chicago), April 14, 1907.

26. *Erie Times-News*, April 9, 1910.

27. *Tribune* (Scranton), February 4, 1906.

28. *Sporting Life*, March 23, 1907.

17. A Season Interrupted

1. "Hot Stove League" was the winter offseason, when fans sat around the heat stove and "talked baseball." (This was in the days before central heating, when "hot stoves" provided heat for homes and shops.)

2. Ralph S. Davis, *Sporting News*, February 17, 1906.

3. Editorial, *Sporting News*, February 17, 1906.

4. Heywood Broun, *New-York Tribune*, April 24, 1914.

5. Quoted in *Inter Ocean* (Chicago), March 19, 1906; and *Cincinnati Enquirer*, March 24, 1906.

6. *Tribune* (Scranton), February 4, 1906.

7. Joe Vila, *Sporting News*, February 17, 1906.

8. *Sporting Life*, October 13, 1906.

9. *Sporting News*, February 17, 1906.

10. The authors found no record of Donlin's standing trial for the train incident.

11. *Pittsburgh Press*, March 12, 1906.

12. *Seattle Star*, February 27, 1906.

13. *Baltimore Sun*, March 17, 1906.

14. *Sporting Life*, March 24, 1906; and Joe Vila, *Sporting News*, April 7, 1906.

15. Quoted in *Sporting Life*, June 24 and July 22, 1905.

16. Alexander, *John McGraw*, 11–14.

17. Alexander, *John McGraw*, 7.

18. Quoted in *Inter Ocean* (Chicago), August 8, 1906.

19. Fleitz, *The Irish in Baseball*, 140. "Dutchmen" was the word used to identify players of German ethnicity.

20. Wm. F. H. Koelsch, *Sporting Life*, June 23, 1906.

21. Francis C. Richter, *Sporting Life*, May 19, 1906.

22. Timothy Sharp, *Sporting News*, February 3, 1906.

23. Timothy Sharp, *Sporting News*, March 7, 1906.

24. Deford, *The Old Ball Game*, 107.

25. Fountain, *Sportswriter*, 123.

26. Quoted in *Sporting News*, February 14, 1918.

27. Quoted in Plannette, "Two Centuries of Baseball," 32 and 31.

28. Joe Vila, *Sporting News*, April 7, 1906.

29. *New York Morning Telegraph*, April 12, 1906, Robinson Locke Collection.

30. Quoted in *Sporting Life*, December 7, 1907.

31. Quoted in *Sporting Life*, February 3, 1906.

32. *New York Evening Mail*, April 13, 1906.

33. Joe Vila, *Sporting News*, May 12, 1906.

34. J. C. Morse, *Sporting Life*, May 12, 1906.

35. Honus Wagner, who was hitting only .277 at the time, would win the batting title with a .339 average.

36. George McCormick, *New York Evening Mail*, May 16, 1906.

37. *New York Evening World*, May 19, 1906.

38. McGraw, *My Thirty Years in Baseball*, 185.

39. Hugh Fullerton, *Buffalo Courier*, June 10, 1906.

40. Joe Vila, *Sporting News*, June 16, 1906. Mathewson's 2.97 earned run average in 1906 was by far the highest of his career until 1914.

41. *Coshocton (OH) Daily Age*, June 16, 1906.

42. *Evansville (IN) Press*, July 2, 1906.

43. Quoted in J. T. Kelly, *Washington Post*, August 2, 1906.

44. Quoted in Plannette, "Two Centuries of Baseball," 27.

45. Deford, *The Old Ball Game*, 109.

46. Quoted in *New York Evening Mail*, August 8, 1906.

47. *New York Herald*, August 9, 1906.

48. Alexander, *John McGraw*, 122, quoting *Sporting News*, August 18, 1906.

49. *New York Evening Mail*, August 18, 1906; and *Pittsburgh Press*, August 23, 1906.

50. J. B. Sheridan, *St. Louis Post-Dispatch*, August 18, 1906.

51. Ruane, "A Retro-Review of the 1900s." This is still the National League record for wins and the Major League record for a 154-game season.

52. *Milwaukee Examiner*, April 28, 1906, Robinson Locke Collection.

53. Unsourced article, November 25, 1906, Robinson Locke Collection.

54. *St. Louis Post-Dispatch*, October 23, 1905.

55. *Republican* (Scranton), February 4, 1906.

18. Their Kind of Town

1. Yuko, "When Baseball Players Were Vaudeville Stars."
2. Klein, *Stealing Games*, 72–73, quoting the *Sporting News*.
3. *Pittsburgh Press*, January 16, 1907.
4. Joe Vila, *Sporting News*, December 29, 1906.
5. *Sporting Life*, February 16, 1907.
6. *Sporting Life*, February 2, 1907.
7. Simkus, *New York Sun*, March 27, 1907; and *Sporting Life*, February 9, 1907.
8. *Sporting Life*, February 9, 1907.
9. Tad, *Cincinnati Enquirer*, April 15, 1907; *Salt Lake Herald-Republican*, January 27, 1907.
10. Quoted in Redmond, *The Irish and the Making of American Sport*, 8.
11. *Sporting News*, January 5, 1907.
12. *St. Louis Globe-Democrat*, April 14, 1907.
13. *Erie Times-News*, April 15, 1912.
14. Crane is quoted in William F. H. Koelsch, *Sporting Life*, February 23, 1907.
15. *Pittsburgh Press*, February 18, 1907.
16. Quoted in *Star Tribune* (Minneapolis), March 10, 1907.
17. Quoted in *Buffalo Courier*, March 21, 1907.
18. Quoted in *Altoona (PA) Times*, March 29, 1907.
19. *Harrisburg (PA) Independent*, March 29, 1907.
20. Joe Vila, *Sporting News*, April 6, 1907. A "four flush" is a poker hand that is one card short of a full flush.
21. Quoted in Frederic North Shorey, *Inter Ocean* (Chicago), April 14, 1907.
22. *Sporting Life*, April 27, 1907.
23. Quoted in Frederic North Shorey, *Inter Ocean* (Chicago), April 14, 1907.
24. Simkus, "Outsiders in the Ragtime Era."
25. Quoted in Frederic North Shorey, *Inter Ocean* (Chicago), April 14, 1907.
26. Yuko, "When Baseball Players Were Vaudeville Stars."
27. McKenna, "Logan Squares." The number of clubs rose to 550 by 1909.
28. Quoted in Mallory, "The Game They All Played," 165–66.
29. *Chicago Tribune*, March 24, 1907.
30. Simkus, "Outsiders in the Ragtime Era."
31. Quoted in Elfers, "Nixey Callahan."
32. McKenna, "Logan Squares."
33. Quoted in Ahrens, "Jimmy Callahan," 53.
34. Joe Vila, *Sporting News*, May 25, 1907.
35. Joe Vila, *Sporting News*, June 15, 1907.

36. Quoted in *Pittsburgh Press*, May 14, 1907.

37. *Pittsburgh Press*, June 22, 1907.

38. Joe Vila, *Sporting News*, July 4, 1907.

39. Joe Vila, *Sporting News*, July 25, 1907.

40. Quoted in *Sporting Life*, August 31, 1907.

41. *Chicago Tribune*, July 7 and 21, 1907.

42. *Inter Ocean* (Chicago), April 1, 1907.

43. Quoted in "Mabel Hite," *Chicago Post*, June 8, 1907, Robinson Locke Collection.

44. Quoted in Frederic North Shorey, *Inter Ocean* (Chicago), April 14, 1907.

19. Become a Changed Man—or Else

1. *Chicago Tribune*, July 29, 1907.

2. John L. Sullivan, *Spokesman-Review* (Spokane), August 25, 1907.

3. Cottrell, "Rube Foster," 149 and 158.

4. Cottrell, *The Best Pitcher in Baseball*, 128.

5. Quoted in J. S. Williams, "Winning the Crucible of White-Hot Competition," 80.

6. Fleitz, "Cap Anson." See, for example, *Chicago Tribune*, August 25, 1907.

7. Schmidt, "The Golden Age of Chicago Baseball," 55.

8. Riess, *City Games*, 117–18.

9. Dixon, *Andrew "Rube" Foster*, 43.

10. Riess, *City Games*, 285n60.

11. Cottrell, *The Best Pitcher in Baseball*, 42.

12. Quoted in Frederic North Shorey, *Inter Ocean* (Chicago), August 11, 1907.

13. Quoted in Cottrell, *The Best Pitcher in Baseball*, 40.

14. *Chicago Tribune*, July 21, 1907.

15. Quoted in Dixon, *Andrew "Rube" Foster*, 109.

16. Frederic North Shorey, *Inter Ocean* (Chicago), August 11, 1907. This was the first (and only) mention of Donlin's impatience at the plate.

17. Quoted in Cottrell, *The Best Pitcher in Baseball*, 40.

18. Quoted in *Times* (Scranton), January 17, 1908.

19. *Sporting Life*, August 17, 1907.

20. Quoted in Lon Richardson, *Salt Lake Telegram*, December 11, 1930.

21. Charles Dryden, *Chicago Tribune*, August 28, 1907.

22. *Chicago Tribune*, August 24, 1907.

23. *Nevada State Journal* (Reno), August 31, 1907.

24. Quoted in *Chicago Tribune*, August 25, 1907.

25. Quoted in *Chicago Tribune*, August 25, 1907.

26. Quoted in Hanson, "Strange and Secret Keeley Cure."

27. When *Time* magazine featured the institute on its sixtieth anniversary in 1939, the institute claimed it had cured four hundred thousand alcoholics, including seventeen thousand doctors, since it opened in 1879. "Keeley Cure," *Time*, September 25, 1939, 34.

28. Quoted in Hanson, "Strange and Secret Keeley Cure."

29. Atropine is the active ingredient in Belladonna, a.k.a. deadly nightshade, which induces hallucinations.

30. Jensen, "Bugs Raymond." See *St. Joseph (MO) News-Press*, January 29, 1911.

31. *Streator (IL) Free Press*, September 19, 1907.

32. *Topeka State Journal*, September 16, 1907; and *Courier* (Waterloo IA), September 14, 1907.

33. Ralph S. Davis, *Pittsburgh Press*, December 29, 1907.

34. *Chicago Tribune*, January 12, 1908.

35. Joe Vila, *Sporting News*, May 27, 1905.

36. Joe Vila, *Sporting News*, September 19, 1907.

37. Joe Vila, *Sporting News*, March 8, 1934.

38. Joe Vila, *Sporting News*, March 8, 1934.

39. *Sporting Life*, March 2, 1907. The account included information about the man's arrest and the pawning of the stud, details that add credence to the account.

40. *Wilkes-Barre (PA) News*, November 28, 1907.

41. Quoted in *Herald and Review* (Decatur IL), November 28, 1907. Other accounts said his 1908 salary was between $4,000 and $5,000.

42. J. Ed Grillo, *Washington Post*, December 2, 1907.

43. The Boston National League club changed its name from the Beaneaters to the Doves in 1907.

20. The Prodigal Returns

1. *New York Sun*, January 25, 1908.

2. *New York American*, December 18, 1907, as quoted in Fleming, *The Unforgettable Season*, 38.

3. Joe Vila, *Sporting News*, February 27, 1908; and *Sporting News*, March 12, 1908.

4. *St. Louis Post-Dispatch*, January 23, 1908.

5. *Pittsburgh Post*, January 19, 1908.

6. Quoted in *Sporting Life*, February 8, 1908.

7. *Washington (DC) Times*, March 5, 1908.

8. Quoted in William Rankin, *Sporting News*, March 19, 1908.

9. Quoted in *Evening Star* (Washington DC), January 13, 1908.

10. Fred Lieb wrote Wagner was holding out for more money. Lieb, *The Pittsburgh Pirates*, 125.

11. *New York Sun*, April 12, 1908, as quoted in Fleming, *The Unforgettable Season*, 38.

12. Quoted in Bogen, *Tinker, Evers, and Chance*, 59.

13. Clarke also managed the Louisville Colonels from 1897 to 1899.

14. Lieb, *The Pittsburgh Pirates*, 64.

15. *New York American*, August 9, 1908, as quoted in Fleming, *The Unforgettable Season*, 161.

16. Quoted in Mansch, *Rube Marquard*, 41–42.

17. *New York Globe*, July 25, 1905.

18. *Washington Post*, July 22, 1906.

19. *Atchison (KS) Globe*, July 18, 1908.

20. Quoted in Robbins, *Ninety Feet from Fame*, 192.

21. *New-York Tribune*, April 23, 1908.

22. *Brooklyn Times*, April 23, 1908.

23. Quoted in *Sporting Life*, October 10, 1908.

24. Quoted in *New York Morning Telegraph*, April 24, 1908, Robinson Locke Collection.

25. Hite, "On Just Being a Fan," 23.

26. Hite, "On Just Being a Fan," 24.

27. *Yonkers Herald*, January 21, 1908. The same paper reported on January 27 that Hite was unable to perform because of an accident to her $100 dummy.

28. Rush, "Orpheum, Yonkers"; and "Mabel Hite," *Variety*, January 25, 1908. Yonkers is a Westchester County suburb of New York City, just north of the Bronx.

29. Amy Leslie, *Chicago Daily News*, February 8, 1908.

30. *Philadelphia Inquirer*, April 14, 1908.

31. Franklin Fyles, "'The Merry-Go-Round' Just Girls and Nonsense," *Chicago Tribune*, May 3, 1908.

32. Nancy Sykes, *Anaconda (MT) Standard*, May 17, 1908.

33. *Brooklyn Eagle*, April 27, 1908.

34. Quoted in *New York Times*, May 30, 1908.

35. Sher, "John McGraw," 209.

36. Deford, *The Old Ball Game*, 156.

37. Quoted in *Chicago Tribune*, February 26, 1934.

38. *Inter Ocean* (Chicago), May 12, 1908.

39. William F. Kirk, *New York American*, May 12, 1908.

40. Joe Vila, *Sporting News*, June 18, 1908.

41. *Chicago Journal*, May 28, 1908, as quoted in Fleming, *The Unforgettable Season*, 80.

42. Jack Ryder, *Cincinnati Enquirer*, July 9, 1908.

43. *Sedalia (MO) Democrat*, July 23, 1908.

44. *Chattanooga News*, February 10, 1908.
45. Quoted in *Santa Cruz Evening Sentinel*, August 29, 1908.
46. Quoted in *Sporting Life*, September 26, 1908.
47. *Sporting Life*, August 1, 1908; and Jensen, "Jimmy Sheckard."
48. Quoted in Ralph S. Davis, *Sporting News*, October 8, 1908.
49. Quoted in William F. H. Koelsch, *Sporting Life*, June 20, 1908.
50. Quoted in R. Edgren, *New York Evening World*, June 11, 1908.

21. The Most Popular Ballplayer

1. Quoted in Ritter, *The Glory of Their Times*, 33.
2. By comparison, Mathewson had a combined 7-7 record against the Cubs and the Pirates, and Pittsburgh ace Vic Willis was a combined 7-5 against them in 1908.
3. Quoted in Murphy, *Crazy '08*, 119.
4. Quoted in Bogen, *Johnny Kling*, 4.
5. *Buffalo Commercial*, August 1, 1908.
6. *New York Times*, July 31, 1908.
7. No other National League player was hitting above .300 at the time.
8. DeValeria and DeValeria, *Honus Wagner*, 183–84. The *New York Evening World*, July 26, 1908, wrote that with each hit Wagner said, "That's 3, Mike," "That's 4," etc.
9. Quoted in DeValeria and DeValeria, *Honus Wagner*, 183–84. Wagner may have been thinking of the September 18 game. See chapter 22 in this volume.
10. *New York Sun*, July 26, 1908.
11. *Pittsburgh Press*, July 26, 1908.
12. Ralph S. Davis, *Sporting News*, August 6, 1908.
13. Wagner's slugging average was .558; Donlin's was .442. Wagner was leading the league in doubles (24), triples (14), and home runs (8).
14. W. M. Rankin, *Sporting News*, July 30, 1908.
15. *New York Globe*, May 17, 1908.
16. *New York Evening Mail*, August 1, 1908, as quoted in Fleming, *The Unforgettable Season*, 147.
17. *New York Evening World*, August 9, 1908, as quoted in Fleming, *The Unforgettable Season*, 161.
18. Quoted in Seib, *The Player*, 69.
19. Robinson, *Matty*, 8.
20. Quoted in Wecter, *The Hero in America*, xxiii.
21. Quoted in Kahn, *The Head Game*, 94.
22. Quoted in Kahn, *The Head Game*, 94.
23. McKim, "'Matty' and 'Ol' Pete.'"

24. Email from Richard Crepeau to Steve Steinberg, October 6, 2021.

25. Plannette, "Two Centuries of Baseball," 24.

26. Quoted in Deford, *The Old Ball Game*, 125.

27. Deford, *The Old Ball Game*, 125.

28. Wecter, *The Hero in America*, xxvii.

29. Quoted in *Washington Post*, August 9, 1908.

30. *Brooklyn Eagle*, August 13, 1908.

31. *New-York Tribune*, August 14, 1908. "Recrudescence" is a revival of activity.

32. *New York Evening Journal*, August 15, 1908, as quoted in Fleming, *The Unforgettable Season*, 169.

33. Hite, "On Just Being a Fan," 24.

34. *New York Sun*, August 25, 1908.

35. *New York Evening Journal*, August 25, 1908, as quoted in Fleming, *The Unforgettable Season*, 169.

36. *Philadelphia Inquirer*, August 27, 1908; and *Lancaster (PA) New Era*, August 27, 1908.

37. Joe Vila, *Sporting News*, August 27, 1908.

38. Humphreys, *Wizardry*, 185.

39. Hopper, "On Tour with the 'Giants,'" 18, 28.

40. Hopper, "On Tour with the 'Giants,'" 30.

41. Hopper, "On Tour with the 'Giants,'" 16. Years later the quote morphed into one credited to Yankees pitcher Waite Hoyt: "It's great to be young and a Yankee."

42. W. M. Rankin, *Sporting News*, July 30, 1908.

43. *New York Evening Mail*, August 29, 1908, as quoted in Fleming, *The Unforgettable Season*, 192.

22. A Pennant Race Like No Other

1. Quoted in Snelling, *Johnny Evers*, 72.

2. Quoted in Snelling, *Johnny Evers*, 11.

3. "Inquisitive Fans," *Chicago Tribune*, July 19, 1908.

4. Editorial, *Sporting Life*, September 12, 1908.

5. W. M Rankin, *Sporting News*, September 17, 1908.

6. *Waterbury (CT) Evening Democrat*, September 17, 1908.

7. *Evening Star* (Washington DC), October 20, 1908.

8. *New York American*, September 19, 1908, as quoted in Fleming, *The Unforgettable Season*, 230.

9. *New York Press*, September 19, 1908.

10. C. B. Power, *Pittsburgh Dispatch*, September 20, 1908.

11. Quoted in *New York Sun* and *New York Times*, September 19, 1908.

12. Ralph S. Davis, *Sporting News*, September 23, 1908.

13. Ralph S. Davis, *Sporting News*, September 17, 1908.

14. *New York Evening Telegram*, September 19, 1908.

15. Quoted in *Chicago Tribune*, May 12, 1929.

16. *New York Sun*, September 19, 1908.

17. Charles Dryden, *Chicago Tribune*, September 23, 1908.

18. *Sporting Life*, August 22, 1908.

19. I. E. Sanborn, *Chicago Tribune*, September 27, 1908.

20. Charles Dryden, *Chicago Tribune*, September 24, 1908.

21. Quoted in Gaines, *The Christian Gentleman*, 95.

22. O'Day told *Sporting Life* that he called the third out because of McGinnity's interference and not Evers's play. Murphy, *Crazy '08*, 193.

23. Mathewson, *Pitching in a Pinch*, 172.

24. Sam Crane, *New York Evening Journal*, September 17, 1908.

25. Alexander, *John McGraw*, 134, quoting "Umpire Bill Klem's Own Story," *Collier's*, April 7 and 14, 1951.

26. Quoted in Ritter, *The Glory of Their Times*, 132.

27. Quoted in Murphy, *Crazy '08*, 268.

28. *New York Evening Mail*, October 2, 1908, as quoted in Fleming, *The Unforgettable Season*, 275.

29. *New York American*, October 1, 1908, as quoted in Fleming, *The Unforgettable Season*, 275.

30. The Pirates had gone 32-9 since August 26. The Cubs had gone 30-8 since that date. The Giants had only an 8-9 record since September 18.

31. Quoted in the *New York Times*, October 6, 1908. Wagner had two hits in the game; he scored one run and knocked in the other.

32. Steinberg, "1908's Forgotten Team," 109–10.

33. *Pittsburg Leader*, October 7, 1908.

34. Quoted in Robinson, *Matty*, 109.

35. Quoted in Dolly Dalrymple, *Birmingham Age-Herald*, February 22, 1913.

36. Tinker's home run had beaten Mathewson, 1–0, on July 17.

37. *New York Globe*, September 9, 1908.

38. Hugh Fullerton, *Atlanta Constitution*, February 13, 1922.

39. Wagner nailed down the batting title in an early September homestand, when he went 18-for-26 and raised his batting average to .350.

40. *Baseball Magazine*, November 1908. Donlin was chosen over the publication's pick for best American League center fielder, Detroit's Sam Crawford.

41. Mark Roth and Sid Mercer, *New York Globe*, May 23, 1908.

42. Nie, *New York Globe*, September 2, 1908.

43. Hopper, "On Tour with the 'Giants,'" 7.

23. Stealing Home

1. *New York Globe*, October 15, 1908.

2. Unsourced magazine, August 28, 1908, Robinson Locke Collection. In 1910 a nonagricultural worker earned $700 a year, and a successful traveling salesman made $1,500 a year. Monod, *Vaudeville and the Making of Modern Entertainment*, 46.

3. Donlin was paid a base salary of $6,000, plus $600 as the Giants' captain, in 1908. *San Francisco Examiner*, June 6, 1909.

4. Quoted in Monod, *Vaudeville and the Making of Modern Entertainment*, 218.

5. Hammerstein's Victoria program files, provided by Andrew Hammerstein. A challenger who stayed in the ring with Livingston for ten minutes earned a $50 prize. No one succeeded in doing so that summer.

6. *New York Times*, October 22, 1911.

7. Laurie, "From Vaudeville," 260.

8. Hynd, *Marquard & Seeley*, 40.

9. Monod, *Vaudeville and the Making of Modern Entertainment*, 4–5 and 10–11.

10. *Sporting News*, August 6, 1908.

11. *New York Globe*, August 6, 1908, as quoted in Fleming, *The Unforgettable Season*, 156.

12. *Sporting News*, August 6, 1908.

13. *Altoona (PA) Times*, January 14, 1909.

14. Quoted in *Star-Gazette* (Elmira NY), November 30, 1908.

15. *Butte (MT) Miner*, April 29, 1909.

16. Quoted in *Washington Post*, January 3, 1909.

17. HEK, *Chicago Tribune*, August 6, 1908. HEK was Hugh E. Keough.

18. *New York Globe*, August 6, 1908, as quoted in Fleming, *The Unforgettable Season*, 156.

19. Quoted in *Chicago Tribune*, January 12, 1909.

20. Quoted in *New York Morning Telegraph*, October 27, 1908, Robinson Locke Collection.

21. Quoted in *Butte (MT) Miner*, April 29, 1909.

22. Monod, *Vaudeville and the Making of Modern Entertainment*, 39.

23. Advertisement, *New-York Tribune*, October 25, 1908.

24. *New York Herald*, October 27, 1908, Robinson Locke Collection.

25. *New York Times*, October 27, 1908.

26. *New York Globe*, October 27, 1908.

27. Quoted in B. Rogers, *Will Rogers*, 115.

28. Bozeman Bulger, *New York Evening World*, October 27, 1908.

29. *Variety*, October 31, 1908.

30. Quoted in Hammerstein's Victoria program files, provided by Andrew Hammerstein.

31. Amy Leslie, *Chicago Daily News*, no date, Robinson Locke Collection.

32. *Variety*, October 31, 1908.

33. *Louisville Courier-Journal*, February 11, 1909.

34. Quoted in Edelman and Betzold, *San Francisco Examiner*, June 6, 1909.

35. Quoted in Colgate Baker, *New York Review*, no date, Robinson Locke Collection.

36. Donlin, "Baseball Acting," 309.

37. *Variety*, October 31, 1908.

38. *New York Press*, December 1908 (exact date unknown), Robinson Locke Collection.

39. Quoted in Monod, *Vaudeville and the Making of Modern Entertainment*, 205.

40. Quoted in *Tribune* (Scranton), December 5, 1908; and *Sporting News*, January 7, 1909.

41. Joe Vila, *Sporting News*, January 7, 1909.

42. *Muskogee (OK) Phoenix and Times-Democrat*, January 14, 1909.

43. Will Rogers, *San Bernardino (CA) Sun*, October 8, 1933, as quoted in B. Rogers, *Will Rogers*.

24. Will He or Won't He?

1. Quoted in *Sporting News*, January 7, 1909.

2. Damon Runyon, *New York American*, October 11, 1926.

3. *Sporting Life*, March 13, 1909.

4. *Buffalo Times*, December 29, 1908.

5. Quoted in *Grand Forks (ND) Herald*, January 1, 1909.

6. Quoted in *Sporting News*, January 7, 1909.

7. Quoted in *Fall River (MA) Globe*, January 9, 1909.

8. *Pittsburgh Press*, January 28, 1909.

9. *Cincinnati Enquirer*, January 4, 1909.

10. *Cincinnati Enquirer*, January 8, 1909.

11. William P. McLoughlin, *St. Louis Post-Dispatch*, July 19, 1909.

12. Reported in Green and Laurie, *Show Biz*, 51–52.

13. *Sedalia (MO) Democrat*, November 27, 1908.

14. *Chicago Tribune*, February 28, 1909.

15. *Inter Ocean* (Chicago), January 9, 1909.

16. *Pittsburgh Leader*, December 29, 1908, Robinson Locke Collection.

17. Unsourced newspaper article, January 1, 1909, Robinson Locke Collection.

18. *Louisville Courier-Journal*, February 11, 1909.

19. *Richmond Times Dispatch*, March 27, 1909.

20. *St. Louis Post-Dispatch*, March 25, 1909; and *Richmond Times Dispatch*, March 27, 1909.

21. *San Francisco Call*, June 17, 1909.

22. Quoted in *Los Angeles Times*, July 4, 1909. Morphine was not regulated as a controlled substance until 1914.

23. Joe Vila, *Sporting News*, March 18, 1909.

24. Joe Vila, *Sporting News*, March 11, 1909; and *Sporting News*, March 18, 1909.

25. Colgate Baker, "Mabel," *New York Review*, undated, Robinson Locke Collection.

26. *Cincinnati Post*, February 26, 1910.

27. *Chattanooga News*, February 10, 1909.

28. *Oregon Journal* (Portland), May 19, 1908.

29. Quoted in *New York Morning Telegraph*, March 4, 1909, Robinson Locke Collection.

30. *Spokane Chronicle*, April 10, 1909.

31. *Hartford Courant*, February 22, 1909.

32. Mabel's financial acumen had surfaced five years earlier. She had recognized and bought a painting (whose value was not recognized) from a New York art gallery. It was priced at $10 and worth $1,000. *New York Evening World*, May 19, 1904.

33. Quoted in *Buffalo Evening News*, February 11, 1909.

34. Quoted in *Hartford Courant*, February 22, 1909.

35. Quoted in *Buffalo Evening News*, February 11, 1909.

36. The couple later did sign contracts extending their stage appearances into the early summer. Joe Vila, *Sporting News*, March 18, 1909.

37. Quoted in *New York Times*, March 17, 1909.

38. Quoted in unsourced newspaper article, April 17, 1909, Robinson Locke Collection.

25. I Play for the Money

1. The absence of Donlin would exacerbate the thinness of the Giants' outfield, as twenty-one-year-old rookies Fred Snodgrass and Josh Devore were not ready to play full time in 1909.

2. *Morning Union* (Grass Valley CA), June 1, 1909.

3. W. W. Aulick, *New York Evening Mail*, April 2, 1909.

4. Quoted in *Baltimore Sun*, April 2, 1909.

5. Quoted in *New York Times*, May 8, 1909.

6. Quoted in *New York Times*, July 17, 1909.

7. Quoted in *San Francisco Examiner*, June 6, 1909.

8. Al C. Joy, *San Francisco Examiner*, May 31, 1909.

9. *Morning Union* (Grass Valley CA), June 1, 1909.

10. Quoted in Julian Johnson, *Los Angeles Times*, July 4, 1909.

11. *New York Times*, July 27, 1909; and *Brooklyn Citizen*, July 15, 1909.

12. *Chicago Tribune*, July 31, 1909.

13. *St. Louis Post-Dispatch*, August 29, 1909.

14. Donlin still "belonged" to the Giants.

15. *St. Louis Post-Dispatch*, August 29, 1909.

16. Quoted in *Variety*, October 30, 1909.

17. Dash, *Variety*, October 16, 1909.

18. *Indianapolis Star*, December 7, 1909.

19. Quoted in Al C. Joy, *San Francisco Examiner*, June 6, 1909.

20. *New-York Tribune*, September 12, 1909.

21. Quoted in *Washington Post*, September 13, 1909.

22. *New York Evening World*, June 4, 1908.

23. John McGraw was a partner in Doyle's pool hall, and notorious gambler Arnold Rothstein was a silent partner.

24. Polsky, *Hustlers, Beats, and Others*, 28.

25. *New-York Tribune*, October 27, 1909.

26. "Donlin Dope," *Sporting Life*, November 13, 1909.

27. Quoted in *Evening Star* (Washington DC), November 2, 1909.

28. E. H. Simmons, *Sporting Life*, December 4, 1909.

29. Quoted in *St. Louis Post-Dispatch*, August 6, 1911.

26. Mabel's Star Continues to Rise

1. *New York Morning Telegraph*, February 4, 1910, Robinson Locke Collection.

2. *Times Union* (Brooklyn), February 12, 1910; and *Buffalo Evening News*, February 4, 1910.

3. Quoted in *San Francisco Examiner*, January 30, 1910.

4. *St. Louis Star*, February 13, 1910; "Wray's Column," *St. Louis Post-Dispatch*, February 11, 1910.

5. W. A. Phelon, *New York Morning Telegraph*, March 20, 1910.

6. Quoted in *Fort Wayne (IN) News*, February 15, 1910.

7. "Donlin on Baseball," *Marion (OH) Star*, May 7, 1910.

8. Quoted in *Washington (DC) Times*, October 21, 1911.

9. *Erie Times-News*, April 15, 1912.

10. *Citizen* (Honesdale PA), May 17, 1912.

11. Edelman, "Baseball, Vaudeville, and Mike Donlin," 52. The average U.S. wage in 1910 was twenty-two cents per hour. The average U.S. worker made between $200 and $400 per year.

12. *Hartford Courant*, January 27, 1910.

13. *Anaconda (MT) Standard*, February 11, 1912.

14. Dietz, *The Complete Book of 1910s Broadway Musicals*, 82.
15. Quoted in *Chicago Tribune*, May 15, 1910.
16. It was not until 1943, with the debut of the musical *Oklahoma!*, that songs were integrated into the narrative of the show.
17. Garrick, *Detroit Free Press*, February 27, 1910. The song includes Mabel's lyric: "It's liberty or death with me; my hair is turning gray. Reno life is simply great, they grant divorces while you wait."
18. Percy Hammond, *Chicago Tribune*, April 13, 1910.
19. Percy Hammond, *Chicago Tribune*, April 13, 1910.
20. Amy Leslie, *Chicago News*, May 12, 1910.
21. *Buffalo Courier*, April 5, 1910.
22. Quoted in Dietz, *The Complete Book of 1910s Broadway Musicals*, 82.
23. *Independent* (Santa Barbara), April 6, 1910, quoting the *Boston Traveler*.
24. See, for example, *Richmond Times Dispatch*, August 6, 1910.
25. See, for example, *New-York Tribune*, July 30, 1910.
26. Quoted in *Richmond Times Dispatch*, August 6, 1910.
27. *Wilkes-Barre (PA) Times Leader*, August 6, 1910.
28. Quoted in *Fall River (MA) Globe*, July 15, 1910. That morning the Giants were in second place, just two games behind the Cubs.
29. *Brooklyn Standard Union*, August 3, 1910.
30. *Boston Globe*, September 11, 1910.
31. *New York Times*, September 25, 1910.
32. *New York Age*, September 29, 1910.
33. *Brooklyn Eagle*, August 5, 1910.
34. These possible diagnoses are based on email exchanges between Steve Steinberg and Dr. Stephen Boren, January 15–22, 2022.
35. While out west the entrepreneurial couple added apples to their portfolio by purchasing an orchard in Oregon. *Salt Lake Herald-Republican*, December 8, 1910.
36. Quoted in *Kansas City Star*, November 10, 1910.
37. *Variety*, October 8, 1910.

27. A Return to Baseball

1. Quoted in A. R. Cratty, *Sporting Life*, March 4, 1911.
2. *New York Age*, April 20, 1911.
3. *Washington Post*, March 22, 1911.
4. F. H. Young, *Philadelphia Telegraph*, March 25, 1911.
5. *New York Times*, April 25, 1911.
6. Mansch, *Rube Marquard*, 79.
7. Quoted in Hynd, *Marquard & Seeley*, 171.

8. Quoted in *St. Louis Post-Dispatch*, August 6, 1911.

9. Donlin now had little leverage and likely signed for less than he had made in 1908.

10. Hynd, *Marquard & Seeley*, 89.

11. Quoted in Schechter, *Victory Faust*, 37.

12. *Sporting News*, October 12, 1911.

13. Quoted in Hernandez, *Manager of Giants*, 67.

14. Quoted in Betzold, "Turkey Mike Donlin," 83.

15. There was no mention of the price Boston paid for Donlin. The Boston club was known as the Rustlers only in the 1911 season; it was a play on owner William Russell's name. Russell was gone in 1912 and so was the name, replaced by the Braves.

16. Tenney had tried to acquire Donlin before the season began, shortly after he agreed to manage the Rustlers. *Oakland Tribune*, January 28, 1911.

17. Quoted in *St. Louis Post-Dispatch*, August 6, 1911.

18. *St. Louis Globe-Democrat*, August 24, 1911.

19. *Kansas City Star*, November 6, 1911.

20. *New York Sun*, October 8, 1911.

21. *Courier* (Harrisburg PA), October 22, 1911.

22. *Erie Times-News*, May 18, 1912.

23. Quoted in *Anaconda (MT) Standard*, August 13, 1911.

24. T. H. Murnane, *Sporting News*, August 10, 1911.

25. *Boston Globe*, August 15, 1911.

26. Hernandez, *Manager of Giants*, 67.

27. Quoted in *Cincinnati Commercial*, September 21, 1911.

28. *Sporting News*, September 28, 1911.

29. Quoted in *Sporting Life*, September 23, 1911.

30. *Chicago Tribune*, December 27, 1911.

31. *Sentinel-Record* (Hot Springs), December 24, 1911; and *Courier* (Hot Springs), March 7, 1912.

32. Quoted in *Lansing (MI) State Journal*, March 15, 1912.

33. Quoted in *Washington (DC) Times*, December 23, 1911.

34. Klein, *Stealing Games*, 273.

35. *Buffalo Enquirer*, January 2, 1912.

36. Quoted in *Washington Post*, December 24, 1911.

37. Quoted in Alexander, *John McGraw*, 160.

38. *Sporting News*, January 4, 1912.

28. A Trade to Pittsburgh

1. *Buffalo Times*, January 7, 1912.

2. Quoted in *Fall River (MA) Globe*, January 9, 1912.

3. Ralph S. Davis, *Sporting News*, February 15, 1912.

4. *Boston Globe*, February 15, 1912.

5. T. H. Murnane, *Boston Globe*, February 16, 1912.

6. Ralph S. Davis, *Sporting News*, February 22, 1912.

7. *Fall River (MA) Globe*, February 23, 1912.

8. T. H. Murnane, *Sporting News*, February 29, 1912.

9. *Pittsburgh Post*, February 18, 1912.

10. James C. Isaminger, *Pittsburgh Press*, February 20, 1912.

11. Grantland Rice, *Washington (DC) Times*, February 23, 1912.

12. Quoted in *Pittsburgh Post*, February 29, 1912.

13. Ralph S. Davis, *Sporting News*, March 14, 1912.

14. W. B. McVicker, *Pittsburgh Press*, March 24, 1912.

15. Quoted in W. B. McVicker, *Pittsburgh Press*, March 24, 1912.

16. *Quad-City Times* (Davenport IA), January 28, 1912.

17. W. B. McVicker, *Pittsburgh Press*, April 10, 1912.

18. W. B. McVicker, *Pittsburgh Press*, April 19, 1912.

19. *Pittsburgh Press*, April 21, 1912.

20. Bill Brennan had also ejected Donlin two days earlier for arguing a call at first base. (He was the first base coach.)

21. *Spokane Chronicle*, April 24, 1912.

22. *Brooklyn Standard Union*, May 12, 1912.

23. *New York Sun*, May 14, 1912.

24. *Times-Democrat* (New Orleans), May 26, 1912.

25. Quoted in James Jerpe, *Pittsburgh Post-Gazette*, May 2, 1912.

26. Quoted in *New York Evening World*, May 15.

27. Ralph S. Davis, *Sporting News*, May 16, 1912.

29. Tragic End of a Loving Partnership

1. A. J. Cratty, *Sporting Life*, June 8, 1912.

2. Quoted in A. J. Cratty, *Sporting Life*, June 8, 1912. "Bull" was slang for a wrong-headed decision.

3. *New York Morning Telegraph*, June 18, 1912, Robinson Locke Collection. Mabel was performing "two-a-days" of *Mabel Hite and Her Clowns*. Other accounts said she collapsed the following day.

4. Erdman was described as "one of the world's noted surgeons" and "the grand old man" of New York surgery in his *New York Times* obituary. *New York Times*, March 28, 1954.

5. *St. Louis Post-Dispatch*, October 23, 1912.

6. *Evening Star* (Washington DC), June 19, 1912. Peritonitis is an inflammation

of the tissue that lines the abdomen and causes a bowel obstruction. It could have resulted from a colon cancer that perforated.

7. Donlin ignored the Giants' star pitcher, Christy Mathewson, who won twenty-three games in 1912. But his 7-3 record on June 10 lagged far behind Marquard's 12-0.

8. Quoted in *Montpelier (VT) Morning Journal*, June 14, 1912.

9. *Pittsburgh Post-Gazette*, June 17, 1912; and *New York Times*, June 18, 1912.

10. *New York Times*, June 16, 1912.

11. Quoted in unsourced and undated newspaper article, *New York Sun* morgue files, New York Public Library.

12. Quoted in *Pittsburgh Post*, June 23, 1912; and *New York Sun*, June 22, 1912.

13. Quoted in *New-York Tribune*, June 22, 1912.

14. Ralph S. Davis, *Sporting News*, June 27, 1912.

15. *Pittsburgh Post*, July 7, 1912; and unsourced newspaper article, July 24, 1912, Robinson Locke Collection. The lease on their apartment expired the end of September, at which time they moved in with Mabel's mother.

16. Quoted in *Pittsburgh Press*, August 19, 1912.

17. *Pittsburgh Press*, August 19, 1912.

18. Ed Wray, *St. Louis Post-Dispatch*, August 21, 1912.

19. Ed F. Ballinger, *Pittsburgh Post*, August 26, 1912.

20. *St. Louis Post-Dispatch*, September 23, 1912.

21. Christian Science sees reality as a shadow and focuses on healing, on the mental act of eliminating fear.

22. Quoted in *New York Evening Journal*, October 24, 1912.

23. Quoted in *St. Louis Post-Dispatch*, September 23, 1912.

24. *South Bend (IN) Tribune*, October 7, 1912.

25. Quoted in *San Francisco Examiner*, September 26, 1912.

26. The Pittsburgh club had sent a telegram asking for permission to have Mabel's car driven to right field, and the request was promptly granted. It was the first game for Mabel since June.

27. Brush, who suffered from locomotor ataxia, a severe progressive disease of the central nervous system, died just two months later.

28. *St. Louis Post-Dispatch*, September 23, 1912.

29. *Erie Times-News*, September 24, 1912. Mike was the "interlocutor" for the Honey Boy Minstrels, announcing for the performers and bantering with them.

30. *Brooklyn Eagle*, October 23, 1912. Doctor Hunt was called in, although he had not been attending Mabel since June.

31. Quoted in *Pittsburgh Press*, October 23, 1912.

32. *Evening Sun* (Baltimore), October 23, 1912.

33. *New York Morning Telegraph*, October 26, 1912, Robinson Locke Collection.

34. *New York Morning Telegraph*, October 23, 1912, Robinson Locke Collection. The article stated her urn would be placed in the Columbarium of the Campbell Funeral Home Company.

35. Email exchanges with Dr. Stephen Boren, January 16–22, 2022. "When I read death certificates from before 1920, I am skeptical of the cause unless it was from trauma," he wrote. "'Intestinal cancer' normally means colon cancer. Rarely is it small bowel cancer. . . . If [Mabel] really had cancer, I would guess it was from her ovaries. Ovarian cancer is very insidious, not rare, and could cause all her symptoms."

36. *New York Morning Telegraph*, October 23, 1912, Robinson Locke Collection.

37. Email exchanges with Dr. Stephen Boren, January 16–22, 2022. "Tuberculosis was very common at that time," he wrote. "While one normally thinks of this being a lung disease, it can occur in the abdomen." Even nowadays it is difficult to diagnose.

38. *Evening Star* (Washington DC), March 22, 1911.

39. Quoted in *Inter Ocean* (Chicago), November 3, 1912.

40. *New York Dramatic Mirror*, October 30, 1912, Robinson Locke Collection.

41. *Kansas City Times*, October 23, 1912.

30. Life Goes On

1. *New York Morning Telegraph*, November 5, 1912, Robinson Locke Collection.

2. *Pittsburgh Gazette Times*, November 10, 1912, Robinson Locke Collection.

3. Quoted in *Pittsburgh Press*, November 11, 1912.

4. *Evening Star* (Washington DC), November 8, 1912.

5. James Jerpe, "Donlin Says Artie Hofman Will Be Great Next Year," *Pittsburgh Post-Gazette*, November 12, 1912.

6. *Philadelphia Inquirer*, December 25, 1912.

7. Ralph S. Davis, *Pittsburgh Press*, December 29, 1912.

8. *Pittsburgh Gazette Times*, November 10, 1912.

9. Quoted in *Paterson (NJ) Evening News*, January 13, 1913.

10. Quoted in *Evening Review* (East Liverpool OH), January 30, 1913.

11. *New-York Tribune*, July 20, 1913.

12. Quoted in *Central New Jersey Home News*, December 31, 1912.

13. Grapewin also appeared in over one hundred motion pictures, most notably portraying Uncle Henry in the 1939 movie *The Wizard of Oz*.

14. Quoted in *Dayton Daily News*, March 17, 1913.

15. *Pittsburgh Post–Gazette Times*, December 6, 1912.

16. Quoted in *Indianapolis Star*, March 18, 1913.

17. Unsourced newspaper article, Grapewin file, New York Public Library, Performing Arts branch.
18. Dolly Dalrymple, *Birmingham Age-Herald*, April 22, 1913.
19. Quoted in *Pittsburgh Press*, May 14, 1913. Donlin was still on Philadelphia's reserve list.
20. *New York Times*, February 11, 2001.
21. *Long Branch (NJ) Daily Record*, August 25, 1913. Rita was not in the original cast. But one night when the actress did not show up, she took the role and kept it for the rest of the run.
22. Quoted in *Inter Ocean* (Chicago), October 13, 1913. Rita's uncle, Charles Ross, confirmed the engagement.
23. Quoted in *Long Branch (NJ) Daily Record*, October 18, 1913.
24. Bozeman Bulger, *New York Evening World*, December 5, 1913.
25. *Houston Chronicle*, November 3, 1913, as quoted in Elfers, *The Tour to End All Tours*, 64.
26. *San Francisco Examiner*, November 14, 1913, as reported in Elfers, *The Tour to End All Tours*, 83.
27. Richter, *Richter's History and Records of Base Ball*, 142–44.
28. *New York World Magazine*, March 29, 1914.
29. *Shreveport (LA) Times*, April 12, 1914.
30. *Pittsburgh Press*, February 29, 1912.

31. Remarriage and a Final Return

1. Elfers, *The Tour to End All Tours*, 237–38, quoting the *New York Morning Telegraph*.
2. Quoted in A. R. Goldberg, *Sporting News*, April 23, 1914.
3. Quoted in Betzold, "Turkey Mike Donlin," 83.
4. *Shreveport (LA) Times*, April 12, 1914.
5. Grantland Rice, *Washington (DC) Times*, April 11, 1914.
6. Thomas J. Gray, *Variety*, March 13, 1914.
7. *Los Angeles Times*, December 19, 1936.
8. *New York Sun*, May 27, 1914.
9. Murdock, *Baseball between the Wars*, 160; and *Erie Times-News*, May 28, 1914.
10. A. M. Corrigan, *Boston Globe*, June 1, 1914.
11. Hernandez, *Manager of Giants*, 84; and Heywood Broun, *New-York Tribune*, August 5, 1914.
12. Donlin would get only one hit in sixteen at bats the final two months of the season.
13. Quoted in Damon Runyon, *San Francisco Examiner*, July 4, 1915.

14. Heywood Broun, *New-York Tribune*, August 5, 1914.

15. Quoted in Christy Mathewson, *Honolulu Star-Bulletin*, September 25, 1914.

16. Quoted in *Los Angeles Herald*, March 8, 1915.

17. *Sporting Life*, October 17, 1914.

18. *Evening Star* (Washington DC), December 6, 1914.

19. Heywood Broun, *Sporting Life*, December 12, 1914.

20. *Miami Herald*, July 18, 1914.

21. *Detroit Free Press*, September 16, 1914.

22. Harry Dix Cole, *Sporting Life*, October 10, 1914.

23. *Sacramento Union*, November 12, 1914.

24. *San Francisco Examiner*, December 10, 1914; and *Sporting Life*, December 19, 1914.

25. Billy Murphy, *St. Louis Star*, December 24, 1914.

26. Mike Donlin photo caption, *Fall River (MA) Globe*, December 31, 1914.

27. *Rochester Post*, December 30, 1914.

28. *Pittsburgh Press*, November 29, 1914.

29. Will Rogers, *San Bernardino (CA) Sun*, October 8, 1933.

30. Donlin said he was still waiting for Mabel's mother to decide on the final disposition.

31. Quoted in *New York Morning Telegraph*, December 6, 1915, Robinson Locke Collection.

32. *New York Morning Telegraph*, December 6, 1915, Robinson Locke Collection.

33. *Sporting Life*, December 18, 1915.

34. Quoted in Ritter, "Ladies and Gentlemen, Presenting Marty McHale," 254. Ritter's interview of McHale was not included in his book, *The Glory of Their Times*.

35. Quoted in Ritter, "Ladies and Gentlemen, Presenting Marty McHale," 261.

36. "The Vaudeville Year," *Variety*, December 25, 1914.

37. Ritter, "Ladies and Gentlemen, Presenting Marty McHale," 254.

38. Hyams and McIntyre, *St. Louis Star*, December 17, 1914.

39. Sime Silverman, *Variety*, November 21, 1914.

40. Wynn, *Variety*, November 28, 1914.

41. *Sacramento Star*, November 10, 1915; *Evening News* (Wilkes-Barre PA), October 9 and 12, 1915; and *Variety*, November 15, 1915.

42. Quoted in *Pittsburgh Press*, February 18, 1915.

43. *Brooklyn Citizen*, March 15, 1915.

44. *Evening Public Ledger* (Philadelphia), April 16, 1915.

45. Quoted in *Hutchinson (KS) News*, August 2, 1915.

46. *New York Age*, April 29, 1915.

47. *New York Age*, June 17, 1915.

48. *Variety*, June 4, 1915.

49. *San Francisco Call*, July 10, 1915. Players were drawn from Bethlehem Steel and the Allentown City League.

50. *New York Age*, July 22, 1915.

51. James Jerpe, *Pittsburgh Post-Gazette*, October 17, 1915.

52. Quoted in *Central New Jersey Home News*, December 31, 1912.

53. Will Rogers, *San Bernardino (CA) Sun*, October 8, 1933.

54. "The Grauman Stage—A Who's Who: Mike Donlin," Grauman's Chinese, accessed April 2022, http://www.graumanschinese.org/whos-who.html #donlin-mike.

32. Mike Enters Motion Pictures

1. Quoted in Czitrom, *Media and the American Mind*, 38.

2. Dirks, "The History of Film." A motion picture is a series of pictures projected onto a screen so rapidly as to convey a sense that it is a continuously moving picture.

3. Quoted in Green and Laurie, *Show Biz*, 49.

4. Quoted in Sullivan, *Our Times*, 3:553.

5. Quoted in Sullivan, *Our Times*, 4:611.

6. Czitrom, *Media and the American Mind*, 42.

7. Trav S. D., *No Applause—Just Throw Money*, 249.

8. Quoted in M. Wallace, *Greater Gotham*, 424.

9. Trav S. D., *No Applause—Just Throw Money*, 217–18, 225, and 243.

10. Dirks, "The History of Film."

11. Quoted in Douglas, *Terrible Honesty*, 61.

12. Quoted in Altman, *Silent Film Sound*, 164.

13. Altman, *Silent Film Sound*, 165.

14. Quoted in Green and Laurie, *Show Biz*, 265.

15. Quoted in D. Wallace, *Lost Hollywood*, 74.

16. Green and Laurie, *Show Biz*, 266.

17. L. Morris, *Not So Long Ago*, 193.

18. Basinger, *Silent Stars*, 470.

19. Only ten of twenty-five silent films about baseball have survived. Most, "Blown Saves," 170.

20. Magazine ad, John Barrymore file, New York Public Library, Performing Arts branch, Robinson Locke Collection.

21. Igoe, *Sporting News*, January 25, 1945.

22. "Mike Donlin," *Variety*, July 16, 1915.

23. *Moving Picture World*, July 31, 1915, Robinson Locke Collection.

24. *New York Evening Sun*, July 13, 1929.

25. *Sporting Life*, November 20, 1915.

26. Wyn, *Variety*, October 1, 1915. See also Edelman, *Great Baseball Films*, 28.

27. Most, "Blown Saves," 169.

28. *Moving Picture World*, September 25 and October 9, 1915, Robinson Locke Collection.

29. Repici, "The Big Leagues on the Big Screen," 144.

33. Memphis Blues

1. *Fort Wayne (IN) News*, January 15, 1916.

2. Honus Wagner, *Pittsburgh Post-Gazette*, January 30, 1916.

3. *Asbury Park (NJ) Press*, February 8, 1916; and *Bridgeport Times and Farmer*, February 9, 1916.

4. *Brooklyn Eagle*, July 10, 1916; and *Sporting Life*, August 12, 1916.

5. *Asbury Park (NJ) Press*, March 10 and June 5, 1916; and *New-York Tribune*, June 19, 1916.

6. Unsourced newspaper article, July 4, 1916, *New York Sun* morgue file, New York Public Library.

7. McCall, "How America's First Shark Panic Spurred a Century of Fear."

8. *Norwich (CT) Bulletin*, December 20, 1916.

9. *Washington Herald*, December 28, 1916.

10. Mrs. John J. McGraw with Mann, *The Real McGraw*, 260.

11. *New-York Tribune*, January 7, 1917.

12. *Nashville Tennessean*, January 7, 1917.

13. Quoted in *Buffalo Enquirer*, January 2, 1917.

14. Damon Runyon, *New York American*, January 9, 1917.

15. Damon Runyon, *San Francisco Examiner*, January 15, 1917.

16. *Chattanooga Times*, January 9, 1917.

17. *Chattanooga Times*, March 2, 1917.

18. Paul Purman, *Knoxville Sentinel*, March 14, 1917.

19. H. C. Hamilton, *Buffalo Times*, March 17, 1917. Hoyt had a 3-9 record and a 3.23 earned run average for the Chicks.

20. Quoted in *Nashville Tennessean*, April 13, 1917.

21. Donlin appeared in sixteen games for Memphis, all in the outfield. He batted .216 for the season.

22. *Chattanooga News*, April 19, 1917.

23. Simpkins, "Kid Elberfeld," quoting an unnamed source.

24. Quoted in *Chattanooga News*, April 20, 1917.

25. Quoted in Henry Vance, *Nashville Banner*, April 20, 1917.

26. Quoted in Murdock, *Baseball between the Wars*, 60.

27. *Nashville Banner*, May 28, 1917.

28. *Asbury Park (NJ) Press*, June 15, 1918.

29. *Rochester Democrat and Chronicle*, June 14, 1917.

30. Quoted in *Sea Coast Echo* (Bay Saint Louis MS), September 8, 1917. Herb Flint was the best known hypnotist of his era.

31. *Sea Coast Echo* (Bay Saint Louis MS), September 8, 1917.

32. Quoted in *Sacramento Union*, May 11, 1920.

33. *Variety*, June 15, 1917. Virtually forgotten now, Stanley was a very popular vaudeville performer at the time.

34. *Variety*, July 20, 1917.

34. Back on Broadway

1. Fowler, *Good Night, Sweet Prince*, 290.

2. *New York Herald Tribune*, September 25, 1933, Robinson Locke Collection.

3. Wid Gunning, "Wid's Films and Film Folk (Jan–Dec 1917)," December 6, 1917, https://archive.org/details/widsfilmsfilmfol03wids.

4. Quoted in *Harrisburg (PA) Telegraph*, May 3, 1919.

5. Film historian Judy Cash identified several films in which Donlin is not credited by the Internet Movie Database (IMDB). Since many films from this era have not survived, it is unknown how many others Donlin appeared in.

6. Segrave, *Extras of Early Hollywood*, 150.

7. Green and Laurie, *Show Biz*, 256.

8. Will Rogers, *San Bernardino (CA) Sun*, October 8, 1933.

9. Vid Larsen, *Sacramento Star*, February 20, 1920.

10. *Pittsburgh Gazette Times*, May 16, 1920.

11. *St. Louis Star*, March 12, 1920.

12. *San Diego Union*, February 29, 1920.

13. "Advertising by Aeroplane," unsourced article, March 1919, Robinson Locke Collection.

14. Quoted in Vid Larsen, *Sacramento Star*, February 20, 1920.

15. *Salt Lake Telegram*, January 15, 1929. Donlin borrowed from his "friends along Broadway" to bet heavily on Dempsey. *Arizona Republic* (Phoenix), March 22, 1920.

16. *North Adams (MA) Transcript*, January 7, 1920.

17. Quoted in John T. Corcoran, *South Bend (IN) Times-News*, November 27, 1921.

18. *Detroit Free Press*, December 12, 1922.

19. O. O. McIntyre, unsourced newspaper article, Robinson Locke Collection.

20. *Washington (DC) Times*, February 14, 1922.

21. *Morning News* (Wilmington DE), March 21, 1919.

22. *Arizona Republic* (Phoenix), March 28, 1920.

23. *Philadelphia Inquirer*, April 6, 1919.

24. *Akron Evening Times*, November 25, 1919.

25. *El Paso Herald*, March 20–21, 1920.

26. Quoted in *Pittsburgh Press*, February 26, 1919.

27. *Variety*, December 30, 1921.

28. *New York Review*, March 23, 1918.

29. Quoted in *Press-Courier* (Oxnard CA), October 15, 1924.

30. "Oh, Doctor! (1925) A Silent Film Review," Movies Silently, May 7, 2013, https://moviessilently.com/2013/05/07/oh-doctor-1925-a-silent-film-review/.

31. Quoted in *Los Angeles Times*, May 22, 1923.

32. John Lardner, *Edmonton Journal*, January 11, 1934.

33. O. O. McIntyre, unsourced newspaper article, Robinson Locke Collection.

34. Frank G. Menke, *Idaho Statesman* (Boise), December 25, 1925. *Childe Harold's Pilgrimage* is a Lord Byron poem that describes the travels and reflections of a world-weary young man.

35. "The Very Breath of Life"

1. Quoted in *Sporting News*, March 7, 1918.

2. Quoted in *Sporting News*, March 7, 1918.

3. Quoted in *Sporting News*, March 7, 1918.

4. Mike also lost his elderly aunt, Mary Cayton, in 1924.

5. Special Collections, Margaret Herrick Library, Academy of Motion Picture Arts and Sciences.

6. *New-York Tribune*, July 23, 1918. Umpires Billy Evans and George Hildebrand mistakenly thought the season had been ended because of World War I. *Salt Lake Telegram*, July 23, 1918.

7. *Variety*, April 18, 1919.

8. Quoted in *Harrisburg (PA) Telegraph*, May 3, 1919. Wagner would be hired as a Pirates coach but not until 1933. He would become a familiar, beloved fixture in ballparks until he retired in 1951. There were few full-time coaches in baseball during Donlin's lifetime.

9. Quoted in *Harrisburg (PA) Telegraph*, May 3, 1919.

10. Quoted in *North Adams (MA) Transcript*, January 7, 1920.

11. Quoted in Sid Mercer, *Oregon Journal* (Portland), June 13, 1920.

12. Quoted in *Los Angeles Record*, March 13, 1920.

13. Quoted in Jimmy Wilde, *Arizona Daily Star* (Tucson), March 21, 1920.

14. Quoted in *Arizona Republic* (Phoenix), March 28, 1920.

15. Mike Donlin, *Los Angeles Herald*, March 19, 1920.

16. *Pasadena Post*, July 17, 1920. The game raised money for southern California orphans.

17. Quoted in *Omaha News*, January 4, 1920.

18. *Fall River (MA) Globe*, January 6, 1921.

19. *Courier-News* (Bridgewater NJ), March 26, 1921.

20. *St. Louis Star and Times*, September 18, 1921.

21. Donlin signed Dick Reichle for the Red Sox. Bill Nowlin, "Dick Reichle."

22. *Rock Island (IL) Argus*, August 7, 1922.

23. *Sacramento Union*, December 17, 1922.

24. *Oakland Tribune*, August 18, 1923.

25. *San Pedro (CA) News Pilot*, November 7 and December 3, 1923.

26. *Dayton (OH) Herald*, January 28, 1924.

27. Quoted in Hugh S. Fullerton, *Atlanta Constitution*, February 13, 1922.

28. Hugh S. Fullerton, *Atlanta Constitution*, February 13, 1922.

29. Hugh S. Fullerton, *Atlanta Constitution*, February 13, 1922.

36. Acting Success

1. *Times Union* (Brooklyn), January 18, 1926.

2. Quoted in Edelman, "Buster Keaton, Baseball Player," 61.

3. Quoted in Nelson, *The Golden Game*, 172.

4. Edelman, "Buster Keaton, Baseball Player," 61.

5. P. Williams, "Byron Houck."

6. Harry T. Brundige, *St. Louis Star and Times*, June 7, 1929.

7. "AFI's 100 Years . . . 100 Movies—10th Anniversary Edition," American Film Institute, 2007, https://www.afi.com/afis-100-years-100-movies-10th-anniversary-edition/.

8. Unsourced book review of Tom Dardis, *Keaton: The Man Who Wouldn't Lie Down*, *Focus on Film*, April 1980, 54, in Keaton file, New York Public Library, Performing Arts branch.

9. Baseball film historian Rob Edelman described the film's lead as a "Ruthian character" who "is an overgrown boy and . . . has no regard for authority. . . . But he is a fan favorite." Edelman, *Great Baseball Films*, 45–46.

10. Damon Runyon, *New York American*, October 11, 1926.

11. Damon Runyon, *New York American*, October 11, 1926.

12. Damon Runyon, *New York American*, October 11, 1926.

13. When Buster Keaton was starring in films for MGM, Sedgwick was the director of many of them. Donlin has an uncredited appearance in one, *Spite Marriage*.

14. *Harrisburg (PA) Telegraph*, December 7, 1926.

15. Quoted in *Warren (PA) Tribune*, May 20, 1927.

16. Quoted in Brian Bell, *Morning Herald* (Hagerstown MD), January 27, 1931.

17. *St. Louis Post-Dispatch*, June 24, 1928. The *Milwaukee Journal* of May 14, 1927, attributed his condition to tuberculosis.

18. A. T. S., *Times Herald* (Port Huron MI), May 11, 1927.

19. Tom Lewis, *Courier-Journal* (Louisville), November 29, 1931.

20. Damon Runyon, *New York American*, October 11, 1926.

21. *Los Angeles Times*, June 8, 1927.

22. *Napa (CA) Journal*, April 7, 1927.

23. William Mayo and his sons started the Saint Mary's Hospital. William had been a surgeon for the Union Army.

24. *Los Angeles Times*, June 9, 1927.

25. Quoted in *Indianapolis Star*, August 7, 1927.

26. Hype Igoe, *San Bernardino (CA) Sun*, March 21, 1939.

27. *Santa Cruz Evening News*, January 27, 1928; and *Pittsburgh Post-Gazette*, April 7, 1928.

28. *Pittsburgh Post-Gazette* and *Minneapolis Star*, April 7, 1928.

29. Brownlow, *The Parade's Gone By*, 169.

30. Edelman and Betzold, "Mike Donlin," 55.

31. Quoted in Brownlow, *The Parade's Gone By*, 566.

32. Brownlow, *The Parade's Gone By*, 566.

33. Quoted in Brownlow, *The Parade's Gone By*, 577.

34. *Wisconsin State Journal* (Madison), May 19, 1929.

35. *St. Louis Post-Dispatch*, June 24, 1928.

36. *Pittsburgh Press*, July 29, 1928.

37. Quoted in *Parsons (KS) Sun*, July 15, 1928. Donlin was hit by a pitch twenty times in his baseball career.

38. James T. Long, *Pittsburgh Sun-Telegraph*, August 31, 1929.

39. Quoted in *Los Angeles Evening Express*, November 2, 1928.

40. *Los Angeles Times*, November 17, 1928.

41. James J. Long, *Pittsburgh Sun-Telegraph*, December 27, 1930.

42. "This One Man," *Playbill*, accessed June 2022, https://playbill.com/production/this-one-man-morosco-theatre-vault-0000002512.

43. Rowland Field, *Times Union* (Brooklyn), October 22, 1930.

44. Mark Barron, *South Bend (IN) Tribune*, October 30, 1930.

45. Quoted in Edward P. Balinger, *Pittsburgh Post-Gazette*, December 10, 1930.

46. Ed Sullivan, *Drumright (OK) Weekly Derrick*, November 24, 1930.

47. Ed Sullivan, *Drumright (OK) Weekly Derrick*, November 24, 1930.

48. *St. Louis Post-Dispatch*, June 24, 1928.

49. Quoted in *Harrisburg (PA) Telegraph*, May 3, 1919.

50. Damon Runyon, *New York American*, October 11, 1926.

37. "Lights, Camera, Action"

1. *Courier-News* (Bridgewater NJ), April 6, 1931.

2. Harold C. Burr, *Brooklyn Eagle*, June 2, 1932.

3. Ralph Davis, *Pittsburgh Press*, May 1, 1929.

4. Damon Runyon, *Evening News* (Harrisburg PA), January 29, 1930.

5. Quoted in Jimmy Powers, *New York Daily News*, March 2, 1930. Brannick worked for the Giants for sixty-five years.

6. Walter Winchell, *Tribune* (Scranton), June 24, 1933.

7. "M-G-M's Ball Grounds," *Variety*, August 28, 1929.

8. *Los Angeles Evening Post-Record*, September 20, 1929.

9. "The Grauman Stage—A Who's Who: Mike Donlin."

10. The 1932 game was sponsored by the Association of Professional Ball Players of America (APBPA). *Los Angeles Times*, June 26, 1932.

11. Edward Ballinger, *Pittsburgh Post-Gazette*, March 30, 1931.

12. *Sporting News*, January 5, 1933. The weekly later reported the Old Timers Baseball Club had booked games in about twenty cities; *Sporting News*, January 26, 1933.

13. Lank Leonard, *Brooklyn Citizen*, March 29, 1933.

14. *San Pedro (CA) News Pilot*, October 28, 1931; and *Standard-Speaker* (Hazelton PA), July 1, 1932.

15. Quoted in Brian Bell, *Morning Herald* (Hagerstown MD), January 27, 1931.

16. Quoted in Mark Barron, *Fresno (CA) Republican*, December 31, 1930.

17. O. O. McIntyre, *Birmingham News*, May 29, 1932.

18. Will Rogers, *New York Times*, March 25, 1932.

19. Ward Morehouse, *New York Sun*, September 25, 1933.

20. "One Way Passage—(Movie Clip) Paradise Cocktail," TCM, Turner Film Classics, 1932, https://www.tcm.com/video/292668/one-way-passage-paradise-cocktail.

21. Quoted in *Los Angeles Evening Express*, June 13, 1931. Donlin had already appeared in two other Garnett films the previous two years.

22. *Evening Sun* (Baltimore), September 20, 1933.

23. Michael Joseph Donlin Death Certificate, Mike Donlin file, Time Inc. New York biography, Special Collections, Margaret Herrick Library, Academy of Motion Picture Arts and Sciences.

24. *San Bernardino (CA) Sun*, September 25, 1933.

25. *Los Angeles Times*, October 8, 1933. Wrigley Field was the home of the PCL's Los Angeles Angels from 1925 to 1957.

26. *Los Angeles Times*, September 26, 1933.

27. *Oakland Tribune*, October 7, 1933.

28. Quoted in *Independent-Observer* (Conrad MT), November 15, 1934.

38. A Life Well Lived

1. Malcolm W. Bingay, *Detroit Free Press*, September 26, 1933.

2. *Oakland Tribune*, October 1, 1933.

3. Will Rogers, *San Bernardino (CA) Sun*, October 8, 1933.

4. Damon Runyon, *New York American*, May 12, 1927.

5. Roundy Coughlin, *Wisconsin State Journal* (Madison), September 30, 1933.

6. Grantland Rice, *Dayton (OH) News*, July 18, 1933. The others on Rice's list were Rube Waddell, Ed Walsh, Tris Speaker, and Heinie Zimmerman.

7. Grantland Rice, *Boston Globe*, September 28, 1933.

8. Billy Murphy, *St. Louis Star and Times*, December 2, 1914.

9. Amy Leslie, *Chicago Daily News*, October 20, 1905.

10. *Milwaukee Sentinel*, May 7, 1906, Robinson Locke Collection.

11. Quoted in Basinger, *Silent Stars*, 207.

12. Will Rogers, *San Bernardino (CA) Sun*, October 8, 1933.

13. Ward Morehouse, *New York Sun*, September 25, 1933.

14. John Lardner, *Edmonton (AB) Journal*, January 11, 1934. Lardner's father, Ring, died prematurely in his sleep from a heart attack, just a day after Mike's death. Ring Lardner was only forty-eight.

15. Edelman, "Turkey Mike Donlin in the Movies," 73.

16. Will Rogers, *San Bernardino (CA) Sun*, October 8, 1933.

17. Jackson, "From the Show to Show Biz."

18. Kaiser, *Baseball Greatness*, 11. Donlin had WAA of 5.0 in 1905 and 4.2 in 1908. He had four seasons of wins above replacement (WAR) of more than 4.0.

19. Fowler, *Skyline*, 12.

20. Damon Runyon, *New York American*, October 11, 1926, and May 12, 1927.

21. *New York Morning Telegraph*, April 12, 1906, Robinson Locke Collection.

22. Damon Runyon, *New York American*, January 9, 1917.

23. Damon Runyon, *New York American*, May 12, 1927.

24. Quoted in Roundy Coughlin, *Wisconsin State Journal* (Madison), September 30, 1933; and Joe Vila, *New York Sun*, September 26, 1933.

25. Quoted in *Indianapolis Star*, August 17, 1935.

26. O. O. McIntyre, *San Bernardino (CA) Sun*, April 26, 1936.

27. *Philadelphia Inquirer*, September 26, 1933.

28. Joe Vila, *New York Sun*, September 26, 1933.

29. Will Rogers, *San Bernardino (CA) Sun*, October 8, 1933, as quoted in B. Rogers, *Will Rogers*.

BIBLIOGRAPHY

Ahrens, Art. "Jimmy Callahan: He Covered All the Bases in Chicago." *Base Ball: A Journal of the Early Game* 7 (Fall 2013): 45–61.

Alexander, Charles C. *John McGraw*. New York: Viking, 1988.

Allen, Lee. *The American League Story: The Official History*. New York: Hill & Wang, 1965.

——. *The Cincinnati Reds: An Informal History*. New York: G. P. Putnam's Sons, 1948.

——. *The Hot Stove League*. Mattituck NY: Amereon House, 1955.

——. *The National League Story: The Official History*. New York: Hill & Wang, 1961.

"All-Star League Teams." *Baseball Magazine*, November 1908.

Altman, Rick. *Silent Film Sound*. New York: Columbia University Press, 2004.

Anderson, David W. "Bonesetter Reese." SABR BioProject. sabr.org/bioproject.

——. *More than Merkle: A History of the Best and Most Exciting Baseball Season in Human History*. Lincoln: University of Nebraska Press, 2000.

——. "Tommy Connolly." SABR BioProject. sabr.org/bioproject.

Appel, Marty. *Slide, Kelly, Slide: The Wild Life and Times of Mike "King" Kelly, Baseball's First Superstar*. Lanham MD: Scarecrow Press, 1999.

Baldassaro, Lawrence. "Ernie Orsatti." SABR BioProject. sabr.org/bioproject.

Baldassaro, Lawrence, and Richard A. Johnson. *The American Game: Baseball and Ethnicity*. Carbondale: Southern Illinois University Press, 2002.

Basinger, Jeanine. *Silent Stars*. New York: Alfred A. Knopf, 2000.

Belletti, Valeria. *Adventures of a Hollywood Secretary: Her Private Letters from Inside the Studios of the 1920s*. Berkeley: University of California Press, 2006.

Bengtson, John. *Silent Echoes: Discovering Early Hollywood through the Films of Buster Keaton*. Santa Monica CA: Santa Monica Press, 2000.

Berger, Ralph. "Marty McHale." SABR BioProject. sabr.org/bioproject.

Betzold, Michael. "Turkey Mike Donlin: One of the Twentieth Century's First Sports Entertainment Figures." *Baseball Research Journal*, no. 29 (2000): 80–83.

Billheimer, John. *Baseball and the Blame Game: Scapegoating in the Major Leagues*. Jefferson NC: McFarland, 2007.

Bjarkman, Peter, ed. *Encyclopedia of Major League Baseball Team Histories: National League*. Westport CT: Meckler Publishing, 1991.

Blaeuer, Mark. *Baseball in Hot Springs*. Charleston SC: Arcadia Publishing, 2016.

Boddington, Clem. "Bugs." In *The Second Fireside Book of Baseball*, by Charles Einstein, 32–35. New York: Simon & Schuster, 1958.

Bogen, Gil. *Johnny Kling: A Baseball Biography*. Jefferson NC: McFarland, 2006.

——— . *Tinker, Evers, and Chance: A Triple Biography*. Jefferson NC: McFarland, 2003.

Bogen, Gil, and David W. Anderson. "Johnny Kling." SABR BioProject. sabr.org /bioproject.

Boorstin, Daniel J. *The Americans: The Democratic Experience*. New York: Vintage Books, 1973.

Bordman, Gerald, and Richard Norton. *American Musical Theatre, A Chronicle*. New York: Oxford University Press, 2011.

Bowery Boys. "Subway Tavern: 'Greasy' Church-Operated Bar Alternative." August 16, 2017. https://www.boweryboyshistory.com/2017/08/subway -tavern-greasy-church-operated.html.

Boxerman, Burton A., and Benita W. Boxerman. *Ebbets to Veeck to Busch: Eight Owners Who Shaped Baseball*. Jefferson NC: McFarland, 2003.

Bready, James H. *Baseball in Baltimore: The First 100 Years*. Baltimore: Johns Hopkins University Press, 1998.

——— . *The Home Team: Our Orioles 25th Anniversary Edition*. Self-published, 1979.

——— . "Play Ball! The Legacy of Nineteenth-Century Baltimore Baseball." *Maryland Historical Magazine* 87 (Summer 1992).

Breslin, Jimmy. *Damon Runyon*. New York: Ticknor and Fields, 1991.

Brown, Walter, and E. De Roy Koch, eds. *Who's Who on the Stage, 1908*. New York: B. W. Dodge, 1908.

Brownlow, Kevin. *The Parade's Gone By*. Berkeley: University of California Press, 1976.

Burk, Robert F. *Never Just a Game: Players, Owners, & American Baseball*. Chapel Hill: University of North Carolina Press, 1994.

Casway, Jerrold. *Ed Delahanty in the Emerald Age of Baseball*. Notre Dame IN: University of Notre Dame Press, 2004.

Cataneo, David. *Baseball Legend and Lore: A Crackerjack Collection of Stories and Anecdotes about the Game*. New York: Galahad Books, 1991.

Cicotello, David. "Bob Emslie." SABR BioProject. sabr.org/bioproject.

Clark, Tom. *The World of Damon Runyon*. New York: Harper & Row, 1978.

Cook, William A. *August "Garry" Herrmann: A Baseball Biography*. Jefferson NC: McFarland, 2008.

Corum, Bill. *Off and Running*. New York: Henry Holt, 1959.

Cottrell, Robert C. *The Best Pitcher in Baseball: The Life of Rube Foster, Negro League Giant*. New York: NYU Press, 2001.

———. "Rube Foster: Negro League Giant." In *The Negro Leagues Were Major Leagues*, edited by Todd Peterson, 147–65. Jefferson NC: McFarland, 2020.

Cox, James A. *World of Baseball: The Lively Ball*. Alexandria VA: Redefinition, 1989.

Cullen, Frank, with Florence Hackman and Donald McNeilly. *Vaudeville Old & New: An Encyclopedia of Variety Performers in America*. Vol. 1. New York: Routledge, 2006.

Cunerd, Stephen. "Vic Willis: Turn-of-the-Century Great." *Baseball Research Journal*, no. 18 (1989): 55–57.

Czitrom, Daniel J. *Media and the American Mind: From Morse to McLuhan*. Chapel Hill: University of North Carolina Press, 1982.

Daniles, Roger. *Coming to America: A History of Immigration and Ethnicity in America*. Princeton NJ: Harper Perennial, 1991.

Dardis, Tom. *Keaton: The Man Who Wouldn't Lie Down*. New York: Limelight, 1988.

Deane, Bill. *Baseball's Who's Who of What Ifs: Players Derailed En Route to Cooperstown*. Jefferson NC: McFarland, 2021.

Deford, Frank. *The Old Ball Game: How John McGraw, Christy Mathewson, and the New York Giants Created Modern Baseball*. New York: Atlantic Press, 2005.

DeValeria, Dennis, and Jeanne Burke DeValeria. *Honus Wagner: A Biography*. New York: Henry Holt, 1995.

Dewey, Donald, and Nicholas Acocella. *The Biographical History of Baseball*. Chicago: Triumph Books, 2002.

Dietz, Dan. *The Complete Book of 1910s Broadway Musicals*. Lanham MD: Rowman & Littlefield, 2021.

Dirks, Tim. "The History of Film: The Pre-1920s." Filmsite, accessed March 2022. www.filmsite.org/pre20sintro.html.

Dixon, Phil S. *Andrew "Rube" Foster: A Harvest on Freedom's Choice*. Bloomington IN: Xlibris, 2010.

Dolan, Jay P. *The Irish Americans: A History*. New York: Bloomsbury Press, 2008.

Donlin, Mike. "Baseball Acting." *The Green Book Album: A Magazine of the Passing Show*, August 1909, 309–11.

Douglas, Ann. *Terrible Honesty: Mongrel Manhattan in the 1920s*. New York: Farrar, Straus and Giroux, 1995.

Doxie, Don. *Iron Man McGinnity: A Baseball Biography.* Jefferson NC: McFarland, 2009.

———. "Joe McGinnity." SABR BioProject. sabr.org/bioproject.

Durso, Joseph. *Casey & Mr. McGraw.* St. Louis: *Sporting News,* 1989.

Edelman, Rob. "The Baseball Films to 1920." *Base Ball: A Journal of the Early Game* 1, no. 1 (Spring 2007): 122–35.

———. "Baseball, Vaudeville, and Mike Donlin." *Base Ball: A Journal of the Early Game* 2, no. 1 (Spring 2008): 44–57.

———. "Buster Keaton, Baseball Player." In *The National Pastime,* edited by Jean Hastings Ardell and Andy McCue, 61–63. Phoenix: Society for American Baseball Research, 2011.

———. *Great Baseball Films: From "Right Off the Bat" to "A League of Their Own."* New York: Citadel Press, 1994.

———. "Lost (and Found) Baseball." *Base Ball: A Journal of the Early Game* 5, no. 2 (Fall 2011): 23–37.

———. "Turkey Mike Donlin in the Movies: Mike Donlin, Movie Actor." *Baseball Research Journal,* no. 30 (2001): 73–75.

Edelman, Rob, and Michael Betzold. "Mike Donlin." In *From Spring Training to Screen Test: Baseball Players Turned Actors,* edited by Rob Edelman and Bill Nowlin, 47–57. Phoenix: Society for American Baseball Research, 2018.

Egenriether, Richard. "Chris Von der Ahe: Baseball's Pioneering Huckster." *Baseball Research Journal,* no. 18 (1989): 27–31.

Elfers, James. "Nixey Callahan." SABR BioProject. sabr.org/bioproject.

———. *The Tour to End All Tours: The Story of Major League Baseball's 1913–1914 World Tour.* Lincoln: Bison Books, 2003.

Erdman, Andrew L. *Queen of Vaudeville: Story of Eva Tanguay.* Ithaca NY: Cornell University Press, 2012.

Fields, Ronald J., ed. *W. C. Fields, by Himself: His Intended Autobiography from His Personal Letters, Notes, Scripts, and Articles.* Lanham MD: Taylor Trade, 2016.

Fleitz, David L. "Cap Anson." SABR BioProject. sabr.org/bioproject.

———. *The Irish in Baseball: An Early History.* Jefferson NC: McFarland, 2009.

———. *More Ghosts in the Gallery: Another Sixteen Little-Known Greats at Cooperstown.* Jefferson NC: McFarland, 2005.

———. *Napoleon Lajoie: King of Ballplayers.* Jefferson NC: McFarland, 2013.

Fleming, G. H. *The Unforgettable Season: 1908: The Most Exciting and Calamitous Season of All Time.* New York: Fireside, 1981.

Foote, Lisle. *Buster Keaton's Crew: The Team behind His Silent Films.* Jefferson NC: McFarland, 2014.

Fountain, Charles. *Sportswriter: The Life and Times of Grantland Rice.* Bridgewater NJ: Replica Books, 1993.

Fowler, Gene. *Good Night, Sweet Prince*. Philadelphia: Blakiston Company, 1943.

——. *Skyline: A Reporter's Reminiscence of the '20s*. New York: Viking Press, 1961.

Frierson, Eddie. "Christy Mathewson." SABR BioProject. sabr.org/bioproject.

Gaines, Bob. *The Christian Gentleman, Christy Mathewson: How One Man's Faith and Fastball Forever Changed Baseball*. Lanham MD: Rowman & Littlefield, 2015.

Gattie, Gordon. "The American League's First Baltimore Orioles: John McGraw, Wilbert Robinson, and Rivalries Created." In *The National Pastime*, edited by Cecilia M. Tan, 7–10. Phoenix: Society for American Baseball Research, 2020.

Gehring, Wes D. *Buster Keaton in His Own Time: What the Responses of 1920s Critics Reveal*. Jefferson NC: McFarland, 2018.

Gilbert, Douglas. *American Vaudeville: Its Life and Times*. New York: Dover Publications, 1968.

"The Golden Age of Vaudeville." *Current Literature* 42 (June 1907): 669.

Gordon, Peter M. "King Kelly." SABR BioProject. sabr.org/bioproject.

Graham, Frank. *McGraw of the Giants*. New York: G. P. Putnam's Sons, 1944.

——. *The New York Giants*. New York: G. P. Putnam's Sons, 1952.

Grayson, Harry. *They Played the Game: The Story of Baseball Greats*. New York: A. S. Barnes, 1944.

Green, Abel, and Joe Laurie Jr. *Show Biz: From Vaude to Video*. New York: Garland Publishing, 1985.

Hammerstein, Oscar Andrew. *The Hammersteins: A Musical Theatre Family*. New York: Black Dog & Leventhal, 2010.

Hanson, Dirk. "The Strange and Secret Keeley Cure for Addiction." *Addition Inbox: The Science of Substance Abuse*, September 11, 2011. https://addiction-dirkh.blogspot.com/2011/09/strange-and-secret-keeley-cure-for.html.

Harper, William. *How You Played the Game: The Life of Grantland Rice*. Columbia: University of Missouri Press, 1999.

Hartley, Michael. *Christy Mathewson: A Biography*. Jefferson NC: McFarland, 2004.

Hernandez, Lou. *Manager of Giants: The Tactics, Temper and True Record of John McGraw*. Jefferson NC: McFarland, 2018.

Hetrick, J. Thomas. *Misfits! The Cleveland Spiders in 1899*. Jefferson NC: McFarland, 1991.

Hite, Mabel. "On Just Being a Fan." *Baseball Magazine*, November 1908, 23–24.

Hittner, Arthur D. *Honus Wagner: The Life of Baseball's "Flying Dutchman."* Jefferson NC: McFarland, 2003.

Holtzman, Jerome. *No Cheering in the Press Box*. New York: Holt, Rinehart & Winston, 1974.

Holway, John. *Blackball Stars: Negro League Pioneers*. Westport CT: Meckler, 1988.

Honig, Donald. *Baseball America: The Heroes of the Game and the Times of Their Glory*. New York: Galahad Books, 1993.

Hopper, James. "On Tour with the 'Giants.'" *Collier's* 16, no. 5 (September 19, 1908): 16–18, 28, 30.

——. "Training with the 'Giants.'" *Everybody's Magazine* 20 (June 1909): 739.

"How Mike Donlin Became a Big Leaguer." *Baseball Magazine*, June 1912, 79–80.

Humphreys, Michael A. *Wizardry: Baseball's All-Time Greatest Fielders Revealed*. New York: Oxford University Press, 2011.

Hynd, Noel. *The Giants of the Polo Grounds: The Glorious Times of Baseball's New York Giants*. New York: Doubleday, 1988.

——. *Marquard & Seeley*. Hyannis MA: Parnassus, 1996.

Jackson, Frank. "From the Show to Show Biz." *Hardball Times*, April 11, 2012. https://tht.fangraphs.com/mike-donlin/.

James, Bill. *The New Bill James Historical Baseball Abstract*. New York: Free Press. 2003.

Jensen, Don. "Bugs Raymond." SABR BioProject. sabr.org/bioproject.

——. "Dan McGann." SABR BioProject. sabr.org/bioproject.

——. "Jimmy Sheckard," SABR BioProject. sabr.org/bioproject.

Johnson, Timothy A. *Baseball and the Music of Charles Ives: A Proving Ground*. Lanham MD: Scarecrow Press, 2004.

Jones, David. *Deadball Stars of the American League*. Dulles VA: Potomac Books, 2006.

——. "Jesse Burkett." SABR BioProject. sabr.org/bioproject.

——. "Patsy Donovan." SABR BioProject. sabr.org/bioproject.

Jones, Maldwyn Allen. *American Immigration*. Chicago: University of Chicago Press, 1960.

Kahn, Roger. *The Head Game: Baseball Seen from the Pitcher's Mound*. New York: Harcourt, 2000.

Kaiser, David. *Baseball Greatness: Top Players and Teams, According to Wins above Average, 1901–2017*. Jefferson NC: McFarland, 2018.

Katz, Jeffrey M. *Plié Ball: Baseball Meets Dance on Stage and Screen*. Jefferson NC: McFarland, 2016.

Keaton, Eleanor, and Jeffrey Vance. *Keaton Remembered*. New York: Harry N. Abrams, 2001.

Keenan, Jimmy. "April 26, 1901: Baltimore Orioles Win Home Opener in a New League." SABR Games Project. https://sabr.org/gamesproj/game/april-26 -1901-baltimore-orioles-win-home-opener-in-a-new-major-league/.

——. "Jack Dunn." SABR BioProject. sabr.org/bioproject.

——. "Joe Kelley." SABR BioProject. sabr.org/bioproject.

Kelley, Brent. *The Case for Those Overlooked by the Baseball Hall of Fame*. Jefferson NC: McFarland, 1992.

Kenny, Kevin. *The American Irish: A History*. Harlow, England: Longman, 2000.

King, Steven A. "The Strangest Month in the Strange Career of Rube Waddell." In *The National Pastime*, edited by Morris Levin, 45–52. Phoenix: Society for American Baseball Research, 2013.

Kirwin, Bill. "Cy Seymour." SABR BioProject. sabr.org/bioproject.

Klein, Maury. *Stealing Games: How John McGraw Transformed Baseball with the 1911 New York Giants*. New York: Bloomsbury Press, 2016.

Kobler, John. *Damned in Paradise: The Life of John Barrymore*. New York: Atheneum, 1977.

Lamb, Bill. "Christy Mathewson: Spitball Pitcher." *The Inside Game: The Official Newsletter of SABR's Deadball Era Committee* 22, no. 2 (May 2022): 27–29.

———. "New York Giants Team Ownership History." SABR BioProject. sabr.org/bioproject.

———. "Ridgewood Park (New York)." SABR BioProject. sabr.org/bioproject.

Lancaster, John H. "Baltimore, a Pioneer in Organized Baseball." *Maryland Historical Magazine* 35, no. 1 (1940): 32–55.

Lane, F. C. *Batting*. Cleveland: SABR, 2001. Originally published by *Baseball Magazine*, 1925.

Lange, Fred. *History of Baseball in California and the Pacific Coast Leagues 1847–1938: Memories and Musings of an Old Time Player*. Oakland: Lange, 1938.

Lardner, John. "The Life and Loves of the Real McCoy." *True*, February 1956.

Laurie, Joe, Jr. "From Vaudeville." In *The Third Fireside Book of Baseball*, by Charles Einstein, 260–62. New York: Simon and Schuster, 1969.

———. *Vaudeville: From the Honky-Tonks to the Palace*. New York: Henry Holt, 1953.

Leavy, Jane. *The Big Fella: Babe Ruth and the World He Created*. New York: Harper, 2018.

Lester, Larry. *Rube Foster in His Time: On the Field and in the Papers with Black Baseball's Greatest Visionary*. Jefferson NC: McFarland, 2012.

Levitt, Daniel R. "Vic Willis." SABR BioProject. sabr.org/bioproject.

Leypoldt, Don, and Don Jensen. "Billy Gilbert." SABR BioProject. sabr.org/bioproject.

Lieb, Fred. *The Baseball Story: Baseball's Most Authoritative Story by Baseball's Top Authority*. New York: G. P. Putnam's Sons, 1950.

Lieb, Frederick G. *The Baltimore Orioles*. Carbondale: Southern Illinois University, 2001. Originally published by G. P. Putnam's Sons, 1955.

———. *The Pittsburgh Pirates*. Carbondale: Southern Illinois University Press, 2001. Originally published by G. P. Putnam's Sons, 1948.

————. *The St. Louis Cardinals: The Story of a Great Baseball Club.* New York: G. P. Putnam's Sons, 1944.

Light, Jonathan Fraser. *The Cultural Encyclopedia of Baseball.* Jefferson NC: McFarland, 1997.

Lord, Walter. *The Good Years: From 1900 to the First World War.* New York: Harper and Brothers, 1960.

Louvish, Simon. *Man on the Flying Trapeze: The Life and Times of W. C. Fields.* New York: W. W. Norton, 1999.

Lowry, Philip J. *Green Cathedrals: The Ultimate Celebration of Major League and Negro League Ballparks.* New York: Walker, 2006.

Macht, Norman L. *Connie Mack and the Early Years of Baseball.* Lincoln: University of Nebraska Press, 2007.

Maguire, John Francis. *The Irish in America.* London: Longmans, Green, 1868.

Mallory, Patrick. "The Game They All Played: Chicago Baseball, 1876–1906." PhD diss., Loyola University, Chicago, 2013. Loyola eCommons, https://ecommons.luc.edu/cgi/viewcontent.cgi?article=1529&context=luc_diss.

Mansch, Larry D. *Rube Marquard: The Life and Times of a Baseball Hall of Famer.* Jefferson NC: McFarland, 1998.

Mathewson, Christy. *Pitching in a Pinch: Baseball from the Inside.* Lincoln: Bison Books, 1994. Originally published by G. P. Putnam's Sons, 1912.

Matthews, George R. *When the Cubs Won It All: The 1908 Championship Season.* Jefferson NC: McFarland, 2009.

McCabe, John. *George M. Cohan: The Man Who Owned Broadway.* Garden City NY: Doubleday, 1973.

McCall, Vivian. "How America's First Shark Panic Spurred a Century of Fear." *National Geographic,* June 12, 2019. https://www.nationalgeographic.com/environment/article/150702-shark-attack-jersey-shore-1916-great-white.

McCusker, Luke F., III. "A Panoply of the Ambitious: Railroaders Big and Small." Irish Railroad Workers Museum, January 28, 2022. https://www.irishshrine.org/big-pivot-posts/a-panoply-of-the-ambitious-railroaders-big-and-small.

McGlynn, Frank. "Striking Scenes from the Tour around the World." *Baseball Magazine,* August 1914, 59–68, and December 1914, 85–88.

McGraw, John J. *My Thirty Years in Baseball.* Lincoln: Bison Books, 1995. Originally published by Boni & Liveright, 1923.

McGraw, Mrs. John J., with Arthur Mann. *The Real McGraw.* New York: David McKay, 1953.

McKenna, Brian. "Logan Squares." SABR BioProject. sabr.org/bioproject.

————. "Reluctant Ballplayer." *Baseball-Fever,* May 28, 2008. https://www.baseball-fever.com/forum/general-baseball/history-of-the-game/42831-mike-donlin-reluctant-ballplayer.

McKim, Donald K. "'Matty' and 'Ol' Pete': Divergent American Heroes." In *The Faith of 50 Million: Baseball, Religion, and American Culture*, edited by Christopher H. Evans and William R. Herzog II, 51–81. Louisville KY: Westminster John Knox Press, 2002.

McLean, Albert, Jr. *American Vaudeville as Ritual*. Lexington: University of Kentucky Press, 2014.

McPherson, Edward. *Buster Keaton: Tempest in a Flat Hat*. New York: Newmarket Press, 2005.

Meany, Tom. *Baseball's Greatest Pitchers*. New York: A. S. Barnes, 1951.

——. "The Real Man of Iron." In *The Second Fireside Book of Baseball*, by Charles Einstein, 256–59. New York: Simon & Schuster, 1958.

Mercer, Sid. "Clippings and Cartoons." *Baseball Magazine*, March 1918, 426.

Monod, David. *Vaudeville and the Making of Modern Entertainment, 1890–1925*. Chapel Hill: University of North Carolina Press, 2020.

Moreland, George. *Balldom: The Britannica of Baseball*. New York: Balldom Publishing, 1914. Reprint: Horton Publishing, 1989.

Morris, Lloyd. *Not So Long Ago*. New York: Random House, 1949.

Morris, Michael A. *John Barrymore: Shakespearean Actor*. New York: Columbia University Press, 1997.

Morris, Peter. *A Game of Inches: The Stories behind the Innovations That Shaped Baseball, the Game on the Field*. Chicago: Ivan R. Dee, 2006.

Most, Marshall G. "Blown Saves: The Fate of Baseball's Silent Cinema." In *The Cooperstown Symposium on Baseball and Culture, 2015–2016*, edited by William M. Simons, 168–82. Jefferson NC: McFarland, 2017.

Mulvoy, Tom. "Arthur Duffy's Odyssey: A Tale of Redemption for the 'Fastest Human of 1902.'" *Dorchester Reporter*, December 27, 2012.

Murdock, Eugene C. *Ban Johnson: Czar of Baseball*. Westport CT: Greenwood Press, 1982.

——. *Baseball between the Wars: Memories of the Game by the Men Who Played It*. Westport CT: Meckler, 1992.

Murphy, Cait. *Crazy '08: How a Cast of Cranks, Rogues, Boneheads, and Magnates Created the Greatest Year in Baseball History*. New York: Smithsonian, 2007.

Nelson, Kevin. *The Golden Game: The Story of California Baseball*. San Francisco: California Historical Society Press, 2004.

Nemec, David, and Eric Miklich. *Forfeits and Successfully Protested Games in Major League Baseball: A Complete Record, 1871–2013*. Jefferson NC: McFarland, 2014.

New England Historical Society. "Eva Tanguay, the Lady Gaga of Vaudeville." Accessed July 2022. https://www.newenglandhistoricalsociety.com/flashback-photo-eva-tanguay-the-lady-gaga-of-vaudeville/.

Nickell, Joe. "Historic 'Gold Cure' for Addiction." Center for Inquiry, March 18, 2016. https://centerforinquiry.org/blog/historic_gold_cure_for_addiction/.

Nowlin, Bill, ed. *Baltimore Baseball*. Phoenix: Society for American Baseball Research, 2022.

———. "Dick Reichle." SABR BioProject. sabr.org/bioproject.

———. "Frank Arellanes." SABR BioProject. sabr.org/bioproject.

O'Connor, Garrett. "Breaking the Code of Silence: The Irish and Drink." *Irish America Magazine*, January 2012. https://www.irishamerica.com/2012/01/breaking-the-code-of-silence-the-irish-and-drink/.

Paranick, Amber. "Eva Tanguay, the 'I Don't Care Girl.'" *Headlines and Heroes* (blog), Library of Congress, January 24, 2020. https://blogs.loc.gov/headlinesandheroes/2020/01/eva-tanguay/.

Peterson, Robert. *Only the Ball Was White*. New York: Oxford University Press, 1992.

Pietrusza, David, Lloyd Johnson, and Bob Carroll, eds., with John Thorn. *The Total Baseball Catalogue: Great Baseball Stuff and How to Buy It*. New York: Total Sports: 1998.

Pietrusza, David, Matthew Silverman, and Michael Gershman, eds. *Baseball: The Biographical Encyclopedia*. Kingston NY: Total Sports Illustrated, 2000.

Pioreck, Richard. "Baseball and Vaudeville and the Development of Popular Culture in the United States, 1880–1930." In *The Cooperstown Symposium on Baseball and American Culture, 1999*, edited by Peter M. Rutkoff, 83–100. Jefferson NC: McFarland, 2000.

Plannette, Jean. "Two Centuries of Baseball: Reminiscences of Mike Donlin." Unpublished manuscript, 1930, LA84 Foundation.

Polsky, Ned. *Hustlers, Beats, and Others*. Piscataway NJ: Transaction Publishing, 2009.

Pope, Edwin. *Baseball's Greatest Managers*. Garden City NY: Doubleday, 1960.

Porter, David L., ed. *Biographical Dictionary of American Sports: Baseball, Revised and Expanded Edition*. Westport CT: Greenwood Press, 2000.

"The Rage for the Frivolous on the Stage." *Leslie's Weekly*, October 24, 1907, 300.

Redmond, Patrick R. *The Irish and the Making of American Sport, 1835–1920*. Jefferson NC: McFarland, 2014.

Reisler, Jim, ed. *Guys, Dolls, and Curveballs: Damon Runyon on Baseball*. New York: Carroll & Graf, 2005.

Repici, Robert. "The Big Leagues on the Big Screen: Character, Culture, and the Mythology of the Majors in the Hollywood Baseball Film." In *The Cooperstown Symposium on Baseball and American Culture, 2013–2014*, edited by William M. Simons, 143–61. Jefferson NC: McFarland, 2015.

Rice, Damon. *Seasons Past*. New York: Praeger Publishers, 1976.

Rice, Stephen V. "Al Bridwell." SABR BioProject. sabr.org/bioproject.

———. "Emmet Heidrick." SABR BioProject. sabr.org/bioproject.

Richter, Francis C. *Richter's History and Records of Base Ball: The American Nation's Chief Sport*. Jefferson NC: McFarland, 2005. Originally published 1914.

Rielly, Edward J. *Baseball: An Encyclopedia of Popular Culture*. Lincoln: University of Nebraska Press, 2000.

Riess, Steven A. *City Games: The Evolution of American Urban Society and the Rise of Sports*. Urbana: University of Illinois Press, 1991.

———. *Touching Base: Professional Baseball and American Culture in the Progressive Era*. Urbana: University of Illinois Press, 1999.

Ritter, Lawrence S. *The Glory of Their Times: The Story of the Early Days of Baseball Told by the Men Who Played It*. New York: Quill, William Morrow, 1984.

———. "Ladies and Gentlemen, Presenting Marty McHale." In *The Complete Armchair Book of Baseball: An All-Star Lineup Celebrates America's National Pastime*, edited by John Thorn, 253–62. Edison NJ: Galahad Books, 1987.

Robbins, Mike. *Ninety Feet from Fame: Close Calls with Baseball Immortality*. New York: Carroll and Graf, 2004.

Robinson, David. *Buster Keaton*. Bloomington: Indiana University Press, 1969.

Robinson, Ray. *American Original: A Life of Will Rogers*. New York: Oxford University Press, 1996.

———. *Matty: An American Hero*. New York: Oxford University Press, 1993.

Robinson Locke Collection of Dramatic Scrapbooks. Billy Rose Theatre Division, New York Public Library for the Performing Arts. Donlin, series II, vol. 130 and series IV, vol. 369, and Hite, series II, vol. 245. Bequeathed to the New York Public Library by Robinson Locke, editor and publisher of the *Toledo Blade*, Toledo, Ohio, 1920.

Roessner, Amber. "The Sinner and the Saint: National Magazine Coverage of Ty Cobb and Christy Mathewson, 1900–1928." In *The Cooperstown Symposium on Baseball and Culture 2009–2010*, edited by William M. Simons, 124–39. Jefferson NC: McFarland, 2011.

Rogers, Betty. *Will Rogers*. Norman: University of Oklahoma Press, 1941.

Rogers, Katharine M. *L. Frank Baum, Creator of Oz: A Biography*. New York: St. Martin's Press, 2002.

Ruane, Tom. "A Retro-Review of the 1900s (the 1901–1909 Edition)." *Retrosheet*, accessed August 2021. https://retrosheet.org/Research/RuaneT/rev1900_art.htm.

Santry, Joe, and Cindy Thomson. "Ban Johnson." In *New Century, New Team: The 1901 Boston Americans*, edited by Bill Nowlin. Phoenix: Society for American Baseball Research, 2013.

Schechter, Gabriel. "Buck Herzog." SABR BioProject. sabr.org/bioproject.

———. "Hooks Wiltse." SABR BioProject. sabr.org/bioproject.

———. *Victory Faust: The Rube Who Saved McGraw's Giants*. Los Gatos CA: Charles April Productions, 2000.

Scheinin, Richard. *Field of Screams: The Dark Underside of America's National Pastime*. New York: W. W. Norton, 1994.

Schmidt, Raymond P. "The Golden Age of Chicago Baseball." *Chicago History* 28, no. 2 (Winter 2000): 38–59.

Segrave. Kerry. *Extras of Early Hollywood: A History of the Crowd, 1913–1945*. Jefferson NC: McFarland, 2013.

Seib, Philip. *The Player: Christy Mathewson, Baseball, and the American Century*. New York: Thunder's Mouth Press, 2003.

Seymour, Harold. *Baseball: The Early Years*. New York: Oxford University Press, 1960.

———. *Baseball: The Golden Age*. New York: Oxford University Press, 1971.

Sher, Jack. "John McGraw: The Little Napoleon." In *Twelve Sports Immortals*, edited by Ernest V. Heyn, 206–33. New York: Bartholomew House, 1951.

Sheridan, George. "The Woman and the Automobile: What the Feminine Influence Has Done to the Motor-Car Industry." *Leslie's Weekly*, November 17, 1910, 518.

Simkus, Scott. *Outsider Baseball: The Weird World of Hardball on the Fringe, 1876–1950*. Chicago: Chicago Review Press, 2014.

———. "Outsiders in the Ragtime Era." *Our Game*, April 1, 2014. https://ourgame .mlblogs.com/outsiders-in-the-ragtime-era-b80cdfb73d4e.

Simon, Tom, ed. *Deadball Stars of the National League*. Dulles VA: Brassey's, 2004.

Simpkins, Terry. "Kid Elberfeld." SABR BioProject. sabr.org/bioproject.

Slide, Anthony. *The Encyclopedia of Vaudeville*. Jackson: University of Mississippi Press, 2012.

Smith, Ira L. *Baseball's Famous Outfielders*. New York: A. S. Barnes, 1954.

Snelling, Dennis. *Johnny Evers: A Baseball Life*. Jefferson NC: McFarland, 2014.

Snyder, Robert W. *The Voice of the City: Vaudeville and Popular Culture in New York*. New York: Oxford University Press, 1989.

Soden, E. D. "The World in Baseball up to Date." *Baseball Magazine*, February 1912, 44–49.

Solomon, Burt. *Where They Ain't: The Fabled Life and Untimely Death of the Original Baltimore Orioles, the Team That Gave Birth to Modern Baseball*. New York: Free Press, 1999.

Sowell, Mike. *July 2, 1903: The Mysterious Death of Hall-of-Famer Big Ed Delahanty*. New York: Macmillan, 1992.

Spalding, John E. *Always on Sunday: The California Baseball League, 1886–1915*. Manhattan KS: Ag Press, 1992.

Spatz, Lyle. *Bad Bill Dahlen: The Rollicking Life and Times of an Early Baseball Star*. Jefferson NC: McFarland, 2004.

Spink, J. G. Taylor. *Judge Landis and Twenty-Five Years of Baseball*. New York: Thomas Y. Crowell, 1947.

Staples, Shirley. *Male-Female Comedy Teams in American Vaudeville*. Ann Arbor MI: UMI Research Press, 1984.

Stark, Benton. *The Year They Called Off the World Series: A True Story*. Garden City Park NY: Avery Publishing, 1991.

Steinberg, Steve. "1908's Forgotten Team: The Pittsburgh Pirates." *Baseball Research Journal*, Fall 2018, 103–11.

———. *Urban Shocker: Silent Hero of Baseball's Golden Age*. Lincoln: University of Nebraska Press, 2017.

Sullivan, Mark. *Our Times: The United States 1900–1925*. Vol. 3, *Pre-War America*. New York: Charles Scribner's Sons, 1930.

———. *Our Times: The United States 1900–1925*. Vol. 4, *The War Begins, 1909–1914*. New York: Charles Scribner's Sons, 1932.

Sunday, W. A. (Billy). "All-American Baseball Team." In *The Fireside Book of Baseball*, edited by Charles Einstein, 333–35. New York: Simon and Schuster, 1956.

Thomson, Cindy. "Mordecai Brown." SABR BioProject. sabr.org/bioproject.

Thorn, John. "The House That McGraw Built." *Base Ball: A Journal of the Early Game* 1, no. 2 (Fall 2007): 115–21.

———. "Presenting Marty McHale, the Lost 'Glory of Their Times' Interview." SABR, December 19, 2012. https://sabr.org/latest/thorn-presenting-marty -mchale-the-lost-glory-of-their-times-interview/.

Tourangeau, Dixie. "Jimmy Williams." SABR BioProject. sabr.org/bioproject.

Trav S. D. (Donald Travis Stewart). "The Barrymores in Vaudeville." *Travalanche*, August 15, 2009. https://travsd.wordpress.com/2009/08/15/stars-of -vaudeville-48-and-49-the-barrymores-and-baby-rose-marie/.

———. *No Applause—Just Throw Money: The Book That Made Vaudeville Famous*. New York: Farrar, Straus and Giroux, 2005.

Vatavuk, Mark K., and Richard E. Marshall. *Baseball in Erie*. San Francisco: Arcadia Publishing, 2005.

Waldo, Ronald T. *Characters from the Diamond: Wild Events, Crazy Antics, and Unique Tales from Early Baseball*. Lanham MD: Rowman & Littlefield, 2016.

———. *Deadball Trailblazers: Single-Season Records of the Modern Era*. Mechanicsburg PA: Sunbury Press, 2022.

———. *Fred Clarke: A Biography of the Baseball Hall of Fame Player-Manager*. Jefferson NC: McFarland, 2011.

Wallace, David. *Lost Hollywood*. New York: LA Weekly/St. Martin's Griffin, 2001.

Wallace, Mike. *Greater Gotham: A History of New York City from 1898 to 1919.* New York: Oxford University Press, 2017.

Wecter, Dixon. *The Hero in America: A Chronicle of Hero-Worship.* New York: Charles Scribner's Sons, 1972.

Wertheim, Arthur Frank. *W. C. Fields, from Burlesque and Vaudeville to Broadway: Becoming a Comedian.* New York: Palgrave Macmillan, 2014.

Wiggins, Robert Peyton. "Jimmy Sebring." SABR BioProject. sabr.org/bioproject.

Wilbert, Warren N. *The Arrival of the American League: Ban Johnson and the 1901 Challenge to National League Monopoly.* Jefferson NC: McFarland, 2007.

Williams, Jeffrey S. "Winning the Crucible of White-Hot Competition." In *The Negro Leagues Were Major Leagues*, edited by Todd Peterson, 75–97. Jefferson NC: McFarland, 2020.

Williams, Joe. *The Joe Williams Baseball Reader: The Glorious Game, from Ty Cobb and Babe Ruth to the Amazing Mets.* Chapel Hill NC: Algonquin, 1989.

Williams, Phil. "Byron Houck." In *From Spring Training to Screen Test: Baseball Players Turned Actors*, edited by Rob Edelman and Bill Nowlin, 113–18. Phoenix: Society for American Baseball Research, 2018.

Wilson, Scott. *Resting Places: The Burial Sites of More Than 14,000 Famous Persons.* Jefferson NC: McFarland, 2016.

Wright, Craig, and Eric Nadel. "Baseball's Greatest Season." *Pages from Baseball's Past*, May 24, 2021. https://www.baseballspast.com/.

Yagoda, Ben. *Will Rogers: A Biography.* New York: Alfred A. Knopf, 1993.

Yuko, Elizabeth. "When Baseball Players Were Vaudeville Stars." *The Atlantic*, April 6, 2017. https://www.theatlantic.com/entertainment/archive/2017/04/when-baseball-players-were-vaudevillestars/521835/fbclid=IwAR3FjiOmZxa07gINqc3BVGs_VnH1wHm2aG8XTzsMtijaskiQyFPN0ZxJAhY.

Zangwill, Israel. "The Future of Vaudeville in America." *Cosmopolitan* 38 (April 1905): 639–46.

Zoss, Joel, and John Bowman. *Diamonds in the Rough: The Untold History of Baseball.* Chicago: Contemporary Books, 1996.

INDEX

Page numbers in italics refer to illustrations.

Donlin, Michael Joseph (*cont.*)
background and overview of, 3,
5–6, 7, 281nn4–5; baseball beginnings of, 7–12; baseball statistics
of, 278; benefit for, 262; café of, in
Harlem, 113–14; cartoon of, *251*; as
a comedian, 122; death of, 273, 274,
275, 279; deaths of those close to,
5–6, 177–78, 205, 211–12, 243–44,
254, 262, 269; fashion statements
of, 124, 183, *184*, *224*, 241; financial
woes of, 218–19, 239, 261–62, 270;
health of, 7, 39, 48, 170, 259, 261–
63, *263*, 269, 282n1; heart disease
of, 261, 262, 263, 273; knifing of,
23–24; legacy of, 276, 277–79; as
manager, 240, 241–44; managerial
position search of, 178, 192, 197–
98, 217, 220, 227–28, 230–31, 239,
257, 271, 276; motorcycle accident
of, 250; personality of, 9, 19–20,
137–38, 247, 269–70, 279; photos
of, as a Cardinal, *22*; photos of, as
a Giant, *118*, *148*, *158*, *224*, *225*, *227*;
photos of, as a Pirate, *200*, *201*;
photos of, as a Red, *43*, *53*; photos
of, as a Rustler, *192*; photos of, for
benefit baseball, *255*, *271*; photos
of, in motion pictures, *165*, *237*,
263; photos of, on stage, *171*, *216*,
249, *267*; photos of, other, *134*, *179*,
184, *187*, *224*, *249*, *251*; popularity
of, 21, 72, 117, 148–50, 157, 278;
post-playing career in baseball
of, *251*, 252–57, 260–61, 266–68,
270–72, 276, 322n37; in prison, 39,
42; robbing of, 137–38; as a scout,
257; swagger of, 9, 13, 30, 117, 170,
191, 275–76; transformation of, in
1908, 144; "Turkey" nickname of,

149, 184, 191; as umpire, 254, 270;
weddings of, 109–10, 228. *See also*
Donlin, Michael Joseph, as actor;
Donlin, Michael Joseph, as fielder;
Donlin, Michael Joseph, batting of;
Donlin, Michael Joseph, drinking
of; Donlin, Michael Joseph, injuries
of; *and specific teams, shows, and
motion pictures*
Donlin, Michael Joseph, as actor: in
motion pictures in 1910s, 235–38,
237, 240, 245, 246–47, 319n5; in
motion pictures in 1920s, 246, 248,
250–52, 259–60, 263–64; in motion
pictures in 1930s, 270, 272–73,
323n21; in theater, 184–86, 189, 247,
248, 266; in vaudeville with Mabel
Hite, 162–67, 169–73, *171*, 179, 185;
in vaudeville without Mabel Hite,
211, 229–30, 248. *See also specific
motion pictures and shows*
Donlin, Michael Joseph, as fielder:
with Cardinals, 21; with Giants, 62,
66, 71–72, 138, *158*, 291n27, 305n40;
with Orioles, 33; with Perfectos,
15–16, 18, 284n18; with Phillies, 217;
with Pirates, 199, 200, 208; with
Reds, 42, 49, 51
Donlin, Michael Joseph, batting of: in
the California League, 11; career,
278; as a Chick, 242, 318n21; as
a Giant (1904), 65–66; as a Giant
(1905), 68, 69, 70–71; as a Giant
(1906), 119; as a Giant (1908), 141,
144, 146–47, 150, 161, 303n7, 303n13;
as a Giant (1911), 196; as a Giant
(1913), 225–26, 315n12; as a Logan
Square, 127; as an Oriole, 31, 33, 38,
287nn30–31, 287n46; as a Pirate,
200, 201, *201*, 204, 207, 208, 209; as

immigration, 4, 5
"I'm on My Way to Reno," 185, 310n17
Indianapolis Freeman, 132
indoor baseball, 45, 80, 138, 289n19
International League, 220, 230, 239
Inter Ocean, 104, 128, 132, 220
Irish baseball players, 51–52, 115. *See also specific players*
The Irish in Baseball (Fleitz), 115
Isman, Felix, 178, 180
Ives, Charles, 73

Jack Doyle's Billiards Academy, 180–81, 239, 309n23
Jackson, Frank, 278
James, Bill, 72
The Jazz Singer, 234, 264
Jeffries, James J., 181, 272, 273
Jerpe, James, 217, 231
Jersey City Skeeters, 220–21, 222
Johnson, Ban: American League and, 27–28, 30–34, 36, 38, 41; barnstorming in Cuba and, 130; Joe Kelley and, 49; John McGraw and, 41, 57, 82; Nap Lajoie and, 56; National Commission and, 47, 139; World Series (1904) and, 63, 64, 65
Johnson, Timothy A., 73
Johnstone, Jim: Cubs and, 160; Giants and, 70, 83–84, 121; Reds and, 52, 55, 57; Rustlers and, 194
Jolson, Al, 94, 96
Jones, Walter, 104–5, 109, 122

Kalamazoo Celery Pickers, 257
Kansas City Times, 99, 212
Keaton, Buster, 94, 259–60, 270, 321n13
Keeler, Willie, 10, 47, 48, 69, 283n34
Keeley, Leslie, 135

Keeley Institute, 135–36, 301n27
Keener, Sid, 6, 13
Keith, Benjamin, 94
Keith-Albee circuit, 94, 229
Kelley, Joe: Mike Donlin and, 49, 51, 55–56, 58, *59*, 253; Reds and, 42, 44–45, 48–52, *53*, 55–56, 58, *59*, 289n16
Kelly, Mike "King," 18, 61, 162
Kelly, Tom, 7, 193, 282n9
Kenny, Kevin, 4–5
The Kid Drops In, 248
Kilbane, Johnny, 240
King, Steven A., 75
Klem, Bill: Cubs and, 160; Giants and, 71, 83, 86, 116, 143, 221; Hank O'Day and, 157; Mike Donlin and, 121, 157, 221, 226
Kling, Johnny, 146, 160, 192, 197, 198
A Knight for a Day, 123, 128–29, 136, 163
Know-Nothing Party, 5

Lajoie, Nap, 33, 47, 56–57, 69, 199
Lane, F. C., 16
Lardner, John, 252, 277
Lardner, Ring, 270, 277, 324n14
Latham, Arlie, 18
Laurie, Joe, 247
Lawndales, 138
Leach, Tommy, 146
Lehigh Valley League, 230–31, 317n49
Leland, Frank, 131
Leland Giants, 131, 132, 186–88
Leslie, Amy, 99–100, *101*, 104, 143, 165–66, 185, 276, 295n6
Lewis, Tom, 215, *216*, 262
Lewisohn, Ludwig, 104
Lieb, Fred, 25, 140
Lincoln Giants, 189, 230
Lipman, Clara, 100
Livingston, Cora, 162, 306n5